Called by Name

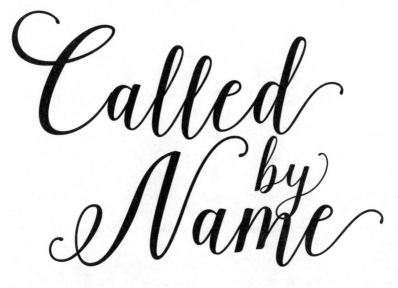

Called by Name

365 Daily Devotions
for Catholic Women

Edited by
Kelly M. Wahlquist, Allison Gingras, & Alyssa Bormes
WINE: Women In the New Evangelization

AVE MARIA PRESS AVE Notre Dame, Indiana

Founded in 1865, Ave Maria Press is a ministry of the United States Province of Holy Cross.

www.avemariapress.com

Paperback: ISBN-13 978-1-64680-070-4

E-book: ISBN-13 978-1-64680-071-1

Cover image © gettyimages.com.

Cover design by: Katherine Robinson

Text design by: Kristen Hornyak Bonelli

Printed and bound in Canada.

Introduction

Imagine the courage it took to brave the darkness before dawn and walk through an area that had been hostile territory just days before, a place where unruly mobs had jeered as an innocent man was led to his death. This was not a safe place to be. It was definitely not safe for a woman to be walking alone at this hour.

Yet one young woman, with a heart tumbling toward despair, dared to make this journey.

The message of love that she and her friends had dedicated their lives to had been rejected. Scenes of hope and celebration just days earlier had given way to hostility and fear. Disheartened, she desperately searched for that which had been taken from her.

It was in that hour, as the sun began to break through the darkness of night, that a man suddenly appeared beside her. The young woman was not afraid. Her quest overcame all fear.

"Why are you weeping?" the man asked.

She responded, not by answering his question, but by begging him to take her to the One she had set her hopes on.

What happened next changed her forever. One moment instantly turned her anguish to joy, her despair to happiness—*she was called by name.*

The man said to her, "Mary."

Turning her head, she suddenly recognized Him—not a gardener, but the One she thought had been lost forever. And she cried out to Him in Hebrew, "Rab-bóni!"—that is, teacher (Jn 20:16).

The moment Mary Magdalene heard the risen Lord call her name, her despair dissolved. Her heart leapt with joy. The Good Shepherd had called her as one of His own, and she was eager to follow Him.

An Intimate Relationship

There is a feeling of comfort that stirs inside you when you hear another call you by your name. A tug on your heart when someone you love says your name tenderly. To be called by name indicates that you are known in a personal way. Hearing your name makes you take notice and lets you know that something important is about to be communicated—especially when you hear your first name followed by your middle name. Yikes! Many are the times my parents would grab my attention by using the name (both names) they gave me. "Kelly Marie, your dirty socks do not belong on my dining room table!"

So important is being called by name that it is a vital step in how we enter into that most intimate of relationships, our relationship with God. At baptism, we are *literally* called by name: "Kelly Marie, I baptize you in the name of the Father, and of the Son, and of the Holy Spirit." (Aha! We are called by our first and middle names—something important is about to happen!) It is important indeed, for "through Baptism we are freed from sin and reborn as sons of God; we become members of Christ, are incorporated into the Church and made sharers in her mission" (*CCC* 1213).

Whether it is a friend calling you by your first name or a parent stringing together your first, middle, and (heaven forbid) last names, being called by name signifies an intimate relationship. That is what the Lord desires to have with you—a personal and intimate relationship. A relationship where you belong entirely to Him.

The Sound of His Voice

The Lord is yearning for a deep relationship with you. He has called you His beloved and longs for you to hear and know His voice. The best way to know His voice is to spend time with Him, listening to Him.

In this daily devotional, we have compiled reflections for each day of the year (leap year included) from eighty beautiful contributors to WINE: Women In the New Evangelization who have spent time listening to the voice of the Good Shepherd.

To help you sit quietly with the Lord and listen to His voice, we have divided each daily devotion into three aspects: read, reflect, and respond.

- *Read* the scripture passage provided: the Lord speaking to you.

    As with all WINE offerings, we encourage you to pray the scriptures through lectio divina—an ancient form of slowly, meditatively, and prayerfully reading sacred scripture. Although we include the verse at the beginning of the devotional, I encourage you to read this devotional with your Bible in hand so you can explore the context more fully. Additionally, you can record what the Lord is saying to you in a journal, such as the WINE journal designed to accompany this devotional. (For more information on the WINE journal, visit CatholicVineyard.com.)

- *Reflect* on the words of your sisters in Christ.

    We are not alone on this journey; we have each other to support, nurture, and encourage us! So, pour yourself a cup of coffee, tea, or whatever relaxes you, and sit down each day with one of your sisters at WINE as she shares a reflection with you, designed to help you open your heart to hear God's voice.

- *Respond* to His call.

In scripture, when the Lord calls someone by name for an important mission, that person responds. The same holds true for us. The Lord is calling us each day to be like Him. If we are to be women in the New Evangelization, we need to respond to the call to be like Him.

An Invitation

My dear sister in Christ, in calling you by name, our Lord invites you into a deeper, more loving relationship with Him. So, what are you waiting for? Dive right in! You need not wait until January 1 to enter into that divine intimacy for which you were created. Begin today!

May the Holy Spirit give you the courage and perseverance to spend time with the Lord each day so that you will come to recognize His voice—and upon hearing Him call your name, may your heart be filled with joy as you respond, "Rab-bóni!"

Kelly M. Wahlquist
Founder of WINE: Women In the New Evangelization

The First Day of the Year

And Simeon blessed them and said to Mary his mother, "Behold, this child is set for the fall and rising of many in Israel, and for a sign that is spoken against (and a sword will pierce through your own soul also), that thoughts out of many hearts may be revealed." Luke 2:34–35

The deep significance of this, the first day of the year, is lost for most of the Christian world. This day marks when the eight-day-old Jesus received the Jewish covenant of circumcision, and His name Yeshua (Hebrew for "God saves") was proclaimed for the first time.

The Brit Milah (covenant of circumcision) is a great celebratory event for a Jewish family, and Mary had certainly witnessed it before. But the mother of our God knew what the mohel did not. Her baby was born to rescue and deliver. He was the Messiah. In Mary's heart, this was the most solemn event. Jesus' circumcision began the trail of His shed blood. It would traverse thirty-three years to a hill in Jerusalem five miles from the place of His birth—and to all eternity.

Mary was always there for Him. From conception to the Cross, she stayed with Him, praying until the end. It is no wonder we pray for ourselves, "Holy Mary, mother of God, pray for us sinners now and at the hour of our death." She stayed faithfully with her Son through the hours of His (and her) agony until His expiring breath.

As we observe New Year's Day, let us remember that the first day of the year marks the first time the Savior of mankind shed His blood for humanity. On the calendar day of Jesus' circumcision, we also remember the solemnity of His mother, whose pure and holy heart was being pierced by a sword.

Prayer: O God, King of the universe, who became flesh for me that I might participate in Your divinity, help me, in the coming year, to know You more fully and love You more deeply. Amen.

Respond to His Call: Today, slowly pray the Hail Mary, pondering each word.

Deborah Kendrick

The Voice of My Beloved

My beloved speaks and says to me: "Arise, my love, my dove, my fair one, and come away." Song of Solomon 2:10

Can you imagine the King of heaven and earth not only noticing you but also speaking tender words of invitation? "I see your heart, my fair one. I see your pain and joys. In this season of new beginnings, remember that with each breath you are given a chance to start anew—an opportunity to love more, pray longer, and come closer to My heart."

Maybe your resolutions tend to come and go. Perhaps this year it is time to move past making resolutions and, instead, commit to a relationship. There is someone out there to whom you belong; He yearns for you, His beloved. Will you keep Him waiting, or will you quench His thirst? Do not be afraid; your Lover is gentle.

If you find yourself burdened by your past mistakes or overcome by your present choices, allow Him into your life. Turn away from sin; look toward the eyes of your Savior. There is nothing you've done that He doesn't already know; His mercy is greater than your guilt. You are always His.

If you think a relationship with the King of heaven and earth is unattainable, remember this: our King humbled Himself and became one of us so we would realize how available and selfless His love really is.

He wants your heart—not just a part of it but your whole heart. Why do you resist? Fix your eyes on Him and allow yourself to be overcome by His goodness and love. Hear His voice calling to you. Will you respond to His invitation? Dear sister, I am praying that, bold in the Holy Spirit, you accept the grace to say yes.

Prayer: Holy Spirit, be with me. Shower me with grace and shine on me the light I need to follow Jesus the Bridegroom wherever He leads. Amen.

Respond to His Call: Make a good Confession. Prepare by thoroughly reviewing your conscience, and go early to the appointed time at your parish. After receiving the sacrament, offer a special prayer of thanksgiving to the Holy Spirit for leading you to the arms of Jesus in the Church, His Mystical Body.

Angela Koenig

Supercop No More

If any one hears my sayings and does not keep them, I do not judge him; for I did not come to judge the world but to save the world. John 12:47

I'm the oldest daughter of the oldest daughter of the oldest daughter. When people ask why I didn't have children, I laugh and say that that line of hyper-responsible, hypervigilant women had to end. (I'm not entirely joking!)

Regardless of your birth order, you may have some of that gene. You know, the one that tells you there's one right way to fold towels and sheets, drive, wrap a present, or dress—and woe to those who don't agree with it. The problem with all that private and sometimes not-so-private condemnation is that when your expectations are that exact, you, those you love, and the world will never live up to them.

What's the point in even trying to please God then? If we can't live up to our own standards, how could we possibly meet His? It's all grace. Through His death and resurrection, Jesus offers us not only freedom from our failures but also healing from our sin and the hope of eternal life.

Yet, Jesus doesn't condemn those who choose not to follow His words. Imagine that! It takes away any power we've given ourselves to condemn. That means no snarky comment about the person with twenty items in the clearly marked ten-items-or-fewer lane at the grocery store or silent seething about the parent who doesn't take the crying toddler out of the sanctuary during Mass.

Jesus sets the perfect example: love, welcome, and accept people as He does. Offer the invitation to the Word, and leave the judging to the Father on the last day. Until then, do what Jesus did: provide gentle correction when the Spirit directs, and distance yourself from those who threaten your salvation—without condemning them.

Prayer: Lord, thank You for loving me just as I am. Teach me to be patient with myself and others. Amen.

Respond to His Call: Today, look for opportunities to be charitable. Before you judge someone, say a little prayer for them.

Melanie Rigney

Our Daily Cross

And he said to all, "If any man would come after me, let him deny himself and take up his cross daily and follow me." Luke 9:23

How beautiful to see our struggles as an opportunity to rely on God. John, the beloved disciple, wrote, "So we know and believe the love God has for us" (1 Jn 4:16). That simple affirmation of faith, coupled with my belief that God orders all for my good, never fails to bring me comfort. These truths relate to both the situation I can see as good and those circumstances where the goodness isn't quite so obvious.

In St. Luke's gospel, Christ tells us if we want to follow Him, we must pick up our cross daily. I've often found it funny that Luke, the physician, includes the word "daily." St. Matthew also shares Jesus' words of wisdom but leaves out the "daily" aspect. It reminds me of the adage "An apple a day keeps the doctor away." Perhaps St. Luke is trying to teach us that carrying our cross each day will keep evil at bay.

Every morning I need to renew my decision to follow Christ and then ask for His help to persevere with my diet, budget, and path to holiness. "I can do all things in him who strengthens me" (Phil 4:13). That's the secret—*in* Christ. The strength comes from Him, and He's always ready to give. But I keep taking it back, thinking I can do it all, maybe afraid to use up all my prayers, like a genie lamp.

Struggles come and go. As long as we are breathing, we'll have them— be it our health, holiness, or family's financial well-being. The flesh is indeed weak, but God is strong: "For when I am weak, then I am strong" (2 Cor 12:10). St. Paul wisely reminds us that Jesus' grace is enough.

Prayer: Lord, whether my cross be heavy or light, may I always yoke myself to You in carrying it. Amen.

Respond to His Call: Make a list of your crosses and contemplate how Jesus is trying to help you carry them.

Allison Gingras

Following Yonder Star

Now when Jesus was born in Bethlehem of Judea in the days of Herod the king, behold, Wise Men from the East came to Jerusalem, saying, "Where is he who has been born king of the Jews? For we have seen his star in the East, and have come to worship him." Matthew 2:1–2

I recently left my job in the Air Force after ten years of service and the arrival of our second child. Sometimes, Jesus asks us to take a great leap of faith and follow Him. I couldn't see the whole road map. Jesus gave just enough to illuminate the next step. It seemed God sent me full speed in one direction only to apply the brakes. The whiplash was stunning.

Imagine how stunning it was to the Magi when, after following a sign in the sky, the brightest star, they arrived at a stable. Faith is mysterious, sometimes sending us on strange paths. Were the Magi surprised when they came to such a humble shelter? Places of greatness may have a very ordinary appearance. Jesus' call may seem ordinary, but He calls us to a new way of life, which will take us on an extraordinary journey. He calls us to follow the Magi's footsteps to an even deeper relationship with Himself, a call that leads to a place of adoration.

Although the Magi brought gifts, the gifts they received were far more magnificent. My trust in God to leave the military was rewarded, but in a very unexpected way. Had I not left my job, I could not have been with my husband when he needed an emergency surgery. Following the star of God's inspiration sent me to a place wholly unknown, yet in the midst of suffering I received gifts, even profound peace.

Not all of us are called to quit our jobs, but everyone is on a journey of conversion to find true peace. Like the Magi, we must follow yonder star to offer our humble treasure to Jesus.

Prayer: Lord, may I recognize the guiding stars in my life. Inspire my heart to remain faithful to following them. Amen.

Respond to His Call: Spend time today with the scriptures. Let the Holy Spirit guide your reading.

Katie Lee Taylor

Odd Gifts for a Newborn

They shall bring gold and frankincense, and shall proclaim the praise of the LORD. Isaiah 60:6

The Feast of the Epiphany celebrates the Magi visiting the Christ child and bringing Him gifts of gold, frankincense, and myrrh. Upon hearing this, one has to think, "Odd gifts for a newborn."

I once saw a plaque that said if the three wise men had been wise women, they would have "asked directions, arrived on time, helped deliver the baby, cleaned the stable, made a casserole, and brought practical gifts." Although the plaque was humorous (and probably true on many points), the Magi's gifts were actually perfect for the newborn Jesus. These gifts fulfilled several key Old Testament prophecies (see Nm 24:17; Ps 72:10–11; Is 60:6).

Frankincense was used to make incense, myrrh was used to prepare the bodies of the dead for burial, and gold was the sign of the wealth of a king. As the baby who received these gifts was God Incarnate, they were perfect. Frankincense represents the prayers made to Him, myrrh points to the salvation He won for us on the Cross, and gold reminds us that this helpless newborn was the King of kings.

During the Epiphany, Christ appeared as God-with-us to the Magi. Today, He appears to us, too. And like the Magi, we can give Him our gold, frankincense, and myrrh. Perhaps our gold is the relationships we hold dear, the activities that bring us the greatest joy, the things we love most—all offered freely to our God. Our frankincense may be the prayers of praise and adoration that we lay before Him. And our myrrh may be our sufferings, the many deaths to self that we must face on this journey. We can bring all these gifts to the altar as we go forward to receive the greatest gift of all—the source and summit of our faith, the Eucharist.

Prayer: Lord, thank You for the gifts that You have given me. Help me to use these gifts to build up Your kingdom on earth. Amen.

Respond to His Call: Give someone the gift of your presence today. Make a point to be attentive to them.

Kelly M. Wahlquist

The Power to Heal

And I tell you, you are Peter, and on this rock I will build my Church, and the gates of Hades shall not prevail against it. Matthew 16:18

When I was a struggling actress on the fringes of the industry, I had an opportunity to create a one-woman act for a performance-art venue. The act, which was well received, was about a creature that survived by feeding on the "fruit" of human emotions. This creature lamented the ready availability of toxic emotional fruit like self-pity, resentment, hopelessness, and rage, and wished for the day when she might feast on forgiveness, mercy, and hope.

The inspiration for this act came from my longing to bring healing to people. When Jesus commissioned His disciples to preach salvation "to every creature," He also said, "They will lay their hands on the sick, and they will recover" (Mk 16:18). As an actress, I'd become especially aware of how desperately people need healing. I used to spend hours people-watching in New York, especially on the subways. Everywhere I looked I saw people who seemed alienated, heartache and loneliness etched into their faces. How I wished to lift their burdens with an act of my will, healing their broken hearts. I liked to imagine their looks of surprise and delight, their eyes sparkling at the miracle of renewed hope.

Today, I teach classes on authentic beauty for teenage girls—and it is so rewarding to see them experience healing from their fears, resentments, and anger. They come to recognize the stunning dignity of the feminine genius—that they are receptive, sensitive, generous, and maternal. And as they heal, they see the healing potential of their own lives.

We are called as the Father's daughters to receive people where we find them, being sensitive to their condition, generous in our response, and maternal in sharing our wisdom. We are to bring healing to the people God places in our path each day—one moment, one act of kindness at a time.

Prayer: Lord, help me to love everyone You place along my path each day—extending one act of kindness at a time. Amen.

Respond to His Call: Today, consider what gifts you have to offer others.

Lisa Mladinich

Perfect Love

> There is no fear in love, but perfect love casts out fear. For fear has to do with punishment, and he who fears is not perfected in love. 1 John 4:18

One night I lay in bed, unable to sleep. I was overcome with anger at someone who had broken my heart. And now, I was facing a ruined relationship and financial devastation. I had no idea what to do or which way to turn. I knew that such consuming anger and fear were not from God, but I felt powerless to control my emotions. I cried and begged God to help me. Then a gentle, steady voice spoke in my heart: "Ask Me for My perfect love." I blinked. "What?" "Ask Me for My perfect love." I was stunned. "What does that mean?" I asked.

"Look, Lord, sure, I want Your perfect love, but I have this problem, and I need help." I waited and prayed for help, but nothing else came to me. "Fine," I said, exasperated. "Give me Your perfect love." Heaving a sigh, I prayed again. "Really, Lord, give me Your perfect love."

I don't know how many times I repeated that prayer that night, but I suddenly realized that I had stopped shaking. My fear and anger were gone. You'd think I'd feel relieved . . . but I panicked and tried to pull those feelings back up. Somehow, I thought the negativity was necessary to deal with the problems I faced. But despite my best efforts, the fear and anger weren't there anymore. The severity of the situation hadn't changed, but now it no longer crushed me. Before long, I fell asleep.

In the morning, I awoke refreshed, rested, and curious. "Why did that prayer work?" I asked God. In reply, a scripture verse floated gently into my head: "Perfect love casts out fear." Today, I use that prayer in every difficult situation—from finances to health to relationships—it's positively miraculous!

Prayer: Lord Jesus, restore my trust in You. Give me Your perfect love, that I may see all things in its light. Amen.

Respond to His Call: If anything, or anyone, is causing you to doubt the faithfulness of God, give the Lord permission to take your perspective and to replace it with His.

Lynne Keating

Five Smooth Stones

And David put his hand in his bag and took out a stone, and slung it, and struck the Philistine on his forehead. . . . So David prevailed over the Philistine with a sling and with a stone. 1 Samuel 17:49–50

In scripture we encounter people with some crazy ideas. Take the story of David and Goliath. What was that crazy kid thinking? None of the Israelite warriors were brave enough to face the giant—but David picked five smooth stones, hurled one with his sling, and the giant fell.

I heard a possible meaning for the five smooth stones. Four of the stones represented courage, confidence, preparation, and trust. The fifth stone, which he used to slay the giant, signified faith. What excellent tools for battle. David put the stones in his shepherd's bag. We could use our purses, briefcases, or diaper bags—or throw them in the passenger seat of the car!

Who are the Davids today, and what Goliath are they going after? We could start with the Goliath of woundedness. The world is bruised, individuals are aching, and the Church has scars. It doesn't seem there is a way to tackle it all. But we don't need to. We just need to begin.

I think women in the New Evangelization are Davids. The WINE website reads, "For such a time as this, the Lord is calling to women, asking us to work in the beauty of our natural gifts as women, and is saying to us, 'Heal my body.'" This David and Goliath business is serious. Let's choose the five smooth stones of courage, confidence, preparation, trust, and faith, and carry them in a satchel marked Mercy!

Prayer: Lord, equip me for battle with courage, confidence, preparation, trust, and faith. Amen.

Respond to His Call: Today, collect five smooth stones. Put them together in a vase to hold flowers for a centerpiece for a table, or perhaps heat them and use them as hand warmers in the cold. Whatever you do with those stones, let them be daily inspirations to take small steps of faithfulness toward whatever battles you're facing.

Alyssa Bormes

Remodels Are Not for Wimps

Jesus answered him, "If a man loves me, he will keep my word, and my Father will love him, and we will come to him and make our home with him." John 14:23

I love makeover shows featuring experts who take old, dilapidated homes and turn them into warm, comfy living spaces. Maybe some of the appeal is that these shows parallel my own work. As a life coach, I love to inspire and guide others to open the closets and sort through the mess of their emotional and spiritual lives, decluttering and bringing beauty into those interior spaces. It can be painful. Some people resist the change. Some make progress, only to sneak old habits back in.

Do you know why it's so difficult to let go of clutter? We fear that we will never have enough and so we hoard what we think will keep us in control. What tremendous energy we spend purchasing, storing, managing, and maintaining it all—only to worry about theft, floods, fires, or a breakup. The same holds true with relationships. How exhausting to be overly involved, micromanaging, and fighting fears of failure, rejection, and abandonment!

God is a master remodeler. He wants to restructure and beautify our interior lives, working with our natural desires to bring order from chaos and holiness from selfishness.

So, ready for a makeover? Make an honest assessment of your life. Open every door to every room, and invite the Lord in. Tell Him your desires, hopes, and greatest fears. Allow Him to draw you into Himself, making you new and beautiful.

Once you open all the doors, our Lord will take over and make His dwelling place in every area of your life.

Prayer: Dear Lord, help me to hold the goods of the world and all my relationships in right order. Fill me with more of You so I need less of everything else. Amen.

Respond to His Call: Spiritual and emotional decluttering is not for the faint of heart. Today, do some research into finding a trustworthy and qualified coach to help you.

Rose Sweet

The Saving Love of a Father

For in Christ Jesus you are all sons of God, through faith. For as many of you as were baptized into Christ have put on Christ. Galatians 3:26–27

A missionary from Ghana came to speak at our high school. When he started giving his witness—sharing the powerful story of his conversion from a tribal religion to Christianity—you could've heard a pin drop! This priest was the firstborn son to his mother and father. He was only a few years old when he became deathly ill. His father, a tribal chief, brought in medicine man after medicine man to heal his son, to no avail. The little boy was getting sicker and sicker.

The chief heard of a Catholic missionary priest nearby. Terrified that his son would die, the chief called on him, asking, "What can you do for my son? Nothing will help him!" The priest responded, "I can baptize him in the name of the Father, and the Son, and the Holy Spirit." The chief asked, "What will that do?" The priest said, "Your son will become a child of God. If he dies, he will be with the God of love forever." Without hesitation, the chief said, "Do it!" So the priest baptized the child. Two days later, the chief's son was healthy again! The chief called the priest back and said, "None of my medicine men could heal my child, but your God healed him. I want you to raise him with the love of your God."

So, the firstborn son was given to the priest's order for instruction. He studied with them, went to seminary, became a priest, and eventually was given the title Monsignor. The little boy saved through baptism would lead the Society for the Propagation of the Faith for the country of Ghana.

Prayer: Dear Lord, how grateful I am for the plans You have for me. Give me peace about whatever lies ahead. Help me to know that You are a gracious Father who works all things together for the good of those who love You. Amen.

Respond to His Call: Put the word "celebrate" in big letters on your calendar on the day you were baptized. When that day comes, give thanks to the Lord, and rejoice!

Patti Jannuzzi

When God Uses Hard Things in His Good Plan

I do not know how you came into being in my womb. It was not I who gave you life and breath, nor I who set in order the elements within each of you. 2 Maccabees 7:22

I lay quietly, waiting to see my baby's heartbeat on the ultrasound screen. The technician, very compassionately and professionally, informed me that there was not one heartbeat but two. Confused, I wondered, *How could my baby's heart have two heartbeats?* But of course, I was carrying twins—a boy and a girl, we eventually learned.

On the day of their birth, I had to have an unplanned cesarean. I was being invited to surrender and trust in a new and deeper way, and all I could do was pray—*Hail Mary, full of grace.* As Mary trusted God with her Son, I had to trust Him with my twins. From Jesus' birth to His death and resurrection, what Mary experienced called for complete surrender. Having twins—and bringing them into the world in such a dramatic way—was not part of my plan and required tremendous levels of surrender!

On the day my twins were born—probably the hardest day of my life—I learned to trust and believe. And isn't that how God works? He brings us through the hardest thing—the thing we don't think we have the strength to do—and transforms it with His grace into something incredibly good. My twins are two of the best things that have ever happened to me. Sure, the early days of their life were a blur, fueled only by coffee and grace. But I am so blessed to be their mom! They are a constant reminder of God's beautiful (and often mysterious) way of bringing us into His divine plan.

Prayer: Thank you, Father, for the gift of children. Amen.

Respond to His Call: Today, while going to work, running errands, or making a meal, make a point to talk with Mary. Ask her to help you surrender to God's plan for your life.

Sarah Damm

The Art of Complaining

Why do you stand afar off, O Lord? Why do you hide yourself in times of trouble? Psalm 10:1

One of the beautiful things about the Psalms is that they teach us there is a godly way to complain. There is no cardboard piety in the Psalms. In these prayers of Israel, God teaches us to express every emotion to Him with complete honesty, whether it be fear, anguish, confusion, discouragement, rage, grief, joy, or hope. The Psalmist tells it like it is.

In the book of Exodus, on the other hand, the Israelites were punished for their complaining, their "murmuring" against the Lord and against Moses any time they were in danger or didn't get their needs met immediately (Ex 16:2–8, 17:3).

What's the difference? What makes one kind of complaining godly and the other ungodly?

First, there is a certain bitterness in the complaining of the exodus generation. You can hear their sarcasm: "Is it because there are no graves in Egypt that you have taken us away to die in the wilderness?" (Ex 14:11). The Psalmist, on the other hand, sometimes expresses perplexity at the Lord's slowness to act but never bitterness.

Second, the exodus generation complained "behind God's back," so to speak. Instead of crying out directly to God, they grumbled among themselves, like a group of disgruntled employees griping about the boss. But the Psalmist always directly addresses God Himself, reflecting his abiding relationship of love and trust with the Lord. That relationship is deeper than any of the ups and downs of life.

Finally, the Psalmist doesn't end with complaints, but always moves toward an expression of trust in God. Often he even thanks and praises the Lord beforehand for the saving deeds that He will accomplish.

Prayer: O Lord, thank You for receiving me with loving arms no matter what my emotional state. Help me turn my complaining into songs of praise, and my mourning into joy. Amen.

Respond to His Call: The next time you're tempted to complain, follow the example of the Psalms and engage in some godly complaining!

Dr. Mary Healy

Keep It Simple

The unfolding of your words gives light; it imparts understanding to the simple. Psalm 119:130

The Gospel is a simple message at its core. But I have a knack for complicating things when I'm faced with difficulties. Maybe that's why I treasure my visits to the adoration chapel. Everything appears so much simpler when I walk into the chapel each week and gaze on our Lord.

In the face of life's complications, we need only turn to the One who can bring light and clarity to a muddled heart. If we were more aware of how each moment of our day comes from God's hand, we would more easily focus our attention back on Jesus, who alone can solve all maladies and misfires. And it doesn't need to be a difficult task.

An acronym my high school math teacher taught me comes to mind—KISS (Keep It Simple, Silly). That's a great lesson. And isn't there something sweet about the word "kiss"? Mother Teresa once said, "Pain and suffering have come into your life, but remember pain, sorrow, suffering are but the kiss of Jesus—a sign that you have come so close to Him that He can kiss you."

Above the monstrance at our church's small adoration chapel, a crucifix hangs. In that simple image, life's complications disappear, returning me to our Lord's beautiful essence. In that chapel I come as close as possible, this side of heaven, to feeling true peace. In His presence, I thank Jesus for His kiss of life, asking that it penetrate my being and equip me to bring His simple, pure love into the world. Do you have any special ways of turning your focus on Jesus, dissolving complications in the simplicity of His presence and love?

Prayer: Thank You, Lord, for Your loving gaze upon me during eucharistic adoration—and I thought it was me coming to gaze upon You! Amen.

Respond to His Call: When you feel alone or abandoned, cry out, "Jesus where are you?" and picture Jesus before you saying, "I am here, my child, carrying you."

Roxane B. Salonen

Thrift Shop Therapy

Now may the Lord of peace himself give you peace at all times in all ways. The Lord be with you all. 2 Thessalonians 3:16

I shop at thrift stores. I can't pass up a good bargain, and thrift stores are full of them. I also like to support a good cause, and many thrift stores are run by charity or service organizations, so we're helping others by shopping there.

But for me, thrift shopping is downright therapeutic. All of those other benefits—saving money, helping others, and so on—are just icing on the cake. It helps me relax, slow down, and think. I head to the thrift stores when I'm exasperated and need to work something out or make a difficult decision. Sorting through all of the merchandise is like an in-between state, not quite here and not quite there. It gives me mental space and lets me push the pause button on my life until I get a grip.

It's not all that uncommon for me to pray while thrift shopping. When I'm having trouble expressing myself, I mentally chant the Hail Mary. It acts like a mantra that calms me down and gets me to refocus. I used to feel guilty about using thrift shopping to work things out rather than praying before the Eucharist. Oh, I still go to adoration, and I love it. But when I'm before the monstrance, I'm there entirely for Him. When I'm thrift shopping, I'm there entirely for me. Once I realized both activities fulfill things I crave and need, I stopped feeling guilty.

I'd like to think that St. Paul would understand my thrift shopping therapy—after all, he prayed that God would give us peace "at all times and in all ways." We shouldn't underestimate those little things that bring us some measure of clarity, rest, and peace. God's grace comes to us in many ways!

Prayer: Lord, help me see the graces You offer in the little, mundane moments of life. Thank You for making Your presence and blessings available to me. Amen.

Respond to His Call: Today, identify a unique activity or place where you experience God's presence—and thank Him for meeting you there.

Marge Steinhage Fenelon

Hoping in His Plan

For I know the plans I have for you, says the LORD, plans for welfare and not for evil, to give you a future and a hope. Then you will call upon me and come and pray to me, and I will hear you. Jeremiah 29:11–12

I once heard the saying, "If God brings you to it, He will bring you through it." Living a life of faith is an adventure! God is always working through each situation He brings. If we're in a difficult struggle, knowing that God in His wisdom has allowed the struggle makes all the difference. With eyes of faith, we can see our trials within the context of His plan— and we can trust that He will equip us with His strength.

Know that God's plan for your life is perfect, even if it involves pain. Rely on His strength to carry you and His love to comfort you. God wants to use the crosses that He allows you to carry to fit you for the tasks that He calls you to do.

Jesus doesn't call us to anything He wasn't willing to do Himself. He also shows us that He doesn't expect us to suffer alone. Staggering under the burden of the Cross, He received help from Simon of Cyrene. And earlier, in the Garden of Gethsemane, Jesus asked His disciples to stay awake with Him for one hour as He cried to God in agony. But ultimately, as the book of Hebrews tells us, Jesus endured the Cross because of the joy set before Him (12:2).

That same joy is set before us, too. Our pain isn't beyond the goodness of God's plan—in fact, it may be instrumental in transforming us into the image of Christ.

St. John Vianney said, "If we do not carry our crosses with joy, then they will be of no use to us." Do you trust that your pain is truly a step in God's good plan for your life? Can you carry your cross with joy?

Prayer: Lord, I wish to carry my crosses with joy so that they will be of use, always bringing me closer to You. Amen.

Respond to His Call: Help someone carry their cross today. Your act of service and kindness may bring great comfort to another.

Kathleen Billings

A Tale of Two Tonys

Let them extol him in the congregation of the people, and praise him in the assembly of the elders. He turns rivers into a desert, springs of water into thirsty ground. Psalm 107:32–33

If you're feeling spiritually lost, bring your search to St. Anthony on his feast today. Never mind that Anthony of Padua, patron saint of lost things, has a feast day in June—today's Anthony the Abbot will help you find just what you need! The dynamic duo of Tonys exemplifies the beauty of both solitude and service.

An unfortunate workweek led me to experience a lost Saturday of the soul. After a grueling morning of work, I was anticipating a glorious afternoon to myself at home. I spent it scouring every surface in sight and picking at projects. However, this wasn't what I was called to do, which resulted in my beautiful afternoon being squandered. I had been invited to rest but had chosen a to-do list.

Quiet time with the Lord is vital for every soul. St. Anthony the Abbot, a desert mystic, realized the value of this solitude. We are invited to encounter Jesus in the desert of our souls. He offers healing waters that wash over the barren disappointments and bleak worries of our hearts, revealing that we can only find ourselves once we learn to rest in Him.

But this doesn't involve hiding from people either! As St. John Paul II often encouraged, "Man finds himself only by making himself a sincere gift to others."

Anthony of Padua found himself through serving others as a friar, teacher, and preacher. Anthony the Abbot's gift was seeking the Lord in aloneness. If you're in a spiritual desert of busyness or a spiritual desert of solitude, take heart: those are both places where God can meet you in a special way. Learn from the examples of these saintly Tonys. Transform your tasks into sincere gift to others, and use your solitude to rest in God.

Prayer: Jesus Christ, guide me to experience Your love and to share that love with others, today and always. Amen.

Respond to His Call: Embrace your desert today. Healing will come when you turn outward and become a gift to others.

Katie Anderson

January 18

Trusting the Unseen Plan

So we do not lose heart. . . . For this slight momentary affliction is preparing for us an eternal weight of glory beyond all comparison, because we look not to the things that are seen but to the things that are unseen; for the things that are seen are transient, but the things that are unseen are eternal. 2 Corinthians 4:16–18

The temptation to give in to despair in the midst of life's challenges is strong. We are women of faith, but we are also professionals, members of society, and co-heads of our families. All's well in the world when I begin my day with morning prayer and crafting a perfect agenda over a hot cup of coffee. But many days, by the time my mug is half empty, my plans have gone awry, replaced by more urgent matters over which I have no control.

Accompanying my aging parents through their many health struggles has become a significant part of my life's mission. The greatest trial I face most days is witnessing their sufferings and being unable to help. I've attempted to strike many bargains with God. "Give me this burden, Lord," I cajole. "I'd rather carry it than see Mom suffer." Yet day after day, the afflictions mount until I question if God hears my pleas.

Lately, I have found peace in understanding that these struggles are not tests for me to pass or fail. Along with being lovingly present to my parents, my job is to trust God's plan, embrace things unseen, and rest in the eternal love of the One who knows each trial and each perfect resolution. When tempted to lose heart, let's allow the Immaculate Heart of our Blessed Mother to pull us into her embrace. We do not lose heart because, despite life's burdens, our Creator waits to welcome us home.

Prayer: Father, You know every affliction and burden, but You have crafted me—just as I am—for such a time as this. Help me to strive for the eternal, trusting that the temporal will work itself out according to Your divine will. Amen.

Respond to His Call: Today, when faced with a problem you cannot solve, thank God for the unknown blessing that accompanies that challenge.

Lisa M. Hendey

Look Up

The watchmen found me, as they went about in the city. "Have you seen him whom my soul loves?" Song of Solomon 3:3

The winter solstice has passed; the days should be growing longer. However, it feels as if we remain stuck in the ditch of midwinter darkness. Days are dingy, the holidays are past, and spring seems even further away than the groundhog can predict. Yet, every day, regardless of the time of year, we are charged with the task of pushing on.

On this day, I realize the sun is rising, and it is beautiful! The sky is pink and barely blue along the horizon, a clear, stunning white across the top. There is a crisp frost on the ground, and my breath mists in the air as I exhale on my morning walk.

Every day is a gift from God, and today is no different. He has blessed us this day. We, His chosen people, have been created with the power to sing His praises. As we take in the beauty of an awakening world, let us offer prayer and praise for those yet to open their hearts to see and believe. We must represent to all the universe how our souls can sing His unending praise.

To quote Matt Redman's song "10,000 Reasons," we should "sing like never before," for "the sun comes up, it's a new day dawning / It's time to sing Your song again." Friends, look up! Have you seen "him whom my soul loves"? He is everywhere—in the cold, frigid morning and in the dawning of the sun. Let our souls sing today!

Prayer: Lord, I can feel my heart vibrate with love for You; let me be a sign of Your grace to all I meet today. Amen.

Respond to His Call: Today, turn on your favorite praise-and-worship song, and lift your eyes and your voice to the Lord.

Julie E. Kenney

Church Ladies Unite

> Whoever would be great among you must be your servant, and whoever would be first among you must be slave of all. For the Son of man also came not to be served but to serve, and to give his life as a ransom for many. Mark 10:43–45

It feels so good to get praise! As a self-professed "church lady," I realize the paradox that has crept into my life. I want to serve our parish and become more humble in my walk—but it feels good to be noticed. Am I alone in this weakness? James and John's request to Jesus for a place in heaven is bold (see Mark 10:35–45), but is it that different from requests we make of Jesus? "Help my child along this path, and I will serve You forever," or "Save a spot for me in heaven, and my works of faith will increase."

Here's a prayer to counter our desire to have our efforts recognized: Lord, let there be less of me so that You may shine through. This prayer for humility accompanies me as I serve. I want to acknowledge my limited role in His plan and convey to others that Jesus alone offers healing and graces.

We can hardly blame James and John for wanting to lock down some of the details of eternal life. We all feel the need for control. My grappling with this desire is evident in the way I fixate on a few aspects of my kids' lives. But parenting four kids has convinced me of the opposite reality: I can't control the outcome. I don't have a guarantee for how things will turn out. This realization can be frightening, but it's freeing too. Instead of worrying about how to control every situation, I pray for Jesus to lead me.

You might be a church lady just like me, trying to follow the call of Jesus in your family. My prayers are with you for humility and recognition of your limitations. May Jesus alone shine; His plan is more excellent, anyway.

Prayer: Lord, I pray for humility. Help me trade the desire for control and recognition for a simple trust in You and Your plan. Amen.

Respond to His Call: Today, each time you are able to serve another, say, "Thank You, Lord, for letting me serve Your people."

Anne Carraux

Conversing with Christ

> The woman said to him, "I know that Messiah is coming (he who is called Christ); when he comes, he will show us all things." Jesus said to her, "I who speak to you am he." John 4:25–26

Can you imagine meeting a stranger while out on an errand who proceeds to tell you everything you've ever done—including parts of your personal history that you're not exactly proud of?

The woman at the well, caught off guard by Jesus' supernatural knowledge about her life, at first assumed he was some kind of prophet. But then something clicked. She remembered a prophecy about the promised Messiah who would "show us all things." She shared this prophecy with Jesus—not asking Him outright whether He was the Messiah but searching to see what He would claim or reveal about Himself.

Prayer is a two-way conversation with Christ. Most of us know how to speak our hearts to Jesus. But *listening* to Christ—really hearing His voice—takes some practice. Christ speaks into our hearts and reveals our history. In doing so, He is a mirror for us. This is important because we need to see ourselves as we truly are in the eyes of God. Yes, God knows everything we have ever done—the good, bad, ugly, and beautiful. He wants us to see our past, present, and future through the merciful eyes of the Trinity.

The woman at the well didn't experience condemnation from Jesus. She experienced the truth that set her free. In recognizing her need for a Messiah and believing in Jesus, she was radically transformed into a new creation. She wouldn't repeat her past because Christ changed her from within. Her Messiah, with whom she conversed at the well, revealed her past, spoke into her present, and gave her a new future. She was redeemed!

Prayer: Lord Jesus, I desire to meet You at the wellspring of prayer and to hear Your voice. Graciously reveal my true identity through the mirror of Your Sacred Heart as You did for the woman at the well. Amen.

Respond to His Call: Place yourself in the scripture scene of the woman at the well. Record your conversation with Christ in your prayer journal.

Kathleen Beckman

Michael and Me

Fear not, for I am with you, be not dismayed, for I am your God; I will strengthen you, I will help you, I will uphold you with my victorious right hand. Isaiah 41:10

About a year ago, during my daily walks to St. Peter's Square, I'd see the same man asking for handouts. He was only one of many homeless in Vatican City looking for alms. Pope Francis has created an extensive network of outreach for the destitute, and many Vatican structures are available to provide aid. There are showers, barbers, medical help, food, and even a twenty-eight-bed dormitory just blocks from St. Peter's.

One day, the Holy Father spoke of the poor and homeless and asked if, when we encounter them on our path, we avoid eye contact and distance ourselves from them—or even cross the street as they approach. Those words were on my mind the next time I walked to St. Peter's Square and saw the same man. This time, I smiled and said, "*Buon giorno.*" He smiled back. Soon, he was always the first to greet me!

One day I said, "We talk to each other, but I don't know your name." He said, "Michael." His smile was a lot broader that day and on subsequent days. Whenever our paths crossed, I'd greet him by name and we'd speak briefly.

I know so little about Michael, but I know his name. I pray for him often. If God has loved Michael from all eternity—called him by name as He called me by name—He must have plans and hopes for Michael.

How many Michaels are there, men and women whom God has made in His image and likeness and called by name, who to us remain nameless? Is there anyone on the margins of your life whose name you should learn?

Prayer: Lord, change my complacency to courage to do as You exhort us: "Truly I tell you, whatever you did for one of the least of these brothers and sisters of mine, you did for me." Amen.

Respond to His Call: Today, look for a way to help a needy brother or sister that shatters your comfort zone.

Joan F. Lewis

If Only St. Paul Had Had a Twitter Account

And the Lord said to Paul one night in a vision, "Do not be afraid, but speak and do not be silent." Acts 18:9

Here is a brief—and not entirely accurate—history of communication in the Church. We start with God telling Adam to stay away from the tree. Then there's Charlton Heston receiving the Ten Commandments (I told you, not entirely accurate). Fast forward to an angel visiting Mary, then a star over the manger, the Sermon on the Mount, the monks and illuminated manuscripts, *Radio Replies* with Blessed Fulton Sheen, EWTN, Pope Benedict XVI tweeting, and this very book! At the heart of it all has been our need to communicate with and about God.

Consider the first evangelists and what they accomplished with the tools they had—their sandals, their voice, and the Word of God. Now consider what is available to us, the new evangelists. We can communicate in real time with someone on the other side of the planet, and what do we do with the amazing tools we have been given? Send photos of cats with hats made of limes. St. Paul could never have imagined the means of evangelization available to us, but we share with him two things: the call to communicate the love of God and the call to spread the Gospel.

Remember, the first evangelists were successful in spreading the Word of God because of their faith, courage, and perseverance. So in our age of evangelization, become like St. Paul! Take your tweets, status updates, and posts, root them in the truth of the Gospel, strap on your sandals, go bravely out into the world, and spread the Good News! "Do not be afraid. Go on speaking, and do not be silent."

Prayer: Pray for us, St. Paul, that we may be preachers of truth to the whole world. Amen.

Respond to His Call: Share Jesus with someone today, using the amazing tools of technology and social media.

Elizabeth Westhoff

Attitude of Gratitude

Make a joyful noise to the LORD, all the lands! Serve the LORD with gladness! Come into his presence with singing! Psalm 100:1–2

There's a sign near my office that says, "Have an attitude of gratitude." Whenever I see it, I can't help but think about my attitude—at work, yes, but also at home, in my relationships with loved ones, and in my relationship with God. When pressed to list all the things I'm thankful for, I can compete with the best. You want ten items? A hundred? Piece of cake.

It's a different thing to move through the day and give thanks moment by moment. Even if I do wake and thank the Lord for a new day and opportunity, I soon get lost in the daily struggle. When doing the breakfast dishes, I grumble at the mess instead of being grateful for food. In traffic, I complain about slow drivers instead of being thankful for personal transportation. When at work, I resent interruptions instead of appreciating the job that uses my gifts.

One day at work, I was surprised by what sounded like a woman singing a song of praise. I looked around, thinking a choir was performing. Other people had the same stunned looks on their faces, trying to understand where the singing originated. I followed the song to another hallway just as the last notes rang, and saw a small group of women hugging each other. The song had ended—but the effects were just beginning. Apparently, an elderly woman with an amazing voice had felt called to sing praises to the Lord. In her own words, "I was called, and I had to obey." Her audible act of expressing thankfulness to God had a huge impact on her immediate surroundings. You may not be called to sing your thankfulness to God—but just imagine how your world might change if you constantly infused it with clear expressions of gratitude!

Prayer: Lord, give me the grace to maintain an attitude of gratitude throughout my day. Amen.

Respond to His Call: Today, make a conscious effort to say, "Thank You, Lord," each time you are interrupted. Say it out loud—it might even make you smile!

Maria Morera Johnson

The Master Weaver

But, as it is written, "What no eye has seen, nor ear heard, nor the heart of man conceived, what God has prepared for those who love him." 1 Corinthians 2:9

God's stitches are intricately woven together. They are the colors of creation—green and blue—so vibrant and full of calming hope. For just a moment, God gives me a glimpse of the detailed tapestry He is weaving. It is a reminder that He is at work; He is in control.

It's easy for me to know, intellectually, that Christ reigns in this world. But sometimes, I'm not so sure I really believe it deep within my soul. As I look upon life, upon what is going on in this broken world, I only see the messy backside of the tapestry. From my limited vantage point, all I can see is jumbled chaos. And I pray, "Where are You, God?"

And God answers with a whispered reminder that He moves amid pandemics, scandals, and injustice. He is in the midst of painful and overwhelming situations. He is present throughout all of this broken and beautiful world that ultimately belongs to Him.

When I forget about the countless ways God is working within His creation, He gently points out His presence, and He gives me hope once again.

God's vision is much clearer, much broader than mine. God sees the big picture. He takes what seems to be chaos and flips it upside down. He sees both sides of life's tapestry and knows how it all works together.

The Holy Spirit, the breath of life, desires to dwell on the earth, as wind and flame, as peaceful strength, to continue God's work of renewing, re-creating, and restoring humanity. And while His work of weaving intricate stitches may seem hidden at times, it is made visible to eyes of faith.

Prayer: Oh Lord, let Your Spirit gather into His wind those who seek Your face, who trust that You are at work in this world, making all things new. Amen.

Respond to His Call: Today, allow the sunshine to warm your face. Rest in the light of God's love. Trust that God is at work in you . . . and in this world.

Sarah Damm

Be a Doer of God's Word

For if any one is a hearer of the word and not a doer, he is like a man who observes his natural face in a mirror; for he observes himself and goes away and at once forgets what he was like. James 1:23–24

The other day, I found an old Bible study workbook on the Epistle of James. Glancing through it reminded me of a discipleship group I teach, where I've witnessed firsthand scripture's power to change and purify, making us more like Jesus. It also reminded me that it's never enough just to read or hear the words of scripture.

As an exercise, ask yourself, "Am I better today than I was a year ago, six months ago, a month ago?" If the answer is no, ask yourself, "What am I doing with God's Word?" We can study and memorize scripture and be part of a small group but still feel stagnant—or even in bondage to old habits. The Word of God is intended to change us, but being readers or hearers is only half of the equation; we must be *doers* of God's Word.

St. James says reading scripture without acting on it is like seeing ourselves in a mirror only to forget what we look like as soon as we walk away. Scripture, like a mirror, reveals who we really are. Who are we? We are women created to bear the very image of God. James adds that if we become doers of the Word—acting in accord with what the mirror of scripture reveals—we will be blessed (v. 25). What woman doesn't want to be blessed?

As a daughter of God, you must make a habit of gazing intently into the mirror of scripture—and taking action based on what you see. The Epistle of James is a great place to start, with practical advice about being quick to listen, slow to speak, and slow to anger.

Prayer: Grant to me a listening heart, O Lord, a sure sign of intimacy and trust between You and me. Amen.

Respond to His Call: Today, resolve to see yourself as you truly are—in the mirror of God's Word. Find a command or call to action in scripture, and do it!

Dianne Davis

You Can Call Me Catholic

When I am afraid, I put my trust in you. In God, whose word I praise, in God I trust without a fear. What can flesh do to me? Psalm 56:3–4

I entered this world long awaited by my parents, who had been praying for a baby for several years. Wanting to honor my grandmother, they gave me her name, Lorraine (Lori for short).

In first grade, the daily roll call was excruciating! Every morning the teacher loudly proclaimed my full name, Lorraine. I quickly realized I was the only six-year-old with an old-fashioned and unhip name—something my fellow first-graders mercilessly reminded me of every day. I still shudder when I think about the humiliation I suffered; the teasing and ridicule made me embarrassed about my name.

In recent years, as my beautiful grandmother reached the end of her life, I came to realize that I had inherited not only her name but also part of her identity—her infectious laughter, her love of travel, and her genuine desire to love people. Knowing that we share these qualities has made me proud to be named after her and less self-conscious about my uncommon name.

In the same way, when Christ calls us to be His followers, we take on parts of His identity and the name "Catholic," which is not always a comfortable thing. Coworkers, family members, and even strangers may make hurtful comments, question our beliefs, or insult and embarrass us.

When I'm feeling afraid to share my Catholic faith or wear the name "Catholic" proudly, I turn to Psalm 56:3–4 and pray for the courage to embrace what I love about my identity in Christ—and my calling to be different from the world around me.

Prayer: Gracious Father, protect me from all that seeks to weaken my identity in You, and help me to trust in Your purpose for my life as a Catholic. Amen.

Respond to His Call: If you find yourself hesitant to share your Catholic faith or wear the name "Catholic" proudly at times, write down what you love about your Savior and where you see those same qualities in yourself.

Lori Ubowksi

Head or Heart?

His divine power has granted to us all things that pertain to life and godliness, through the knowledge of him who called us to his own glory and excellence. 2 Peter 1:3

Is faith a matter of the head or the heart? A popular "church-y" phrase is that faith must *move* from the head to the heart, implying that for faith to be authentic, it must transform from head knowledge *about* Jesus to a relationship *with* Jesus. While our interior relationship with God is a necessary cornerstone of faith, it's not true that knowledge of God must *move* from the head to the heart. It should reside in both.

Today's patron saint, St. Thomas Aquinas, is the epitome of this truth. His faith was equally intellectual and personal. This is what allowed him to write both the scientific, philosophical proofs of God's existence and the poetic, personal *Adoro te Devote*. During times of intense intellectual thought, Thomas would lay his head against the tabernacle for guidance and clarity—beautifully embodying the union between head and heart.

At various times in our faith journeys, we can tend toward one extreme or the other. Sometimes we may spend more time reading books or listening to podcasts about our faith than in prayer. Other times we may converse with God regularly in prayer but neglect to learn more about our faith. Our goal should be to integrate the two, always seeking to build both our intellectual and our personal knowledge of God.

The wells of our Catholic intellectual tradition and of God's heart are both deep enough that we will never fully consume them. So let us drink with equal fervor! In this way, we will always be ready to give an intelligent and personal testimony for the faith we profess.

Prayer: "I am not like Thomas, wounds I cannot see / but can plainly call thee Lord and God as he / Let me to a deeper faith daily nearer move / daily make me harder hope and dearer love" (St. Thomas Aquinas, *Adoro te Devote*).

Respond to His Call: Pick a concrete way to cultivate your intellectual and personal faith this week. For example, begin reading a book by a saint, and add a specific prayer to your daily routine.

Annie McHugh

A Fruitful Life

But those that were sown upon the good soil are the ones who hear the word and accept it and bear fruit, thirtyfold and sixtyfold and a hundredfold. Mark 4:20

Today marks the anniversary of my mom's sudden passing. Her life was fruitful, vibrant, and joyful, but it was also quite ordinary. She was a devoted farm wife and loving mother of eight daughters. The thousands who came to her funeral made it clear that in some mysterious way, her ordinary life veiled something extraordinary.

Our home was busy, lively, often chaotic, and messy. Home was holy ground where grace abounded. Now I understand the transformational power of my mom's simple faith; it was the most precious gift she gave us, and it multiplies in her ten grandchildren. She gave her heart to Jesus, her yes. In the day-to-day grind of ordinary life, extraordinary graces began to unfold. The Divine Sower was mysteriously at work, never letting a small act of love go to waste.

If she read this, my mom would be shocked at the lofty description of her ordinary life. She knew heaven as home, but did she know that she brought heaven to her home in loving Jesus?

Do you find meaning in the grind of your vocation? Is the ground you traverse holy? Jesus will use any doubts and insecurities to till receptive soil in your heart; He waters with mercy and love. The moments of obscurity in your life can be tender moments of intimacy with Him.

When we yield to Jesus, fruit not only appears; it multiplies and overflows. By allowing the Divine Sower to produce lasting fruits in us, may we be filled with holy wonder as we contemplate the extraordinary graces hidden in our ordinary lives. Then, like my mother, may we quietly sow seeds in God's kingdom, right in our ordinary lives.

Prayer: Lord, I will remember every day as Your gift to me. My gift to You is to bear fruit in return. Amen.

Respond to His Call: Remember the fifth commandment: Honor your father and your mother. Today, pray for them—and perhaps give them a call.

Kristin Molitor

Jesus Has the Wheel

And a storm of wind came down on the lake, and they were filling with water, and were in danger. And they went and woke him, saying, "Master, Master, we are perishing!" And he awoke and rebuked the wind and the raging waves; and they ceased, and there was a calm. Luke 8:23–24

"Calgon, take me away." That phrase is from a popular 1970s commercial for bath products featuring a stressed-out working mom desperately trying to get a few minutes of quality time alone. In a moment of frustration, she blurts out those words before settling into a welcoming bath.

One afternoon, that commercial was running on a continuous loop in my brain. I was heading to Confession in a foul mood. I had just about had it with the stress and the angst of the world as well as my radio audience, to the point of wondering if God wanted me to work in Catholic media any longer. So, I prayed, "Lord, Your will. Not mine."

While I was whining to God, I stopped at the church office to pick up the mail for my husband, who is a deacon. A prayer card dropped out of the envelope; it was the ordination card from our associate pastor. I am not sure how the prayer card ended up in my husband's mail since the priest had been ordained several years earlier. But when I looked at the quote on the card and the image accompanying it, I realized it was meant for me to see at that moment. The picture was Jesus calming the storm on the sea of Galilee. And the quote was from St. Padre Pio: "Stay in the boat in which the Lord has placed you. You will not perish. It appears to you that Jesus is sleeping, but His heart diligently watches over you."

At the right time, He will awake to restore your calm. I had my answer. I think I knew it all along. Don't give up. Take a break or a bath once in a while. But never forget, when you step out of the tub and back out on deck, who is at the wheel.

Prayer: Lord, Your will, not mine. Jesus, take the wheel. Amen.

Respond to His Call: Restore your calm. Treat yourself to a nice bubble bath.

Teresa Tomeo

Until God Opens the Next Door, Praise Him in the Hallway

Have no anxiety about anything, but in everything by prayer and supplication with thanksgiving let your requests be made known to God. Philippians 4:6

I remember watching *The Sound of Music* on television each Easter. One of Maria's lines always stuck with me: "Where the Lord closes a door, somewhere He opens a window." I often recall this message of hope when I encounter an opportunity lost—a door closing. It is a message that always proved to be accurate.

Then one day, a door closed, and I waited, and I waited . . . and it seemed as though God didn't know someone had shut the door on me. As time passed with no opening in sight, I began to feel anxious. Why weren't Julie Andrews' words of wisdom coming through for me?

Then, I realized, it wasn't the words of Julie Andrews I needed to rely on; it was the Word of God. So, I opened my Bible and found this passage: "Have no anxiety about anything, but in everything by prayer and supplication with thanksgiving let your requests be made known to God." I took comfort, but I still didn't see the window opening.

What do you do when the window stays shut? Easy; you praise God! Here are three simple ways:

1. *Pray*. Every time we pray, we communicate with our Father.
2. *Sing a song*. Through song, we can reflect on His great love and mercy.
3. *Offer it up*. When we unite our sufferings with Christ, we add meaning to them.

So, Fräulein Maria was right. But sometimes that window takes longer to open than we had hoped. It's up to us what we do while we wait.

Prayer: Lord, help me live one day at a time. Please help me not to worry about tomorrow but to trust that You will take care of my every need. Amen.

Respond to His Call: Today, blast your favorite praise-and-worship song and sing along!

Kelly M. Wahlquist

The Healing Power of Confession

Create in me a clean heart, O God, and put a new and right spirit within me. Cast me not away from your presence, and take not your holy Spirit from me. Restore to me the joy of your salvation, and uphold me with a willing spirit. Psalm 51:10–12

As a little girl, I often dreamed of a fairy godmother granting me three wishes. My usual picks? Money, fame, and world peace (the last one thrown in with the hope that it somehow would garner me extra wishes). As an adult, although I'd like to say differently, my wishes are about the same. The difference now is that I recognize the sin that can be attached to those desires and often ask God to keep me steadfast in faith and to stir in me a desire to avoid temptations.

If given a chance, I wonder if I would ever use one of those precious wishes to be granted a spirit impervious to sin. Could I forgo the false idols, tempting comforts, and fading treasures of this earthly life for the unseen hope of eternal glory?

Fairy godmothers do not exist, of course. But God does, and He is there in every moment as I choose between grace and temptation.

Psalm 51 reminds me of the powerful healing available in the Sacrament of Reconciliation. Confession, an encounter with Jesus, reconciles and heals us. Jesus creates a clean heart in us, one free from the shame and guilt of our poor choices and fallen nature. He renews in us a determination to do better the next time through the Holy Spirit living within.

This great gift of a heart reconciled to God is not as limited as my dream of three wishes from a fairy godmother—I can partake of it as frequently as I need! This treasure far outshines money, fame, or any other desire a girl could dream of. And as far as world peace goes—God is working on it one heart at a time through the peace of Christ that surpasses anything this world has to give.

Prayer: O Lord, place in my heart the courage and humility to bring my sins to You. Amen.

Respond to His Call: Make a mercy date with Jesus. Find a convenient Confession time (and location) and put it on your calendar.

Allison Gingras

The Law of Love

And every priest stands daily at his service, offering repeatedly the same sacrifices, which can never take away sins. But when Christ had offered for all time a single sacrifice for sins, he sat down at the right hand of God. Hebrews 10:11–12

In first-century Israel, there was only one place where devout Jews could make reparation for their sins against each other and the Lord—the great Temple in Jerusalem. At least once a year, every Jew made a pilgrimage to the holy city and entered the Temple, carrying lambs, goats, and turtledoves. Priests waited at an altar just below the Holy of Holies to receive their offerings. One type of offering was required shortly after a child's birth: every new mother offered a sacrifice for her purification.

Imagine the scene as Mary, Joseph, and Jesus arrived at the Temple for Mary's ritual purification. They entered the gates, Joseph carrying the offering of two turtledoves, Mary with Jesus in her arms. As Mary and Joseph entered the Temple with the infant Jesus, no one realized that something astonishing was taking place. The Son of God had entered into the story of salvation in the most unexpected way. Not as a warrior, coming to overthrow the Romans. Not majestically, in a pillar of fire or a blazing chariot but as a child—small, innocent, and vulnerable—in His mother's arms.

Only the aged prophet Simeon and prophetess Anna—and Mary and Joseph—were allowed to glimpse this extraordinary reality as it unfolded. Only they had some inkling that this baby would be the Lamb of God, the sacrifice to end all sacrifices, the one to conquer sin and death forever.

As you celebrate Candlemas, look to the child Jesus as the Lamb of God who, out of love for each of us, offered Himself as the one sacrifice that truly washes away our sin.

Prayer: Simeon and Anna, pray for me to recognize Christ in my midst, and to grasp the fullness of God coming as an infant. Amen.

Respond to His Call: Make an offering to God: give Him your prayers, works, joys, and sufferings of this day.

Stephanie Landsem

Anna the Prophetess

And there was a prophetess, Anna . . . she was of a great age . . . [and] did not depart from the temple, worshiping with fasting and prayer night and day. And coming up at that very hour she gave thanks to God, and spoke of him to all who were looking for the redemption of Jerusalem. Luke 2:36–38

I love Anna! Anna is one of those bubbly, over-the-moon-with-joy grand-mothers about the Christ child. Maybe my exuberant love of Anna is motivated by what I didn't have as a grandchild: a grandmother. Deter-mined to be a loving mother and grandmother, I support, encourage, talk about, and rave about my children and grandchildren every chance I get.

So I identify with Anna the prophetess, the one longing with love, listening to the Holy Spirit's whispers for decades, adoring in the Temple. Can you imagine her joy when she finally encounters the long-awaited Child? She touches Him gently, holds Him with failing physical strength. She memorizes His face—and, in that moment, nobody can keep her heart from overflowing with joy and love. I imagine that Anna's joyful proclamations may have sounded something like these familiar Christmas lectionary readings: "Children . . . your sins have been forgiven for his sake" (1 Jn 2:12) and, "Ascribe to the LORD the glory due his name; bring an offering, and come into his courts! Worship the LORD in holy attire" (Ps 96:8–9).

Speak again, Anna, tell us the story again! Prophesy to us about the Child who dwells in the Eucharist, so that He will grow and become strong within us. Help us to know His wisdom and the favor that God has brought to us. A holy day has dawned. Come, you nations, and adore the Lord. Today a great light has come upon the earth!

Prayer: O Jesus, give me the power to prophesy! I want to announce You to the world and to the people You have given to me to know and love. Help me to spread Your name wherever I am. Amen.

Respond to His Call: Speak to a friend or family member about some-thing in your life that changed for the better because of Jesus.

Dr. Carol Younger

Ugly, Sensible Shoes

The LORD sees not as man sees; man looks on the outward appearance, but the LORD looks on the heart. 1 Samuel 16:7

I have a dear friend who was deeply, emotionally attached to her wardrobe. Growing up in the Great Depression, she typically had a total of three plain cotton dresses to choose from on a given day. So perhaps it's no surprise she eventually defined success as the ability to buy gorgeous clothes with shoes to match.

But in the years before she died, my friend suffered a few minor strokes and kept falling down. Since she had no family nearby, the neighbors took her to the ER.

One well-meaning neighbor bought her a pair of safe, sensible shoes—with rubber soles—that would help keep her from falling. My distressed friend called me, crying, "The shoes are so ugly! So today, I didn't wear them. I put on the cute ones that go with my slacks." Then wistfully, "I hope I don't fall."

She reminded me of a child, protesting the practical slickers her mother wants her to wear in the rain. But I sensed that she'd had enough people telling her what she needed to do; instead, I decided to lighten her mood. "Well," I said, "if you slip and fall and die when you're wearing the cute shoes, at least those who stand over your dead body will see how well put together you are! And you would never be buried in ugly, sensible shoes!" She giggled with delight.

How often we let appearances override good sense! My friend probably should have opted for the ugly, sensible shoes. But that's not the real lesson here. Rather than criticism or a word of common sense, what my friend's heart really needed in that moment was compassion, empathy, and a little bit of humor.

Prayer: Lord, help me to see what others really need, not just what I think they need. Amen.

Respond to His Call: Is someone in your life making choices you think are silly or foolish? Don't shame them! Instead, pray about how you can gently meet their needs and provide the right kind of encouragement.

Rose Sweet

Blessing God

Lord, now let your servant depart in peace, according to your word; for my eyes have seen your salvation which you have prepared in the presence of all peoples, a light for revelation to the Gentiles, and for glory to your people Israel. Luke 2:29–32

Simeon reveals his eagerness to see the face of Christ, his anticipation to gaze upon the salvation of his people. Simeon's desire was fulfilled when he took the infant Jesus into his arms and "blessed God." Wait . . . how does *that* work? Simeon "blessed" God? How can one bless God? God is the giver of all blessings! So, after reading this passage in Luke, I did a little research on the Presentation in the Temple.

Let's take a closer look using etymology, the study of the sources of words. The Greek word for "bless" is *eulogeo*. It's made up of two components: *eu*, meaning "well done, good, or rightly"; and *logos*, meaning "a word, or a divine announcement."

Stay with me on this. There is no question that what Simeon said was "right" and "well done." Jesus is a light to the world, a glory for all people. And what Simeon said qualified not just as truthful and eloquent: with the Holy Spirit as his guide, Simeon proclaimed a divine announcement of the arrival of salvation for all people. So this is one way we can bless God—by using our words to proclaim His truth and His message!

Jesus, the one to bring salvation to all people, was brought to the Temple by His parents, Mary and Joseph. Unlike Simeon, Joseph is not known for having been a man of many words; yet he proved to be a virtuous husband to Mary and a foster father for Jesus. In his own way, he blessed God—not through eloquent words but through humble actions.

We are blessed by the example of both of these holy men—Simeon's ability to bless God by proclaiming a divine announcement, and Joseph's silent virtue.

Prayer: Jesus, make me eager like Simeon to see Your face. Show me how I can bless You today, whether with words or through virtuous actions. Amen.

Respond to His Call: Are you outspoken like Simeon or silent like Joseph? Ask the Lord how He desires you to proclaim His love and salvation.

Susanna Parent

Do Not Worry!

Look at the birds of the air: they neither sow nor reap nor gather into barns, and yet your heavenly Father feeds them. Are you not of more value than they? Matthew 6:26

Whenever I feel burdened by a particular situation, I am encouraged by how God speaks to me through this scripture. *Do not worry. You are of special value to Me. If I care for the daily needs of the birds, how much more can you—My dear child created in My image—depend on Me for all your needs?*

Our Father in heaven pursues and protects us because He deeply loves us. Does this mean that we will never fall or experience pain? Of course not. We will experience hardship, but God will ensure that our crosses work to our good, molding us to follow His will.

Just as an animal fiercely protects her young from danger, so also God protects us from the evil that threatens to steal His precious life in our soul. But we have a responsibility to preserve our own souls from outside threats that can crowd out Christ's presence within us. Jesus names one of the biggest obstacles to our ability to sense His love: worry. It's natural to focus on having enough food, clothing, and shelter. But it's vital that we see our lives as a continual gift from our loving heavenly Father, rather than as a possession to be guarded at all costs.

If we open our eyes and declutter our hearts, we will see examples of God's faithful love all around us. Worry forgets God's love and focuses on the things that might go wrong. Faith rests in God's love and believes nothing can stop His good plan for our lives. Worry sees suffering as evidence that life is going off the rails. Faith sees suffering as an opportunity to grow in virtue and draw nearer to Christ.

Prayer: Lord, ease my heart from its burdens. Remind me that You will provide for my every need. Amen.

Respond to His Call: Where in your heart is worry crowding out your experience of God's care and love? How can you replace that worry with faith? Put it in writing. "Today I am worried about _____, but I have faith that God will _____."

Kathleen Billings

The Bounty of Sisterhood

They said to him, "He will put those wretches to a miserable death, and lease the vineyard to other tenants who will give him the fruits in their seasons." Matthew 21:41

While reading the parable of the wicked tenants in Matthew's gospel, I was moved by these words: "Therefore I say to you, the kingdom of God will be taken away from you and given to a people, producing the fruit of it" (Mt 21:43). Although all may seem lost, the vineyard owner, God, remains in control of the vineyard. With these words, Jesus assures a place in the vineyard for anyone aiming to bring glory to God through faithful service.

Have you ever considered the harvest God provides for you and the opportunities He gives you to work in His vineyard? Our families, our Church community, our friends, and our coworkers are all fertile ground for sharing God's kingdom. We must be Christ in the world and share what we believe. People may not wish to hear our words, but as the old hymn reminds us (echoing John 13:35), "They will know we are Christians by our love." Sometimes our witness is best expressed by a simple invitation. My return to the Catholic Church began with one woman's gift to me of a book, along with an invitation to join a reading group in her home.

What joy I've discovered in my small group as we share everyday struggles and triumphs in our faith journeys. The days we feel we labor in vain, we are buoyed by our friends' recognition of our efforts to please God—and by their efforts to do the same. It gives us tremendous courage to see we are not the only ones seeking to know God and His will, and to share in the hope that we will be the vine growers with whom God will choose to share the vineyard.

Prayer: Lord, may my efforts to remain faithful not only please You but also produce beneficial fruit, especially when joined with the fidelity of my sisters in Christ. Amen.

Respond to His Call: Reach out to a friend today. Invite her to join your small group or ask her to help you start one.

Allison Gingras

The Gift of Giving a Name

Your eyes beheld my unformed substance; in your book were written, every one of them, the days that were formed for me, when as yet there was none of them. Psalm 139:16

Before we were married, my husband and I agreed on names for our first boy and first girl. The names we chose honored our parents and some close friends. We always wanted a larger family, but we didn't think beyond those two names. And we didn't consider that it wouldn't be until child number four that our girl name became relevant!

Time and again, we brought this gift of giving a name to prayer. *Lord, what do You want this child to be named? How will You call this child to Yourself?* Some of the answers we received were names we'd never considered. A name simply popped into one of our minds. But when we spoke each name out loud, we knew it was right.

As we get to know our children better, we revel in how these names so beautifully fit the people they are. This incredible insight was never clearer than with our second child, whom we lost to a miscarriage. We chose the name Ethan. I didn't know it when we named him, but "Ethan" means "permanent, firm, enduring"—fitting for a saint who rests eternally with the Lord.

Naming our children has been an exercise in trust and a lesson in confidence in God's provision for us. To God, we are not just some*thing*, but some*one* whom He loves and cherishes personally. Naming our children is a small reflection of the reality that God intimately knows and deeply cares for each of His children, calling us by name to be part of His family, the Church.

Prayer: Lord, help me to hear how You are calling out to me. Help me to see myself with Your eyes, to identify myself with the name You have for me. And give me the grace to live this identity with joy. Amen.

Respond to His Call: Look up the meaning of your name or of your parish patron's name. Ask the Holy Spirit to show you how this name connects with your particular calling to love.

Lindsay Schlegel

God's Temple Needs You

So then you are no longer strangers and sojourners, but you are fellow citizens with the saints and members of the household of God, built upon the foundation of the apostles and prophets, Christ Jesus himself being the cornerstone, in whom the whole structure is joined together and grows into a holy temple in the Lord; in whom you also are built into it for a dwelling place of God in the Spirit. Ephesians 2:19–22

So much separates us: culture, race, age, religion, sex, opinions, temperaments, and a million other things. We can feel lonely even in the midst of family, friends, and work that energizes us. The world sees our smiling social-media avatar and counts us lucky, yet there's an aching emptiness in the center of our being that only God can fill. Sometimes we blame that unmet longing on the people around us.

St. Paul's letter to the Ephesians reveals that, in Christ, we are being built together into "a dwelling place of God in the Spirit." How consoling to think that our loving Jesus is drawing us into communion, holding us together, and molding us into something sacred.

When we trust God to satisfy our deepest longings, we become ambassadors of this "holy temple in the Lord," an architecture so great in beauty that it is inhabited by the very Spirit of God. In this mysterious structure, we are no longer strangers and sojourners because our connection no longer relies on agreement or human understanding. We stand on a foundation that mortars us to divine love, life, and fulfillment.

Prayer: Lord Jesus, You alone are the way to peace. Make my heart a sanctuary of Your limitless, unconditional love, and then speak that love to others through my every thought, word, and action. Amen.

Respond to His Call: Tell someone in a very specific way that you love them for how they are uniquely and wonderfully made by God.

Lisa Mladinich

Ultimate Elevator Pitch

But in your hearts reverence Christ as Lord. Always be prepared to make a defense to any one who calls you to account for the hope that is in you, yet do it with gentleness and reverence. 1 Peter 3:15

Early in my career, I belonged to several professional organizations. We often learned to market ourselves with an "elevator pitch"—a description of our organization or job in thirty to sixty seconds, roughly the time of an elevator ride. Years later, I learned the Bible has its own directive for an elevator pitch. St. Peter tells us to "always be prepared to make a defense to any one who calls you to account for the hope that is in you." The hope we have in Jesus will not fail us: "Suffering produces endurance, and endurance produces character, and character produces hope, and hope does not disappoint us" (Rom 5:3–5).

While walking the Way of St. James, or the Camino, in Spain, I came to recognize the anchor as a symbol of hope. At one point on the trip, I met a younger woman with a necklace with three charms: a cross, an anchor, and a heart. She shared that it was the only present she ever received from her father, and the charms represented faith, hope, and love. Later, a priest led us through a reflection on our journey, asking that we choose a symbol that represented something meaningful we'd learned. One of the men chose the anchor because he'd offered hope to a friend who happened to share his love of sailing. Ever since that trip, when I think of hope, I think of an anchor that we can rely on to keep us steady no matter how rough the waves get.

Today, we need to be anchors of hope for one another. And we need to be ready to share the *reason* for our hope in Jesus. Is your elevator pitch ready?

Prayer: Lord, help me to trust in You as You call me forward. You will equip me with all the graces I need. Amen.

Respond to His Call: Write down your elevator pitch. How would you share Jesus with another in thirty seconds? Practice it in front of the mirror—it will come in handy someday!

Lucy H. Johnson

The 1.3-Mile Witness

. . . who shows no partiality to princes, nor regards the rich more than the poor, for they are all the work of his hands. Job 34:19

It was May 1982. I didn't have a date to the prom, which was called a dinner dance, which meant you could still go if you didn't have a date. Another friend was dateless as well. My dad drove us to the prom. It was only a 1.3-mile drive, but it was a ride I'll never forget.

On the way, my dad told us about his pilgrimage to Lourdes in 1950. He was riding on the night train, on the cheapest seat available—a wooden bench shared with other passengers. The train stopped. Four impoverished people climbed aboard. Their clothes were tattered, they smelled, one man had no arms. My father hoped they wouldn't sit near him, but there weren't any other spots.

Arriving in Lourdes, my father was in a dark mood from not being able to sleep on the train. He walked away from his four benchmates with a sense of superiority; although he was poor, he wasn't that poor. He took consolation in knowing he would never have to see the four travelers again.

It seems Mary had a healing for my dad at the grotto. He saw the four people from the train again, and his heart was struck when he saw the armless man fitted with a harness. The harness allowed him to carry cots with the infirm to the healing baths. This was Dad's healing. He had wrongly judged them; he knew that he would never judge others again without knowing them. Each of my siblings recalls my father saying, "People are people, and vice versa." In other words, don't show partiality, because we're all created in the image of God. My family can attest that he lived by this principle.

My dad was just driving me to the prom, but his witness drove me the first 1.3-mile leg of my 4,535-mile pilgrimage to Lourdes in 2005.

Prayer: Our Lady of Lourdes, pray for us! Amen.

Respond to His Call: Today is the Feast of Our Lady of Lourdes. Ask her for a healing, one you don't even realize you need. Settle in for the surprise.

Alyssa Bormes

A Little Coffee and a Whole Lot of Jesus

We love, because he first loved us. 1 John 4:19

I love coffee. One of my favorite memes uses the five "love languages" of Gary Chapman to express the joys of coffee. It reads something like this: Words of Affirmation—Your coffee is delicious. Acts of Service—I made you coffee. Receiving Gifts—Here's a coffee. Quality Time—Let's go get a coffee. Physical Touch—Let me hold you like a coffee.

The concept of love languages offers fascinating insights into how people tend to give and receive love. There is incredible fulfillment in being loved as we desire to be loved. We know our love will never reach perfection this side of heaven, which makes us long for paradise. However, God does allow us to experience glimpses of that fulfillment here on earth in our relationships.

Beyond human love, we are perfectly loved by God the Father, Son, and Holy Spirit. Consider how the Lord loves us in our daily lives:

- Words of Affirmation—He wrote the most stunning love letter to us, holy scripture!
- Acts of Service—He not only died for us but also continues His saving work today through the Church's ministry.
- Receiving Gifts—The Holy Spirit gives us knowledge, fortitude, understanding, piety, counsel, wisdom, and fear of the Lord.
- Quality Time—The Lord delights to sit with us in adoration and gaze on us with love in the Most Blessed Sacrament.
- Physical Touch—The Lord touches our bodies and souls in the Eucharist each time we receive Holy Communion.

Prayer: Thank You, Lord, for loving me so perfectly. Please open my heart to receive Your love in a new way today. Amen.

Respond to His Call: Make your own list of love languages with the Lord. Set aside time each day, week, and month to let Him love you.

Katie Anderson

King of Hearts

Do not be conformed to this world but be transformed by the renewal of your mind, that you may prove what is the will of God, what is good and acceptable and perfect. Romans 12:2

My life continues to become easier as I remind myself of this simple truth: God loves me too much to leave me as I am. Sometimes He will even allow my heart to break. When we learn to follow the leadings of the Holy Spirit in that brokenheartedness, our lives are transformed.

Recently, Jesus spoke to the stillness of my heart: *I am always leading My people. . . . You think I am leading you to success. . . . I am leading you to My Heart.*

In the moment of His whisper, a door of understanding opened for me. We often perceive His purposes through the lens of our desires and believe He leads us to success. When we hit that heartbreaking bump, we accuse ourselves of failure. Those are the moments when it is fortifying to remember that He loves us too much to leave us as we are.

Bumps on the road of life, like speed bumps on streets, are there to guide us. When our hearts break, we come to know the only One who comforts, heals, and brings lasting peace. These are the times when life is not easy, but they are also the times that make us.

I am reminded of a story. Two maestros were marveling at the voice of a new young soprano. "She has the voice of an angel; it is as if heaven opens when she sings," said the younger maestro. "Ah yes," replied the older one. "She sings beautifully, but she will sing even more beautifully when her heart is broken."

The essence of divinity flows into and out of humanity's brokenness: "The Spirit of the Lord GOD is upon me . . . [and] sent me to bind up the brokenhearted" (Is 61:1). Jesus is still binding up the brokenhearted. He is the King of Hearts.

Prayer: Lord, I place my heart in Your hands. Help me to see the depths of Your love in the scars of the Hand that holds my heart. Amen.

Respond to His Call: Meditate on Jesus' nail-scarred hands. Then, in your mind's eye, see your own heart being held by His hands.

Deborah Kendrick

It's All about Love

> But when you pray, go into your room and shut the door and pray to your Father who is in secret; and your Father who sees in secret will reward you. Matthew 6:6

"This is going to be the shortest homily you've ever heard," our priest announced. It was 6:30 a.m. Mass, and he wanted to reassure the crowd gathered for ashes that they'd get to work on time. "Jesus sums up our Christian life in three things in today's gospel," he said, and then spoke a few words about almsgiving, prayer, and fasting. "They're all in Matthew 6:1–6 and 16–18," he said. "Go home and pray over that and ask the Lord what He'd have you do."

Great advice, especially the part about going home to meditate on the scriptures. Spend time reflecting on that gospel and you'll see that prayer, fasting, and almsgiving are not only for Lent; they also define who and what we are as Christians. That's because all three of those practices spring from love. When we truly love God, we spend time with Him in prayer. When we truly love others, we give generously to them. And when we truly love ourselves, we fast, redirecting our appetites away from self-indulgence and toward that which is truly satisfying.

I love how this gospel pairs with 2 Corinthians 9:6–11, which turns giving from a chore to a joy. Why? First, because God gives us more than enough so that we can give in turn; and second, because whoever gives a lot will receive a lot. If you doubt God's generosity, spend some time with verse 8 and notice all the superlatives: "And God is able to provide you with every blessing in abundance, so that you may always have enough of everything and may provide in abundance for every good work." How can you give out of that abundance today?

Prayer: Lord, I believe every good and perfect gift comes from You. Today, may I not only receive Your love but also share it with others. Amen.

Respond to His Call: Prayerfully consider what the Lord might be calling you to do to love Him or others through prayer, fasting, or almsgiving. What is one thing you can give today from the abundance of His gifts to you?

Sarah Christmyer

Dating Jesus

Wash yourselves; make yourselves clean; remove the evil of your doings from before my eyes; cease to do evil, learn to do good; seek justice, correct oppression; defend the fatherless, plead for the widow. Isaiah 1:16–17

I had issues as a young girl accepting that I was beloved by our Creator. I hid from God's truth, and I paid the price with my choices. Then, as a young woman, I received advice from my sister-in-law. She told me that I needed to fall head over heels in love with Jesus. To a single twenty-one-year-old, this seemed crazy. I had never been wildly in love with anyone, let alone Jesus. I mean, I loved Jesus, but fall in love with Him—what did that mean?

Even though it seemed crazy to me, I knew I needed to do something. I had spent years completely numb to emotion; I was willing to try anything. So I figured I would start dating Jesus. Then, I felt Jesus ask me to date Him by going to daily Mass. This became the start of our love story.

At Mass, I could feel Jesus speaking to me. The readings addressed my struggles, my lifelong burdens. The revelations left me crying at Mass each day. Now, most people would tell you to stay away from boys who make you cry, but when the Holy Spirit brings the tears, they are accompanied by love. Jesus was wooing me; I fell in love with Him—head over heels, butterflies-in-the-stomach love. Years of inadequacies were gone. Jesus revealed that the walls I had built to avoid pain were doing the opposite; they were excluding others. By not allowing them to love me, I was not allowing Jesus to love me. Jesus desires an intimate relationship with each one of us. Dating Him will be different for everyone, as He loves us individually. Tell Jesus you want to date Him. Then allow Him, the ultimate gentleman, to woo you; be prepared for fireworks.

Prayer: Jesus, today I will allow You to love me, and I will see myself as worthy of that love. Amen.

Respond to His Call: Put a date on your calendar to spend special time with Jesus. Then be there.

Angela Koenig

Trusting God's Providence

I sought the Lord, and he answered me, and delivered me from all my fears. Psalm 34:4

If only we would follow the commandments and live according to God's will, rather than our own—what a difference this would make in our lives! I struggle mightily with abandonment to God's will. I often pray the words, and I am certain of my earnestness in the moment. Most of me wants to align myself entirely with God's will in my life. But a tiny—yet significant—part of me, in a reticent, self-protective corner of my mind, fears what this kind of love demands of me.

I fear being asked to sacrifice too much. I fear I am not enough. I fear I won't be able to handle what comes my way. I fear! It can be paralyzing to give in to this fear, yet Jesus is right there, with His consolation and strength.

Consider how many times in the Bible we are told not to be afraid. Various forms of the phrase "Do not be afraid" appear dozens of times in the scriptures, making it one of the most common commandments in the Bible.

When I feel paralyzing fear rearing its ugly head, I find comfort in the Gospel of Matthew: "Look at the birds of the air: they neither sow nor reap nor gather into barns; and yet your heavenly Father feeds them. Are you not of more value than they?" (6:26). This particular discourse is a call to trust in God's providence. Just as He provides for even the smallest creature in His creation, He will give us the graces we need to face the challenges in our lives. Ultimately, we need not fear to live according to His will—He will provide everything we need to do so.

Prayer: Dear Lord, thank You for Your presence in the littlest details of our lives. Give us the grace of faith, that we may trust in You in all things. Amen.

Respond to His Call: Meditate on the beautiful image of the Divine Mercy. Pray, "Jesus, I trust in you." Know that God loves and values you.

Maria Morera Johnson

Be Present. Be Hope. Be Love. Look Up!

Rejoice and be glad, for your reward is great in heaven, for so men persecuted the prophets who were before you. Matthew 5:12

We live in a world where so many people are looking down, both physically and figuratively. How many times have you had to say, "Look out," in order for someone to avoid running into you? Have you ever been in a room filled with people who are looking down at their phones? We live in a country that God has truly blessed, and yet so many of us miss the most precious blessing of all, being 100 percent present to one another.

In the Beatitudes (Mt 5:3–12), Jesus is saying, "I see you. I hear you. I feel your struggle. I am present to you and with you, in all of the challenges you are enduring." Jesus says this to the poor, the persecuted, the oppressed, the disenfranchised, the despairing and brokenhearted, the meek and lowly, those who hunger for justice and peace.

To hunger and thirst for righteousness is to desire intensely that the will of God "be done on earth as it is in heaven." Christ exhorts us to recognize, empathize with, and do all we can to relieve human suffering. Jesus desires that each of us be a peacemaker, ready to subjugate the quest for power, wealth, and fame to the aspiration that all may know the infinite love of God. Only as peacemakers will we recognize that every human being comes from one Creator. That makes us all brothers and sisters. All of us are, equally, the children of God.

The Beatitudes command us: Love those who hate you. Return good for the evil done against you. Bless those who curse you. Pray for the people who do you wrong. Do everything you can to bring about respectful, peaceful relationships among all human beings.

Prayer: Dear loving God of humankind and all creation, help us share Your love with all, despite trials, hardships, and challenges. Amen.

Respond to His Call: On YouTube, view the song "Look Up," by ValLimar Jansen and Sarah Hart. Be inspired to have at least one daily, in-person conversation where you are 100 percent present.

ValLimar Jansen

Wise Women Seek Him

When they saw the star, they rejoiced exceedingly with great joy.
Matthew 2:10

The Epiphany celebrates the Wise Men's historic visit to adore Jesus. We, like those kings of old, are called to seek Jesus. The surest path to finding Jesus is to allow Him to fill us with grace. Prayer, sacrament, and scripture keep us plugged into this treasury. Prayer is simply a conversation. We can chat with the saints, Mary, or, of course, Jesus. These conversations open our hearts to follow God's will and increase our virtue. There is no wrong way to pray.

When we seek Jesus through the sacraments, we always find Him. If we want to truly emulate the Wise Men, we can seek out Jesus in eucharistic adoration. Adoration became a transformative part of my faith journey about ten years ago. Sitting in the quiet with the scriptures and good spiritual reading, along with a favorite writing pen and journal, gradually inflamed my faith. I've since made a date with Jesus every week, just like date night with my husband.

The last of the grace trifecta elements is scripture. If you have been seeking to hear Jesus' voice in your life, opening His Word may be the key to ending the silence. How can you recognize what you've not heard? Spending time with the Bible, particularly the gospels, will open your mind and heart to receive God's Word more effectively than ever before. The Wise Men "were overjoyed at seeing the star" because they knew it would lead them to Jesus. We, too, will be overjoyed when we recognize and follow the spiritual guiding stars in our lives that lead us directly to Jesus. As with the wise men of old, when the Spirit moves a wise woman's heart, she will always seek Him.

Prayer: Lord, count me among the wise who still seek You. Teach me the sound of Your voice, so I may recognize when I have found You. Amen.

Respond to His Call: Today, spend five minutes with the scriptures, learning to recognize the voice of Jesus.

Allison Gingras

Most Precious Gift

I also will give my answer; I also will declare my opinion. For I am full of words, the spirit within me constrains me. Job 32:17–18

Job suffered not only because of his circumstances and from feeling abandoned by God but also because of his friends' unfair rebukes. Eliphaz accused Job of being impatient, while Bildad and Zophar told Job to accept what God had put before him, saying it was a consequence of his sinfulness. They pled with Job to turn to God in repentance, yet Job was convinced his suffering was not due to his sin. In fact, Job's suffering was a testament to God's deep love and respect for him. God did not hesitate to test Job because He had great confidence that Job would remain faithful. Job's perseverance amid his trials exemplified his radical trust in God and, therefore, his righteousness.

In Lent, we strive to be diligent in prayer, fasting, and almsgiving. Just as Job's friend Elihu was "full of words . . . like new wineskins ready to burst" (Job 32:18–19), so too is the *Catechism of the Catholic Church*. However, the *Catechism* points us in a different direction. It exclaims the righteousness that we have in Christ.

When we are baptized, we bring nothing of our own. When an infant is brought to the holy water font, her parents must carry her there. It is like winning the lottery without even knowing it! The *Catechism* teaches us that in the Sacrament of Baptism, "the *sign of the cross*, on the threshold of the celebration, marks with the imprint of Christ the one who is going to belong to him and signifies the grace of the redemption Christ won for us by his cross" (1235).

This Easter, let us rejoice that God does not operate as Job's friends thought He did. Instead, let us recognize that we have been redeemed in Christ and are God's most precious gift.

Prayer: Jesus, in my suffering, help me to place my trust in You. Amen.

Respond to His Call: Reflect on the day of your baptism and the grace bestowed on you through the sacrament. Say a prayer of gratitude for those who helped bring you to this sacrament.

Susanna Parent

God Offers Himself

And demons also came out of many, crying, "You are the Son of God!" But he rebuked them, and would not allow them to speak, because they knew that he was the Christ. Luke 4:41

Nestled within the healing verses of Luke's gospel is this curious passage about Jesus exorcising demons. What I find especially intriguing is that the demons recognize Jesus. They believe (correctly) that He is the Son of God, and identify Him as such.

This story reveals something important about the nature of faith. Faith cannot merely be belief—in God, or a set of teachings—because "even the demons believe—and shudder" (Jas 2:19). Knowing what faith encompasses is of primary importance, for "without faith it is impossible to please him. For whoever would draw near to God must believe that he exists and that he rewards those who seek him" (Heb 11:6).

Believing God exists is the first necessary step. Obedience is also essential, but not enough. After all, the demons obeyed Christ! Genuine faith adds something beyond mere belief and obedience: it desires Him and seeks to love Him. The heart of faith obeys not because Jesus grants or withholds rewards according to our behavior but because it knows that the more we are conformed to who He is, the more of Him we can receive. Faith understands that the reward God offers is Himself.

The Gospel says Jesus heals those who desire Him. He gives Himself to them. Once they experience Him, they fall in love with and cling to Him. Faith begins with belief and goes on to obey, but it must not end there. Do we love the God we know? Do we seek Him in daily prayer and scripture reading?

Prayer: Dear Jesus, how much of my faith is just belief in what I've been told? How much is dutiful obedience? I want to believe You, rather than just believe in You. Please come near, Lord, as You pass by today. Stay with me. Touch me. Heal me. I am searching for You. Amen.

Respond to His Call: Read your parish bulletin and select one item to respond to this week with love. Some examples: donating food, helping with a catechesis program, or becoming an RCIA sponsor.

Sonja Corbitt

Love as the Gift within the Gift within the Gift . . .

The first is, "Hear, O Israel: The Lord our God, the Lord is one; and you shall love the Lord your God with all your heart, and with all your soul, and with all your mind, and with all your strength." The second is this, "You shall love your neighbor as yourself." There is no other commandment greater than these. Mark 12:29–31

My daughter came to me from the other side of the world when she was just fifteen months old. Born in a noisy industrial town in the middle of Siberia, she brought grace into my life. Blessings followed her tottering steps through the door as we started a new life together. Everything changed.

Having lived within walking distance of a Catholic parish for more than a decade, I enrolled my daughter in the school. It was then that it occurred to me to walk into the church. Once we walked through those doors, everything became new. I came back to the Church through the gift of my daughter. I'd floundered for so many years before His plan came to fruition; God's timing is perfect.

Years have passed, my daughter has grown, and the Holy Trinity works alongside us. Love continues to take me by surprise. At Mass, tears of sincere gratitude fill my eyes, often after I receive the Eucharist. I am filled with love pouring into me. I am made new again. I'm continually renewed by the memory of those times when my only task was to pour love into my little girl kneeling beside me, when I hugged her tightly and whispered love into her ears. To love my child and to speak God's love to the one who was instrumental in my own journey to becoming a child of God is truly a gift within a gift.

Prayer: Dearest Father, I thank You for the gift of freedom to worship You in the Eucharist, through which I am being transformed and renewed. Here I am, Lord. Open my heart to receive the gift You are offering right now. Amen.

Respond to His Call: Tonight, count your blessings as part of your night-time prayers.

Jill Mraz

Look Forward

> Jesus said to him, "No one who puts his hand to the plow and looks back is fit for the kingdom of God." Luke 9:62

I once heard a college professor say, "Don't should all over yourself." Although I thought it was clever, the wisdom of that comment did not sink in for years.

At some time in your life, you've probably thought, *I should have done this, or that—then things would have worked out differently.* When I was in my twenties, a difficult breakup left me reeling and heartbroken. In that season of immense grief, moving on seemed impossible. I didn't blame God; I blamed myself. My mind filled with thoughts like, *God gave me what I wanted and needed, but I totally screwed it up. . . . I should have appreciated what He gave me.* It wasn't God's fault that the relationship ended—it was mine. I created my hell. The truth is everyone screws up. Everyone falls. We all miss the mark sometimes. But what's also true is that God's plan for each of us incorporates our strengths and weaknesses.

God loves us more than we can comprehend, and nothing is impossible for Him. Just imagine if Peter spent the year after Jesus' death beating himself up over the fact that he denied Jesus three times the night the Lord needed friends the most. Imagine if instead of moving on and working for God's glory, Peter said, "I'm not worthy—God needs someone else to be the rock on whom He builds His church."

We need to trust God with our vocation, our work, and our current circumstances. We need to look forward. We need to embrace God's forgiveness. We need to stop dwelling on the past. God's plan is bigger than our mistakes. God wants us to be fit for His kingdom.

Prayer: Dear Lord Jesus, help me not to dwell on the mistakes I have made but to look at each day with joyful enthusiasm, ready to love You and serve others. Amen.

Respond to His Call: Ask yourself, What can I do today that will both spark joy in another person and delight God? Then do it.

Amy Brooks

February 23

Called to Be New

Behold, I am doing a new thing; now it springs forth, do you not perceive it? Isaiah 43:19

When I am exhausted, it is easy to see the areas of my life that seem unchangeable. Habitual sins plague me: Pride. Anxiety. A short fuse with a friend, child, or spouse. A tendency to vent or complain. If you're like me, hyperawareness of your failures (which reflect disordered desires), coupled with your unique wounds and difficulties, can make change seem unattainable.

In the daily grind we may overlook answered prayers and personal growth. We often suffer from spiritual amnesia, forgetting where we have been and where God has already brought us. Exhaustion can leave us blind and untrusting, doubtful that we can ever really change. But we have a God who longs to raise us, every part of us. "Behold, I am doing a new thing," God says, "now it springs forth, do you not perceive it?"

You are called by name to be a new creation in Christ. There is no part of you too broken, addicted, inadequate, or worn out for God to renew. Pope Francis wrote, "If you have lost your inner vitality, your dreams, your enthusiasm, your optimism, and your generosity, Jesus stands before you as once He stood before the dead son of the widow, and with all the power of His resurrection He urges you: 'Young man, I say to you, arise!' (Lk 7:14)" (*Christus Vivit*, 20).

Isaiah 43:19 goes on to say, "I will make a way in the wilderness and rivers in the desert." No matter how lost we may feel, God promises to come into our hot mess and imperfections to make our way straight. The parts of us that seem dry He fills with water—to renew us, quench our thirst, and help us bear great fruit in the desolate places.

Prayer: Lord, help me perceive all that You are doing in my life. Replace my heart of stone with a heart of flesh. Pour Your renewing water into my soul, straightening out the mess when I cannot see a way out. Amen.

Respond to His Call: Spend a moment reflecting on where you have already been healed and made new. Then name one current struggle, and ask God to pour in His water and heal you.

Katie Lee Taylor

Whack-a-Mole

And every one who thus hopes in him purifies himself as he is pure. 1 John 3:3

When my kids were young, they used to love to go to the arcade and play Whack-a-Mole. You know the game. It has seven holes, and silly little moles pop out of the holes while you frantically use a padded sledgehammer to knock them back underground. The satisfaction of landing that hammer squarely on the head of one of those moles is short-lived, as another mole pops up immediately. As exciting as the game can be, it seems like the moles always win!

That game is a pretty accurate illustration of my struggle with sin. It seems that once I identify and start working on one of my sinful tendencies, another pops up. When I divert some attention and prayer to that one, the first one pops back up again.

Is the struggle with sin futile? Why bother trying when it seems you're stuck repeating the same sins over and over again? If you ever feel that way, I have some encouraging news: the very recognition of the "moles" in your life is proof of the hope that Christ gives us. Working on particular sins in an effort to become closer to God is part of the journey we're all called to make. As Mother Teresa said, "We are called upon not to be successful, but to be faithful."

We certainly need help in whacking those sins down again and again. Confession gives us that help—even when we feel as if we're just confessing the same sins over and over. Confession is the sledgehammer that keeps sin in check as we make progress on the path to God.

Prayer: Dear Lord, help me to recognize sinful tendencies in my thoughts and actions. Help me to replace them with love and to learn to love as You do. Give me courage to continue battling sins that keep coming back, knowing that You have won the final victory over all sin. Amen.

Respond to His Call: Plan to go to Confession this month. It is the best sledgehammer to attack sin!

Sharon Agnes Wilson

One Powerful Ordinary Moment

To the Lord our God belong mercy and forgiveness; because we have rebelled against him. Daniel 9:9

While I was visiting my daughter Gemma at Benedictine College for a family weekend, a little girl caught my attention as we left Mass at the abbey. The little girl was repeatedly banging on the confessional door. Her mother calmly struggled to pull her away, but her daughter's tiny feet fluttered right back to the confessional and her stout hands continued to pound on the door. In an attempt to quiet her child and appease her curiosity, the mom reluctantly opened the confessional door to allow her tenacious daughter to see what was inside. But as soon as she shut the door, her daughter once again started banging on it.

As I witnessed this ordeal, I couldn't help but think, *Shouldn't we all be banging on this door?* If we genuinely comprehended how life-changing the Sacrament of Confession has the potential to be, we would be just as determined as that little girl to march right back to the confessional door, confess our sins, and receive absolution as often as possible.

Sin clogs our souls and blinds us to truth. Sin weighs us down. When we go to Confession, the weight is taken from us, and we are free to move and act with the Holy Spirit as our guide. Absolution of our sins allows God to work in and through us in all the ways that He desires.

I am grateful for the example I witnessed in the innocence of that little girl. Her behavior unintentionally pointed to a profound truth. We all have fears, yet our Lord compassionately calls us to the Sacrament of Confession so that no sin will keep us from Him. He beckons us to "be not afraid" and trust His plan for our lives.

Prayer: Lord, please forgive the sins that clog my soul and keep me from living in the freedom You won for me on the Cross. Amen.

Respond to His Call: End your day with an examination of conscience, asking for forgiveness for those things you did and failed to do that offend the Lord.

Kathleen Billings

The Early Bird Grows Grumpy

For the kingdom of heaven is like a householder who went out early in the morning to hire laborers for his vineyard. Matthew 20:1

In the parable of the workers in the vineyard, we might not recognize at first the focus on the landowner. The landowner who hires idle workers represents God. We hardly notice it is His vineyard. He hires all day, watching for anyone unemployed and in need of a salary. He desires that no one hoping for a place in His vineyard is left out. There is work enough for all. Honorable, real work: dress the vines, feed the vines, gather the grapes, fellowship with other workers, job security with the promise of a reward.

But trouble comes when early workers compare their recompense with what workers of the last hour receive. Their sense of justice is offended: they worked harder, longer, and under more challenging conditions—so they feel they deserve greater payment than the latecomers. But that's not how it works with this landowner. Generosity is the rule by which God pays His workers. Every hireling receives recompense far beyond anything he or she earned by the hour! And the vineyard needs the skills of all hirelings at just the right hours. And so, the early birds in the vineyard didn't get the worm—they became grumblers.

So many lessons in this passage! Am I one of the idle ones? Have I expressed my gratitude that God has invited me to work in His vineyard? Do I remember that my task is designed exactly for my talents, skills, and my life's hour? Do I welcome other workers, or judge them as latecomers to Jesus? Do I rejoice in the grace given to other hirelings? I mumble my answers to these questions, realizing again how far I am from Jesus' command: "Be perfect, as your heavenly Father is perfect" (Mt 5:48).

Prayer: O Jesus, help me open my heart wider for Your grace in the vineyard. I trust in Your will for me; help my lack of trust. Amen.

Respond to His Call: Find an opportunity to tip extravagantly some person who has done you a service. Offer that extravagance to God for all His many graces you have neglected in your past.

Dr. Carol Younger

Create in Me a Clean Heart

Create in me a clean heart, O God, and put a new and right spirit within me. Psalm 51:10

A clean desktop on my iMac makes life seem less stressful and offers a good metaphor for life: Clean your heart, simplify your life!

There's always been something about a clean space that helps me think, work, create better. Perhaps that's one way I am made in the image and likeness of God, for He, too, began with a clean slate. God started with an earth "without form and void, and darkness was upon the face of the deep" (Gn 1:2). Now, I'll admit my iMac may sometimes seem like a formless wasteland as I get in a rut of saving things too quickly to my desktop, but what a wonderful feeling to see it all wiped clean and witness the beauty of the picture that lies underneath.

This is how I feel in life sometimes. I get in a rut with sin: same old sins, just increasing in quantity and piling up on the desktop of my soul. How blessed I am to have the forgiveness of my heavenly Father. Without a doubt, one of my favorite things about being Catholic is knowing that the Sacrament of Reconciliation brings forgiveness of sins and restoration of God's grace. The *Catechism of the Catholic Church* tells us that those receiving Reconciliation with a contrite heart experience a true "spiritual resurrection" (*CCC* 1468), which is followed by peace and serenity of conscience. That's it! That is the beauty I experience as I join in an intimate friendship with my Creator. Sometimes a clean desktop is all I need to ensure a good night's sleep, but a clean soul is what I always need to ensure serenity of heart and to safeguard me from a total reboot.

Prayer: Create in me a clean heart, O Lord, and put a new and right spirit within me. Amen.

Respond to His Call: Go to that one drawer that needs to be cleaned out, and offer this up for penance. Discard what is no longer useful, clean and rearrange that which can contribute to your future good, and donate that which can help another person.

Kelly M. Wahlquist

Fashioned for Christ

Your hands have made and fashioned me; give me understanding that I may learn your commandments. Psalm 119:73

Not long ago, I was at an event chatting with other middle-aged women who you would have thought had long moved beyond high school gossip. They hadn't—and I was silently judging them. But as I sat there in judgment, I thought suddenly of some of the reality television I consume. My excuse for watching these shows (at least, what I tell my husband) is that I need to pray for these people. Ironically, I morph into a Pharisee every episode as I judge their spoiled, egotistical behavior. I start thinking, *At least I'm not as bad as all of these people!* Self-righteousness is not a new tendency for me. I was suddenly aware of the fact that I was using the morally bankrupt behavior of people I observed in these shows to excuse my own bad habits. Wow, what a wake-up call!

As I sat with these thoughts after that event, the Holy Spirit reminded me of how Jesus interacted with the people He encountered, especially those with a broken moral compass. He befriended many people we would not consider choosing as friends, and yet we see in the scriptures that they became frontrunners to enter heaven.

I imagine myself standing in line on that last day, waiting to meet Jesus with hopes of entering heaven, and seeing one of those reality stars I judged getting in ahead of me. I know my reaction would be, *Really, Lord, them before me? Really?* One of the main drawbacks of a tendency to self-righteousness is that we miss the chance to find beauty and goodness in unexpected people and places. Oh, that God would protect us from the blindness and isolation of a self-righteous attitude, opening our hearts to confess our own sins and see the goodness in those around us!

Prayer: Lord, protect me from my tendency to judge others and to excuse myself. Refashion me according to Your merciful love. Amen.

Respond to His Call: Today, identify one thing that triggers self-righteousness in your heart—and take practical steps to avoid or counteract that thing.

Michelle Nash

A Leap of Faith

Now faith is the assurance of things hoped for, the conviction of things not seen. Hebrews 11:1

I teach a class called "Faith and Reason" to high school sophomores. Now, the course title doesn't always grab their attention, so I thought incorporating a high ropes challenge into the class would! This adrenaline-packed treetop course cleverly shows how faith and reason are the two wings that guide our journey home.

The course begins with community-building exercises designed to simulate life-threatening situations and to get students to think about how they would work together to survive. Through these exercises, the kids learn to recognize each other's wisdom and the importance of the virtues of listening, humility, selflessness, and courage.

Next, they tackle a high ropes course. The students are harnessed and shown how they will not fall to their death due to the belay system. Together they climb a 100-foot tree, walk across a treacherous swinging bridge, and land on a small platform from which all are encouraged to jump into midair. While facing a 100-foot jump, it is easy for them to think, *You will die if you jump!* However, encouraging cheers from the supportive team drown doubts and quell fear. Most students jump and are greeted with joy by their teammates

After the course, we discuss how these activities illustrate the link between faith and reason. Students easily relate the treetop leap to the leap of faith of the first evangelists, who gave their lives to spread the Gospel. They risked their lives because they knew their mission was lifesaving. Students walk away from the lesson with the confidence to be evangelists, knowing Jesus assures us we will be eternally rewarded for our leaps of faith.

Prayer: Lord, thank You for this extra day of the year with which we can choose to take a leap and strengthen our faith in You. Amen.

Respond to His Call: Take a simple leap into a cookbook today. Choose a challenging dinner recipe, prepare it for a neighbor, and deliver it with a note offering a half hour of prayer for their family intentions.

Patti Jannuzzi

Brave New Step

We know that in everything God works for good with those who love him, who are called according to his purpose. Romans 8:28

I had a plan. He was pretty much perfect, and I knew exactly how things would go for us. The future seemed inexpressibly bright and full of hope. Then that conversation happened. You know the one when he says you're not the one. How in the world do we look forward to the future when the future just crumbled before our eyes?

As a working musician, I continued traveling and performing and writing music after that breakup—but in my heart, I stood still for months. One rainy afternoon I walked into my friend Kirsten's house. Tears streamed down my face as I told her of my inability to let go of my version of happily ever after. She looked at me lovingly and explained that I wasn't alone. And then she said something strikingly beautiful: "Our neat and tidy idea of the future is never secure, but we are always securely held by the Father."

We wandered toward the piano, and the lyrics began to flow with the tears: "I don't have the answers that I wish I had. . . . At the end of my questions is one brave new step. I don't have tomorrow. Just one more deep breath. At the end of my sorrow is one brave new step."

In just hours, "Brave New Step" was written. As Kirsten and I exchanged stories about friends who had miscarried, lost jobs, or lost loved ones, I realized my heartbreak wasn't the only thing going on in the world; many were taking *much* braver steps than I.

We are all living unplanned and unforeseen lives, but our Father knows the plan He has for us. God wants us to be brave, brave like Our Lady, whose *yes* to a change of plans changed the world.

Prayer: Father, You have a purpose and plan for my life. Give me the grace to trust in Your perfect plan and to let go of the future I think I need. Amen.

Respond to His Call: Remember a time when big plans in your life changed and God was faithful through it all. Smile knowing He's got whatever you are going through today too.

Marie Miller

Return to Me with Your Whole Heart

"Yet even now," says the LORD, "return to me with all your heart, with fasting, with weeping, and with mourning; and tear your hearts and not your garments." Joel 2:12–13

On Ash Wednesday, church attendance peaks. Why do people return at this time? It's not a holy day of obligation. Instead, it is a reminder of our death: "You are dust, and to dust you shall return" (Gn 3:19). The ashes are an outward expression of sorrow for our sins and a desire to repent. The rise in attendance indicates being drawn to God when contemplating death and searching for purification.

God calls us to rend our hearts, our most private interior. There, He reveals mercy. In contemplating interior change, we discern what to give up for Lent and what to offer additionally in prayer, living beyond an outward appearance, in order to transform our hearts.

As I am writing this, my husband continues his battle with cancer, which is why we live near his medical center, away from home. This struggle happens to coincide with Lent. But it's not really coincidence, is it? I've come to recognize providence at work here. This is God's timing. Being denied the comforts of home is a sacrifice appropriate for Lent. The outward appearance of a new home points to a hoped-for interior transformation, physical and spiritual. We will focus on God, His mercy, and our desperate need for His grace. We did not choose this road, but there are blessings in the sacrifice. Denying ourselves the things we love because of our hope to obtain physical health is akin to our long-term goal of sacrificing spiritually for our eternal goal of heaven. No sacrifice is too great for purification and life everlasting.

Prayer: No trouble will weigh upon my heart that can separate me from You, my Lord and my God. Amen.

Respond to His Call: This Lent, give up the things that mean the most to you, thereby creating space for God in your heart. He will not just brush your outer garment but also penetrate your soul. True sacrifice through suffering brings transformation.

Jennifer Beutz

God's Creative Genius

From your lofty abode you water the mountains; the earth is satisfied with the fruit of your work. You cause the grass to grow for the cattle, and plants for man to cultivate, that he may bring forth food from the earth. Psalm 104:13–14

When I read Psalm 104, I can't help but join in the Psalmist's awe of God's creative genius. This psalm sings of the earth and sky, the wind and sea, the earth's creatures, and the blessings of food and drink. Here in Minnesota, after a long winter avoiding the elements and a wet spring spent inside, summer is a perfect time to recognize and give thanks for our God's amazing creativity. Whether in your yard, on vacation, or anywhere in between, take a moment to wonder at creation.

Close to home, flowers, gardens, and fruit trees are thriving, reminding us of God's bounty and generosity. The Creator has given us not just plants that provide food to sustain us but also flora of endless variety and beauty to delight our senses—lush trees and vines, fruits and vegetables in a myriad of colors and flavors, and flowers of every shape and hue. How can we not be amazed at His goodness?

As we gaze in wonder at God's creative genius, let us stand in awe of His divine power and offer a prayer of thanksgiving to our Father in heaven, who has given us so much and asks for nothing but our love in return. Praise the Lord along with the Psalmist: "I will sing to the LORD as long as I live; I will sing praise to my God while I have being. May my meditation be pleasing to him, for I rejoice in the LORD" (Ps 104:33–34).

Prayer: Lord, what a wonderful world You have given to us. Today I will see You, with thanksgiving, in all of creation. Amen.

Respond to His Call: Tap into your creative genius! Color a picture of God's beautiful creation. This can be calming and prayerful. (Find *visio divina* resources at CatholicVineyard.com.)

Stephanie Landsem

Listening to His Voice

Fear not, for I have redeemed you. . . . When you pass through the waters I will be with you; and through the rivers, they shall not overwhelm you; when you walk through fire you shall not be burned, and the flame shall not consume you. Isaiah 43:1–2

As a Catholic theology teacher, I have met many holy missionaries, including some who have put their lives on the line for the spread of the Gospel. One afternoon, I met a very holy Liberian priest. He gave a talk to my class that I will never forget.

Father was the pastor of a parish in Liberia when civil war broke out. In the middle of the night, he learned that a vicious rebel attack on his parishioners was imminent. Immediately, Father gathered his parishioner families, which included the sick, elderly, and very young children, before the Blessed Sacrament. In the presence of our Lord in the Eucharist, he explained that they were in grave danger of being killed by a rebel machete attack. He told them that they could not risk taking time to collect food or necessities if they hoped to survive since the rebels were very close to the church.

In the dark of night they fled without shoes, food, or water. Father led his parishioners through the rugged rain forest of Liberia, praying and listening to the Lord's voice every step of the way. Father relied solely on the Lord to direct him over roaring rivers and through dense woods. The rebel forces were always close behind in pursuit.

After a perilous week-long journey, Father and all of his parishioners made it to safety. Echoing Isaiah 43:1–3, Father described his journey with humble simplicity: he trusted and God saved! Father implored my students to pray, study scripture, and listen to the Lord's voice. This story always reminds me that the Lord will lead me if I listen and follow His voice. He calls me by name! I am His, and He is mine.

Prayer: Lord, lead me in the way You want me to go. Help me to hear and follow Your voice. Amen.

Respond to His Call: Today, consider how you can best listen to the Lord's voice.

Patti Jannuzzi

What Judas Missed

The Lord GOD has given me the tongue of those who are taught, that I may know how to sustain with a word him that is weary. Morning by morning he wakens, he wakens my ear to hear as those who are taught. Isaiah 50:4

I've come to realize that spiritual growth is more about what we allow God to do in us than what we try to do in ourselves.

I'd like you to imagine two people who have chosen disparate paths, though the option of God's love and mercy is set before both of them. The first person walks the path of the Suffering Servant, Christ; she unceasingly trusts in the Lord and bears a great deal of hardship to witness to the truth. The second person follows the way of Judas the betrayer, refusing to trust Jesus and turning away from Him.

I can't help but ask myself where I fall between these two extremes. Judas does not call on God. He looks only for what he will gain. At the Passover meal, a hint appears that he already knows he's fallen: "Is it I, Master?" (Mt 26:25). He looks to Jesus for affirmation, but he knows the truth as well as our Lord. His heart is hardened, and it is he who will betray Jesus. Why didn't he look to Christ earlier? Might he have repented? But Judas wasn't looking for the Lord's help. He was only looking as far as he could reach on his own.

Though Christ does not stand before us in the same physical manner in which He stood before Judas, He remains with us. He is in our hearts, our families, and the Eucharist. He's still calling us to let the love of the Father live through us. Are you going to choose the way of Judas—and miss out on all that He's calling you to? Or will you open your heart to all that God wants to give you?

Prayer: Lord, give me the courage to suffer, and to rejoice in the amazing gifts You bestow, knowing this only happens if I lean on Your grace. Amen.

Respond to His Call: Close your eyes and picture Jesus standing before you with His arms wide open. What does He say to you? How do you respond?

Lindsay Schlegel

Holy Thursday Pedicures

Then he poured water into a basin, and began to wash the disciples' feet, and to wipe them with the towel that was tied around him. John 13:5

As my turn approached for the priest to wash my feet on Holy Thursday, I slipped off my shoe and sock, exposing my desperate need of a pedicure. I laughed, feeling simultaneously humbled and filled with gratitude for this moment. The tears welled and I lowered my head, partly to shield my face from those witnessing and partly to keep the moment from slipping away too fast. Like Peter at the Transfiguration, I wanted to remain in this moment with my Lord. Each Holy Week, we have this amazing opportunity to transport ourselves back to those days when the world was changed forever. When Jesus, who humbled Himself to live among us, offered Himself to expiate our sins.

Jesus' most remarkable act was not the cleansing of our feet but the cleansing of our souls. Jesus referred to Judas as the one who is not clean (Jn 13:11). I often feel more like Judas than Peter. Although I was cleansed at baptism, I've been dirtied by my travels and I know my soul requires cleansing. The Sacrament of Reconciliation is the "washing of the feet" for my soul. I feared this incredible gift for years—partly because I was embarrassed about what I had to confess but also because I was skeptical of its power.

The more I learned about Jesus, the more I understood the extraordinary gifts He offers us. He humbled Himself, descending to unimaginable depths to serve and save His beloved children—including you and me. Don't let pride get in the way of receiving those gifts of grace! Don't let embarrassment stop you from letting God Himself wash your feet.

Prayer: Lord, help me open my heart to the Sacrament of Reconciliation, the "washing of the feet" for my soul. Erase any pride that keeps me from experiencing Your extravagant grace. Amen.

Respond to His Call: Today, set aside any excuse that's keeping you from experiencing the joy of reconciliation with God. Humbly, go to Confession and connect with a Savior who washes your feet.

Allison Gingras

Looking Forward with Hope

I am the vine, you are the branches. He who abides in me, and I in him, he it is that bears much fruit, for apart from me you can do nothing. John 15:5

As I prepared to leave my job, a friend gifted me a farewell basket of assorted wines. The 2012 Aquinas Pinot Noir was noticeably the stoutest and heaviest bottle—how fitting is that? The perfect antidote for the grieving that accompanies a huge—albeit good—life change. There is sadness at leaving dear friends, productive work, a familiar setting, and the security of an identity forged over time. But as the august Dominican friar and theologian St. Thomas Aquinas helpfully noted, "Sorrow can be alleviated by good sleep, a bath, and a glass of wine."

The funny thing about transition is that it gives you time to think. I confess that my thinking during seasons of transition hasn't all been spiritually and emotionally constructive. There's the self-criticism when I consider all the projects and goals I didn't see to completion, the anxiety of starting something brand new, the self-centeredness of holding on tightly to past accomplishments, and the self-doubt of wondering whether I'm up for this journey through the unfamiliar. It's normal to be vulnerable to such thoughts, but ruminating on them can become a subtle, slippery slope that moves the focus off of Christ and squarely onto self. Here's the thing, dear sisters: we're not the vine—Jesus is.

As branches, we get to display those beautiful ripe clusters of fruit, but we don't nourish them on our own. He bears them through us. It's not our private vineyard we're working; it is His vineyard, and He's promised to take care of it—branches, fruit, workers, and all. When we can't overcome the snares of temptation and self-centeredness by ourselves, our Beloved is waiting to refresh us, lift us, and grant a new start full of hope and joy.

Prayer: You are the vine, and I am a branch. When I am grafted to You, I can produce beautiful fruit. Help me abide in You, the true vine. Amen.

Respond to His Call: Choose a different parish near you and attend Mass there, and don't forget to read the bulletin. Then, write a list of praises to Jesus about that other branch of His vine.

Sharon K. Perkins

A Bruised Reed

A bruised reed he will not break, and a dimly burning wick he will not quench; he will faithfully bring forth justice. Isaiah 42:3

The Church sings in an ancient hymn, "Lord, You have worn Yourself out looking for me. O that Your labors will not have been in vain." The words from this hymn rang true for me in my journey back to the full embrace of Mother Church.

Raised in a Catholic family of eight children, I left home at seventeen to marry my high school sweetheart. Six years later, I found myself divorced with two small boys, filled with heartache. Almost immediately, I began searching for someone to fill the deep void in my life to be loved—a need that only God can ultimately fulfill. In haste, I remarried outside the Church.

Several years later, in 1989, my mother invited me to eucharistic adoration at a small chapel in the Ozark Mountains, near where she and my father lived. At that time, my second marriage was in trouble. Feeling like a broken failure, I cried many tears that night as I sat before Jesus in the monstrance. Instead of condemnation, I felt a river of His mercy washing over me, cleansing me, bathing me. I was the fragile bruised reed, most in need of His mercy. My "smoldering wick" He gently brought back to life.

The next day after Confession—where, Jesus said to St. Faustina, "the greatest miracles occur" (*Diary*, 1448)—the priest gently told me, "For your penance, you are to spread the message of Divine Mercy the rest of your life." Many graces followed. My marriage was convalidated in the Church. The Lord gave me the song "Divine Mercy Flood My Soul" and set my feet on a path to spread the message of His beautiful mercy.

Prayer: "The Mercy of the Lord I will sing forever. Before all the people will I sing it. For it is God's greatest attribute. And for us an unending miracle" (St. Faustina, *Diary*, 522). Amen.

Respond to His Call: Today, strive to become more patient and merciful, realizing there are many who might be the bruised reed and smoldering wick most in need of His mercy.

Annie Karto

Never Give Up on Prayer

And he told them a parable, to the effect that they ought always to pray and not lose heart. Luke 18:1

As I celebrated my fortieth birthday, a sadness tinged my heart. I had so many incredible blessings to be grateful for: a loving and merciful God; a kind, caring husband; healthy, happy children; a warm and cozy home. And yet, I felt burdened, exhausted, and stuck. No longer did I want to watch the days pass by; I wanted to live each one in His joy and peace. I asked God to change my life, to help me move forward.

As I prayed for change, I continued to do the same old things, just in a different order. I insisted on keeping the same commitments, and I kept trying to juggle it all. Essentially, I was on a hamster wheel, and I desperately needed to jump off. I persisted in my prayer for change, and eventually I realized that the change God wanted to give had to begin deep within me. I had to halt the craziness. I had to be brave enough to say no to demands on my time and energy. I had to be okay with not doing it all on my own. I needed to surrender.

God invited me to take a big leap of faith. And when I finally did, I landed safely in His arms. There, He was finally able to give me the change I much desired. God encourages persistence in prayer because it changes our hearts. The more we pray, the more we become in sync with God's will. And when we live in His will, we find peace.

Prayer: Thank You, Lord, for always hearing my prayers and for answering them in the most generous ways. Amen.

Respond to His Call: Today, choose a deep desire and offer it to God in prayer with complete openness about how His mysterious plan and timing could bring about the answer.

Sarah Damm

Cross My Heart to You

What then shall we say to this? If God is for us, who is against us?
Romans 8:31

As a little girl, I always dreamed of graduating from college, becoming a wife and mother, and living happily ever after. But then life happened—and things didn't work out quite so neatly.

Instead of walking a straight line from my childhood dreams to a completely fulfilled reality, I traveled a long, winding road of loss, trials, and depression. Eventually, God sent an inspiration into my hopeless heart, and I began to surrender to the One who died for my sins. As the flame of belief kindled in my heart, I started to believe again that God had a purpose and a plan for my life—even if it wasn't what I'd imagined.

My transformation started in a new city with new people. Little did I know that my painful past would be my eternal salvation. When I placed all my crosses at the foot of His Cross, they became the very blessings I so desperately hoped for. I submerged myself in the Word of God, attended daily Mass, and prayed the Rosary and novenas. Jesus became real and constant in my life. Only three short months after that move to a new city, Jesus revealed Himself to me in a special way: I "met" Him within my husband-to-be. These words were given to my husband, part of a song he sang at our wedding: "I hear Christ speaking to both of us. I cross my heart to be the one to give you love, where there is none. In everything and all that I do. And every breath I'll breathe by you. I cross my heart, my promise to you. To make each wish and a dream come true, I cross my heart for you."

Prayer: O my Jesus, I know nothing can separate me from Your love. Keep me and guard me with Your grace, so I may return Your love with my life and be happy with You in heaven. Amen.

Respond to His Call: Make a list of all the disappointments and hurts that you think have drawn you away from Christ. As you pray the Our Father, tear that list slowly into tiny bits, and place them beneath the Cross.

Donna Luna Hernandez

The True Value of Generosity

Every good endowment and every perfect gift is from above, coming down from the Father of lights with whom there is no variation or shadow due to change. James 1:17

Imagine that someone walks toward you with a prettily packaged gift, extends her hand, and says, "I picked this out just for you." Your first reaction would probably be sheer delight that you were in the thoughts of this person! Next, you'd take the gift and, fighting the urge to rip through the pretty wrapping to see what's inside, gently open it. Lastly, with a grateful heart, you would thank the giver.

God is a generous giver. He gives abundantly, and just when you think there is nothing left, He gives more. In WINE's Lenten book, *Walk in Her Sandals*, we accompany Huldah, a beautiful fictional character, as she offers to help a friend in need. One of the gifts God has bestowed on women is an innate generosity—a natural giving of self. This type of generosity comes from Jesus Himself. Recall the first Holy Thursday Passover meal, when Jesus offered the greatest sacrifice. He strayed from the traditional Seder meal and offered His Body, Blood, Soul, and Divinity to His disciples. That moment was the culmination of something He taught with every step, action, and word throughout His ministry: pour yourself out in service and love to those around you.

In *Walk in Her Sandals*, Huldah is drawn to Jesus. She wants to be close to Him and listen to Him. Taking to heart Jesus' command, "What I have done for you, you must do for others," Huldah discovers that when she serves with generosity, she finds her own purpose and value.

Will you, like Huldah, listen to the voice of Jesus and embrace your identity as a generous giver?

Prayer: Lord, make me a channel of Your peace and unconditional acceptance of others. Amen.

Respond to His Call: Today, give to a sister in Christ your time, your attention, or even an invitation to join you in a book club. (You can even give her a copy of *Walk in Her Sandals* and join her on the journey.)

Reagan Franklin

Fighting Temptation

Man does not live by bread alone, but . . . by everything that proceeds out of the mouth of the LORD. Deuteronomy 8:3

Lent's start seems a little like New Year's Day to me; both dates are new beginnings marked by a personal resolution to make life changes. While our New Year's resolutions might include exercising more or learning a new skill, we're more likely to begin a new spiritual practice or give something up during Lent. It doesn't matter what I give up; the temptation to cave a little on my Lenten resolution gets stronger week by week.

Knowing that Jesus was tempted at the end of His long retreat in the desert gives me consolation and offers me a model for defeating my own temptations. After forty days of fasting, surely Jesus was not only hungry but also tired and a bit lonely. Facing His adversary while in this condition, Jesus used a weapon we also have at our disposal: God's Word. To Satan's suggestion that He make bread for Himself, our Lord responded with Deuteronomy 8:3: "Man does not live by bread alone." The devil doubled down with two more temptations, but Christ returned fire with Exodus 34:14 and Deuteronomy 6:16. Jesus definitely had the last word in that encounter—and it was a word of scripture.

We can't claim that "the devil made me do it" when we sin—we're ultimately responsible for our actions. But Satan gives us that extra push of temptation. Sadly, he doesn't have to push all that hard sometimes.

The Bible tells us that if we resist the devil, he will flee (Jas 4:7), as he did after he tempted Jesus. Our Lord shows us that scripture is the best weapon to overcome temptation. Let's practice finding encouraging, life-giving scriptures and keeping them nearby. Gradually we can learn to use this two-edged sword, so we're ready when the enemy approaches.

Prayer: Father, give me the strength to overcome temptation, in whatever form it comes. Amen.

Respond to His Call: Is there a place where you know you're going to encounter temptation? Make copies of psalms that speak to you (try Psalms 39, 40, 42, 61, 84, 92, 112, 121, and 128), stack them in that place, and pray one when you're tempted.

Susan Klemond

The Rugged Road of Lent

When you send forth your Spirit, they are created; and you renew the face of the earth. Psalm 104:30

As I drove the rocky road toward the retreat center, I couldn't help but compare it to how rugged the road of my own life had been for me that Lent. Flashing through my mind unbidden were the many times over the past forty days that I'd fallen and failed in my Lenten promises. "But I'm here, Lord!" I cried out—as if my sacrifice would somehow wipe the dirty slate clean.

Reluctantly, I entered the room filled with familiar faces. Standing on the periphery, as I often tend to do, I watched old friends embracing and witnessed new friendships being forged. I so badly wanted to be a part of it as I stood there pleading with the Lord to help me get out of my own way. When we moved into the chapel for Mass, it felt like the Upper Room with an infusion of the Holy Spirit into our hearts. My earlier feelings of loneliness began to fade away, making room for something wholly new. These women prayed using their innate gifts of receptivity, generosity, sensitivity, maternity, and the Holy Spirit. The Lord's presence was tangible in a way I'd never before experienced.

God had been listening! Though He'd taken me out of my comfort zone, He'd brought me into the zone of His comfort. The Lord knew what I'd done and failed to do, yet through these beautiful sisters in Christ, He was letting me know that He longs for me still. He walked to Calvary for me. And, likewise, He walked for you! The rugged road this Lent has been fruitful after all. He's alive! He lives in you and in me. It's up to us to share with others the unique gifts He's given us as women so that they, too, will know He's alive within them.

Prayer: I am here, Lord. Despite my fears and failings, I am here, Lord, with You. Amen.

Respond to His Call: Step out of your comfort zone and offer to pray with someone today who you sense needs prayer. Ask the Holy Spirit to guide you.

Paige Freeman Rosato

The Best-Laid Plans

The plans of the mind belong to man, but the answer of the tongue is from the LORD. All the ways of a man are pure in his own eyes, but the LORD weighs the spirit. Commit your work to the LORD, and your plans will be established. Proverbs 16:1–3

I have the best intentions, lofty goals, and an ambitious spirit. But after carefully crafting daily to-do lists and long-term Excel sheets, I often find myself ignoring them. The best-laid plans fail when they do not change my heart first. And therein lies my problem: this model of perfection is one that I envision for myself—it isn't the one that the Lord intends for me. The devil is quick to say I'm disappointing God. Discouraged, I continue to seek an unattainable perfection. Instead of turning to Jesus, the source of goodness, truth, and beauty, I allow my desire to be perfect to continue. But, thanks be to God, He is always there to remind me that my name is not St. John Vianney, St. Faustina, or St. Thérèse. I am not called to be any of those people because I was created to be me.

You'll still find me with my schedules and highlighters, chomping at the bit to color-code. But I no longer try to design my life to be something more. I strive to pattern my life to be something less—less of me and more of the Creator, fewer have-to-dos and more get-to-dos.

If your Lenten resolutions are slipping off the wagon, now is the perfect time to reflect on how to be less, not more, in the coming weeks. Less worried, less anxious, less focused on self-judgment, less discouraged because you've given in to temptation. When we focus less on ourselves and more on our Father, our Savior, and our Consoler, His best-laid plans suddenly seem so much better than anything we could imagine.

Prayer: O my Jesus, thank You for the encouragement and the grace to follow You. Give me the courage to go wherever You want me to go. Please accompany me. Amen.

Respond to His Call: Set aside five to ten minutes daily during Lent to sit quietly and simply listen to the Lord.

Angela Koenig

Victory through Faith

For whatever is born of God overcomes the world; and this is the victory that overcomes the world, our faith. 1 John 5:4

I have a little sign next to my coffee maker that says, "Life happens. Coffee helps." Who can't relate to that? However, as good as coffee is, it doesn't offer solutions to the unexpected (and sometimes tragic) trials in life.

A few years ago, our family learned some devastating news. It was the kind for which you can never be truly prepared, the kind that makes your breathing stop until you are gasping for air. Sometimes, tragic news can be so overwhelming that we fall into a spiritual sadness and no longer enjoy the good that God offers us each day. To add to the tragedy, we put our faith on pause for better times—when it is that very faith that will help us overcome the trial.

To be victorious in our trials, we may need to picture ourselves at the foot of the Cross. There we find our Blessed Mother, John the Apostle, Mary Magdalene, and a few other faithful women. They stood fearlessly in a time of great sorrow. They offered each other solidarity and a witness to courageous faith in the most awful and painful circumstances.

God created us to relate to each other in the joys and sorrows of life. But while sharing a cup of coffee with good friends will offer some needed consolation, there is no pause button for our faith. There is no victory in the trials of life without a courageous faith. Life happens, faith overcomes. In every trial, may we have the courage to say with St. Joan of Arc, "Hold the cross high, so I may see it through the flames."

Prayer: Dear Jesus, You know me and You know my heart. Help me to see where my faith is weak and will not withstand a trial. Please, Jesus, send down on my heart all the virtues I need to be strong and steadfast in my faith so that I may overcome any unexpected trials that come my way. Amen.

Respond to His Call: Prayerfully reflect on your weaknesses through the lens of the Church's teaching on the seven deadly sins. Pray that God would strengthen your faith in those areas.

Letitia M. Peyton

When It Storms

And a great storm of wind arose. . . . But he was in the stern, asleep on the cushion; and they woke him and said to him, "Teacher, do you not care if we perish?" And he awoke and rebuked the wind, and said to the sea, "Peace! Be still!" And the wind ceased, and there was a great calm. He said to them, "Why are you afraid? Have you no faith?" Mark 4:37–40

In Mark's opening chapters, Jesus healed a demoniac, a leper, a paralytic, and many more. His fame spread throughout the land, and crowds began to follow Him, begging for His help. Besieged by masses of desperate people, constantly preaching and healing, He must have been exhausted. Is it any wonder He fell asleep in the boat? Then a storm came. And what did the disciples do? They woke Him up!

I don't know about you, but if I'd been preaching and healing nonstop and I finally got a chance to catch a little shut-eye, I would not have been thrilled if someone woke me up. There's a good chance whoever woke me would have ended up in the drink.

But what did Jesus do? He calmed the storm. His disciples should have known that no storm was going to harm them—I mean, come on, they'd seen Jesus drive out demons! Still, they got scared. It's no wonder Jesus rebuked them: "Do you not yet have faith?"

I once had a terrific moment of clarity while watching the movie *The Passion of the Christ* during a very troubled time in my life. I was watching the actor playing Jesus, bloodied and half dead, dragging the Cross up the hill, when all of a sudden I heard an interior voice saying, "What else do I have to do to get you to trust Me, Susan?"

Jesus wants us to trust Him in the storms. Sometimes that can seem like a lot to ask. Trust Him anyway.

Prayer: Jesus, I trust in You. Amen.

Respond to His Call: The Sisters of Life have written a beautiful Litany of Trust (sistersoflife.org/litany-of-trust). Get to know this life-changing prayer.

Susan Vigilante

Grit and Stamina

You will be delivered up even by parents and brothers and kinsmen and friends, and some of you they will put to death; you will be hated by all for my name's sake. But not a hair of your head will perish. By your endurance you will gain your lives. Luke 21:16–19

As I visited the holy places of Ireland, I was struck by the number of remnants of centuries-old churches, monasteries, abbeys, and friaries. It's clear that Ireland's history is built around the Church and the heroic religious who brought the faith there. One place impacted me more than the others—Ballintubber Abbey, known as "the abbey that refused to die."

Ballintubber Abbey is the starting point of the old chariot road on which St. Patrick traveled. The history of the abbey reflects the grit and stamina of the Irish people in preserving their Catholic faith despite adversity. It speaks of the people whose faith not only survived but grew strong through persecution and famine. Ballintubber flourished until the reign of King Henry VIII. This dark period for Catholics witnessed the dissolution of monasteries and the enactment of anti-Catholic Penal Laws in Ireland. The wooden roof of Ballintubber Abbey was burned in 1653, but somehow complete destruction was kept at bay. Efforts were made through the years to restore the church, but not until 1966 was the nave rebuilt, in time for the 750th anniversary of the abbey's founding.

Remarkably, through all of this, Mass was celebrated there without interruption. As I looked at ruins and renovated buildings, I was deeply touched by the perseverance of the Irish people in fighting for their Catholic faith in the face of calamity, poverty, and hardship. Today, the Irish people talk about the Penal Laws and the famine years in an accepting, matter-of-fact way. *What happened, happened.* The faith lives on and so do they.

Prayer: Lord, the Church will continue to persevere through hardships. Bless me with grit and stamina to remain steadfast in my faith. Amen.

Respond to His Call: Recall a friendship lost to you through argument, death, or distance. Have a Mass said, or devote an hour of prayer before the Blessed Sacrament, for that person's faith in God.

Marge Steinhage Fenelon

To Be Transfigured Is to Become More Beautiful

. . . who saved us and called us with a holy calling, not in virtue of our works but in virtue of his own purpose and the grace which he gave us in Christ Jesus. 2 Timothy 1:9

I once had a friend who asked a great question after the reading of the Transfiguration at Sunday Mass: "What's the difference between being transformed and being transfigured?" To be transformed means to be changed, but to be transfigured means to become more beautiful and elevated. Christ revealed His beauty at the Transfiguration. Is there some way in which we are to follow Christ in the matter of transfiguration?

Remember, we were made in God's image and likeness. We are beautiful for merely being our Lord's creation. But we are also called to grow in how we use the gifts we've been given. In the season of Lent, why not go beyond sacrifices of fewer desserts, simpler meals, and less shopping? What if we gave up our need for control, our pride, our fears and doubts, choosing instead to use our gifts to serve humbly?

At this point in Lent, you probably feel some emptiness. Something I find sustaining when I'm feeling this way is to remember the goal of all these sacrifices: to be transfigured into a more beautiful image and likeness of our God.

In sacrificial seasons of purging and scaling back, stay focused on that ultimate goal of finding your full beauty in heaven. Personal transfiguration only happens through participating in the Passion, Death, and Resurrection of our Lord Jesus Christ. His Transfiguration is a call for our transformation—and someday, God willing, our transformation will result in our being fully transfigured with Him.

Prayer: Jesus, help me empty my life of the habits that distract me from You. Guide me to be filled up and elevated by Your sacred love. Amen.

Respond to His Call: Choose a day to go without a shower or cosmetics, and visit a nearby church for an hour of prayer. Begin with Psalm 135.

Lindsay Schlegel

His Own Fiat

When Joseph woke from sleep, he did as the angel of the Lord commanded him; he took his wife. Matthew 1:24

St. Joseph is an incredible example of faith whom we can turn to for prayer not only in our work but also in our pursuit of greater trust, humility, and love. Joseph is often overlooked because of his holy hiddenness. We see this immediately in Matthew's gospel: "Joseph, being a just man and unwilling to put her to shame, resolved to send her away quietly" (1:19). However, the angel Gabriel approached Joseph in the quiet stillness of a dream to tell him that this was not to be. Like Mary, Joseph gave the Lord his fiat by doing "as the angel of the Lord commanded him" (v. 24), taking his wife into his home.

With great masculinity and self-control, Joseph respected Mary's call to give herself entirely to God. His love and care for Mary were part of his vocation and therefore his path to heaven. The love between Joseph and Mary reflects the spiritual communion that Dietrich von Hildebrand speaks of in *Man and Woman: Love and the Meaning of Intimacy*: "Jesus is the theme of this relationship that for each partner the other's salvation is of primary concern, that they each participate in the love of Jesus for the other . . . this relationship then has a glow and an ardor."

In *Redemptoris Custos* (*Guardian of the Redeemer*), St. John Paul II said, "It is in the Holy Family, the original 'Church in miniature (*Ecclesia domestica*),' that every Christian family must be reflected." We can look to the model of Joseph and Mary's relationship in our effort to give our fiat to the Lord. Joseph and Mary will surely help us in our effort as they witnessed for themselves a perfect example of a virtuous life in Jesus, their Son.

Prayer: Jesus, help me to give myself entirely to You, just as Joseph and Mary did through their fiat. Amen.

Respond to His Call: Ask the Lord how He wants you to reflect the virtue and love of the Holy Family in your own home.

Susanna Parent

Loving in Deed

Little children, let us not love in word or speech but in deed and in truth. 1 John 3:18

It had been one day since we moved my stepdad into hospice. His body was settled in his bed, his eyeglasses and other necessities within reach; but his mind was very unsettled. He was grasping at imaginary things in the air, and he even roughly pushed away the familiar soft, wet nose of my dog, who had come with me to help make him feel comfortable.

My stepdad had a hard life, and at times he could be very difficult to love. He wouldn't accept help, and even as dementia ravaged his once-capable brain, and lung cancer ate away at his robust health, he fought it. When he could fight no longer, my mother took exquisite care of him, insisting that none of us would ever be saddled with the job.

As a result, the opportunity to care for him presented itself only a few times as he grew sicker. He couldn't easily hear the words, but I longed to show my stoic stepdad that I loved him through my actions. That night in his hospice room, he asked me with confusion on his face, "What's going on?" I had my opening. "Dad," I said, squeezing his hand, "what's going on is that you are here with people who love you very much, and most of all, God loves you." He looked at me briefly with a flicker of recognition. He died the very next day.

Prayer: Jesus, help me love those who are difficult to love and show them Your love through not only my words but my service as well. Amen.

Respond to His Call: Who in your life is difficult to love? Find a way to show them your care through a small act of kindness.

Sherry Kennedy Brownrigg

Broken and Wasted Lives

Mary took a pound of costly ointment of pure nard and anointed the feet of Jesus and wiped his feet with her hair; and the house was filled with the fragrance of the ointment. John 12:3

When the woman at Bethany poured the precious oil over Jesus, some of His followers scoffed, calling it a waste. But Jesus told them she was anointing Him for His burial (see John 12:1–8). In advance of His suffering, Crucifixion, and death, she prepared His body for the grave, anticipating the final reverence before it was wrapped in linen and the tomb was sealed. Her profound, heartfelt act would be remembered in the telling of Jesus' story throughout the entire world.

While the disciples were assessing the monetary value of the oil, this dear woman was providing us with an exemplary lesson of a life poured out to God. Only when the bottle was broken could that which was precious flow out. And so it is with our lives. Our Father, in His eternal mercy, loves us too much to leave us as we are. We are created to know God and to love Him—and we are being changed from glory to glory. Brokenness is a vital step in that journey.

Brokenness is often mistaken for failure. Herein lies a sublime choice: Jesus encourages us to fall upon the stone and be broken voluntarily, thereby sparing the stone falling and crushing us. When the painful circumstances that produce brokenness present themselves, what will you choose? Bitter resistance? Or holy acceptance? When we choose the latter, our brokenness allows that which is most precious to begin to pour into and ultimately out of us. May God grace us to find ourselves "wasting" our lives on Jesus.

Prayer: Lord, help me to embrace the cracks and broken places in my life. Bring to me Your stillness and peace that I may pour myself out on You. Amen.

Respond to His Call: Can you identify something in your life that is valuable and sealed that could be broken open and poured out to Jesus, His Church, and His kingdom? Commit that thing to the Lord in prayer, and ask Him to show you the best way to offer it to Him.

Deborah Kendrick

Turning Sacrifice into a Gift

Even if I am to be poured as a libation upon the sacrificial offering of your faith, I am glad and rejoice with you all. Philippians 2:17

Every year for Lent I give up wine. Sometimes this sacrifice requires the drastic measure of taking a just-opened bottle and pouring it down the drain lest it prove too tempting. One time, I made a little ritual out of this act of pouring out a nearly full bottle of wine—I made it a libation or drink offering. Libations were offered in conjunction with other sacrifices in ancient Israel. A small amount of wine was poured onto the burning lamb or ram or bull, "topping off" the main sacrifice. I read once that it was a kind of supplement to the offering that showed an extra measure of thankfulness.

I wish I'd thought to pour my libation out on a fire, so I could see the steam rise to heaven. Instead, I poured it on the ground, offering in thanks the merlot that I would not drink as a "topping off" sacrifice to the larger, Lenten offering I would make of myself.

I wonder what, exactly, St. Paul meant when he spoke of being "poured as a libation" in Philippians 2:17? Was he speaking of his suffering, of giving everything for the cause of Christ? I can't help but see Paul's offering as a "topping off" of Christ's sacrifice. He has given his whole life to God. Perhaps as his own life draws to an end, Paul is willing for his own blood to be shed as a drink offering, poured out in thanks for the greater, once-for-all sacrifice of the Paschal Lamb, Jesus.

As we head into Holy Week, let's consider how we too can enter into that pouring out of life—how we can become a libation, "topping off" Christ's sacrifice, offering up our sufferings with His and giving thanks.

Prayer: Jesus, I offer my life as a libation. Accept it and turn it into something that glorifies You. Amen.

Respond to His Call: Meditate prayerfully on Romans 12:1 or Philippians 2:17. What is one way you can "top off" the sacrifice Christ made for you?

Sarah Christmyer

Begin Each Day on the Right Foot

Take heed to the path of your feet, then all your ways will be sure.
Proverbs 4:26

While on retreat as a young teenager, I heard a wise priest suggest that if we do not give the first moments of our day to God, then the enemy is eager and waiting to step in and take the lead. These words were etched in my heart the moment they fell on my ears, and they came to mind whenever my day started to go off the rails.

Eventually, I formed a habit of offering each day to God. Before I step foot out of bed, I present to God my agenda for the day, ask Him to align my hopes with His plan, and then beg for the grace to do His will and not my own. Starting my day with this short and simple prayer sets my feet on the right path and gives me the assurance that I am walking in the direction God desires me to walk that day.

Inevitably, there are days that I veer off the path. That's okay. The important thing is that I recognize it and ask God to set me back on the proper track. Luckily, God is always listening. He hears my plea, and, being the loving Father that He is, with each new day, in His mercy He gives me the opportunity for a do-over.

When you ask God to direct your life, are attentive to the path you are walking each day, and seek eternal life as your ultimate goal, you can be confident that you are living your best life, one day at a time.

Prayer: Lord, please lead me each day on the path that is directed toward eternal life with You. Amen.

Respond to His Call: At the beginning of each day, as your feet hit the ground, ask God to lead you on the path destined for heaven.

Kathleen Billings

I Just Want to Love God

> Do all things without grumbling or questioning, that you may be blameless and innocent, children of God without blemish in the midst of a crooked and perverse generation, among whom you shine as lights in the world. Philippians 2:14–15

Following Jesus is hard. I didn't realize that at first! After my conversion, I decided to become a radical Jesus-follower. Becoming a disciple, I thought, would be pretty straightforward—it was simply a matter of loving Jesus, right?

This went well for a while. Dwelling on the Word of God filled me with love and sparked my curiosity. My vision of discipleship was then a comfortable sort of love—an uncomplicated, almost instinctive experience of being loved by God and loving Him back. But one day, while studying the origins of the word "disciple," I discovered it came from the same root word as "discipline." My first thought was, *Who wants discipline? I just want to love God!* But real love requires discipline and sacrifice.

Loving Jesus requires that we grow in our knowledge of the things of God, so we see more clearly our faith's sometimes complex beauty and embrace more fully what the Cross means for our daily lives. Acquiring that knowledge takes discipline, and loving Jesus involves the hard work of changing our old habits and developing new habits of holiness.

Sometimes we're graced with an instantaneous transformation or sudden revelation—but usually, spiritual growth involves discipline. We need to identify triggers for sin and come up with practical steps to change the way we act and think. We need to pray every step of the way.

Cherish those times when discipleship comes easily. But when the going gets tough, let the disciplines of prayer and self-examination sustain you.

Prayer: How I long to live every day in Your presence, Jesus, and to be Your disciple. Amen.

Respond to His Call: Consider adding the discipline of an examen at the end of every day. Get into the habit of asking yourself, *Did I live the day in God's presence? Was I His disciple?*

Sharon Agnes Wilson

Free to Fiat

And Mary said, "Behold, I am the handmaid of the Lord; let it be to me according to your word." Luke 1:38

"Come with me!" my sister implored. Impulsively I agreed. Little did I know that this unplanned fiat would be a challenging act of surrender for me. I thought it would be easy to give up the satisfaction of crossing items off my to-do list to spend a day with my sister. But instead, I felt fretful, distracted, and resentful—and that led to feeling angry at myself for failing to be present and attentive to my sister. With tears stinging my eyes, I heard the Lord whisper, "Katie girl, are you here because it's what you want or because it's what I want?" My spirit softened. I *could* be fully present. For the rest of the day, sweet graces unfolded from my small fiat and the million little deaths of my "perfect plans."

I prayed on the ride home, Lord, how many of these glorious moments have I missed because I feared that saying yes to Your invitation would crowd out the things I thought were important? A fiat is no small feat. No wonder the enemy is so quick to knot our souls with doubt when we cooperate with God's plans. Who better than Mary to help undo these knots? Mary empathizes with souls hesitant to say yes to God's surprising ways. The planner in me is floored by Our Lady's response to the annunciation. Hers is the prayer my heart needs most: "Let it be done unto me."

The annunciation. isn't an event trapped in history. Every yes we offer the Lord is an echo of Mary's fiat, which opened the pages to the greatest story: a Father who loved the world and gave His only Son to save us from our dreaded knots. How can we refuse?

Let us ask Mary to bring our knotted lives to the Untangler of Souls, who will free us to say yes. Yes by yes, surrendering to the Father's will is the best plan we'll ever make.

Prayer: Blessed Mother, you see the knots in my life, how they entangle and bind me. Please bring my petitions to your Son, that all the knots may be undone. Amen.

Respond to His Call: Pray the Novena to Our Lady, Undoer of Knots.

Katie Anderson

We Work, He Converts

And I am sure that he who began a good work in you will bring it to completion at the day of Jesus Christ. Philippians 1:6

Years ago, one of my sisters left the Catholic faith and embraced Hinduism. I was determined to bring her back. I read the pantheistic Hindu scriptures to find common ground with her. For about a year, I prayed and sweated over my mission, searching for the perfect argument to turn her heart back to Christ. Then one day, she called and said, "I want what you have."

I dropped to my knees and said, "Let's pray together."

After prayers of thanksgiving, we discussed what she meant by "what you have." As she was explaining, it became clear that she wanted faith to function like a crutch—something that could prop her up and comfort her. "Then you're looking in the wrong place," I said immediately. "Christianity will challenge you down to your toenails. It's no crutch."

Pondering for a moment, she said, "I still want it. It has nothing to do with anything you've ever said or written." My heart sank. *Had all my hard work been irrelevant?*

"Then what was it?" I asked.

"I could see the Holy Spirit working in your life," she stated.

This conversation, recalled from a distance of many years, is clear evidence that we don't bring about conversions—God does. Yet, God blesses and uses our care for souls. The efforts may be ours, but the power is all His. Loving someone enough to meet them halfway, listening to them with a genuine desire to understand, accepting them where we find them, and being ready to boldly but respectfully declare our beliefs—God can use all of these efforts to open the door of their hearts.

Prayer: Mary, my mother, enfold me with your blue mantle of peace as you guide me into a deeper relationship with your precious Son, Jesus Christ. Amen.

Respond to His Call: Go for a walk. Take your rosary with you and pray for Our Lady of the New Evangelization to shower you with the graces to share her Son with confidence.

Lisa Mladinich

A Prepared Heart

Lead me in your truth, and teach me, for you are the God of my salvation; for you I wait all the day long. Psalm 25:5

Dying on the Cross, Jesus looked down at His mother standing with the beloved disciple, John. To her, He said, "Behold your son," and to John, "Behold your mother." Jesus wasn't talking about a regular mother-son relationship. John's biological mother was present, after all. Rather, Jesus was saying to John, as He would have said to any of the other disciples had they been there, "This is My mother. She gave birth to Me and walked with Me. She will walk with you in the days ahead. She is a gift to Me, and I am giving Her to you."

From the dark terror of that Friday afternoon through the unknown of Saturday to the empty tomb on the first day of the week, Mary was there for the disciples. As Jesus ascended to heaven after forty days, He told them to wait in Jerusalem for the fulfillment of the promise of the Holy Spirit. Mary knew with certainty how glorious it was to be filled with the Holy Spirit. She knew that in a prepared heart that desires the fullness of God, the Holy Spirit can conceive the presence of Jesus. If any of the disciples were inclined to wander, despair, or depart, she would prevail on them to stay with her and pray.

The Church was birthed on the day of Pentecost, and Mary is the mother who saw it through. She remains with us now, to take us to a new Pentecost for the New Evangelization, as we welcome the Holy Spirit to breathe on us. Mary desires that not one drop of His Blood be shed for naught, that all will be heirs of Her Son's inheritance.

Prayer: Our Lord and our God, in Your dying breath You bequeathed to us Your very own mother. May we avail ourselves of her help as we prepare our hearts each day to receive Your Holy Spirit. Amen.

Respond to His Call: Just as Mary facilitated the Church's birth through the disciples' reception of the Holy Spirit, she can help you receive the Holy Spirit, too. Today, ask her for special aid as you seek Jesus' presence and invite others into His kingdom.

Deborah Kendrick

Shouldering One Another's Burdens

And as they led him away, they seized one Simon of Cyrene, who was coming in from the country, and laid on him the cross, to carry it behind Jesus. Luke 23:26

Luke's gospel points our attention to the passerby, Simon of Cyrene, who was forced to carry the Cross for Jesus. I wonder what Simon was thinking. *Why me? How did I land in this spot?* Maybe he even wondered how embarrassing it would be if he couldn't handle the physical labor of carrying that Cross. The fact is, Simon was specially chosen by God. Of all people, he was chosen to share in the heavy burden of carrying the Cross for Jesus. What an amazing privilege!

Often we focus on our own crosses—the burdens of our sorrow, our losses, and our pains. Meditating on Simon helps me realize that when we help others carry a heavy cross, we are helping them fulfill their mission in Christ, just as Simon was helping Christ with His mission. Perhaps we don't feel strong enough or wise enough. But as we saw with Simon, simple obedience is all it takes—a willingness to be the shoulder that allows someone to fall without injury, find some solace even in moments of grief, or walk another step. Padre Pio, who received stigmata in the shoulder, once said, "When the Lord entrusts a soul to me, I place it on my shoulder and never let it go." It was as if he bore this extreme pain for all of his spiritual children, sharing physically in their burdens. St. Pio was chosen. Perhaps you've been chosen, too.

Prayer: Dear Lord, make my shoulder strong enough for those in need. Give me the grace to be obedient to the task. You say that love hurts. Let the pain of shouldering another's burden remind me of how much You love each of us. Amen.

Respond to His Call: Reach out to a friend or parishioner who is alone or in need. Offer them a shoulder to lean on or cry on.

Margie Mandli

The Truth of Lent
Is the Goodness of God

Therefore, since we are justified by faith, we have peace with God through our Lord Jesus Christ. Through him we have obtained access to this grace in which we stand, and we rejoice in our hope of sharing the glory of God. Romans 5:1–2

I have tasted and seen the goodness of the Lord. He has blessed me time and again, in ways that were apparent right away and in ways that took me some time to comprehend. Sometimes, I still wonder, *Is this God all that He says He is? Will He provide for me?*

Lent is not about what we can give the Lord. It's about surrendering to what He's given us—which is not always easy. Too often, my prayers are a series of suggestions for which I am expecting God's enthusiastic stamp of approval. But perhaps the places I'm looking for God aren't where He intends me to find Him. Do you ever find yourself expecting Him to fall in line with your ideas? I know I do. If He asks something of you that you didn't anticipate, do you trust Him enough to respond with obedience?

Ideally, the answer will be a resounding yes—a fiat. Saying yes to God is difficult for hearts that are distracted and pulled in many directions. Lent is a season for setting aside those distractions. The things we give up make space for us to say an even bigger yes to God. And paradoxically, we find that in giving up many small things we receive something much better—the goodness of God. May our hearts stay soft—quick to believe that God is good, ready to receive His presence, and eager to say yes to every blessing and task that He has for us.

Prayer: Jesus, I trust that You are who You say You are. I surrender my desires to Your will. I offer you my fiat. Help me see that saying no to my desires and yes to You prepares me to receive Your wonderful goodness. Amen.

Respond to His Call: Make a list of some things Jesus might ask you to do. For example, serve one day in a soup kitchen, or clean out your clothes closet and gift the excess to the poor. Choose one—and *do it!*

Lindsay Schlegel

A Life of Yes

In the sixth month the angel Gabriel was sent from God. . . , to a virgin . . . and the virgin's name was Mary. Luke 1:26–27

After First Saturday Mass at our parish, we strolled over to the parish hall for breakfast and Rosary devotions. I was surprised to find the table adorned with two statues of Mary. A small crucifix was positioned near the statues. I wondered, *Who would put two statues of Mary side by side?* In my heart, I heard a voice so loud it could not be ignored: "These are the bookends on Mary's life of yes to God!"

The first statue showed Mary's bowed head and prayerful hands at the annunciation. *Yes,* Mary replied to God, without even knowing what the request to bear God's Son entailed. Her yes was immediate and wholehearted.

Even before her yes, Mary's life was a mix of sorrow and joy. Penance was hers throughout life as well: living in poverty; experiencing exile in Egypt; following her Son's public life; witnessing His rejection, Passion, and death; and nurturing the early Church.

All these same things are part of our lives: ordinary daily tasks, some poverty of food and drink, and some mortification of the body as we serve others in our work, follow Jesus in our sacramental life, and nurture our families.

The second statue showed Mary's assumption into heaven as Queen of Heaven and Earth. Seeing these images side by side showed me how the Rosary documents Mary as the first disciple of Jesus. Her discipleship began with the annunciation, and the coronation proclaims her reward as queen in eternity. The Rosary is our call to a disciple's life, preparing us for the reward of eternal life with Jesus, her Son.

Prayer: O Mary, watch over me as I follow your life mysteriously in union with your Son, Jesus. I wish to imitate you in your yes to God. Amen.

Respond to His Call: Choose a person whom you love, and pray all twenty decades of the Rosary with that person in mind.

Dr. Carol Younger

A Pilgrimage with Mary Magdalene

Now when he rose early on the first day of the week, he appeared first to Mary Magdalene, from whom he had cast out seven demons. Mark 16:9

It's weird how a pilgrimage to one place can take you someplace else. On March 31, 2005, I went to the grotto of St. Mary Magdalene in Sainte-Baume, France. I had to travel by way of train, bus, and cab—though the cab was more like a carpool—and then by foot. It was magnificent. Perhaps my favorite thing was the altar with a statue of Mary Magdalene. There, she is forever adoring Jesus in the tabernacle.

To get to the grotto, you have to walk up a mountain; to get home, you have to walk down the mountain. You could fall down the mountain, which is what happened to me. To be fair, I didn't fall down the whole mountain, just one fantastic wipeout that burst the bursa in my knee. I can't really explain what that means, except it's painful. This led to some ugly limping to the cab/carpool, which took us to the bus. We changed our tickets to leave the next evening, as my knee begged to return to home base in Rome.

By 7:30 a.m. on April 2, I was enjoying breakfast with fellow students, who asked if I was going to St. Peter's Square. "Why?" I asked. They answered, "Because the Holy Father is dying."

It was 9 a.m. when we got to the square. By 9 p.m. many thousands of people had joined us there, and millions more were holding vigil around the world. At 9:38 p.m., Pope John Paul II died.

That whole experience was life-changing for me, in more ways than I can list here. But I like to think that Mary Magdalene gave me a push to get me back to the Eternal City a bit early, sending me on an unplanned and incredibly meaningful spiritual pilgrimage. It was quite a gift!

Prayer: St. Mary Magdalene, pray for us! Please pray that we may have a relationship with Jesus that is as close as yours. Amen.

Respond to His Call: Make a physical or virtual pilgrimage (online visit) to the parish where you were baptized. After looking around, pray the Divine Mercy Chaplet for all those who were present when you were baptized.

Alyssa Bormes

A Fool for Christ

We have become a spectacle to the world, to angels and to men. We are fools for Christ's sake, but you are wise in Christ. 1 Corinthians 4:9–10

Sometimes Easter falls on All Fools' Day. In the eyes of the world, no doubt, the joke's on us, the fools who have fallen for Christ. Of course, we *are* fools. The real question is, what kind of fool? A fool of the world or a fool for Christ?

While we who believe in Christ are yet in the world, mightn't we still be of help to those poised to fall into holy fooldom? We can pray that the hearts of these would-be fools will open to joy, sprung from the Resurrection, revealing God's plan for salvation. We can pray that these seekers cast their lot fully onto the Cross in a plea for reparation. We can pray that they be overcome by the Holy Spirit, who flows in fiery waves from the Father to the Son and back in a torrent of consummate love, whispering that our lives are meaningless unless ordered to God. We can pray that this final realization of His everlasting mercy will usher in a swell of gratitude and humility so complete as to cause them to fall, soundly thudding to their knees in utter surrender and relief—and we can do no better than to tumble down beside them, most readily.

If you know souls who fear the world's opinion, I urge you to witness by your life, speak up, and pray that they might find the courage to fall as one more beloved fool willing to suffer gladly for Christ. Foolishness for Christ is the willingness to be wrong in society and wrong according to our time—but right according to our conscience, as guided by the Holy Spirit.

Prayer: Lord, give me the courage to fall as one more beloved fool, willing to suffer gladly for Christ. Amen.

Respond to His Call: Identify someone who does not know you are Catholic and plan a conversation with them. Invite them to share their faith journey. Tell them about your relationship with Jesus, and share why you love your Catholic faith.

Jill Mraz

Winner, Winner, Easter Dinner

Peter then came out with the other disciple, and they went toward the tomb. They both ran, but the other disciple outran Peter and reached the tomb first. John 20:3–4

I saw a meme one Easter on social media that went like this:

John: "I won!"

Peter: "Who's ever going to know?"

John (whispers): "Everyone will know . . ."

I chuckled at the thought of Peter, the loser in this footrace, downplaying John's win. How often do we do this? "I didn't want that promotion anyway!" But John, the dissed victor, has an ace up his sleeve: he's going to write a gospel, and his words (including this little detail about outrunning Peter) will echo throughout the centuries at the holiest of Christian celebrations!

We are each given a role in building God's kingdom on earth, and we should not be jealous of the role of another. Instead, we should pray to recognize that role and respect it. And we should pray to recognize our own role and virtuously live it. Mother Teresa of Calcutta said, "You can do what I cannot do. I can do what you cannot do. Together we can do great things." When we embrace this philosophy, we enhance the gifts of one another and build up the Body of Christ.

John may have been a faster runner, but it's what he did when he stopped running that matters: he waited in humility. John let Peter—the leader of the twelve apostles, whom Jesus had identified as the rock upon which His Church would be built—enter the empty tomb first. It was that action that made John the winner. And what was his reward? John received the gift of faith. "Then, the other disciple, who reached the tomb first, also went in, and he saw and believed" (Jn 20:8). When you walk (or run) in faith with a humble heart, you will experience the greatest reward.

Prayer: Lord, help me to see and believe, like St. John, that I am the disciple You love. Amen.

Respond to His Call: Today, compliment someone you see doing what you cannot do and building up the Body of Christ.

Kelly M. Wahlquist

A Reflection of Beauty

So God created man in his own image, in the image of God he created him; male and female he created them. Genesis 1:27

God always wants to bless us. Instead of giving up on His people, who continually fall from grace, He made the ultimate gesture of blessing by sending His Son. God has called humans from the beginning as His special image-bearers to share in His creative activity; but God also gave us the freedom to embrace or reject that role.

Everything God created is beautiful. In Genesis, we read that God saw His creation as "very good" (1:31). The Hebrew word translated "good" also carries the idea of beauty. God is not just moral but also aesthetic! Creating this beautiful world filled with beautiful things was an artistic enterprise for God. Creation reflects both His goodness and His beauty.

Human sin smudges the beauty of creation. Our rebellion is like a mark on a precious work of art, a mark that not only defaces God's image in our own souls but also damages creation itself.

Have you noticed that the stories in Genesis and the rest of the Bible follow a simple pattern? First, God gives us a beautiful gift, and we respond with sin. Consequences ensue. But in the end, God's grace—not our rebellion—has the final say. Again and again, in response to our insistence on choosing sin and death, God gives grace and life. That pattern culminates in Jesus Christ. He is the most amazing grace, the true Image who heals and restores our broken humanity, the ultimate expression of God's abundant grace that refuses to let our sin have the final say.

Prayer: Come, Lord Jesus! We await Your arrival with joy and hope. In You we can become true image-bearers, living lives of justice, peace, and mercy. Amen.

Respond to His Call: Do you have a habit or pattern of behavior that smudges the beauty of God's image in your life? Write it down on a piece of paper, and pray on the hour for nine hours a prayer of your choice focused on holiness. At the end of the day, tear up or burn that piece of paper, and ask the Holy Spirit to heal and renew you.

Lynda MacFarland

Be Amazed

Moreover, some women of our company amazed us. They were at the tomb early in the morning and did not find his body; and they came back saying that they had even seen a vision of angels, who said that he was alive. Luke 24:22–23

It's only three days after Easter and I've already raided my kids' Easter baskets. I am also eating up Luke's gospel, which contains the well-known account of two of Jesus' disciples walking with Him on the road to Emmaus. As familiar as this story is, this time I was struck by what the two were sharing with Jesus on the journey. Since the travelers had yet to recognize Jesus, they recounted to Him all that had happened in the last few days, including that Jesus' body, which had been placed in the tomb after His death, had since disappeared. Women from their group had reported this disappearance and their vision of angels announcing He was alive. The disciples' astonishment about the women's discovery and the magnitude of what had been revealed to them profoundly moved me.

I love that such a powerful experience was shared by women. My heart has been touched by experiencing Jesus and his work in our lives with other women—especially His forgiveness and healing.

Ladies, we are better when we walk together on our journey with Christ. God gives us gifts in the presence of our sisters. Seek the support of other women striving in their faith. Sharing and hearing how God blesses, heals, and transforms is a powerful, vital encouragement for your faith journey. Maybe you can join a parish group or Bible study, or perhaps God is calling you to start a book club or moms' group. The possibilities are endless and rewarding! May each of you reading this be surrounded by women who love you and are a constant reminder of Christ in your life.

Prayer: Lord, You give me reasons every day to be amazed. Please provide me with a community of sisters who are eager to share their wonder at Your goodness. Amen.

Respond to His Call: Visit CatholicVineyard.com and learn more about the sisterhood of WINE.

Lori Ubowski

The Truth Will Set You Free

Jesus then said to the Jews who had believed in him, "If you continue in my word, you are truly my disciples, and you will know the truth, and the truth will make you free." John 8:31–32

On April 5, 1993, we lost our son to sudden infant death syndrome; the anniversary is emotional. Although Jordan and his twin sister, Courtney, were born prematurely, they both seemed healthy. As you can imagine, the shock of having a child die suddenly wreaked havoc on our lives—spiritually, emotionally, and physically. Death is part of the cycle of life, but it is out of order for a parent to lose a child.

The emotions I feel on this anniversary have changed over the years. For many years, I remained angry with God, demanding an answer to why Jordan died. But during the Jubilee Year of Mercy, I made an intentional effort to focus on forgiveness. I offered a prayer for forgiveness daily. I recalled people in my life who had wounded me and prayed to forgive them. It didn't happen all at once, but I came to realize something in the truth of daily forgiving. When I was chained to anger about my wounds, I was never really free.

For me, freedom came from the truth that while I need to be a disciple, I do not need to have all the answers. There is comfort in knowing that I am simply called to imitate Christ and trust in His plan. I don't need to have everything figured out.

It's a bit counterintuitive: I don't know the reason for my son's death, but through the discipline of embracing forgiveness, my trust in God has grown and my anger is only a memory. God is the truth; His truth is love, and He holds my son safely in that love.

Prayer: Jesus, I lay every bitterness and disappointment at the foot of the Cross. Help me to forgive. Help me embrace the truth that I don't need answers to all my questions—I can regain peace in each situation by simply trusting in Your love. Amen.

Respond to His Call: Call to mind something in your life that's a source of pain or bitterness. Then pray, "Jesus, I trust in you. I do not need answers or vindication—I just need You."

Sharon Agnes Wilson

What Can I Do for You Today?

Now Samuel did not yet know the LORD, and the word of the LORD had not yet been revealed to him. 1 Samuel 3:7

When the Lord called Samuel, it took a few tries before Samuel realized what was going on. But Samuel's response, once he'd figured it out, is beautiful—and instructive. He said, "Speak, LORD, for your servant hears" (1 Sm 3:9). With these simple words, the boy Samuel expressed complete readiness to listen and obey.

This passage has become a short prayer that reminds me of what I am called to do. Accepting God's will for our life can be difficult. But if we remember that God will provide whatever resources we need to do His will, we can rely on His words and relax in His love. Because this trust takes time to develop, we must continually ask for guidance, grace, and courage.

I knew from the day of my cancer diagnosis that God had a plan for me. It took time for me to let go of what I thought my life was supposed to be like and let God take over. I thought I was doing a decent job, but then something new would enter my life to test my trust in Him. I have come to believe, with my whole heart and soul, that I was put on this earth to always praise Him, even through my cancer returning. I have seen the mercy God has shown me in ways both small and great. Each time I recognize His mercy, I thank Him for it, and my trust in Him grows.

Today, thank God for the blessings in your life. Ask Him, "What can I do for You today?" Then sit quietly and listen. Open your heart, and pay attention to what your body and mind are doing. If someone comes to your mind, God may be asking you to do something for that person.

Prayer: Thank You, God, for the many blessings in my life—not only those I recognize but also those that I struggle to see as blessings. Amen.

Respond to His Call: Ask God, "What can I do for you today?" Write down the thoughts that come to you and the things that God puts on your heart.

Rhonda Zweber

The Combination

And to keep me from being too elated by the abundance of revelations, a thorn was given me in the flesh. 2 Corinthians 12:7

My bag was packed—swimsuit, kickboard, towel. This new commitment
to working out was great. With bag in hand and ready to go, I realized
that I had forgotten one thing—my padlock for the locker. After rummaging through drawers and containers, I concluded that the padlock
was lost. (If you find it, the combination is 36-4-10; go ahead and use it.)

On that day of nearly swimming, I did have the idea that I could stop
by the hardware store on the way to the pool to purchase a replacement
lock. However, I had a better idea: how about a bath? Cool—with a bath
bomb in hand and a good book, I successfully avoided exercise! Then,
on the following day, I was in the confessional. No, I did not confess the
missed swim day, but I did confess a habitual sin—the thorn in my side.

Without asking, Father knew I had been neglecting my daily Rosary. I
was to begin it again that day. I did, but my swimming avoidance and lack
of attention to the Rosary kept bothering me. Then the "aha! moment"
arrived: there was a connection between missing my swim and neglecting
my daily Rosary. I used to do my half-hearted swim-walk routine for
an hour at a time. And because it isn't easy to keep yourself in the pool
moving in your lane for that long without being wildly bored, I would
pray the Rosary. Thirty minutes was one Rosary, sixty minutes was two.

So now I've got a new padlock, and I'm back in the pool praying the
Rosary. Every other day, I have an aquatic holy hour in my pink-flowered
swimsuit. It might be funny looking, but the combination is good!

Prayer: Father, help me maintain a regular schedule of prayer. I know this
is the spiritual equivalent of taking my daily vitamins, and it's vital for my
well-being. Amen.

Respond to His Call: Separate yourself today from the distraction of
screens and use that time to go walking, swimming, or biking. Pray during
your exercise for the Lord to help you balance your spirit, mind, and body!

Alyssa Bormes

Prayers of an Army Wife

In the Lord I take refuge. Psalm 11:1

I've been reading the Psalms and trying to apply them to my life. Psalm 11 is about trust in God. I work on this *all* the time! I try mightily to give everything up to God: my worries, challenges, loved ones, desires, fears. But then I find myself taking my concerns back out of God's almighty hands. If we want them back, He just lets go of them. God has never been in the business of coercing us, nor does He get in our way if we decide to ruin our lives. Free will is a two-edged sword.

As an army wife who relocated with her soldier twenty-one times, I felt as if we were always moving or getting ready to move. I have spent a lot of time wondering what this perpetual state of transition is supposed to mean for me. Sometimes I think about how it affects my husband, or its impact on our children and grandchildren. But one morning, I realized I'd spent an exorbitant amount of time asking what was in it for *me*. The guilt overwhelmed me—not only for the time spent, but for the question asked.

My life is incredibly blessed, containing more goodness than I can express. I need to be thankful and let God lead. We placed each move in God's hands because we had no idea what was best for our family. Now, in retirement, I can see how the challenge of constant relocation was actually an amazing faith journey. But it wasn't easy to see the blessing along the way. I was clinging to a "poor me" narrative unfit for a daughter of the King, a daughter married to a son of that same King. We are all children of the King, so let's rejoice and give thanks!

Prayer: Lord, I thank You for the life, the family, and the community in which You have placed me. Thank You for those military families sacrificing to serve our nation. Amen.

Respond to His Call: Think of one item you lost when you moved or changed jobs, and estimate its dollar value. Set aside that dollar value (or a token amount, if expensive) and donate it to a charity or your church parish, asking Jesus to refresh your trust in Him alone.

Lynda MacFarland

Increase Our Faith

Humble yourselves before the Lord and he will exalt you. James 4:10

The apostles said to Christ, "Increase our faith!" (Lk 17:5). As a military wife, I am familiar with opportunities to increase my faith: *Where will the military send us? Will the kids make friends? How will we all transition? How will this affect our marriage?*

Uncertainty is the norm for military families—and in some ways, that uncertainty is a blessing. It keeps us from holding our hopes and plans too tightly. We humans tend to develop a set agenda, with our lives ordered and scheduled according to a particular vision. However, God is calling us to live beyond our plans and schedules. It is His timetable that matters. Embracing that truth requires faith.

The apostles desired something elusive: complete abandonment to God's will. We have an opportunity to make the same request: "Lord, increase our faith." I experience some tension in my heart when I say that prayer. On one hand, I really do desire a deep, unwavering faith; but on the other, I harbor some concerns about what that kind of abandonment to God's will might entail. Is my faith strong enough to withstand the trials that are essential to build up my faith further?

We attempt to control God by controlling our surroundings and calendars. Yet, we discover that our plans aren't always His, or on His timetable. God's plans and His timeline are perfect. But we struggle to surrender, to lay our desires at the foot of His Cross. Giving God control of our lives may be scary, but building deep faith requires it. Releasing our cares and fears to God helps us build faith. In this sometimes difficult process, remember the disciples' request: "Lord, increase our faith."

Prayer: Lord, I surrender to Your will. Increase my faith and reduce my anxiety as I discover Your immense, never-ending love for me. Amen.

Respond to His Call: Choose someone you encounter daily, and set aside a significant portion of a day to serve them in a meaningful way. There's nothing like serving others to help you break away from anxiety about your own life.

AnnAliese Harry

Seek God and Begin Again

And immediately there was in their synagogue a man with an unclean spirit; and he cried out, "What have you to do with us, Jesus of Nazareth? Have you come to destroy us? I know who you are, the Holy One of God." But Jesus rebuked him, saying, "Be silent, and come out of him!" And the unclean spirit, convulsing him and crying with a loud voice, came out of him. Mark 1:23–26

Sometimes it is easy to close our eyes to the reality of evil in the world. But when we scrutinize our own sinful desires—or hear the whispers from the world urging us to prioritize glamour, materialism, or pleasure above God—we know that evil is present and that our weak human nature is tragically susceptible to its allure.

In Mark 1:23–26, Jesus not only sees evil but also commands it to leave with great authority. Jesus may not vocally rebuke evil in our hearts in the same way, but he may speak quietly and urgently to our spirit about changing our ways and seeking good instead of giving in to earthly temptation. Jesus is our ultimate authority, and He speaks to us in a variety of ways—including the internal proddings of our conscience and the external voices of those who love us and want us to keep trying to be the people God intended us to be.

In this season of Ordinary Time, let us reflect on our sinful tendencies and take steps to increase our faith and pursue holiness. As we observe our weaknesses, let us ask God to replenish our strength. Let us seek God in the Sacrament of Reconciliation and begin again to resist evil and work toward selfless sainthood. May God bless you with a glimpse of beauty to sustain your faith during the journey.

Prayer: Lord, shower me with the grace I need today to resist temptation. Grant me the strength to work continually toward sainthood. Amen.

Respond to His Call: As you read or watch the news today, identify a virtue that is especially needed to resist evil in our time. Make nine visits to the Blessed Sacrament asking for replenishment of that virtue.

Anne Carraux

Airport Interactions

I know, O Lord, that the way of man is not in himself, that it is not in man who walks to direct his steps. Jeremiah 10:23

When you surrender your day to the Lord and trust in His promise to bring good in all circumstances, He delivers. I learned this when I was stuck in an airport one day. What could have been hours spent simply waiting around turned into a series of divine appointments.

First, I met Joan, a retiree who had plans to spend a week with her sister in sunny Florida. As we commiserated about the stresses of travel delays, I revealed that my writing dealt with trusting the Lord. Joan opened up about how she struggled with anxiety, confessing that she would get angry with herself when she wasted time worrying about things she couldn't control. The Lord gave me this beautiful opportunity to share my lifelong battle with anxiety and the strength my faith has offered. We laughed together over the silly things we often worried about, while also being honest about the difficulty of trusting in an unseen God.

I next encountered Wanda, a feisty wisp of a woman with a face deeply wrinkled and eyes that reflected an inner sadness. Wanda was also traveling to spend time in a warmer climate with family. The members of her family were dwindling, and the losses weighed on her heart. Wanda shared a photo of her brother, Eddie, who had passed away in the Korean War. A sweet, boyish face smiled out from the plastic slot in her wallet. The Lord directed me to speak the hope of heaven into her sadness. I shared the recent loss of my beloved spiritual director and described how prayer had brought me through so many difficult times. As we spoke, Wanda's lovely gray eyes filled with tears. "I'm so glad I sat here," she said. After a pause, she added, "You know, my daughter always says that prayer is everything, and now I'm starting to see why."

Prayer: May my heart always be open to receive the blessings of surrendering my day to You, Lord. Amen.

Respond to His Call: Before leaving the house today, offer your day to the Lord. You never know what opportunities He'll give you to share His goodness with someone in need.

Allison Gingras

More Than Meets the Eye

Now on the first day of the week, Mary Magdalene came to the tomb early, while it was still dark, and saw that the stone had been taken away from the tomb. John 20:1

It's interesting how many times John refers to "seeing" in his account of the morning of the Resurrection. Mary Magdalene saw the stone removed. John and Peter came to see for themselves. Peter saw Jesus' headcloth in a separate place. Finally, John entered the tomb, and he saw and believed. There was nothing to see—and yet, there was more here than met the eye. Jesus' body wasn't there, and that in itself was astonishing. He left burial cloths behind, rolled up the headcloth, and left. Signs that Jesus was elsewhere were everywhere!

John is gracious about some of the disciples' lack of sight: "For as yet they did not know the Scripture, that he must rise from the dead" (Jn 20:9). But what did John see? At first, he saw the burial cloths from outside of the tomb. When he went inside, he saw signs that this was not a case of body theft; this was a miracle of a body risen!

What John had heard from the lips of Jesus was now fully revealed in the light of the Resurrection. Death cannot hold the Son of God. He arose out of the bonds of burial cloths and death. Yes, we humans are dust, and to dust we shall return—but that's no longer the end of the story.

Death has died and the God-Man has risen. After the Resurrection, we can see death as something we leave behind, like the burial cloths Jesus left in His tomb. When we die with Him, we will rise with Him. Alleluia!

Prayer: O my Jesus, help my eyes to see You risen in the world around me and let my life reveal Your glory to others. Help me to live Your promise of resurrection so that I can proclaim to the world Your promise to be the Way, the Truth, and the Life. Amen.

Respond to His Call: Visit the grave of a relative, or a cemetery at a nearby church. Spend some time praying for your deceased relatives and the souls in purgatory to receive the blessings of Jesus' Resurrection.

Dr. Carol Younger

A Firm Foundation

Do not think that I have come to abolish the law and the prophets;
I have come not to abolish them but to fulfil them. Matthew 5:17

With Christ, it is always more, not less. In saying that He has come to fulfill God's laws, Jesus shows us a deeper reality. God's laws are revealed in the Old Testament and fulfilled in the New. God does not change, but as we grow, we can more fully accept, embrace, and live what God wrote on our hearts. "Not an iota, not a dot, will pass from the law until all is accomplished" (Mt 5:18).

God's laws are eternal and not subject to fashions or philosophies of the day. What is good and holy now was good and holy then, and it is a great comfort to know we do not need to wring our hands or wrack our brains to understand this; it merely is. In this day, when much of our world embraces moral relativism, the unchanging reality of God's truth and goodness—from creation to the Cross to our hope of heaven—provides a firm foundation. God is our rock, and our spirit can rest in the knowledge that what was true yesterday is still true today—and ever shall be true.

Christ isn't in the business of making the way to heaven unknown. He is continually revealing to us that what God desires is written on our hearts and always available to those who seek. The more we seek, the more we will discover God's infinite love and how we should live as His followers.

Prayer: Jesus, thank You for giving us clear standards about how to live. Give me the grace to seek Your will and the humility to follow Your call. Help me rest on the firm foundation of Your truth. Amen.

Respond to His Call: Your conscience is a great gift from God that helps you know His truth and hear His voice—but it can become improperly calibrated! Ask God to reveal any areas where your conscience needs to become more closely aligned with His truth.

Sherry Antonetti

A Puddle of Time

For everything there is a season, and a time for every matter under heaven. Ecclesiastes 3:1

When I was young, I loved to splash in puddles. Sometimes the street near us would flood, and we would joyfully ride our bikes through the knee-high "river." Those rain puddles and temporary rivers seemed made to be enjoyed, splashed about, navigated. As children, we find something irresistible in those tiny ponds: the stomp of a rain boot results in the triumph of a splash. Today, I maneuver around puddles of water; I have a longing for a different sort of puddle, a puddle of time.

What is a puddle of time? It's one of those rare, sometimes astonishing "in-between" moments—the breathing space between laundry, work, groceries, appointments, and everything else. Whether planned or a surprise, time puddles are lovely opportunities. Do we splash in that extra time? Or maneuver around it? Are we busy being busy? Or do we joyfully savor the moments down to our toes?

I've enjoyed time puddles by sharing a laugh with a friend before we get in our cars, by gazing at the changing leaves, and by getting my pillow just right for a five-minute retreat.

Time puddles drain away after only a short time, so store their memory in your heart to splash in them again later. Time puddles are elusive, and that's part of why they are precious. They shouldn't be maneuvered around. They are little gifts from God that help get us through the rest of life. I've discovered the best way to spend a time puddle is by splashing with galoshes full of gratitude. Now go find a puddle of time and make the most of it!

Prayer: Lord, my heart is filled with gratitude for the blessings You bestow today. Allow me the opportunity to sit in the quiet and enjoy special time with You. Amen.

Respond to His Call: Carve out some puddle time, and spend it with Jesus.

Alyssa Bormes

All Things New

Blessed are the merciful, for they shall obtain mercy. Blessed are the pure in heart, for they shall see God. Blessed are the peacemakers, for they shall be called sons of God. Matthew 5:7–9

Concerned about the state of the world, I often find myself yearning for the kingdom of God here on earth. I want to live in the New Jerusalem, with no more death or mourning or pain, where God dwells with the human race. Where is that place?

Despite that longing, I find myself fearing the "new" part. I like familiarity. I'm timid when it comes to putting myself out there. I'm stuck between wanting something new and fearing the change. What if I get hurt? What if I'm wrong?

I discover the answer to my fear in scripture. Jesus gives me a new commandment—to love as He loves. Elsewhere, scripture tells me that love is patient, kind, and merciful. Love is never rude or proud, self-seeking, or volatile. Love forgives everything. *Everything.* Can I do that, Lord? And if I do love as You love, what will happen then? Will Your kingdom come? What will it look like? It has been said that courage isn't the absence of fear; rather, it is the decision that there is something more important to me than the fear I face.

I'll confess I've sometimes been tempted to dismiss the Beatitudes as a list of impossible platitudes. But what if I close my eyes and ponder those words deeply within my heart? Will I get a glimpse of that kingdom of God? Will I hear the Lord describe it to me, this New Jerusalem? Perhaps that's what the kingdom of God is all about—encountering the new commandment and embracing it. And rather than fearing the "new" as if it were a crashing wave, I'll swim out to meet it—and dive right into the kingdom of God.

Prayer: O Jesus, I want Your kingdom to come now, in my lifetime. Though sometimes I fear, I do long to live in Your kingdom, and I beg for the grace to live here and now as You want, with love and mercy for others. Amen.

Respond to His Call: Learn the Chaplet of Divine Mercy from St. Faustina. Pray it every day for a week for your city or community.

Lynne Keating

April 16

Into the Light

The light shines in the darkness, and the darkness has not over-come it. John 1:5

Easter marks the anniversary of my return to the Catholic Church. Out-wardly, before my Confirmation, it was a flurry of activity. But inwardly, my journey home was contemplative. A slow dance was in progress as my soul unfolded into newness with waves of love silently crashing against my heart.

The Easter Vigil arrived. I remember well the tears that surprised me and flowed steadily down my face as the priest laid his hands on my bowed head. I was blessed at that moment. Claimed. My life was changed forever. Reflecting on all that has come to pass since that night when my heart was pierced as the Holy Spirit rushed upon me, I pray that I will continue to surrender my will to the one who so beautifully captured it with His fierce and tender love.

I love the dark: dark mysteries, the twilight, riding a bike down dark streets on summer nights. Even my dark past, with all its failings, bad decisions, and lost opportunities, has served its purpose. How I love, too, the silence that accompanies the middle of the night. As the sun rises, we begin again. Similarly, at the Easter Vigil, I stood still in the dark. With my trembling candle, I walked into the church as light replaced the dark-ness. When the priest finally laid his hands on my head, my heart sang with joy. I am filled with gratitude for the Catholic faith, for my friends, and even for the dark days of my past.

How apt is the exultant cry in the liturgy, "O happy fault that earned so great, so glorious a Redeemer!"

Prayer: My God, how I love You! As we move toward longer, brighter days, give us the grace to rise and begin again in our most beautiful Catholic Church, ever ancient, ever new. Amen.

Respond to His Call: Recall when you felt the furthest away from Jesus, and write Him a thank-you note for the rescue He provided from that dark-ness. Be sure to include how His grace helped you move to brighter days. Bring that note with you to read in front of the Blessed Sacrament.

Jill Mraz

Finding My Prayer Voice

Likewise the Spirit helps us in our weakness; for we do not know how to pray as we ought, but the Spirit himself intercedes for us with sighs too deep for words. Romans 8:26

Have you ever found yourself thinking, *There's so much that needs prayer—where do I start? Is it selfish to pray for personal things when there is so much need in the world? Will God think my intercessions are trivial?* Honestly, those kinds of worries have sometimes hurt my prayer life. Maybe it's my all-or-nothing mindset, but unless my prayer addresses all the world's problems, I perceive it as a failure. That's where Paul's words in Romans come in to save the day.

What a comfort to know that I don't have to know where to begin! I don't have to know how to pray. When I'm overwhelmed by the breadth and gravity of the issues at hand that need prayer, the Spirit reads my heart and intercedes. I mean, if that doesn't just completely take the weight of the world off your shoulders, I don't know what will. Whenever we come to the Lord in prayer, we should remember that God doesn't expect perfection. He doesn't want polished or pristine. He doesn't expect pitch-perfect prose. He wants our hearts. The raw, authentic heart has His ear, even if it might not know where to start when interceding for this crumbling world and its hurting people.

The important thing is to begin. There is power in prayer. And there is nothing the world needs more right now than a praying people. Prayers for peace. Prayers for health and safety. Prayers for equality and justice. Prayers for the lonely and brokenhearted. Prayers for the oppressed and persecuted. Prayers for love to drive out hate.

Prayer: Holy Spirit, come and fill in the gaps when I pray. Intercede where I've missed or overlooked things. Thank You for being my Intercessor when I've lost my prayer voice. Amen.

Respond to His Call: Sit quietly for ten or fifteen minutes (set a timer so you don't watch the clock). Remain as quiet as possible, just listening to sounds you hear with no interpretation, ending the time with the quiet whisper, "Thank You, Holy Spirit."

Caralyn Collar

His Glory Revealed

And the glory of the LORD shall be revealed, and all flesh shall see it together, for the mouth of the LORD has spoken. Isaiah 40:5

How did Jesus spend the first day of His forty days on earth after the Resurrection? By revealing Himself. On the same day He arose, Jesus was seen five times. First, He appeared to Mary Magdalene, who was alone in the garden. Then He appeared to the women who left the empty tomb to tell the disciples. He next appeared to Peter, then to two disciples on their way to Emmaus, and finally that night to the eleven apostles together.

How does Jesus reveal Himself to us? He asked the men on the way to Emmaus what they were discussing. He acted as if He knew nothing. In doing so, Jesus made room for them—their questions and uncertainty—and gently drew them into His wisdom and presence.

I have often pondered this occurrence on the road to Emmaus, wondering what Jesus might have said to the disciples. Approaching Emmaus, Jesus feigned that He was traveling farther. "Stay with us," they urged, and He did. Yet they still did not recognize Him. When He took the bread, blessed it, broke it, and gave it to them, their eyes were opened. The moment they realized who they were dining with, He vanished. Later, when the two disciples recounted Jesus' explanation of the scriptures to them, they said, "Did not our hearts burn within us?" (Lk 24:32).

Where is your heart today? Do you, like the men traveling to Emmaus, ache to remain near Jesus, holding onto Him and begging Him to stay? Even when our hearts are far from Him, He says ever so tenderly, "Stay with Me, that I may visit you. The veil is torn in two; I am fully present to you at all times."

Prayer: Jesus, You are both the God who hides Himself and the one who reveals Himself when we seek You. Your ways are higher than our ways. Show us Your glory. Amen.

Respond to His Call: Meditate on Jesus' mysterious ways. Mysteries beg to be unraveled—and when the veil is parted, we see as He sees. Ask God to help you recognize Him wherever He's present and speaking to you today.

Deborah Kendrick

Loving without Reserve

So we know and believe the love God has for us. God is love, and he who abides in love abides in God, and God abides in him. 1 John 4:16

My grandmother lived to be almost 104. She was a woman of great faith and decided at age 100 that God had kept her on earth to pray for her grandchildren. Many graces came to me through her prayers!

Grandma lived in a Catholic assisted-living facility that celebrated Mass every day. On Wednesdays, I attended Mass with her. The sacristan eventually asked me to serve as a eucharistic minister, and I felt so blessed to bring Jesus to those who could not make it up to the altar. They would watch me coming down the aisle, their bodies leaning forward and their eyes moist in anticipation. They were so focused on Jesus and couldn't wait to receive Him.

One day, I was working my way down the pews and came to a slight break before the next person. She was a few pews away, and I picked up the host in the ciborium in preparation to give her Communion. I could feel this woman's longing for Jesus, and much to my surprise, I suddenly could also feel Jesus' longing for her. It was as if Jesus would leap out of my hand for love. Tears flowed down my cheeks as I realized the incredible gift I had been given. Jesus was showing me how to live. These seniors in the twilight of their lives had stripped away the trappings that keep us from focusing entirely on Him. They loved Jesus without reserve, and in return, He wanted to be completely united with them.

Prayer: Lord, help me to remove the things that keep me from focusing on You. Amen.

Respond to His Call: What is keeping you from focusing on Jesus? Ask the Lord today to show you, and He will.

Sherry Kennedy Brownrigg

Living in Shalom

Peace I leave with you; my peace I give to you; not as the world gives do I give to you. Let not your hearts be troubled, neither let them be afraid. John 14:27

Our God deeply desires that we know true peace. And while that sounds good, many of us do not experience peace, even if we have been Christians all our lives. Jesus' promise that we can know His peace may seem too good to be true as we wrestle with fears, disappointments, and anxieties. Complicating this is the fact that many people have a limited understanding of the word "peace." Some people think of peace as the mere absence of conflict—but it's so much more.

The word "peace" in the Old Testament is usually translated from the Hebrew word *shalom*. Such a small word, but so full of meaning! While it does mean tranquility or calm, the truest sense of shalom is wholeness. Wholeness includes concepts of completeness, harmony, and fulfillment. All the things that God intended for His good creation, all the things that were broken and lost because of sin, and all the things we look forward to in the fulfilled kingdom of God can be described as shalom—perfect harmony within creation and between all creatures and God.

You were designed by God to desire and know His peace. The peace or shalom of God is a precious gift of the Holy Spirit. Peace comes from knowing that God is with you in every area of your life as you surrender to His love and His faithfulness.

Do you need peace? Bring God your conflicted heart. Does your home need peace? Entrust your family to His hand. When you are wrestling with fears and disappointments, keep turning toward Him, surrendering your circumstances and sufferings to His hands.

Prayer: Heavenly Father, I thank You that You are bigger than anything we face in this life. I lay every one of my burdens before You. Lord, bring the peace into my heart that surpasses all understanding, as I surrender to Your strength. Amen.

Respond to His Call: Give specific praise to God for His peace, accepting the promise of peace that Jesus gives you no matter the circumstances.

Barbara Elaine Heil

Exercise Humility

Do not be conformed to this world but be transformed by the renewal of your mind, that you may prove what is the will of God, what is good and acceptable and perfect. Romans 12:2

At age forty-six, after my husband's courageous two-year battle with cancer, I became a widow. The title was difficult to speak and even more difficult to accept. Left alone with three children, I struggled to understand how my husband, who was so vibrant and strong, faithful, and devoted to his family, could be taken. When he was very sick, he told me, "If I die from this disease, you'll be sad; you'll grieve. Things will be confusing. But I'm telling you, don't question why this is happening. Don't ask why. No good can come of asking that question."

We assume that questioning deepens our understanding of our world. Seeking truth is good and noble, but we should not presume there is always an answer to be found. We can become prone to the sin of pride in thinking that if we study hard enough, research extensively, or pray long enough, we'll know all the whys of the universe. Pride can fool us into thinking we can discover all the answers and know the will of God.

My husband's advice was wise: no good comes from demanding answers from God. The question would only bring futile frustration. I am not meant to know God's will at all times. It takes humility to accept—without feeling entitled to understanding why—someone so wonderful being taken from this world and his family. Obeying God's will is a daily decision, sometimes made moment by moment. We must humbly accept God's will whether or not we understand it so that He will lead us to our shared eternal life.

Prayer: Lord, help me to humbly accept the path You have laid out for me even when I feel challenged and despairing. Please give me the grace each day, through prayer and the sacraments, to acknowledge that carrying my cross unites me more closely with You. Amen.

Respond to His Call: Today, exercise humility in your actions. Let a stranger have your spot in line; let your friend know a trait you value in them; let your family member have the last word.

Jennifer Beutz

April 22

Tiny Seeds, Plentiful Branches

Truly, truly, I say to you, unless a grain of wheat falls into the earth and dies, it remains alone; but if it dies, it bears much fruit. John 12:24

Reflecting on Jesus' description of a grain of wheat, I am amazed at how much He reveals in a few simple words about . . . farming. As a midwestern kid with a mother who loved to garden, I know all about seeds. I have fond memories of my sister and me germinating seeds in damp paper towels, readying them to plant in the vegetable patch. We checked on them every day, hoping to see that radicle pushing through—that first sign of life. It is a miracle that something can start so small and grow so large.

Our faith is like that seed. It was probably planted by our parents, and its germination began with the cleansing waters of baptism. Soon our little sprouts thrive and stretch stems toward the Son. Rooted in Christ Jesus, we become mighty through the seasons of life, pushing through the dark soil of adversity to break free into the light. Before any of this can happen, however, the seed must first break open. We cannot become the women of faith we are supposed to be without allowing our hard, exterior shell to crack open and reveal our inner selves, in need of God and His grace.

Spiritual growth can be a challenge; we struggle to bloom. Yet, if we remain seeds unsoftened by water and earth, we cannot serve the world. Just as the proverbial mustard seed grew to become a refuge for the birds to rest their wings, we must grow large and open, offering ourselves in service to others. This growth is not just for our benefit but also for all those to whom God sends us.

Prayer: Jesus, You have planted me in Your vineyard. Help me respond to the many gifts, promptings, and graces You provide for me to grow. I desire to be Your wheat for the many who hunger for You. Amen.

Respond to His Call: How are you a seed, afraid to break open and grow? Sit with the Father today in the shade of His love and the sunshine of His Son, and ponder how you are called to grow.

Angela Koenig

God Knows You

Are not five sparrows sold for two pennies? And not one of them is forgotten before God. Why, even the hairs of your head are all numbered. Fear not; you are of more value than many sparrows.
Luke 12:6–7

Look back at your life. Do you recall something that you were worried about that stole your joy? Often the things we worry about never come to pass, or when they do, we have the grace to get through them. When stuck in worry, we can get so focused on the future that it becomes difficult to enjoy the present. But God knows our needs and what lies ahead of us. He knows every hair on our head. If He loves the sparrows and takes care of them, how much more does He love us?

When we allow the worries and anxieties of life to take over, we miss out on God's peace reigning in our hearts. If we are patient and persevering in prayer, things we worry about will eventually pass. Afterward, a deepened faith will emerge if we let it. The enemy will do everything he can to keep us in a state of unrest because God works through us most powerfully in moments of calm attentiveness to Him. The enemy wants us to be distracted and self-focused so that we won't be available to hear God's voice or help those around us. Yet our very joy connects us with others, allowing God's love to flow in our hearts.

God knows you. He knows your tears, your sufferings, and what keeps you up at night. He suffers with you and is holding you in His arms right now. You have been chosen for a unique purpose. No one else can be who God created you to be. God wants you to walk in confidence and peace as His beloved child. Don't let worry steal your joy any longer. Rest in the knowledge that the Lord loves you and desires to see you smile!

Prayer: Jesus, please forgive me for worrying and help me to trust that You will provide all that I need. Amen.

Respond to His Call: Name one thing that you worried about in the past that never came to be. Let that memory encourage you to take what you are worrying about today and give it to Jesus.

Joelle Maryn

A Little Mary, a Little Martha

But the Lord answered her, "Martha, Martha, you are anxious and troubled about many things; one thing is needful. Mary has chosen the good portion, which shall not be taken away from her."
Luke 10:41–42

At one point in my life, I was immersed in volunteer work. I loved it. But it also kept me from some pretty important things: prayer, family, and writing. After several months of discernment, I finally surrendered the decision to God. The conviction to resign from my volunteer position grew so strongly that I couldn't ignore it. The Lord was inviting me to enter a time of increased prayer and contemplation.

Stepping away from that work was a difficult decision for me. Many people thought I was crazy for leaving my high-profile volunteer position, but I had to trust God instead of them. I knew it was vital for me to remain attentive to His still, small, and steady voice instead of their loud opinions.

This experience reminds me of the story of Mary and Martha. In it, Jesus does not reprimand Martha for her generosity and hospitality. Instead, He addresses her anxiety and worry. Jesus knows that Martha's work is good, but it could be more fruitful and joyful if it were balanced with time seated at His feet—a place that her sister Mary recognized as "the better part."

Over time, I received clear confirmation that I had chosen "the better part." Time with my family at home was more joyful, and my writing improved. I felt less stress and more peace—all because my work flowed from a place of prayer.

Prayer: Lord, thank You for delighting in the woman You created me to be. Always help me to approach the unique work You have for me from a place of prayer, praise, and thanksgiving. Amen.

Respond to His Call: Today, before you do anything on your to-do list, spend time at the feet of Jesus, listening to His loving guidance. Note how this simple practice impacts the rest of your day.

Sarah Damm

Wonder Bread Crumbles in Comparison

Then the woman went her way and ate, and her countenance was no longer sad. 1 Samuel 1:18

"Just eat a sandwich. You'll be fine!" These pragmatic words of my late Grandpa Dave were our longtime household remedy for every fatigue and ailment. He lived by this mantra, as did the rest of us. A piece of peanut butter toast to calm the child who couldn't sleep. A pitcher of lemonade to refresh the youngsters playing outside. A pail of cookies to cheer the weary college student. I've come to believe Grandpa's words. But physical food doesn't address every kind of hunger. We also experience spiritual hunger, which can only be satiated by the Bread of Life, Jesus.

Before His Passion, Jesus had an extraordinary supper with His disciples. He blessed, broke, and shared bread with His friends—just as His body would be blessed, broken, and shared with the whole world on Good Friday. He explains numerous times throughout the gospels that He is the Bread of Life. He nourishes us and makes our bodies and souls strong. Every time we gather around the table to celebrate Mass, we remember His love for us. We receive that love through the Most Holy Eucharist in Communion.

Many an ice cream cone has left me less than satisfied. This world can only offer us so much, especially when our desire for things created distracts from or even replaces our desire for the Creator. The Lord invites us to His table with words of welcome and a promise to meet every need: Come, you who are weary. Receive His invitation and open wide the door to your heart. You shall be filled, and you shall be made well!

Prayer: Sweet Jesus, Bread of Life, make me aware of Your presence in a new way today. Fill my body, mind, and soul that I may have the strength to love others and receive all the love You have placed in my path. Amen.

Respond to His Call: Feeling hungry, emptied out, needy? Visit an adoration chapel to be in the presence of the Bread of Life, and to receive all the "crumbs" of goodness Jesus desires to fill your heart with!

Katie Anderson

Rock of Ages

There is none holy like the Lord, there is none besides you; there is no rock like our God. 1 Samuel 2:2

I can still hear my father's voice, calling me the nickname he gave me all those years ago. "Rock, do you see that little yellow bird? It's a western meadowlark," or, "Rock, let's go on a drive in the country and pick some buffalo berries." Others called me either by my full name, Roxane, or other variations. Dad alone chose "Rock." Not until after his death did I begin to reflect on what my father may have been trying to communicate through this choice. Now, I see my nickname as a summons—to stay strong and to persevere and keep my eyes on the Lord.

I think of the heartaches I have endured as a mother—miscarriage, the pain of seeing my children hurting, the sorrow of watching them question God—and as a wife, journeying with my husband through two open-heart surgeries and other worrisome moments. I have needed to be a rock through these tumults, even when feeling incapable. "And I tell you, you are Peter, and on this rock I will build My Church," Jesus said to His friend (Mt 16:18). How daunted this disciple must have felt! I wonder if he anticipated that this commission would ultimately end in martyrdom. Even if not, he likely felt unworthy, as I do most days when I'm called to be a rock for my domestic church.

What allows us to go forward in faith is knowing our limits. Human rocks are but pebbles next to the Rock of Ages. With this Rock near, we can move confidently forward, joining our littleness with His almighty power to help grow the kingdom of God on earth.

Prayer: Dear Lord, You had a purpose in giving me my name, and You have imprinted a mission on my very soul. Help me know more clearly each day the road You have laid out before me. Give me confidence to step into this thoughtfully plotted pathway, knowing that You, the true Rock, will provide everything I need to carry out Your call. Amen.

Respond to His Call: Meditate before the Eucharist on God's unique call for your life. Thank Him for being the Rock who gives you the strength and security you need to fulfill that calling.

Roxane B. Salonen

Grace Is My Middle Name

And he came to her and said, "Hail, full of grace, the Lord is with you!" Luke 1:28

It's a grace that in junior high school, at the time of my Confirmation, I had some understanding of the commitment I was making by accepting the sacrament. My heart was all in when it came to beginning my journey as an adult in the Catholic Church. I didn't know much about the saints, so I didn't already have a heavenly friend to honor when choosing my name. I did know I wanted one that meant "grace." I searched baby-name websites for options but didn't find one that felt right.

Eventually, I settled on Grace, plain and simple. I prayed for clarity but didn't experience an earth-shattering reply that made me as thrilled about my choice as I'd hoped. To my teenage soul, the name felt direct, rather than poetic or powerful.

Fast-forward seven years to my wedding day. I stood in the same church beside a man who had been confirmed that same day. Entering into marriage, I chose to change not only my last name but my middle name as well. Legally and spiritually, Grace became my middle name.

A few years later, my father-in-law suggested that with this name, I could claim all Marian feast days as my own—which at our house, with young children, primarily manifests as being able to choose what's for dessert! But at a deeper level, it meant that I could claim Mary as my own—as my mother but also as my sister in faith. I'd unwittingly chosen a name connected to the Blessed Mother, someone I'd come to know, love, and trust, someone on whom I could lean as I grew in faith. Grace, for sure—it's my middle name.

Prayer: Holy Spirit, who came upon me in a grace-filled way at the time of my Confirmation, renew Your gifts within me, that I may share them with everyone I meet today. Amen.

Respond to His Call: Recall why you chose your Confirmation name, and consider how this name is relevant to your current state of life.

Lindsay Schlegel

Pray for Wisdom

Settle it therefore in your minds, not to meditate beforehand how to answer; for I will give you a mouth and wisdom, which none of your adversaries will be able to withstand or contradict. Luke 21:14

As a counselor, I feel that I am often in the midst of what St. Luke is talking about in chapter 21, verses 12–19. I encounter much sadness and brokenness in those I counsel. I read in the news about modern culture's rejection of the family and the Church and threats to religious freedom. I have friends and family who have left the faith, left Christianity, and followed the latest glitter and bling on offer from the world. They look at me as if I have two heads when I want to say grace over a meal or go to Mass or talk about God. I sometimes wonder if I am crazy—or if what is going on around me is what's crazy.

Then I remember, I am living in a war zone. I know who wins the war, but the current battle is for souls. So I soldier on and wait for the day when the lost souls around me are ready to be found. I pray for wisdom, remembering the punch line of today's scripture: "I will give you a mouth and wisdom."

God Himself is going to provide me with the ability to speak His truth. I know that God is real. I know that God loves me. Even amid the darkness, the battle, the pain, and the suffering, those truths don't change. Some days I don't feel it, but each day I can choose to believe it and stand in that belief until the time when I *do* feel it. "But not a hair of your head will perish. By your endurance you will gain your lives" (Lk 21:18–19). Thank You, Jesus!

Prayer: Lord, fill the places I lack wisdom. Amid darkness, troubles, and suffering, secure my decisions and hope with Your Holy Spirit. Amen.

Respond to His Call: Write down ten concerns that take up too much of your attention. Fold up the paper and place it under your Bible. Then read Psalm 34 several times, slowly and reflectively, until the worries shrink in size inside your mind. Close the Bible, throw away the folded paper, and thank God.

Katsey Long

Trust the Vine Grower

If a man does not abide in me, he is cast forth as a branch and withers; and the branches are gathered, thrown into the fire and burned. If you abide in me, and my words abide in you, ask whatever you will, and it shall be done for you. By this my Father is glorified, that you bear much fruit, and so prove to be my disciples.
John 15:6–8

Five times in John 15:1–8, Jesus tells His disciples to "remain in me" like branches on a grapevine. A branch can't bear fruit by itself, He points out—and neither can you be fruitful if you don't remain in Jesus, attached to Him, with His life flowing through you as the life of the vine flows through its branches.

How often do I force a side-by-side relationship with Jesus instead of remaining in him and allowing Him to live through me? Rather than drawing my strength from the Lord and waiting on His plan, sometimes I prefer to do my own thing. Or how often, when it seems as though He's not active, am I tempted to get started on my own power?

Instead of taking advantage of that "wintertime" to send my roots deep into His Word and sacraments and fill myself up with His presence, I may choose to spend my strength growing a lovely long branch with lots of showy leaves. I may set out to accomplish my works, hanging fruit on the branch. But a decorative branch can't carry Christ's life if it's not connected to the vine.

Jesus wants fruit that remains. Fruit that feeds others and reproduces. And He wants to bear fruit in me (and you!). The Vine Grower has our flourishing in mind, even when it seems we've been abandoned or when we can feel the cut of the pruning shears. He chose us to bear fruit, and He will make us fruitful—in His time and in His way.

Prayer: Lord, help me to remain in You. Feed me and fill me with Your life-giving water. Whatever drought or difficulties come my way, help me to trust myself to the loving hands of the Father. Amen.

Respond to His Call: Prayerfully consider ways that you might attach yourself more fully to Jesus, so as to remain in Him and draw on His strength.

Sarah Christmyer

Speak Lord, Your Servant Is Listening

Therefore Eli said to Samuel, "Go, lie down; and if he calls you, you shall say, 'Speak, LORD, for your servant hears.'" 1 Samuel 3:9

With a looming deadline and the need for quiet and divine guidance, I went to St. Walburga Abbey for a writing retreat. Yet every time the bells chimed, I felt God nudging me to join the nuns praying the Divine Office. So I halted my writing and walked the quarter mile to the chapel . . . five times a day! As I was hustling back to my cabin at sunset, I grumbled, "How do these nuns run a farm and get anything done when they stop to pray all day?" Then I chuckled at myself as I heard, "That is exactly how they get it all done!"

I used to say my daily prayers on the run. I'm quite busy doing His work, you know. In 1 Thessalonians 5:17, Paul tells us to "pray constantly," so I rambled on to God, petitions mostly, all day long. But He gently guided me to a better way: "Be still, and know that I am God" (Ps 46:10). Eventually, I committed to setting aside at least fifteen minutes a day, every day, to be still and pray—for it is there in the silence that we hear the divine guidance in our lives. Instead of, "Listen up, God, your servant is speaking," it became, "Speak, Lord, your servant is listening." God didn't say, "Keep real busy and work crazy for Me." He said, "Be still, and know that I am God."

Over and over in scripture we hear that Jesus went alone to a quiet place to pray. If Jesus needed that, how much more do we? Jesus meets us in the stillness of our souls. It is there that He communes with us. But stillness is hard to find in speed and noise. Create a quiet place where you can meet God daily. Wait in His presence and listen. Be still.

Prayer: Lord, show me the time and place to be still and feel Your presence, to hear Your voice. Help me keep this commitment to You. Amen.

Respond to His Call: Today, look at your schedule prayerfully; then write in the time you will be still each day to pray . . . and listen.

LeeAnn Thieman

The Gift of Wisdom

If any of you lacks wisdom, let him ask God, who gives to all men generously and without reproaching, and it will be given him.
James 1:5

My short definition of wisdom is this: Wisdom is learning from other people's mistakes. That is the best shortcut I have found in life so far. Before you say how unfair that sounds, consider this—the Bible is a book that explicitly details the flaws, mistakes, errors in judgment, and outright sins of many who are named in it. All of this has been preserved and given for our benefit. This is where we begin to learn from the mistakes of others. When we wash our minds with the Word of God, His wisdom enters our hearts.

So how does this wisdom come to us? Spending time in prayer is a good start. Solomon simply asked God for wisdom. When Solomon made that request, God granted his desire—and so much more. Solomon had not asked for riches, honor, victory over his enemies, or even long life for himself. But God gave him all these things in addition to wisdom and knowledge.

Wisdom also comes through reading scripture. Not only is the Bible full of stories that teach wisdom and people whose lives provide examples both good and bad but also entire books within the Bible (for example, the book of Proverbs) are known as "wisdom literature." These books impart practical advice for making wise choices that honor God.

Prayer: Lord, today I seek wisdom above all else. May I know Your thoughts and ways. Let Your kingdom come and Your will be done on earth and in me, as it is in heaven. Amen.

Respond to His Call: Read one chapter of Proverbs every day this month; conveniently, there are thirty-one chapters. After trying it for a month, you may find that you want to keep up the habit!

Deborah Kendrick

The Only Perfect Mother

Whoever does the will of God is my brother, and sister, and mother. Mark 3:35

Ordinarily our parish recites the Rosary together before Mass, but on one occasion Father asked us to pray it in silence as the choir would start singing soon. My friend's niece, who has Down syndrome, sat between us. She misunderstood Father, thinking he didn't like the Rosary, and began crying. We started to explain, but just then the choir started and it all made sense. Now calm, my friend's niece began to explain to us how to pray the Rosary. The beads on her rosary were heart-shaped and pearl-colored. She told us the prayers for the little beads, the big beads, and the cross, and then she turned to the medal. Her voice full of awe, she declared, "This is Mary. She is the only perfect mother."

Tears rolled down my face. This young woman with Down syndrome was a sort of mystic. Her words pierced my heart, my friend's heart, and surely the heart of God. At that moment, I was able to forgive my mother for her occasional mistakes in raising her children. I was able to forgive myself for my own failures as a mother; my two children had died through abortion.

There are many mothers among us—some with grown children, others with young ones, some with many, some with few, some whose children have been lost to abortion, others who lost their children to disease or accident, and there are spiritual mothers as well. From time to time, ponder the words of this young woman and forgive yourself for the ways you fall short. Rejoice in the gift of motherhood.

Prayer: Lord, doing Your will is my desire, but my broken places sometimes become obstacles. Forgive me my trespasses, especially those that have left me the most broken. Amen.

Respond to His Call: Take a rosary, and pray the first decade for your mother. On each bead, mention something you need to forgive her for, and say a Hail Mary. Pray the second decade for yourself. On each bead, mention something you need to forgive yourself for, and say a Hail Mary.

Alyssa Bormes

Childlike Faith

Truly, I say to you, unless you turn and become like children, you will never enter the kingdom of heaven. Whoever humbles himself like this child, he is the greatest in the kingdom of heaven. Whoever receives one such child in my name receives me. Matthew 18:3–5

My life changed when we had children. Time and money were no longer our own. We became focused on our children's health and lives. But despite all the new complexities, we also gained (or regained) a perspective of simplicity. We started to look at the world through childlike eyes.

My children reawakened some of the traditions, prayers, and games of my childhood. I had forgotten the simple Guardian Angel prayer until I started teaching it to my children. My children are now young adults, and although I don't sit bedside and say evening prayers with them as I did when they were little, I do pray for them. And I start with the Guardian Angel prayer.

Jesus calls us all to be more childlike. Not silly like children—although a bout of silliness is often a good thing! But we are called to be childlike in our trust in God, and filled with grateful wonder when receiving His gifts.

Trust and gratitude are lifelong endeavors. But simple acts can continually lead us back to the childlike perspective that God delights in. Are you quick to tell God, "I trust You," expressing the kind of faith that lets a child leap fearlessly from a great height into her father's open arms? Do you say "thank You" every chance you get, like a child who runs to sit in her mother's lap, utterly grateful to be there?

Prayer: Angel of God, my guardian, ever close to my side, please guide me, enlighten me, and make straight my path to heaven. Amen.

Respond to His Call: Write out the Guardian Angel prayer and tape it to the inside driver's corner of the windshield. Pray it every time you start the ignition for a full week. You may just find that after a week you want to keep it up!

Sharon Agnes Wilson

God's Gift of Enough

Let not yours be the outward adorning with braiding of hair, decoration of gold, and wearing of robes, but let it be the hidden person of the heart with the imperishable jewel of a gentle and quiet spirit, which in God's sight is very precious. 1 Peter 3:3–4

Growing up, I often felt that I wasn't enough. I may have looked confident and assured to the outside world, but deep down, I suspected it was just luck or pity that kept people around. Nagging doubts and a deep-seated lack of confidence have forever plagued me. In adulthood, I recognized how these things had been detrimental driving forces in my life, and I prayed for change.

God knows, in His infinite wisdom, how to best answer our prayers. He knew that my insecurity was rooted in a kind of pride—and He knew that I needed to go through the process of being stripped of my pride. Only when I'd reached a place of humility could He gently lead me to discover my true worth. In that process, I found that God had made someone who isn't yet perfect but is loved beyond measure by her Father. I am a daughter of the King, loved so intensely that He would have died on the Cross to save me even if I were the only person on earth. That love tells me that I am enough.

Whatever doubts you are harboring, ask the Lord to help you experience His deep, eternal, mystical love. Ask Him to crush your doubts about whether you are lovable or worthy. Don't wait another minute to start your journey to believing that you are a daughter of the King. You are enough!

Prayer: Lord, I trust Your infinite wisdom to answer my prayers. Your love is all I will ever need. You are truly enough! Let me see myself in the clear light of who You say I am and who You've called me to be. Amen.

Respond to His Call: Volunteer for a month at the children's liturgy at your parish, and take note of what children say to God in response to His Word. Allow their expressions of simple faith in their Father God to infuse your prayer life with childlike faith.

Sherry Kennedy Brownrigg

First Holy Communion

At that time Jesus declared, "I thank you, Father, Lord of heaven and earth, that you have hidden these things from the wise and understanding and revealed them to infants." Matthew 11:25

I moved to a Catholic school from public school in second grade. I remember a lot about second grade at Holy Spirit Catholic Parish School. I was pretty special there, and I often even sat at Sr. Marina's desk! The only second-grader able to read, I read stories aloud to my classmates frequently. The big event, though, was everyone's first Communion.

In Matthew 11, Jesus says that although the Father hides things from the wise and the learned, He reveals them to "infants," or as the Douay-Rheims translation says, "little ones." Little ones like me in second grade. Jesus also says, "No one knows the Father except the Son, and any one to whom the Son wishes to reveal him" (Mt 11:27). Well, Jesus revealed the Father to our family that year.

By the end of the school year, my father, my brother, and I had all been baptized and my parents had their marriage convalidated in the Church. That's a lot of sacraments! And I was invited to the communion rail in Holy Spirit Parish Church for my First Communion.

The rest, as they say, is history. Today, my three children are all married in the Catholic Church, and First Communions continue for their children and their children's children.

We are all chosen. If you are reading this, you are chosen. Jesus has shown you His Sacred Heart, and He beckons you. The Lord has set His heart on you and has chosen you just as He chose Israel. So, the next time you receive the precious Heart of Jesus in the Eucharist, receive Him as eagerly and sincerely as if this were your First Communion.

Prayer: O Sacred Heart of Jesus, draw me nearer to You with each Eucharist I am blessed to receive. May Your sacraments in this life keep me as a child close to You so that I may live in happiness with You eternally. Amen.

Respond to His Call: Offer your next Communion for those who are prevented now from receiving Jesus in the Eucharist because of war, lack of freedom, or sin.

Dr. Carol Younger

From Me to We to He

Therefore do not be anxious about tomorrow, for tomorrow will be anxious for itself. Let the day's own trouble be sufficient for the day. Matthew 6:34

I am a strong, independent woman. For years, I have prided myself on my ability to take care of myself and rise above controversy, heartache, and struggle. It took my marriage falling apart to make me realize that I needed Jesus. But even after all that, I always had my career, and I derived a lot of my self-worth from my work. So I was shell-shocked when my boss told me it was time to start looking for another job. I was a successful career woman. How could this be happening? But my fiancé had been watching me come home from work increasingly tired, stressed, and sometimes even in tears. When I told him that I'd lost my job, he comforted and encouraged me—and asked if maybe this was a sign that it was time to take a much-needed break and relax.

That Sunday, as Mass began, I contemplated my fiancé's words. I felt God telling me I had gotten swept up in my pursuit of success and financial security. My mind went back to how I'd responded when my fiancé asked what was most important to me: *my son and family*. I began to feel a growing sense of peace about what I was supposed to do. Then God spoke to me as the priest read from Matthew's gospel: "Look at the birds of the air: they neither sow nor reap nor gather into barns, and yet your heavenly Father feeds them. Are you not of more value than they?" (6:26).

So I allowed my "independent" self to lean on another for help. My relationship with my fiancé flourished. I made God the focus of my life. And I had peace that my heavenly Father would eventually lead me to the perfect job.

Prayer: Dear God, help us look to You in times of crisis for grace and reassurance that You have good plans for our future. Remind us that our job is not to worry but to trust in You. Amen.

Respond to His Call: Is there something God is calling you to let go of? If so, be brave, go forward slowly, listen for clues, and wait quietly and prayerfully for His guidance.

Julie E. Kenney

Remembering Mothers

But he replied to the man who told him, "Who is my mother, and who are my brethren?" Matthew 12:48

When we bought our first house, we joined St. James Church. We had two small children, and I missed my mother deeply. The ladies at church reminded me of her; they quickly filled that hole in my and my children's lives. As a new member, I got involved quickly, working and learning alongside those church ladies. Through the years, we shared advice, hardships, spirituality, and faith.

When I was in charge of the funeral luncheons at church, I was a point of contact for parishioners who were making arrangements for a loved one who had died. Since ours was a small parish, I often knew the deceased and could relate a story or two if we had worked together over the years. It wasn't until my mother passed, and I was on the receiving end of those stories, that I truly appreciated the gift of this interaction.

I treasured the stories my mother's caretakers shared at her funeral. The nursing home attendants told me that they would wait to tend to my mother last so they could spend time talking with her. She often provided comfort to them. She gave away scapulars to anyone who inquired about the one she had pinned to her pajamas.

Sharing mothers' stories, both mine and others, helps me better understand Christ's words in Matthew's gospel: "Who is my mother?" (12:48). For years, I wondered if Jesus was rejecting His mother. Yet, as my understanding grew, I realized how rich this comment is and that it foreshadows the moment at the Crucifixion when Jesus entrusted John with His mother. Jesus wasn't rejecting His mother; He was expanding the invitation to anyone who hears His words and does His Father's will to become part of His family.

Prayer: Lord, I accept Your invitation to be a member of Your family. What a special gift, to be given Your mother as my own. Amen.

Respond to His Call: Request a Mass to be said for your mother, whether alive or deceased. Bring a few flowers for the side altar of the Blessed Mother, who mothers you both as her children in the order of grace.

Lucy H. Johnson

A Honey-Do List for the Lord

And the LORD came and stood forth, calling as at other times, "Samuel! Samuel!" And Samuel said, "Speak, for your servant hears." Then the LORD said to Samuel, "Behold, I am about to do a thing in Israel, at which the two ears of every one that hears it will tingle." 1 Samuel 3:10–11

How often do we ask God to listen to all that we have to say? I know I often show up to Mass or prayer with a laundry list of "Honey dos" for our Lord.

But how often have I come before Him and said, "Speak, for your servant hears"? It is a request, begging to hear the voice that is Love. His is the voice that said, "Let there be light" (Gn 1:3)—and there was light. That same voice spoke to Moses from the bush and said, "I AM WHO I AM" (Ex 3:14). Elijah heard the "still small voice" of God (1 Kgs 19:12). The quieter our hearts, the better we can hear His still, small voice.

We can come to the Lord like St. Martha, expressing our anxieties over many things (Lk 10:40). He is gracious and will listen patiently. But we should remember that a quieted heart, willing to listen to Jesus, chooses the better portion.

"Speak, for your servant hears." Saying that requires a docile spirit, willing to do God's will. When you ask the Lord to act in your life, He acts. When you ask God to command you, He offers you the opportunity to obey. The more we obey, the more we discover the nature of God's plan for our lives.

Today, dare to listen to God.

Prayer: Lord, speak—Your daughter hears. I come to do Your will. Amen.

Respond to His Call: Ask God to show you three things you can do for Him today, and do them with joy. Amen.

Sherry Antonetti

Mary and the Word of God

And Mary said, "My soul magnifies the Lord, and my spirit rejoices in God my Savior. . . . For behold, henceforth all generations will call me blessed; for he who is mighty has done great things for me, and holy is his name." Luke 1:46–49

Some of Mary's most profound lessons come from her model of listening, discerning, and responding to the Word of God. Because we encounter His Word most readily in scripture, it is vital to spend time daily reading the Word of God, asking the Holy Spirit to guide our reading. Consider how Mary's example can enrich your time with the Bible.

Mary was receptive to the Word of God. When the angel first revealed to her that she would be the mother of "the Son of the Most High," she replied, "Let it be to me according to your word" (Lk 1:32, 38). How quick are we to respond with joyful acceptance to God's words to us?

Mary responded to the Word of God with sincere and humble thanksgiving. Every day holds a built-in opportunity for thanksgiving. Does your soul magnify the Lord, rejoicing that He has reached out to you with love and grace?

And Mary models a persistent attitude of meditation. In the days that followed her Son's birth, scripture tells us that she "kept all these things, pondering them in her heart"(Lk 2:19). I've discovered that no matter how tired I am, I can sleep much better if I take some time to draw my heart away from the world and toward the things of God. It may be fifteen fewer minutes of sleep, but it is guaranteed to be time well spent!

Through Mary's intercession, we can learn to listen and respond to God's Word as she did—with receptive hearts, abundant thanksgiving, and constant meditation. Doing so will allow us to have an ever-deepening relationship with God.

Prayer: Blessed Mother, your model of holiness inspires me. Pray for me to grow in discernment of God's Word and his will in my life. Amen.

Respond to His Call: Open your Bible to Luke 1:46–55. Read the Magnificat aloud *slowly*, inserting "I" in place of "Mary" in line 46. Meditate for a few moments on how you might praise God like that daily.

Marge Steinhage Fenelon

Miracle of Life

And when Elizabeth heard the greeting of Mary, the child leaped in her womb; and Elizabeth was filled with the Holy Spirit. Luke 1:41

One of my favorite experiences of motherhood occurred before I officially became a mom. When I felt my first baby move inside me, I smiled and was entertained by what felt like her pushing against the wall of my womb. I tried to imagine what she was accomplishing with her movements. Was she figuring out how to stretch her legs and arms, or was she just looking for attention?

When Mary, who was carrying Jesus in her womb, approached Elizabeth, Elizabeth's own unborn child, John the Baptist, leaped for joy. Having felt those kinds of movements from my girls, I can place myself in that Bible story!

Attending the March for Life ignited my daughter Hailey's passion for standing for life. One year, the march was even more moving than usual. During a bus ride to the Basilica of the Immaculate Conception in Washington, DC, the group leader announced to the kids that Hailey's dad (my husband, Val) was having emergency surgery for a tumor that extended from his esophagus to his stomach. The leader asked that everyone pray during Mass for the surgery's success.

After Mass, Hailey learned that her father's surgery had been nothing short of miraculous. Instead of taking out his entire esophagus and part of his stomach, the surgeon, guided by our Divine Physician, removed only the tumor. That day, Hailey experienced not only tens of thousands of people marching for the lives of unborn children but also God's healing grace as her team poured out their hearts in prayer for a man many of them didn't even know.

Prayer: Divine Physician, please bring healing to all who are sick. Protect the lives of the innocent. May we cherish the miracle of life. Amen.

Respond to His Call: What can you do to help the unborn? Consider joining your parish's Respect Life committee or volunteering at a nearby pregnancy center. Most of all, pray daily for the rights of the unborn.

Rhonda Zweber

Savor and Stretch

Give thanks in all circumstances; for this is the will of God in Christ Jesus for you. 1 Thessalonians 5:18

Does it ever seem that in the busyness of life time is slipping through your fingers? This feeling was amplified in me when I had three children in three years. Amid the brain fog and sleepless nights, I was constantly reminded by strangers to "enjoy it, it goes so fast!" True words—but when I found myself feeling frustrated with motherhood, I would beat myself up for letting the happy moments pass too quickly.

That changed one day when I was eating a piece of cheesecake. Since cheesecake is a favorite delicacy of mine, I savor every bite. That day it hit me: I need to savor my children like little pieces of cheesecake. When moments are particularly sweet and special, I should stop and soak them in. I needn't worry about what difficulty might be looming or what task I *should* be doing. I need only stop and savor the moment. The joy.

What about the rough moments I would prefer to swallow quickly and leave behind? While in labor, I had another "mini epiphany" that frames the challenging times. The physical suffering and stretching of labor also stretch a mother's soul, making room for the image of God she is blessed to nurture. The painful moments stretch us. We can allow them either to make us bitter or to stretch us into the holy women God desires. If our response is one of docility to the small suffering that God allows in that moment, we will grow.

"Savor and stretch" became my interior disposition toward parent-hood—and for every state in life. When all is right with the world, stop and savor the blessing. Do not think about how it is probably going to get hard soon. When faced with a challenging moment, pray for the grace to stretch into the holy woman you are called to be.

Prayer: Father, grant me the grace to savor life's pleasant moments and stretch my soul through every suffering. Amen.

Respond to His Call: Look at each moment as an opportunity to *savor* or *stretch* . . . and thank God for that piece of cheesecake that offers such peace!

Annie McHugh

May 12

Advice for Worried Moms

There is no fear in love, but perfect love casts out fear. For fear has to do with punishment, and he who fears is not perfected in love. 1 John 4:18

Moms, especially new moms, tend to worry. So I want to share some advice I received when I became a mother, as well as the lessons I learned. Maybe I can help those of you who are struggling with worry.

Live a life of faith, talk to your children about God, and make your Christian beliefs a part of your everyday experience. Always keep lines of communication open. Don't let fear keep you from allowing your kids to be part of the culture. Explain things as best as you can, follow up with discussion, ask your kids questions, and respond with love and patience to theirs. If God is just as much a part of your life as your spouse and children are, connecting with Him will be natural and not just something you do on Sundays. Discuss books and movies and music with your kids, not in a condemning way, but teaching them to think about the messages. You can help develop their critical thinking skills as you enhance their faith.

Fear is not of God. Pray for your children and pray that the Holy Spirit will give you wisdom in dealing with them on faith matters. Ask to know not only what to say but also when to keep silent. Remember that youth is for making mistakes. And be there to pick them up if they fall. If you give them a loving but firm foundation, they'll come back one day even if they wander. Never stop praying for them!

Finally, make sure you know the faith and scripture so you can answer their questions. If you always treat youngsters respectfully, even when their questions seem misdirected, they will continue to ask and continue to talk with you, respecting your values and opinions.

Fear not! God is with you!

Prayer: Holy Spirit, Counselor, Paraclete, I come to You today for wisdom, discernment, and understanding in matters of faith. Amen.

Respond to His Call: List five significant life events when your trust in the Holy Spirit for wisdom was rewarded.

Lynda MacFarland

The Sinless Virgin Mary

> But he said to them, "Not all men can receive this precept, but only those to whom it is given. . . . He who is able to receive this, let him receive it." Matthew 19:11–12

As a non-Catholic researching my way into the Church, I cannot overstate my complete incredulity regarding the Church's teachings on Mary. I was scandalized by the Church's assertion that God predestined, created, and preserved Mary in lifelong sinlessness and virginity. It seemed impossible. Yet, I read the primary sources. I knew the Church had received and maintained these teachings from the apostles. So I began to wrestle with why God would preserve Mary as both the perpetual Ark of the New Covenant and the sinless, ever-virgin New Eve.

The answer is eschatological and lies in Jesus, all the way forward in salvation history to His Second Coming and the marriage feast that will consummate the new heavens and new earth.

We think so small, like Israel in its expectation for the Messiah. Every Israelite alive expected a human messiah with a regular kingdom, and every married woman in Israel hoped to be his mother in the usual way. Yet, Mary is mother by direct action from God with no human intervention. This new, divine motherhood will embrace all. We are the Body of Christ, and Christ was born of Mary. Precisely because the kingdom to come is to be fulfilled in flesh and blood, it begins in the mother. Mary's motherhood signifies our new covenant with God. Her perpetually sinless, virgin motherhood is the beginning and prototype of the Church.

Mary remains both sinless and virgin because her motherhood is completely and eternally spiritual and pure—giving birth to the Word in innumerable spiritual children, all conceived by the Holy Spirit and born of God. She nurtures our holiness so that we, too, can give birth to the Word in the world through faith.

Prayer: Hail Mary, Mother of God, spiritual mother to all the world, pray for me. Amen.

Respond to His Call: Pray to the Holy Spirit for His gifts of wisdom, understanding, counsel, fortitude, knowledge, piety, and awe of the Lord.

Sonja Corbitt

Barefoot on Holy Ground

Then he said, "Do not come near; put off your shoes from your feet, for the place on which you are standing is holy ground." Exodus 3:5

I used to do all of the "environment" at our parish. Environment in this case is another way of saying decorating the church. We use that term to differentiate it from the way we decorate our homes. In the church, all decoration must be pertinent, directed to the liturgy, and pointed to the Eucharist.

It was special having keys to the church. My children were young, and I would often go to church after I put them to bed, leaving my husband to man the household while I did my church work. Walking into the church alone at night was prayerful. Changing vases of flowers and exchanging an altar cloth are holy acts when done with love and reverence.

This passage from Exodus reminds me of all the times I took my shoes off at church. It was easier to move without my shoes, but it also reminded me that I was on holy ground. If we can remember that we are on holy ground, we realize all things can be made holy.

When I wash the dishes, am I doing it begrudgingly, or do I remember the blessing of my family with gratitude? When I meet with a friend with whom I have disagreed, am I recognizing God's child in front of me?

God reminded Moses that he was stepping on holy ground. I may not remove my shoes when facing a difficult person or situation, but I try to imagine the One who is in front of me, who I serve.

Prayer: Lord, instill in us the firm belief that all the world, created in Your likeness and image, is holy ground. Help us to treat it, and all those we encounter on it, with love and respect. Amen.

Respond to His Call: Create a prayer space with a crucifix or some small reminder of God's love in a place where you usually take off your shoes. Whenever you can, pause and offer a prayer.

Sharon Agnes Wilson

Running toward Heaven

Do you not know that in a race all the runners compete, but only one receives the prize? So run that you may obtain it. 1 Corinthians 9:24

I'm not much of a runner. Few things can compel me to lace my sneakers—except my sister. When we run together, it's not just bodily exercise. We use the time for prayer and for offering each other spiritual encouragement. Today's run would lead us down some new spiritual paths.

My strides shrank as the terrain inclined. My sister encouraged me, "Think about your arms." I thought I misheard her, but she added, "Your legs will only go as fast as your arms." Hmm, how do I use my arms each day? Are they folded, keeping other people from my heart? Do they welcome friends with warm embraces? Are they supportively around the shoulders of weary souls? Focusing on my progress only leads to exhaustion. Perhaps we live most abundantly when we focus on others. On the running path and in life, our legs will only go as far as our arms extend to others.

My sister suggested we run another mile, asking for whom I would offer it. I suggested we offer our steps for whoever needed it most. Each stride felt heavy. Bolstering my weary soul, she reminded me, "Every step is a prayer." What if we offered every step, dirty dish, and patient conversation for those who suffer? Perhaps we would find the humility and perspective to persevere, drawing strength from God.

Reaching the end of the road, my sister smiled and said, "Let's go home." This simple nudge forward hides in the background of every busy day. Lesser incentives sometimes distract me from the glorious hope of heaven. But I strive today for humility to set aside worldly motivations of success and adopt this mission of love: I run this race for Jesus.

Prayer: Lord, give me humility to seek Your kingdom and not be sidetracked by the rewards and distractions of this world. Amen.

Respond to His Call: Take ten minutes this morning to consecrate your day to the kingdom of God. Walk around your house while you say the Morning Offering (see versions online or in a Catholic prayer book).

Katie Anderson

He Knows Me by Name

O LORD, you have searched me and known me! . . . You discern my thoughts from afar. Psalm 139:1–2

For most of my life, I've borne the self-imposed burden of feeling unknown and misunderstood. In His goodness, God placed a friend in my path that gave me the precious gift of her time. Over many years and many gut-wrenching conversations, I finally came to feel like someone knew me—and loved me anyway.

One morning on my way to Mass, I momentarily forgot that precious gift. The lifelong burden of feeling unknown and misunderstood loomed over me. I startled myself as I heard my desperate plea: "Lord, do You care? Do You even know who I am?"

Thirty minutes later, I knelt in my regular spot, praying the Rosary. When Mass was over, I remained behind to complete my daily prayers, but I could hear several women in the vestibule, engaging Father in conversation. "Undeserved forgiveness," one woman said. "Laughter," interjected another. "Affection," exclaimed a third.

Having finished my prayers, I exited the pew. As I genuflected and made the Sign of the Cross, I heard Father ask, "Paige, you settle this. What is the greatest gift one can give another?" I don't think Father expected an answer, but I stood ready to give one, as his question was a timely reminder of my friend's precious gift. Boldly, I responded, "The greatest gift given to me was the gift of being known." The other women looked at me a little confused, but Father slowly nodded his head and smiled. To feel truly known and loved by another person is to experience, in some small way, the merciful, compassionate love of the Father.

Prayer: Father, we thank You for the precious gift of being known and loved by You. Grant us the courage and willingness to be Your hands and feet for others so that they, too, will come to know and trust in Your promises. Amen.

Respond to His Call: Knowing how valuable it is when someone makes time to listen to the worries of your heart, today reach out to someone in need of your time and specific treasure and freely offer it to him or her.

Paige Freeman Rosato

Overcoming the World

I have said this to you, that in me you may have peace. In the world you have tribulation; but be of good cheer, I have overcome the world. John 16:33

Want to know a secret? I sometimes don't like being a Catholic weirdo. I sometimes resent the ways in which faithfulness to Jesus makes me different from others or seems to make my way of life more burdensome than other people's. But that only happens when I forget who Jesus is and that He doesn't call us to anything alone. He is always with us, every step of the way.

The world does not exactly celebrate our faith. You only have to take a look at Twitter or a cable-news broadcast to discover that. Anyone who is serious about their faith will pay a price for it sometimes. We may not be called to die for our faith, but we may be the only ones whose kids are not allowed to see the latest movie, the only ones who decline sports events on Sunday mornings, or the only ones who speak out in opposition to some immorality in the workplace. And these are not comfortable things.

When life is challenging, especially when it is challenging because of our faith, we should not be surprised. Jesus never promised it would be easy, but He did remind us that He is all we need: "I have said this to you, that in me you may have peace. In the world, you have tribulation; but be of good cheer, I have overcome the world."

We don't have to do anything on our own. When the world gives us trouble, we must remember to turn to Jesus, who is always with us. He has overcome the world. He is the only one we need, the only one who gives us lasting joy.

Prayer: Lord, help me to see Your presence in my life today and give me grace to follow Your way, even when it is uncomfortable. Teach me Your ways and draw me closer to You. Amen.

Respond to His Call: Put a holy card on your bathroom mirror to remind you to say a prayer at the start of each day, offering your entire day to God.

Danielle Bean

Healing Attention

And when Jesus saw her, he called her and said to her, "Woman, you are freed from your infirmity." Luke 13:12

Jesus Christ spoke these words to a woman in Luke's gospel who was bent over with an ailment for eighteen years. Imagine her amazement and joy at receiving Christ's healing attention. Seeing her great need, and knowing of her years of suffering, Jesus lavished divine healing upon her. She was precious in His sight. His heart went out to her. He desired for her to walk upright, not bent over; to be well, not sick; to be free, not imprisoned.

Whatever is weighing you down today, whatever is wearing you out, zapping your joy, or blocking your love—be it physical or spiritual infirmities—draw close to Christ now. Reflect for a moment in silent receptivity. Imagine that you are the woman in Luke's gospel to receive Christ's words: "Woman, you are freed from your infirmity." Let these words fill every atom of your being—receiving them as a pure gift of grace.

Imagine yourself as a new creation in Christ—one who is truly free to walk upright, well, joyful, and animated by divine love. Allow yourself to experience the joy of being chosen, known, and loved by God, who heals all things in His perfect time. Surrender yourself to divine providence with confidence that God knows how to work all things for your salvation.

Prayer: Lord Jesus, help me to let go of all that weighs me down as I place my intentions within Your Sacred Heart. Thank You for making me a new creation, widening my perspective, and seeing what is best for me now and forever. Amen.

Respond to His Call: Consider people in your circle of family and friends who need a healing word of love and encouragement today—and make it happen.

Kathleen Beckman

May 19

The Burning of Babel

To each is given the manifestation of the Spirit for the common good. 1 Corinthians 12:7

On Pentecost, the birthday of the Church, tongues of fire settled on the apostles. The same fire ignites our souls in the Sacrament of Confirmation. What scattered at Babel, as a consequence of "making a name for ourselves" (Gn 11:4), is restored through the Holy Spirit. With God, there is unity; without Him, there is chaos. So often, we think that we need to build towers to reach heaven on our own—towers of wealth, power, perfection, or pleasure. But these towers prevent us from placing our trust in the Holy Spirit. There is no tower we build that can get us to heaven.

Jesus did not leave us alone in the world. It's time to burn down our towers, with the fire of the Holy Spirit. Let wisdom, knowledge, counsel, and understanding consume our need for wealth and power. Allow fear of the Lord to burn our desire for perfection in the eyes of the world. Let fortitude and piety set fire to unholy cravings for pleasure. God gave us the Holy Spirit, who can set the world on fire through us if we allow Him.

St. Paul tells us that the Spirit is given for some benefit. We glimpse the power of the Spirit in the Acts of the Apostles: wisdom, healing, courage in the face of death. The apostles became the fire whose embers passed that same fire of the Spirit through generations. Ask yourself: What power does the Holy Spirit manifest in you? What flame is in your heart for the sake of the kingdom? Allow Pentecost into your heart. You are the flame of the Holy Spirit who can set the world ablaze.

Prayer: Lord, send Your Holy Spirit anew to the earth to enflame the Church to proclaim You. O Jesus, set me afire with love that can stir hearts to turn to Your Father, through the Holy Spirit. Amen.

Respond to His Call: Light a candle in church or in your home. Pray the Novena to the Holy Spirit, with the special intention of the proclamation of the Gospel to unbelievers outside the Mystical Body of Christ, the Church.

Angela Koenig

Godspeed, Mom!

When the LORD saw that he turned aside to see, God called to him out of the bush, "Moses, Moses!" And he said, "Here am I."
Exodus 3:4

Certain phrases in the Bible are comforting. I especially like "Here am I."

On May 20, at 3 a.m., we were called to the hospital; my mother was dying. Fr. Joseph had anointed her on the previous Sunday and was now joining us in her last moments, to grant her apostolic pardon and guide her to eternity. When he arrived, he began by saying, "Karol, it's Fr. Joseph. I'm here now because Jesus will be calling your name very soon. When He calls your name, you say, 'Here I am,' and you go right to Him. Until He calls your name, keep repeating, 'Jesus, I trust in you. Jesus, I trust in you.'"

His voice was so sure; nothing was held back. His voice was soothing, yet still filled the room. There was a firmness—a giving of instructions. At the same time, Father was confirming for my mother that she has known the way for her whole life. Follow the sacraments, the saints, the angels, follow your entire life of service, your amazing yes to life—follow all these things back to their beginning.

I don't suppose that my heart ever broke more entirely than at the death of my mother, but right in the midst was a sense of gratitude and joy. Jesus was going to call her name. And her whole life to that moment was a confirmation that she knew the answer: "Here I am!"

Godspeed, Mom!

Prayer: Eternal rest grant unto [*name of a loved one*], Lord. Let perpetual light shine upon them. May they rest in the peace of Your loving embrace. Amen.

Respond to His Call: Pray a Divine Mercy Chaplet for someone who has recently passed away.

Alyssa Bormes

Little Acts Equal Love in a Big Way

Let the greatest among you become as the youngest, and the leader as one who serves. For which is the greater, one who sits at table, or one who serves? Is it not the one who sits at table? But I am among you as one who serves. Luke 22:26–27

"Kerry, you've got to hear this!" came a cry from the other room where my book club gathered. Absorbed in slicing cake, I had nearly missed the conversation. "When I went to visit Mother at the hospital, I found her sitting quietly. I could see how unkempt she looked, so fragile and innocent. She had aged visibly during this latest bout of sickness. Her long hair hadn't been combed all week. I was overcome with compassion. I gently combed her hair until all the knots were gone. My movements became rhythmic; I could feel the tension and anger that we held toward each other melt. We finally felt peace."

For several months, my friend and her husband had been struggling to care for his sickly, live-in, elderly mother while raising three young children. There were trips to the ER and doctors' offices, late nights, and long days of worrying, all of which led to frustration and resentment. Our book club was studying Thérèse of Lisieux, known for her "little way" of showing love to others through small, selfless acts of kindness.

As she sat combing her mother-in-law's hair, my friend thought about St. Thérèse. She realized that she was becoming Christ to her mother-in-law with each loving stroke of her hair. She finally understood her role as caretaker. It was her cross to bear now. She could learn to love it and persevere in difficult times. Joy and peace filled her heart.

May we follow in the footsteps of St. Thérèse, doing everything for love of our Father and neighbor, thereby making the ordinary extraordinary through gentle humility, loving service, and childlike faith.

Prayer: Lord, make me meek and humble of heart, to serve You every day of my life. Amen.

Respond to His Call: Today, rise beyond your discomfort, and do something special for someone.

Kerry McGuire

Forgiveness Lessons

So whatever you wish that men would do to you, do so to them; for this is the law and the prophets. Matthew 7:12

Arriving late for vacation Bible school with three cranky kids, the mounting heat, and anxiety about navigating a new parish triggered a major panic attack for me. The woman at the registration desk handed me a yellow shirt. I was expecting a blue one, indicating that my daughter Faith, whom we had newly adopted, would be in the kindergarten group. The yellow shirt was for the preschool group. I had purposely selected the older group, feeling it was a better fit to interpret to her in American Sign Language. Uncharacteristic rage swelled and tumbled out at this unexpected switch. I yanked the shirt from the VBS director and said, "It's fine," and stormed off, leaving her startled with tears welling. Furious, I dragged my daughter, barked orders at my sons to stop sulking, and angrily signed the words to the opening song about "love and joy." Oh, the irony!

Opening activities complete, we were dismissed to our group rooms. Faith and I walked into the yellow-shirt room and saw the other campers (including two other little girls with special needs). We met her group leader, who was a special education teacher by trade. I instantly knew I had made a colossal mistake. The Holy Spirit had guided us to the perfect camp for Faith. I realized I could either pretend my morning tantrum had never happened or admit my pride and beg for forgiveness.

I decided to apologize. However, when I finished expressing my regret at my outburst, the director's eyes teared again! She took a breath and explained that I was not the first to treat her that way during registration—but I was the first to apologize. She not only graciously accepted my apology and showed me great mercy but also became my first friend at our new parish. She remains one of my dearest friends to this day.

Prayer: Lord, sometimes I need to forgive, and other times I need to ask for forgiveness. Give me the words and the courage for each. Amen.

Respond to His Call: Is there someone you need to ask forgiveness from? Pray and discern if today is the day to do that.

Allison Gingras

Pentecost: Just Wait

If you then, who are evil, know how to give good gifts to your children, how much more will the heavenly Father give the Holy Spirit to those who ask him! Luke 11:13

Waiting is a vital part of salvation history; it builds trust and faith. One of the most significant times of waiting is Pentecost. Before His Ascension, Jesus was dining with His apostles. He told them not to leave Jerusalem but to "wait for the promise of the Father" (Acts 1:4). The apostles knew they were to continue the mission of Jesus, preaching the kingdom of God and doing all that Jesus had taught them. They had been with Him for three years, observing Him and learning from Him.

What more did they need? They needed power. They needed the Holy Spirit, who would strengthen them to share the Gospel and be witnesses to the world. Without the power of the Holy Spirit, they would continue to hide, afraid of persecution. So they waited.

With the Blessed Mother, the apostles spent nine days in the Upper Room, always in prayer. On the tenth day, the Holy Spirit came. The apostles received the ability to speak different languages; no longer were they afraid. Instead, they were filled with holy boldness! They became exactly who God created them to be: witnesses to the world.

Each of us is called to the mission of sharing the Gospel in a new Pentecost. We need to pray in an "upper room" with expectant faith. We were sealed with the Holy Spirit at our Baptism and Confirmation. We can renew these sacraments through prayer, giving us courage for our mission.

Pray for a tsunami of the Holy Spirit over all the earth. Pray for the conversion of the world. Jesus wants to use you as one of His witnesses. He will give you the power to do it. You have prayed and waited. Now it is time to go on mission.

Prayer: Holy Spirit, pour out Your power on this earth and convert every heart. Amen.

Respond to His Call: Choose a way to fast for the Lord. Offer that sacrifice for the conversion of the world.

Dianne Davis

Mary's Greatest Intervention

Jesus also was invited to the marriage, with his disciples. When the wine failed, the mother of Jesus said to him, "They have no wine." John 2:2–3

Have you ever intervened? As a school counselor and administrator, I have intervened with students, teachers, parents, and even police in emotionally charged situations. This intervention required alert observing, compassionate listening, and the offering of options. The goal? To get everyone back to learning, leaving the conflict and hurt behind. Often, my interventions went unnoticed, but I knew and thanked Jesus, the real miracle worker.

At a wedding in Cana, Mary intervened, leaving to Jesus and the servants the miraculous and material help. Wine was running short, and Mary knew that Jesus was already aware of the situation. She simply told Him she had noticed the problem, and then surrendered the solution to Him. Mary knew Jesus didn't need her help. But she also knew from the annunciation that Jesus chooses to use our yes. So Mary told the servants, "Do whatever he tells you" (v. 5). This moment at Cana introduces us to Mary's role as an intercessor; she intervened by going to her Son with a prayer and a request, and offered direction to others. And the miraculous response brought an overflowing of the choicest of wines!

Let's imitate Mary by going to her Son with our needs. There are people and situations around you in need of intervention. First, tell Jesus about the loss or lack of wine (joy, hope, peace). Then, surrender everything to His loving care. Be open to doing whatever He tells you. Then stand back and watch the miracle!

Prayer: Dear Jesus, You know where I am needed. Attend to the situation You're sending me into today. Inspire me to see and to intervene. I ask You to heal, change, and sanctify the people I encounter. I request the material help they need for Your sake and the sake of Your kingdom. Amen.

Respond to His Call: If you know someone who is alone much of the day, invite them over for a visit or a meal. Or send a spiritual bouquet to someone who needs your prayers. Pray for them at Mass or adoration.

Dr. Carol Younger

Childlike Calm in the Storm

He drew me up from the desolate pit, out of the miry bog, and set my feet upon a rock, making my steps secure. He put a new song in my mouth, a song of praise to our God. Psalm 40:2–3

Since our sons were children, it has been our family tradition to spend a week at the beach on Florida's Gulf Coast. It has become a cherished week of quality time together. One picture-perfect day our whole family was playfully enjoying the beautiful gulf waters. The waves were higher than usual, and my grandsons took full advantage of it. While my son and I held onto a huge raft, the boys dove headfirst into the waves. Two hours later, our youngest grandson, exhausted by his quest to conquer the best wave, put his head down on the raft and fell asleep. The waves stirred up around him, the raft continued to jolt from side to side, but he remained asleep, perfectly calm in the middle of the turbulence.

In prayer, I heard the Lord say, "Become like this child. This child trusts, even as he sleeps, that his father is keeping him safe. I call all of My children to this same level of trust. When David fought Goliath, he knew that he had something much greater than that Philistine had—David was in a covenant relationship with Me. David knew he was protected and that there was no giant larger than My love for him. You are My children, and there is no giant larger than My love for you."

Children of God, unless we become like children, we will never enter the kingdom of heaven. We need to turn back to Him and enter into His righteousness, peace, and joy because that is the kingdom. When we trust our Father, we find peace and calm, no matter how choppy the waters are around us.

Prayer: Lord, I desire more of You. Let me experience a personal Pentecost. Engulf me in Your Spirit so that I can become Your witness to the ends of the earth. Amen.

Respond to His Call: Envision yourself on the shoulders of your heavenly Father, looking down at any fear that has held sway over your life. Tell that fear that it has no more power over you, in the name of Jesus!

Dr. Carol Razza

With Mary, We May

But you shall receive power when the Holy Spirit has come upon you; and you shall be my witnesses. Acts 1:8

We were celebrating another family commencement a week after I received my bachelor's degree. My car—laden with corporate clothing and apartment necessities—evidenced the significant firsts to come. The celebrations gave way to an uncertain adventure. Rosary in hand and tears wiped from my cheeks, I bid farewell to my parents.

I admit to having a sense of unrest during life's grand finales. We think the story is wrapped in a neat little bow, while the divine Author sees a new chapter to unwrap. When my story is set to change, the Ascension fills my worry-inclined heart with hope. I imagine gazing at Jesus while standing alongside the disciples and Mary. Jesus looks at us with love before inviting us on a mission: "You shall be my witnesses . . . to the end of the earth."

Does Mary watch Jesus ascend with a tearful smile, or does she fall to her knees in prayer, remembering another grand invitation fraught with uncertainty? She couldn't foresee what God had in store for her when she first gave her fiat. Mary teaches us to embrace the uncertain path ahead by giving our yes to the Lord.

Springtime is full of farewells and commencements. Every chapter of life is shrouded in uncertainty, but we needn't walk this journey alone. The mysteries of the Rosary offer exceptional peace whenever our story reaches another bend in the road. The Blessed Mother walks us home with sure confidence. As St. Maximilian Kolbe said, "Our dear little, little mother, the Immaculate Mary, can do anything for us. We are her children. Turn to her. She will overcome everything."

Prayer: Mary, my mother, accompany me through all my commencements in life, helping me to trust God along the way. Amen.

Respond to His Call: List two commencements you expect in the future. Write down what Mary might advise for the two new beginnings, and tuck the paper in your Bible.

Katie Anderson

Good Fruit

You will know them by their fruits. Are grapes gathered from thorns, or figs from thistles? Matthew 7:16

I love my local farmers' market. It's practically a party—music, pizza, beer—and of course, the fruits and vegetables. Like any shopper, I try to bypass the bad fruit. For me, "bad" isn't about misshapen, too small, or bruised; it's about wormholes and the like. But some types of rotten fruit aren't as evident; think about the times you've found mold at the bottom of the berries and had to discard them all.

Bad spiritual fruit isn't always easy to identify, either. Our world is filled with false prophets with alluring messages. They offer counterfeit solutions for our problems, peddling vanity, lust, and greed. Now, not all of the world's experts bear bad fruit. However, discernment is necessary. We must ask whether their advice aligns with God's will. Part of the discernment process involves judging them by their fruits. As Christians, if we are diligent in investigating their offering, we can discern what is profitable.

A friend of mine was faced with a choice between two men, both gentlemen, both of whom cared for her. "Choose the one who will help you get to heaven," her mother advised. She chose the man who was involved in their parish, whose life displayed the fruit of a heart devoted to God. Thirty-plus years later, they're still married. The good fruit they have borne together includes three children and the support of dozens more through a global humanitarian organization.

I often think about my friend's mother's words: "Choose the one who will help you get to heaven." Her advice follows me in all my relationships. And we can identify the people who will help us to heaven by their fruits.

Prayer: May I be the friend, parent, and spouse that journeys alongside my loved ones to heaven. May my words, prayers, and example be a source of a blessing, producing good fruit. Amen.

Respond to His Call: Recall those individuals who are helping you to heaven. Make a spiritual bouquet (a Mass, visits to the Blessed Sacrament, or a Rosary) for each person. If you'd like, share your bouquet with them.

Melanie Rigney

Spirit-Filled Woman

Jesus said to them again, "Peace be with you. As the Father has sent me, even so I send you." And when he had said this, he breathed on them, and said to them, "Receive the Holy Spirit. If you forgive the sins of any, they are forgiven; if you retain the sins of any, they are retained." John 20:21–23

There's something especially beautiful about a Spirit-filled woman. How she carries herself and relates to others emanates a supernatural beauty. It shines in her eyes, floats on the melody of her voice, and spreads through her words and actions—a holy presence proclaiming she's claimed for Christ. I pray about my desire to become a Spirit-filled woman throughout the year, but especially during the days after Easter when the scriptures trace the apostles' adventures as they spread the Good News. These brave men had once been cowards, abandoning our Lord in the Garden of Gethsemane the night before His Passion. Now, filled with the Holy Spirit, they exhibit courage and an unshakable sense of mission.

The apostles were on fire with the message of Christ, and it showed in their words and actions. There's a scene from the Gospel of John that I'm especially drawn to. The disciples, hiding fearfully in a locked room, are shocked when Jesus suddenly appears in the room with them. After all, just days earlier, they'd witnessed His death. So Jesus said to them, "Peace be with you," and showed them the wounds in His hands and His side. With a dawning sense of joy, the disciples start to celebrate—and that's when Jesus "breathed on them," telling them to "receive the Holy Spirit." Oh, that Jesus would come to us through any locked door and give us His Spirit!

Prayer: Jesus, unlock the doors of my heart and rescue me from all that keeps me from being courageous in faith. Breathe Your Holy Spirit into my soul; make me a Spirit-filled woman. Amen.

Respond to His Call: Write four sentences describing yourself as a Spirit-filled woman. What would you look like? What habit would identify you? What would you stop doing? What daily habit would you add? Post this paper where you will see it at the beginning of every day.

Marge Steinhage Fenelon

Called to Cheerfully Give

God loves a cheerful giver. And God is able to provide you with every blessing in abundance, so that you may always have enough of everything and may provide in abundance for every good work. 2 Corinthians 9:7–8

"God loves a cheerful giver." A woman's feminine genius is grounded in her orientation toward others. Our relationships in marriage, motherhood, work, and friendships allow plenty of opportunities to give to others. At times giving can offer us great fulfillment and joy. However, it can also leave us feeling drained and overextended. But the scripture continues, "God is able to provide you with every blessing in abundance, so that you may always have enough of everything and may provide in abundance for every good work."

These words challenge my exhausted heart. They remind me that I can only give when I am resting entirely in Him. We need daily prayer to recharge, reset, and refocus. We must invite Jesus to help us and be the source of strength for everything we do. By offering our empty hands for Jesus to fill, we achieve far more than through our own grit alone.

His generosity challenges us to tithe through giving ourselves. Jesus provides an example of how sacrifice bears abundant fruit. Through sacrificial acts, we are granted growth opportunities to rest more profoundly in the Lord's embrace. When we allow Him to lead and carry us, the burden and yoke are light.

St. John Paul II wrote that one "cannot fully find himself except through a sincere gift of self. . . . To say that man is created in the image and likeness of God means that man is called to exist 'for' others, to become a gift" (*Mulieris Dignitatem*, 7). Let us be a gift to those near us, a conduit of grace and an image bearer of the most high King.

Prayer: Lord, help me be a cheerful giver. I surrender my tired heart and invite You to be a gift to others through my sacrifices. Amen.

Respond to His Call: Write out a list of what seems impossible and surrender it to God. Ask Him to accomplish His will through you. Imagine Him beside you in these tasks.

Katie Lee Taylor

A Visitation in the ICU

The LORD is near to the brokenhearted, and saves the crushed in spirit. Psalm 34:18

On Memorial Day, I ended up in the ER with a dangerously slow heartbeat. They pumped me full of nausea-inducing dopamine to get my heart rate up, and then they told me I would be getting a pacemaker as my parting gift.

After my pity party, I realized with joy that the surgery would take place on the Feast of the Visitation. It felt like a kiss from Mama Mary. The Body of Christ lifted me in love and carried me along on a cloud of grace. I had never been so at peace. As surgery pierced my heart, I knew Jesus wanted to pierce my soul to give me a greater capacity for love and a greater receptivity to the movement of the Holy Spirit. What I didn't know then was that He would do this through suffering.

As I prepared to resume life as usual, the bigeminy arrhythmia began. The weeks wore on; I became exhausted, immobile, short of breath, and depressed. The doctor said there was no cure and that we would try different meds to manage it. I did my best to smile for my family, yet I was bereft of any comfort or consolation.

Then, just as suddenly as the bigeminy came on, it disappeared. My only response could be—and still is—profound gratitude. I was soon back to my sassy old self, but the trial left me humbled and more compassionate toward those who suffer.

Are you hurting right now? Do you feel—as I did—that God has abandoned you? Know that God loves you more than you can fathom, and He has plans to work all of this for your good. God desires your ultimate good, and He will not allow you to suffer without providing the grace you need each day—all you need do is humbly ask and receive.

Prayer: God, how grateful I am for Your promise to never forsake me. Strengthen my heart to hold the compassion You lavish on me. Amen.

Respond to His Call: Today, be watchful for God's presence in your life. Thank Him for even the smallest sighting.

Kitty Cleveland

Jump for Joy

And Mary said, "My soul magnifies the Lord, and my spirit rejoices in God my Savior." Luke 1:46–47

Imagine what it must have been like for Mary the day the angel Gabriel visited her. Mary, likely in her early teenage years, awoke to find an angel in her room. The angel told her she was going to have a son. She would conceive of the Holy Spirit, her baby would be the Son of the Most High, He would be a king in the line of David, He would reign over the house of Jacob forever, and His kingdom would have no end. Wow! That's a pretty big morning for a teenager! And what was the first thing Mary did after receiving this big news? She went in haste to visit her cousin Elizabeth.

Perhaps Mary went in haste to help her older cousin in her time of need. Or, maybe she hurried along because she was overcome with an uncontrollable eagerness to share the awe of what was happening within her with someone who could understand. Whatever the reason, the moment the two women met, Mary immediately shared with Elizabeth what she had received. She shared Jesus.

At the Visitation, Mary, overshadowed with the Holy Spirit, models perfectly how we should bring Christ to others. The first thing Mary did when she saw Elizabeth was to radiate joy. When Mary arrived at Elizabeth's home, she was so full of the joy of the Holy Spirit that she couldn't contain her joy. She burst into song, and her soul magnified the Lord!

That's evangelization—allowing the Holy Spirit to work through you and being so in love with the Lord that you can't contain it. That kind of joy leads others to Jesus.

Prayer: Lord, overshadow me with Your Spirit. May I enthusiastically share the Gospel with renewed confidence, conviction, and hope. Amen.

Respond to His Call: On this Feast of the Visitation, let the joy of the Lord overshadow you. Today, share your relationship with Jesus with another and let them leap for joy.

Kelly M. Wahlquist

God's Got This

But he, desiring to justify himself, said to Jesus, "And who is my neighbor?" Luke 10:29

When I heard the Good Samaritan story, I used to ponder how I could show mercy to others. However, once I needed and received help, my perspective changed. One fall, I walked the Camino in Spain by myself. The theme of my forty-day pilgrimage was trust and surrender. On the second-to-last day of my journey, my Good Samaritan story began.

Knowing that day's walk would be more miles than usual, I started about two hours before sunrise. When I left the hostel, rain was pouring and the sky was dark. I planned on taking a shortcut to save time and avoid a large hill. After about an hour, I realized I was lost. I was in a highway construction zone. As the roadwork began, I realized I couldn't go back, so I kept going forward.

Finally, I saw an approaching car roll to a stop on the side of the road. Had he seen my headlamp? Would he help? No. Instead of helping, he yelled at me in Spanish. I could only reply, "Camino?" and pantomime "You drive me?" He locked the doors of his car, turned his back, and walked away. Then a truck passed. The middle-aged driver slowed, but he would not help either.

Finally, a young man drove up. As I repeated my attempts to communicate, he said, "*Si*," and allowed me in. I could only say "*gracias*" over and over. I never would have found the path on my own, but this kind man took me right to where I needed to be.

As I look back on that experience, I am amazed that I had inner peace throughout the ordeal. I knew God would protect me. I had lost my way trying to avoid hardships, but God was faithful. He didn't lose sight of me.

Prayer: No matter how lost I become, Lord, help me to know that You are faithful and never lose sight of me. Amen.

Respond to His Call: Make a virtual pilgrimage by reading or researching about St. Peter's Basilica or St. Paul Outside the Walls, both located in Rome.

Lucy H. Johnson

Battling Indifference

Thus, when you give alms, sound no trumpet before you, as the hypocrites do in the synagogues and in the streets, that they may be praised by men. Truly, I say to you, they have their reward. Matthew 6:2

Jesus warns against doing righteous deeds for the sake of advancing your own reputation. Giving alms should come from your heart, that hidden place where you choose Christ and learn to desire what He desires.

Our parish priest shared during a recent homily of his encounter with almsgiving. As a foreign national studying and ministering in the United States, he lived on a meager monthly stipend. One day he took the whole allowance—a fifty-dollar bill—and headed out to purchase his monthly necessities. At the store entrance, a homeless person was begging for money. Father was about to walk past, but a thought challenged his heart: *Am I a Christian or not?* With no further hesitation, he gave his entire stipend to the homeless person. He then went into the store, only to realize he no longer had any money. Father was at a loss, but at that moment a couple from his parish greeted him and asked him why he was there. Despite his lack of funds, he said, "I'm shopping!" The couple promptly placed two hundred dollars in his hand.

Father was deeply touched by this unexpected (and timely) gift. How amazing that his own burst of generosity was immediately met and exceeded by the generosity of others! But in pondering his initial indifference toward the beggar, Father was reminded of the rich man who ignored the beggar Lazarus until it was too late (Lk 16:19–31). Father concluded that indifference was the sin we need to be concerned about, not whether we extend the charity. Do you observe the needy with indifference? Or does their neediness move you to generous action?

Prayer: Jesus, replace my indifference with genuine love. Fill me with a desire to meet the needs of others. Amen.

Respond to His Call: Instead of indulging in a dessert or an extra coffee, anonymously donate the amount you would have spent on that indulgence to a charity, or put it in the poor box or collection at church.

Dr. Carol Younger

Courageous in Christ

And Peter answered him, "Lord, if it is you, bid me come to you on the water." He said, "Come." So Peter got out of the boat and walked on the water and came to Jesus. Matthew 14:28–29

As I stand on the beach at the ocean's edge, it seems that the water continues without end. The ocean's vastness helps me recognize God's majesty. I become aware of how small I am and how God, who made the sea, is bigger than our biggest problem. It gives me a glimpse of God's power.

Why do we shrink in fear in times of trial? Do we think God isn't big enough for what we are going through or that He doesn't care? Fear makes us run away, only to get stuck in life's muddy swamps. But God wants to bathe us in the ocean of His mercy. He calls us to walk on the water with Him so He can raise us above our suffering. He asks us not to be afraid. Being courageous doesn't mean that we won't feel frightened; it means trusting God and doing the scary things anyway.

Perhaps, like Peter, you want to walk on the water—but as soon as you see the waves and storms in life, you lose sight of Jesus and begin to sink. What if we trusted enough to rise above our problems with Christ instead of drowning in them? Imagine the works the Lord could do through us!

When we keep our eyes on Jesus and His majesty, miracles can happen. When we embrace His calling for our lives and give Him our yes, He will always provide the grace and the strength. No wave can knock us over. We will see that He is King of the waves. Whatever our problems or obstacles, He can crush them with one wave of His love, one wave of His mercy, one wave of His truth.

Prayer: Jesus, please call me to join You on the stormy sea and lift me up out of these troubled waters. I need You and I trust in You. Amen.

Respond to His Call: Spend three minutes in silence and let God's truth wash over you today. Hear Him say to you, "I love you. Come to me, do not be afraid."

Joelle Maryn

Good Soil

And he told them many things in parables, saying: "A sower went out to sow." Matthew 13:3

Out by my driveway is an army of spider flowers: tall, pink, spiky flowers that never give up until the first frost. When the long seed pods have matured, my kids love to take them in their hands. One gentle touch and they explode, sending a shower of seeds every which way. Every year, some of those seeds find a home in a pocket of soil and take root there, ready to leap to life the next summer. It's my kind of flower: something that seeks out soil to grow in.

Jesus told a parable about sowing seeds in Matthew 13. The sower doesn't carefully place each seed but tosses them around carelessly. They hit the path, the rocky ground, the weeds. Only some of the seeds land in the type of soil where you'd expect them to grow. And sure enough, many of the seeds never have a chance to germinate: birds gorge on some, some get scorched by the sun, and weeds choke others. But those that fall on good soil pay off big time.

Where is the good soil for the message of the Gospel? Certainly, it helps to prepare the ground. But Jesus scattered the seed of His Word regardless of the soil. Where I might skip a patch of weeds, He let some fall. He gave everyone the chance to take that seed and grow it.

Thank God we have a choice: To receive or not receive. To truly hear or not to listen. Thank God He throws that seed wherever there might be a little crack to catch it. Maybe you know what it is to feel His life inside, transforming you. Perhaps you long to share that experience, spreading the seeds of your faith, trusting Jesus will prepare the good soil.

Prayer: Lord, give me the grace to scatter the seed of my faith. Help me avoid the temptation to hoard it, waiting for what I think is the right time or place or person. Make me open to a harvest You might bring where I least expect it. Amen.

Respond to His Call: Who in your life have you judged to be poor soil for the Word? Plan one way to spread the seed of the Gospel in his or her direction next time you are together.

Sarah Christmyer

From Ascension to Pentecost

Therefore I want you to understand that no one speaking by the Spirit of God ever says "Jesus be cursed!" and no one can say "Jesus is Lord" except by the Holy Spirit. 1 Corinthians 12:3

On the day of the Ascension, Jesus' instructions were specific: Do not leave Jerusalem; wait for the Holy Spirit. The apostles, still focused on earthly dominion, asked, "Lord, will you at this time restore the kingdom to Israel?" (Acts 1:6). So Jesus repeated: "You shall receive power when the Holy Spirit has come upon you, and you shall be my witnesses" (Acts 1:8). Jesus ascended out of sight, and the apostles became marked men. They would receive the promise—the seal of the Holy Spirit in their lives. There would be no turning back.

The Holy Spirit empowered me in a Pentecostal church, in the baptism of the Holy Spirit. My life changed instantly. The Holy Spirit became a constant companion, speaking instruction, breathing wisdom.

One day, as I was reading my Bible, a scream pierced my solitude from a pregnant woman who had fallen down a full flight of steps. As I held her in my arms, she stopped breathing. I said, "God help us."

I will never forget the power that came upon me. I suddenly knew how to help her. As I breathed life into this woman, a voice of commanding authority spoke through me into her, ordering her, "Live!" I alternated that with "Breathe!" I do not know how long I contended for her life. Then came a miraculous moment, when I witnessed this soon-to-be-mother return to her body. I watched death lose its power and release its grip over another person's life—actually, over three persons' lives, as she was carrying twins. To God be the glory!

Water the seed. Watch it grow. And when His power comes upon you, you will be witnesses to the ends of the earth, just as Jesus promised.

Prayer: Holy Spirit, come, welcome guest of my soul! Lead me into truth; give me Your wisdom so I may reveal Your glory with my life. Amen.

Respond to His Call: Find the Sequence of the Holy Spirit from the liturgy of Pentecost and pray it as a novena for someone who needs intercession.

Deborah Kendrick

God Never Hides

Then you will call upon me and come and pray to me, and I will hear you. You will seek me and find me; when you seek me with all your heart. Jeremiah 29:12–13

How do we know the plans God has for us? We seek, for God does not hide. If we seek Him, we *will* find Him. If we come to Him in the silence, He'll not take long to show Himself and His heart.

One morning, I awoke with some unusual questions on my mind: *What are my long-term goals? What do I aspire to accomplish in my work?* Now, I'm a busy person. So my days typically focus more on checking off an endless to-do list. This day, before my feet touched the ground, I had reframed the question: "Lord, what is Your goal for me?" Unfortunately, I didn't make any time to hear His reply.

For days, I wrestled with daily tasks without giving those questions another thought. But finally, when it was time for my adoration holy hour, I brought spiritual reading with me and settled in to hear from God. There, in the quiet, with my gaze upon Jesus, He spoke. As I read someone else's words, I heard within them the voice of God. Popping off the page was the response to my "work-goal" question. Confident in the source, I marveled at the simple message: *I want you to love Me. Your work's goal is heaven. Whatever you accomplish from your to-do list will matter little if your work does not lead you to a closer relationship with Me.*

Next, I reached for my Bible and read Jeremiah 29. The scriptures reminded me that not only does God have plans for us (v. 11) but also that those plans always include Him. We're not in this alone; the answers are just a prayer away. Our prayers are heard, and the answers always lead us to fulfill our ultimate goal—heaven. Maybe my work will not lead to riches, but I'm comfortable seeking heavenly retirement benefits instead.

Prayer: Lord, I believe the plans You have for my life are for my good. Restore any peace lost when I lose sight of this truth. Amen.

Respond to His Call: Write down three ways you can seek God today.

Allison Gingras

The Almighty Has Done Great Things for Me

For behold, henceforth all generations will call me blessed; for he who is mighty has done great things for me, and holy is his name.
Luke 1:48–49

I recently hit a milestone—my third decade. As I reflect on my journey so far, I have one overwhelming feeling: gratitude. I am so thankful for my life. It hasn't always been easy. I've long battled insecurity. I thought it was a battle I couldn't win. I felt that my worth was rooted in what I could accomplish—so I crumbled when I couldn't attain perfection. What a horrible way to live! But it was all I knew. God never intended for me to lose this battle—but I was trying to fight alone.

I wore self-sufficiency as my armor and carried the sword of independence with pride. But the protection I received was superficial—a lie of the enemy who sought my destruction. Battle after battle, I swung the sword, and my pride led me to believe I was winning. However, I was tired, lonely, and broken. I had to surrender. I needed someone to save me. As soon as I acknowledged my weakness and relinquished control, my Savior provided. I began to trust Him and His protection. The sword of independence dropped from my grasp, as did the pride and self-sufficiency that were suffocating me. I looked to the Father and saw myself as He does—His beloved daughter, the daughter for whom He will always fight.

Now, when I picture myself in front of my Father, Mary's Magnificat is on my lips: "My soul magnifies the Lord, and my spirit rejoices in God my Savior" (Lk 1:46–47). My worth is not based on what I can do—my value is in Him, as is yours. You are loved. What unholy armor are you wearing that keeps you from seeing yourself as the Father does? Set it aside. You are willed, wanted, and wonderful. Life is a blessing; go live it!

Prayer: Lord, thank You for my life. Thank You for Your unyielding love. Thank You for creating me willed, wanted, and wonderful. Amen.

Respond to His Call: Call a friend and tell her how wonderful she is, what she means to you, and how much you believe God loves her.

Angela Koenig

They All Rejoiced

. . . that there may be no discord in the body, but that the members may have the same care for one another. If one member suffers, all suffer together; if one member is honored, all rejoice together. 1 Corinthians 12:25–26

Recently, we found a family member, although she was never lost in the sense of being physically lost. Her natural father, who was my uncle, left her and her mother. She was an infant in Thailand, and he returned to the United States. That was fifty years ago. Sadly, he passed away before she could meet him. As a very young and curious child, I had seen a picture of the young couple in my grandmother's photos, although I didn't know who the woman was, and it was not discussed. The picture was taken in Thailand and always held so much mystery to me.

Now, through DNA testing and a lot of perseverance, the daughter of that union has found a family she did not know existed. Strangely enough, those of us who are her closest living relatives were not surprised. I think we always felt there was something more to the mystery of that man and woman in that small black-and-white photograph.

We have been rejoicing now that she has been found. It's been beautiful to share stories of family traditions and compare all the similarities despite being strangers for half a century. While there are many what-ifs, we must focus on the present moment and what will be in the future.

Perhaps God's timing was to remind us of all our family members, known and unknown. God calls us to live together in love and peace and to care for each other in sorrow and rejoicing and always with honor. "If you want to change the world, go home and love your family," said St. Teresa of Calcutta.

Prayer: Dear Lord, shower Your peace and the love that surpasses all understanding on my family. Heal any discord and grant us the gift of rejoicing in each other. Amen.

Respond to His Call: Today, bring out some old photos and discuss with your mom and dad or children your family's origin and how faith has played a role in your family's generations.

Letitia M. Peyton

June 9

A Day at the Beach

For the LORD takes pleasure in his people; he adorns the humble with victory. Psalm 149:4

Over several days of vacation, we fell in love with the sun, sand, and waves. Now, we were savoring our last day at the beach before we headed home. All of us were in the ocean. Some of my kids tossed a football with my husband. Others rode the waves on boogie boards. My youngest covered his legs with wet sand and then laughed hysterically as it instantly slipped off when he ran into the water.

I was in the middle of it all—delighted, content, at peace. With my arms and legs outstretched to keep afloat, I bent my neck back so that my face was directly in the sun. The sound of the waves, the softness of the breeze, the coolness of the water, and the swirl of seaside colors encompassed me. Everything else dissolved. At that moment, God's love washed over me like a gentle, giant wave. And I knew without a doubt that I was right where I was supposed to be, content and peaceful within His creation. God saw me being present to the moment He gave me, and He was delighted.

They say that vacation is an escape from the daily grind. But I would beg to differ. My encounter with God on the beach was more real than everyday life. It stripped away the accusation that I am less than anyone else. It freed me from the masks I often hide behind. And it allowed me to be who I truly am in the image and likeness of God. As one more breeze brushed over my face, God whispered to me, "Ah, there you are. The girl I created. Oh how I love and delight in you." As I basked in all the joy the beach offered, it felt good to simply be me and be loved by Him.

Prayer: Heavenly Father, thank You for the times when I can simply be in Your presence. It is where I find rest and refreshment. Amen.

Respond to His Call: Spend time with God today. Notice how He approaches you, and feel His presence. There is no need for words or actions. Simply be you. Simply be with Him.

Sarah Damm

The Garden of Your Soul

And that Christ may dwell in your hearts through faith; that you, being rooted and grounded in love . . . Ephesians 3:17

My husband and I are both avid gardeners. We have a small vineyard, several fruit trees, and an enormous vegetable garden. There is a unique thrill that comes from witnessing something you plant grow and blossom. Many are the hours we delight in gazing on the garden and walking through the vineyard, seeing our labors bear fruit.

Gardening offers many life lessons. All living things thrive best when properly tended to in a healthy environment. If I hope to have an abundant harvest, I must provide fertile soil for my plants, water them frequently, and remove weeds that threaten to compete for vital nutrients. Likewise, if I desire to have a healthy and fruitful life, I must have fertile soil to grow in, so I have ample opportunity to flourish.

God's love is the fertile soil for our souls, perfectly balanced and waiting for our lives to take root. It is here, in the foundation prepared for us before time, where authentic love grows, and we experience the optimal opportunity to blossom in the unique ways God intended. This fertile seedbed is shaped and reworked through each sacrifice we offer and each act of genuine love we make.

Prayer is like water to the garden bed of our soul. It gives us the necessary nutrients to thrive and provides the inner strength to weather the tumultuous seasons of life. And one of the greatest gifts given to us by the true Vinedresser, the Divine Gardener, is the Sacrament of Confession, which allows us to weed out all that threatens to destroy God's life in our souls.

Prayer: Lord, may my soul be a seedbed of faith for Your love so that I may glorify You through my life. Amen.

Respond to His Call: Examine the atmosphere of your soul. What changes do you need to make to cultivate a healthier environment for God's love to grow in you?

Kathleen Billings

Our Hope Does Not Fade

And when Moses had finished speaking with them, he put a veil on his face; but whenever Moses went in before the LORD to speak with him, he took the veil off, until he came out; and when he came out, and told the sons of Israel what he was commanded, the sons of Israel saw the face of Moses, that the skin of Moses' face shone. Exodus 34:33–35

Moses's face glowed as he descended Mt. Sinai with the Ten Commandments. His face was veiled after talking to the people, and only unveiled later while speaking to God. Little details in scripture like this nag at me. Why did Moses veil his face? Some research led me to Paul's second letter to the Corinthians: "Since we have such a hope, we are very bold, not like Moses, who put a veil over his face so that the Israelites might not see the end of the fading splendor" (2 Cor 3:12).

Moses didn't want the people to see the glow fading from his face. If the glow faded, so might their hope. Paul's letter to the Corinthians reminds us that we are not like Moses. In Christ, our hope does not fade.

When I converted, I fell in love with God hard, and I remember thinking that I must even look different because I felt so different. Knowing God loves you changes you. Years have passed since the big conversion, and I have experienced ups, downs, and times when I didn't "feel" His love. However, mature love surpasses mere feeling. As I have grown in my faith, I have learned that God's love for me depends not on feeling, but on my continuing to hope in that love.

When others see me, do they know a woman aglow with God's love? I need to make sure, in those occasional times when I feel doubt, that I veil my face and take it to God, lest I give the impression of my hope fading.

Prayer: Lord, set the fire of Your love on me that all who see me will know I am a woman aglow in Your amazing love! Amen.

Respond to His Call: Today, find ways to praise God with the great joy that He calls you to in His Name.

Sharon Agnes Wilson

Answering God's Call

Before I formed you in the womb I knew you, and before you were born I consecrated you. Jeremiah 1:5

Life can be uncertain and downright scary at times. Too often, we begin to doubt the path we are taking, and the anxieties compound so that we have difficulty knowing whether our actions are leading toward Christ. Sometimes, we don't know where to turn for support, love, and encouragement. But no matter how heavy our life feels or how much doubt we battle, there is one constant: God.

God is love. As our Creator, He made us to know, love, and serve Him. We are individually created by God and for God. He gently calls us into His embrace. God wants us to invite Him into our hearts and the uncertainty of our daily lives. He asks us to lay our worries at His feet and allow Him to shoulder the heavy burdens in our life.

It can be challenging to hand over control to God, but He asks us to remember a few things as He stretches out His loving hands:

- God has known you since the beginning of time. He knows you today, just as He knew you at the beginning of time.
- God knows the life you have experienced and will experience. He wants to walk the path of your life with you daily.
- God has created you specifically for today's time. Life will not necessarily be easy, but with confidence you shall persevere.
- God has called you by name. He delights in you. He finds you beautiful, even when life around you seems messy.

Will you answer His call?

Prayer: Dear Lord, thank You for the times You have shouldered my burdens. Help me to always remember to turn to You. Amen.

Respond to His Call: Today, gaze into your reflection in a mirror, and repeat the words: "God is gently and lovingly calling me by name. God loves me fiercely, and I am His."

AnnAliese Harry

Our Loving Father Will Call Us Home

For God so loved the world that he gave his only-begotten Son, that whoever believes in him should not perish but have eternal life. John 3:16

Sometimes the pain of life is so acute that even those not directly affected by a tragedy feel it. Recently, our parish experienced the loss of two young fathers with complicated illnesses. They were steadfast in belief, clinging to their faith and calling for family prayer in the midst of suffering. How could God allow these young husbands and fathers to go so early when it seemed their work was not done? Many of us prayed for a miracle, but death came instead.

Our understanding of a miracle may not align with the unimaginable beauty God has planned for us. Who but a loving Father could "show the immeasurable riches of his grace in kindness" (Eph 2:7), in contrast to what we might deserve?

I frequently stumbled throughout my upbringing, yet my dad walked with me, even when I fell. His belief in me persevered. His encouragement was endless, calling me back to goodness. He shared with me the bounty of family life, love, and joy—treasures whose value I didn't realize. In the same way, our God is a loving Father who walks alongside us, calling us to light and goodness, beckoning us to shine His love to others.

John 3:16 points us to the miracle God had in mind all along for those two young men, and for all of us: life beyond suffering, in the arms of a loving Father. What parent does not wait joyfully for their children to return? We all want to be received with bountiful love after our work here on earth is done. We must keep faith with sight unseen, and seek comfort in imagining the beauty and bounty of family life in heaven with the Father.

Prayer: Jesus, please heal us as we mourn; walk with us and support us when we stumble. Send us an image of the bounty that awaits, the glorious, unimaginable day when we meet the loving Father. Amen.

Respond to His Call: Today, write John 3:16 on a piece of paper, and tuck it some place where it will remind you how much God loves you.

Anne Carraux

Disjointed Thoughts

For God is not a God of confusion but of peace. 1 Corinthians 14:33

Oh, I have nothing to say—there are just disjointed thoughts spilling forth.

It is my father's birthday today. I remember his hugs. . . . I miss you these thirty years since you died. Do you hear me when I talk to you? Do you still wipe my tears?

When my windows are open, I love the sound of the birds.

My city has been on fire. Nothing makes sense.

Confession after Confession, sin still visits me, and my heart breaks at my weakness. It nearly breaks again when You forgive me. Your grace is overwhelming.

Today when I awoke, I placed my trust in You, Jesus. I will serve You; what will You have me do?

Another boot cast? How is it that I can break my heel while attempting to write a thank-you note? No wonder writing them is a lost art. This will be hilarious, not tragic.

Having my hands in pie dough reminds me of my mother and grandmother. The dough becomes a meeting place where I pray with them.

Being a lector at Mass humbles me. I feel unworthy allowing Your words to fall from my lips.

It was so good to speak to my big brother John recently when I was frightened and alone.

What an odd time—my heart breaks and exults all at once. My thoughts tumble yet dance. My body once more is home to a cast; the pain is an offering in laughter.

We live in strange times. I don't know what to do. Which is why today, I placed my trust in Jesus.

Prayer: Help me to place my trust in You anew every day, Lord Jesus. I will serve You; what will You have me do? Amen.

Respond to His Call: Throughout the day today, journal any of your disjointed thoughts. Then, thank God for each during your evening prayers.

Alyssa Bormes

Our Father Teaches Us to Pray

Do not be like them, for your Father knows what you need before you ask him. Matthew 6:8

For most of my life, the Lord's Prayer seemed rote—words that I simply recited, not being mindful of their deeper meaning. One day, I took the time to ponder that Jesus doesn't just give us words to recite repeatedly. Instead, He uses the Lord's Prayer to invite us into a deeper relationship with Him and His heavenly Father.

The Lord's Prayer gives praise: *Our Father who art in heaven, hallowed be thy name.* God alone is holy and worthy of praise. Therefore, it is good to begin any prayer with praise, for it honors God for who He is.

The Lord's Prayer expresses firm purpose: *Thy kingdom come. Thy will be done on earth as it is in heaven.* God desires that His kingdom reign on earth and in heaven. I pray to transform my desires into God's. I pray His will may be done in and through me.

The Lord's Prayer reflects trust: *Give us this day our daily bread.* I have made this line my daily mantra. It inspires me to trust God in the present moment and not succumb to worry and anxiety.

The Lord's Prayer asks forgiveness: *And forgive us our trespasses as we forgive those who trespass against us.* If I desire God's forgiveness and mercy, I cannot hold onto hurts caused by others. Asking God to help me forgive brings me deeper into His merciful love.

The Lord's Prayer requests protection: *And lead us not into temptation, but deliver us from evil.* The enemy does not want me to be close to God. Therefore, it is vital to ask God for His constant help and protection.

The Lord's Prayer is powerful and essential. I am so grateful that it brings me into a deep and personal conversation with God, my Father.

Prayer: Thank You, Jesus, for teaching me how to pray. Amen.

Respond to His Call: Is there a prayer that you recite without contemplating? Pray it slowly and carefully, and rediscover its beauty and meaning.

Sarah Damm

He Gives Us Himself

And he took bread, and when he had given thanks he broke it and gave it to them, saying, "This is my body which is given for you. Do this in remembrance of me." Luke 22:19

When life is hard, it can be tempting to think that God does not care about us, at least not in a personal or intimate way. But we need look no further than the nearest crucifix to see that this is not so. There hangs our God, bleeding and dying, pouring out all for love of each of us. Not for all of humanity in some general way, but for each of us personally, deeply, without limits, and without ceasing. That is the all-giving, all-loving God we meet in the Eucharist. He is present and dwells among us even today. He is present in our tabernacles, monstrances, and in eucharistic processions, and in whatever Communion line you might find yourself in next Sunday.

I'll never forget the time years ago when our parish held Mass in the gymnasium while the church was being renovated. There, under basketball hoops and yellow lights, with clocks humming on the walls and bleachers rising around us, we received Jesus. The great gift of the Eucharist. Jesus came to dwell among us in that humble, uninspired place.

He comes to battlefields and hospital beds. He comes to tiny chapels and great cathedrals—all for love of us. Jesus comes to us, no matter who or where we are. He comes to fill our hearts with His grace and love. He comes to heal us where we are wounded, fix us where we are broken, and strengthen us where we are weak. He gives us the gift of nothing less than Himself.

Prayer: Jesus, thank You for the gift of Your Real Presence in the Eucharist and in every moment of my day. Help me to see You, know You, and love You more each time I receive the Eucharist. Amen.

Respond to His Call: Memorize an act of spiritual communion and make a habit of praying it on any day that you cannot go to Mass and receive the Eucharist.

Danielle Bean

The Sweetest Love

Come to me, all who labor and are heavy laden, and I will give you rest. Matthew 11:28

Recently, as I was catching up on the latest news, a popular song from the sixties kept running through my head: "What the world needs now is love, sweet love. It's the only thing that there's just too little of." Those lyrics, originally sung by Jackie DeShannon, seem just as meaningful now as they were in the turbulent sixties—an era that included the Vietnam War, the Detroit riots, and other conflicts that divided our nation. Many of the problems we grappled with then are unfortunately still with us today.

We're still in need of love, and not just any kind of love. The love of God, in our hearts and toward our fellow man, is and always has been the thing we need more of in this world. If we're looking to spread God's Fatherly love, we should look to the Feast of the Sacred Heart of Jesus, which, not coincidentally, occurs close to Father's Day. Could there be any better way to contemplate love, especially that of our Father in heaven, than by reflecting on the beautiful Sacred Heart of Christ?

Our Catholic faith teaches us that the solemnity of the Sacred Heart stems from the visions of St. Margaret Mary Alacoque in seventeenth-century France. The image of the Sacred Heart is closely associated with the blood and water that poured forth from Christ's heart as He was dying on the Cross. Nothing but pure, sacrificial love emanates from that divine image. It's the Father of all fathers saying, as we heard in Matthew's gospel, "Come to me, all you who labor and are burdened, and I will give you rest."

Prayer: Father, today I come to You weary from my burdens. Grant me the rest You promise in Your divine love. Amen.

Respond to His Call: Today, make a point to tell those you love that you love them.

Teresa Tomeo

All Heart

When I am afraid, I put my trust in you. Psalm 56:3

I remember the day my pregnant sister arrived at my door. She'd gotten the results of her amniocentesis. She and her husband had already cried; here she was, asking her older sister for a different kind of support.

There was something wrong with the baby's heart. The arteries were in the wrong locations, and there was a hole between the chambers. The prognosis was unknown. The baby could be born in crisis and need surgery immediately; it could be stillborn; it could need oxygen and life support upon delivery; or it could have a limited life expectancy.

I hugged my sister while she cried. Then something happened: Jesus showed up. He inspired me to tell my sister, "Doctors don't know everything. God can work miracles. This could be the perfect opportunity for God to show the world how amazing He is." I reminded her how often the Bible tells us to not be afraid and to trust the Lord.

Our family steeped ourselves in prayer for the next four months. My sister shook her tendency to be private and shared the baby's condition with everyone who inquired, unafraid to ask for prayers. She and my brother-in-law named the baby Valen, inspired by the love that is outpoured on St. Valentine's Day and how Valen's own heart needed so much special attention.

Throughout those months, and up until the baby's delivery in June, if anyone asked my sister how she was coping, she would simply answer, "God's got this." And He did. Valen was born with no complications, perfect oxygen saturation, no machines necessary. To date, he hasn't needed surgery either. We don't know what the future holds for Valen, but we do know one thing for certain: "When I am afraid, I put my trust in you."

Prayer: Dear Jesus, thank You for coming to our rescue whenever we need You. Please calm the storms in the hearts of all mothers in need. Amen.

Respond to His Call: Ladies of WINE, go forward today with hope in your hearts. Know that God has your thoughts and prayers clasped firmly in the palm of His hand; trust in Him today.

Julie E. Kenney

A Lonely Place

And he said to them, "Come away by yourselves to a lonely place, and rest a while." For many were coming and going, and they had no leisure even to eat. Mark 6:31

While on a pilgrimage through the Holy Land, my friend Thomas took our spiritual director and me to "a lonely place to rest a while." The place was indeed lonely. It was a cave hidden in the side of a hill that looked out over the Sea of Galilee. As we sat in this secluded cavern and opened our Bibles to the Gospel of Mark, Thomas explained that it was in this "lonely place," or in Greek, *eremos topos*, that Jesus came to embrace solitude and to pray.

Mark 6:30–34 describes a busy scene. The apostles are returning to Jesus, eager to share with Him all they had done and taught. Many were coming and going, so busy that they didn't even have time for lunch, and others, seeing Jesus and His disciples leave by boat, were running from nearby towns trying to beat them to their destination. The scene is high paced and action-packed. At first glance, all this action is good—proclaiming the Good News, running to where you know you will encounter the Lord. But notice what Jesus asks amid all this commotion. He asks his disciples to come away, by themselves, to a lonely place and to rest. In the same way, He asks us to enter deeper into our contemplative spiritual lives—to find our *eremos topos*.

We don't need a cave between Capernaum and Magdala to enter into this retreat of the soul. We can find refuge in the Word of God. Meditating on the scriptures, we can retreat to a lonely place—lonely in the sense that all distractions are gone, and our entire focus is on Jesus. It is here where we can truly rest a while.

Prayer: O Lord, instill in me a passion for sacred scripture. Open the eyes of my heart, and show me how to meet You in Your Word. Amen.

Respond to His Call: Today, go to your *eremos topos*. Read Psalm 62:5 and rest a while in quiet prayer.

Kelly M. Wahlquist

All the Single Ladies

And the unmarried woman or virgin is anxious about the affairs of the Lord, how to be holy in body and spirit. 1 Corinthians 7:34

I decided to "put myself out there" in the online dating world. I spent an entire weekend setting up my profile, reading other profiles, and searching for a match. It took a lot out of me. I felt the rollercoaster of emotions run among scared, excited, and downright awful. It was a good exercise in being vulnerable. However, when it came time to finally having a date, I spiraled into a panic.

When I feel inundated with anxiety or doubt, I like to open my pocket Bible and ask the Lord for help. I asked, "Lord, tell me: what do I need to know?" And I opened to 1 Corinthians 7:25–40, the passage headed "More concerning Marriage."

The message of that passage is that an unmarried person is happier if she remains as she is. In her unmarried state, she remains especially available to the Spirit of God, content in her undivided devotion to the Lord. I heard the message. I laughed. God certainly has a sense of humor and the best timing, reminding me to seek Him before anyone else!

So what did I do? I prayed and asked for a blessing over my date. I went. I felt strange but protected. Oscillating between doubt and trust, I held space for God to come in. Afterward, I reflected on how I could continue to seek and keep the Lord first by maintaining my faith and remaining in love with Jesus.

So, for all you single ladies, when navigating the sea of love, turn to St. Paul's counsel. Seek first the Lord. Having an anchor of devotion to the Lord will help us swim in the deep water of romance where sometimes there's ground—and sometimes not.

Prayer: Lord, when I am facing situations far out of my comfort zone, please fill my heart with the wisdom needed to move where you send. I pray the scriptures always bring me the solace and strength I seek.

Respond to His Call: Consider how you ensure you are first securing devotion to the Lord before any other relationship in your life?

Hilary Scheppers

Pebbles from the Hand of God

So David prevailed over the Philistine with a sling and with a stone, and struck the Philistine, and killed him; there was no sword in the hand of David. 1 Samuel 17:50

I was recently on vacation in a particularly beautiful part of Montana where a small lake, tucked away in a mountain valley, beckoned swimmers to its clear waters. Having just finished a hike, I hurriedly stripped off my boots and socks for an icy but refreshing foot soak.

I couldn't help but notice that instead of sand, the beach consisted of millions of small stones, worn smooth over time. They were perfect for practicing my rock-skipping technique and reminded me of the biblical story of David. Young David went to meet the Philistine warrior Goliath with nothing more than five smooth stones and a sling. What sort of crazy person does that? Would it not have been more prudent to calculate the threat, acquire the necessary weaponry, and strategize?

And yet, David picked up weapons already at hand—objects of ridicule to Goliath—and declared boldly, "This day the LORD will deliver you into my hand . . . that all the earth may know that there is a God in Israel" (1 Sm 17:46).

So many times, when I face a problem, my default position is to rush to a solution or wrack my brain for some sort of strategy. Whether confronted with a mountain or a molehill, I often forget that God has permitted that challenge in my life to deepen my trust in Him. Most of the time, I already possess the answer and simply need to be thankful for God's grace while moving into action with confidence. The bonus? My act of trust becomes a witness to others that there is a God who cares about all our concerns.

Prayer: Lord, You gave David the ability to conquer Goliath with simple weapons, close at hand. Help me trust that You have already given me exactly what I need to overcome any challenge I face today. Amen.

Respond to His Call: Before searching for your own solution to a particularly challenging problem today, stop, confess your trust in the Lord, and thank Him who has already given you the tools you need.

Sharon K. Perkins

The Voice of the Sacred Heart

"Teacher, which is the great commandment in the law?" And he said to him, "You shall love the Lord your God with all your heart, and with all your soul, and with all your mind." Matthew 22:36–37

How easily I lose track of time when I'm contemplating the Great Commandment. In fact, I can spend hours on just the word "all," which appears three times in this scripture. "All" implies complete, total engagement.

This central commandment poses a challenging question in today's secular world: How do we love God with *all* our heart, soul, and mind? More than a century ago, a modern-thinking pope did something to help the faithful embrace this commandment. In 1899, Pope Leo XIII consecrated the world to the Sacred Heart of Jesus.

I have a special love for the Sacred Heart of Jesus, instilled in me since childhood. Growing up, I was accustomed to seeing images of the Sacred Heart of Jesus and the Immaculate Heart of Mary above my parents' bed. First Friday devotion to the Sacred Heart was a given in our home.

My seventh-grade teacher, Sr. Mary Alacoque, bore the name of the saint to whom Jesus revealed His Sacred Heart. In her last vision, Sr. Margaret Mary Alacoque saw Jesus' heart engulfed in flames and surrounded by thorns. She heard Jesus promise, "I will bless the home in which the image of My Sacred Heart shall be exposed and honored."

By the time I attended nursing school and university, the commandment of God's love and caring through the Sacred Hearts of Jesus and Mary was etched in my heart and soul. I am blessed in my professional life to promote nursing as a transcultural, caring science and art. Offering our poor hearts and listening to the Sacred Heart helps us understand the voice of Love, giving us courage, wisdom, and spiritual comfort.

Prayer: O most holy Heart of Jesus, fountain of every blessing, I adore You, I love You, and with a lively sorrow for my sins, I offer You this poor heart of mine. Make me humble, patient, pure, and wholly obedient to Your will. Amen. (taken from the Sacred Heart of Jesus Prayer)

Respond to His Call: Spend time reflecting on the image of the Sacred Heart of Jesus.

Dr. Marilyn A. Ray

Pruned from the Vine

I am the true vine, and my Father is the vinedresser. Every branch of mine that bears no fruit, he takes away, and every branch that does bear fruit he prunes, that it may bear more fruit. John 15:1–2

As I was reading John's gospel on the vine and the branches, the verse above struck me. I'm not a gardener, so the concept of pruning is perplexing. When I was young, I would watch with confusion as my mother removed robust roses in the name of pruning. How could that be beneficial? She always assured me that the plant would grow back healthier, fuller, and stronger; she was right.

Pruning is hard, but God reminds us, "He prunes, that it bears more fruit." Oddly, the prospect of being pruned fills me with hope and anticipation. God is at work right now in our adversity, pain, uncertainty, and fear. He is working to make us stronger and more spiritually healthy, laying the foundation for an abundant harvest later. We can think about harvesttime through the lens of earthly pessimism, or we can imagine where we'll be once God has accomplished the work He is doing in each of us. God's timing is never accidental. His ways are intentional. He will use everything for good.

I've been pruned before. Thirteen years ago, I couldn't understand why I had to endure a nearly fatal case of anorexia. However, now I see the tremendous fruit that came from that incredibly painful pruning. By enduring that season of suffering, I gained faith and dependence on God. By His grace, my story has been used to help others.

The promise about pruning is straight from Jesus' mouth. It gives me hope to think of the collective fruit that will come from our current sufferings. Imagine: it could be enough to change the world!

Prayer: Jesus, although I may wish to avoid Your loving pruning, I thank You for each occasion of it, knowing the good fruit You produce through it. Amen.

Respond to His Call: On your next grocery trip, select a small plant to care for and remind you of God's work of pruning you.

Caralyn Collar

A Man Sent from God

And they made signs to his father, inquiring what he would have him called. And he asked for a writing tablet, and wrote, "His name is John." And they all marveled. . . . For the hand of the Lord was with him. Luke 1:62–63, 66

St. John the Baptist is an incomparable saint. He was conceived miraculously in the womb of a woman past her childbearing years. His name was bestowed by heaven, his coming birth heralded by an angel.

The Gospel tells us that John first encountered the Savior when his mother Elizabeth welcomed her cousin Mary, both women carrying infants in the womb. At this meeting, the unborn baby John leaped for joy (Lk 1:44).

Later, John withdrew into the wilderness until the day he came forth baptizing and preaching the gospel of repentance. It was John who would baptize Jesus after fully preparing the way for Jesus' earthly ministry (Mt 3:13).

How overlooked John was then, as he is now. He lived among the wild beasts, wore a loincloth, ate locusts and wild honey, and never touched wine or strong drink. He was not of this world, so much so that the people accused him of "having a demon" (Lk 7:33). Yet, John is the only saint to have both his birth and his death celebrated by the Church, and he gave us the greatest, shortest, and most pointed instruction for spiritual growth: "He must increase, but I must decrease" (Jn 3:30).

For all these reasons and more, John is my go-to saint for many of the world's ills. The Bible tells us our struggles are not against flesh and blood, but against powers and principalities, rulers of darkness and spiritual wickedness. John never cowered. In today's vernacular, he spoke truth to power, and it cost him his life. Truly, John was a man sent from God.

Prayer: Most Holy St. John the Baptist, as you continually prepare the way for Jesus to come, pray for us that through our words, prayers, and deeds, we may be carriers of divine life to those in darkness. Amen.

Respond to His Call: Find a charity that helps pregnant women and consider a way you may help.

Deborah Kendrick

Trusting the Lord in All Things

Now faith is the assurance of things hoped for, the conviction of things not seen. Hebrews 11:1

My husband was diagnosed with an aggressive form of cancer, which has shaken our family to the core. We now pray more. We have slowed our lives as God has provided us a new direction. Friends are praying for his complete healing. Am I allowed to do that? Can I ask for everything? Out of desperation, I have tried to bargain, "What sacrifice or prayer will shrink the tumor so he'll make it to Christmas?"

Providentially, God places people to deliver messages. A friend told me she asks God for everything she wants. I now pray for complete healing; anything is possible with God. In our vulnerability, our trust in God grows. We give Him our hearts completely, revealing our deepest needs. Sometimes fear keeps us from raising our hopes. To live in fear is not of the Lord; it is not His will for us. We can desire our spouse's health, but our trust may be stretched when we ask for His will to be done, not ours.

The examples of the saints can nurture trust. St. Faustina teaches, "Jesus, I trust in You." Abraham offered Isaac in trust. Do I have that much trust in God to make such an offering? Jesus wants us to trust His mercy, especially during times of struggle. I offer acts of service and prayerful petitions for my husband. Any work of mercy we can do for others not only brings them but also ourselves closer to the Lord.

Praying with the Divine Mercy image and scripture, I trust He can do anything. Let my heart transform to His will. When His will is not what I desire, may I humbly trust and accept His will, especially as it pertains to my husband.

Prayer: Boldly, Lord, I pray today for the needs of my family, my community, and my nation. Humbly I stand before You, trusting Your will for each of us. Amen.

Respond to His Call: Call someone who has need of support. Assure them of your prayers, and (if they feel comfortable with it) pray with them.

Jennifer Beutz

Carrying the Cross

Whoever does not bear his own cross and come after me, cannot be my disciple. Luke 14:27

Before my cancer diagnosis, I thought only Jesus carried a cross. Now the concept of carrying a cross is part of my everyday life. Jesus tells us to be His disciples; that means we must carry our cross. While this may sound difficult, seeing our cross as part of His plan makes it easier to accept and to bear with joy.

Do you recall a time when Jesus' plan was different from your own? That time, for me, came on the day of my diagnosis—a day that changed my life forever. Lying on an exam table, I felt a prayer come to my heart: "Thy will be done; just give me the strength to get through it." Thirteen words etched on my heart. At that moment, I accepted Jesus' plan for my life over my own. Learning that I had cancer opened my heart to desire a real relationship with our Lord.

Before my diagnosis, I went through the motions of being a good Catholic. My three daughters went to a Catholic school, I volunteered at school and church, and we attended Mass every Sunday. I had no idea what I was missing. It took me a couple of years after my diagnosis to realize that the words that came to my heart on the exam table that day were a prayer, accepting Jesus' invitation to walk with Him and believe that He was walking with me. Almost thirteen years later, my relationship with Jesus continues to strengthen. He has never left my side, especially when breast cancer has moved throughout my body. He continues to show me the pathway to heaven as He guides my daily actions.

Prayer: I surrender myself to Your divine mercy, my Lord and my God. Jesus, I trust in You. Jesus, I trust in You. Jesus, I trust in You. Amen.

Respond to His Call: Reflect on the crosses your friends carry, as well as the crosses that you carry. Keep these friends and yourself close in prayer today.

Rhonda Zweber

In Light of Littles

Be mindful of your compassion, O Lᴏʀᴅ, and of your merciful love. . . . Remember not the sins of my youth, or my transgressions; according to your mercy remember me. Psalm 25:6–7

I was four years old when I blew out my first birthday candles; previously, my older (and quicker) siblings had gleefully deprived me of this magical moment. However, when we remember the good old days, the not-so-grand moments dissipate in light of the loving journey of life. Family videos fill me with a sense of hopeful wonder. (Most videos, anyway. Some clips would be better left unwatched!)

Our best remedy for fighting discouragement about yesterday comes from the Psalmist: "Remember not the sins of my youth, or my transgressions; according to your mercy remember me." The Lord remembers, but not for the sake of scrutinizing past mistakes or analyzing old ways. He sees every blunder with the compassion of a parent who knows the child's heart. No kid likes to be sad or scared, but they sure know where to turn when life hurts. Every warm embrace and inviting lap reflects the love of our heavenly Father and our Blessed Mother.

Remembering implies a backward glance. Though I have great aspirations for my elderly years, my best chance at remembering the light of love is to hold on to my childlike spirit of simple play, bellyaching laughter, and an unquenchable hope in our heavenly Father.

Home videos of sweet littles speak the same truth as the Word of the Lord: Nobody can steal the brilliant glow of God's burning love for His children. Whether you're ages old or years young, the Lord faithfully remembers you through every stage. May we seek to recollect our childlike joy and find wonder in each day.

Prayer: Father, help me remember that sometimes You calm the storm and sometimes You calm the child. Whichever You send this day, help me to receive it with childlike wonder and awe. Amen.

Respond to His Call: Recall your favorite childhood birthday and the people who were there. Say a Hail Mary for each person.

Katie Anderson

Take a Selfie

No servant can serve two masters; for either he will hate the one and love the other, or he will be devoted to the one and despise the other. You cannot serve God and mammon. Luke 16:13

In this passage from Luke, I propose that we replace the word "mammon" with "self" for a new perspective. It can help us distinguish which master we are serving. If I am serving myself, I'm surely not serving God. It's impossible to do both at the same time. Suppose I want my life to be easy, free of responsibility, and full of pleasure. That sort of existence requires that I pawn things off onto others and trample on the poor and needy. That is the complete opposite of what God calls us to do. To serve God is to serve others.

I watched a documentary featuring two young men who had high-paying jobs but felt empty. They decided to downsize and got rid of everything they owned except for a few well-chosen items. The young men then felt happy and free, which was their primary objective. But under it all, they were still serving themselves in their self-made poverty. If I downsize to make myself happy, that isn't serving God. I need to have the attitude of St. Francis, who chose to be poor to serve the poor. And then I become happy because I am helping others, not solely because I pleased myself.

What if, instead of sending out a selfie, we post a "godie"? What would that picture look like? How can we portray caring more for others than for ourselves? Can you capture a prayer for a hurting friend, an extra hug for a loved one? A "godie" would show the acts of kindness we do as we serve God and not ourselves.

Prayer: Dear Lord, let me mirror Your heart of love. Help to remember that only in You will my soul be at rest. Amen.

Respond to His Call: Next time you snap a selfie, examine your heart to see whether you are serving God or yourself. If you are serving yourself, decide at that moment to repent and to find a way to put God first.

Emily Cavins

A Heavenly Courtship

He who has the bride is the bridegroom; the friend of the bridegroom, who stands and hears him, rejoices greatly at the bridegroom's voice; therefore this joy of mine is now full. John 3:29

I couldn't take my eyes off the picture of Jesus above my desk. Drawn to that picture, I realized, finally, that Jesus was again courting me. When I realized this, all I wanted was Him. I still had time to get to the adoration chapel near my house before it closed. And I spent a beautiful hour and a half reading the Song of Solomon, listening to what Jesus had to say to me in those words. I am His beloved. As I write these words, the love I receive from God floods my soul. A simple love it is, yet the love we all so desperately need.

The love we experience in prayer, especially in front of the Blessed Sacrament, is a reminder that we are willed and desired by a King whose majesty outshines all others. Yet, He was humble enough to come to us in His human body, and now remain with us in the Blessed Sacrament. Jesus didn't just love you when He sweated blood, knowing what lay ahead in His Passion, nor when He suffered at the pillar. He loved you completely when He took His last breath to deliver you from sin. He loves you still today. Pure, beautiful, and eternal is His love for you. His love never fails.

Do not miss out on Jesus' daily love, holding out for earthshaking explosions. Jesus will shatter the earth if He needs to get your attention, but we are more likely to get those little glances from across the room on a daily basis, just as with His picture in my room that night. Glances reminding us that, in the eyes of the Lord, we are His beautiful bride.

Prayer: I love You, Lord Jesus. Teach me to love as You love, forgetful of self and focused on others. Let me see Your gaze in the faces of others who need my attention and care. Amen.

Respond to His Call: Take your Bible to adoration and read John 4:1–26, the meeting between Jesus and the Samaritan woman. Speak to Jesus about what you want to know about Him.

Angela Koenig

Before All Time

For I know the plans I have for you, says the LORD, plans for welfare and not for evil, to give you a future and a hope. Jeremiah 29:11

Called by name! Is there anything more beautiful than hearing our name called out? A word that defines us as a unique, irreplaceable, inimitable human being, a word that, when used by our parents, siblings, friends, teachers, colleagues, mentors, or pastor, brings specific (and hopefully positive) qualities to mind: happy, generous, faithful, funny, wise, loyal, thoughtful, moral, Christian. Sometimes it's the reverse: a trait such as happy, generous, or faithful brings to mind a specific person.

The first gift our parents gave us was life. And the second was our name—our lifelong ID card. Yet, before we were a twinkle in their eye, we were known and loved by God. God knew our name before all time. As we read in Isaiah 43:1, "Fear not, for I have redeemed you; I have called you by name, you are mine." How can we understand love that great!

"I have called you each by name"—words that are seared onto my soul! I, Joan, am known by God, called by name from all time! If my parents had hopes and dreams for me, how much greater could God's plans and hopes be for me? And I realized that each step in my life, whether or not I was aware of it, was God's doing. He made sure His plan would come true, every step of the way, even if I did not understand. Now I try to start each day by saying, "Okay, Lord, what's on the agenda? Whatever it is, help me do it or through it. Thy will be done."

Prayer: In Your loving goodness, Lord, You gave me the gift of life. In Your loving mercy, grant me the gifts of the Holy Spirit so that my life mirrors Your will. Amen.

Respond to His Call: Remember today that everything you do, every person you meet, every challenge you face, every joy you receive is part of God's loving plan for you.

Joan F. Lewis

The Time of Our Lives

For if you keep silence at such a time as this, relief and deliverance will rise for the Jews from another quarter, but you and your father's house will perish. And who knows whether you have not come to the kingdom for such a time as this? Esther 4:14

Esther's people were in grave danger. Only by breaking the law and appearing before the king uninvited could she have any hope of saving them. Both she and her cousin Mordecai knew that if she did this, she could be executed. Not exactly an easy choice.

I'm writing this in the summer of 2020. If you knew God had chosen you to be a part of the times of a global pandemic and serious social upheaval, would you have said, "Great!"? Or would you have lobbied for a better deal? I'm not sure what I would have done. Remember that Mordecai, who is asking this question of young Queen Esther, isn't exactly sure this is what she was born for, either. As he puts it, "Who knows?"

Nevertheless, this is where we find ourselves. We live in the age of a pandemic. Worse, we live in an age of confusion on every front: on marriage, on sexuality, on human nature, on culture as a whole. Confusion is not a good thing. If God is a God of order, confusion does not come from Him. Confusion is a tool of Satan—one of his most effective tools.

God did not create us to be confused. He created us to know the truth with certainty. That truth is found in the person of Jesus, who alone is "the way, and the truth, and the life" (Jn 14:6).

There is one path to certainty—keeping the Lord at the center of our lives. If we keep Him front and center, then confusion in the world won't shake us. We will stay on course, no matter what the times throw at us.

Prayer: Lord, in these dark days, shine brightly in our hearts and minds. Give us unshakable faith in You and show us Your path in every situation we encounter. Amen.

Respond to His Call: Meditate on the crucifix for one minute every day. Notice how that one, small act helps put this world in perspective.

Susan Vigilante

The Grace of Spiritual Friendship

And blessed is she who believed that there would be a fulfilment of what was spoken to her from the Lord. Luke 1:45

The first chapter of Luke captures the beauty of the Visitation. Every line has such profound meaning, from the joy of two cousins greeting each other, to the joy of two mothers-to-be celebrating, to the stunning words of Elizabeth to Mary when her child leaped at the presence of the Lord.

I often put myself in this scene, marveling alongside Elizabeth at the wonder of Mary's gift within her. When I pray this mystery of the Rosary, I often pray for my friends, especially those dear women with whom I share a spiritual friendship.

What an example of selfless friendship is captured in this record of Mary's visit to Elizabeth. We traditionally meditate on Christ's presence in the womb, but I also reflect on the beauty of the relationship between these two women and how they love each other.

Consider how the Blessed Mother, the first tabernacle of our Lord, took Him to her kinswoman and how Elizabeth received Mary and Jesus, giving praise!

In my prayer, I often ask for the grace to go into the world, bearing Christ as Mary did. I also pray for the grace to be like Elizabeth, quick to recognize Jesus' presence in my life and immediately give Him praise.

Isn't that a magnificent example of evangelization for us to follow?

Prayer: Dearest Jesus, give me the courage to take You with me wherever I go, to carry Your love to my friends, family, and all those I encounter in my daily living. Amen.

Respond to His Call: Think of one thing you can do today to strengthen a spiritual connection with a friend. Pray a Rosary for her. Offer a Mass for her. If you're comfortable, share prayer intentions with her and pray together.

Maria Morera Johnson

Imitate Jesus

Be imitators of me, as I am of Christ. 1 Corinthians 11:1

We don't just follow Jesus; we imitate Him. We do what He did! We love, we serve, we pray, we heal, we share the truth. Disciples imitate the Master. Disciples of Christ model their lives after His, which often means we too carry our cross.

St. Paul says, "Be imitators of me, as I am of Christ." Tradition is handing on what we know or have learned. Paul is pleading with the Corinthians, and all of us, to do what he does because he is doing what Christ did. It's not about Paul, and it's not about you and me. It's about Jesus, His mission, His love for us, His mercy, and His forgiveness through His ultimate sacrifice.

Consider Jesus on the Cross. That's forgiveness for eternity because the Eternal sacrificed Himself for us. Jesus is always with us. Baptism begins His presence in us, and Confirmation amplifies or enhances His presence in each of us. God never lets go of us, but we can and often do release our grip on Him. Never doubt His mercy and grace.

Jesus doesn't send us on the mission of making disciples alone. As the consummate Big Brother, He's got our back. We simply need to trust Him and remember to call on the grace the Holy Spirit provides. We are a team. The Father, Son, and Holy Spirit are with us, as are the Blessed Mother and the Communion of Saints.

Disciples are sent to evangelize. Jesus wants us to teach His commands to those who do not know Him. What does He command? To love God with everything we have, and to love everyone as ourselves.

Prayer: Jesus, as I gaze on You on the Cross, I pray for strength to never doubt Your mercy and the gift of Your grace. Amen.

Respond to His Call: What are some ways you can imitate Christ? Choose two of those ways that you will try today.

Lynda MacFarland

This Land That I Love

Blessed is the nation whose God is the LORD, the people whom he has chosen as his heritage! Psalm 33:12

I love patriotic music! It fills me with wonderful memories of Fourth of July celebrations on the lake, in full red-white-and-blue costumes, dancing in the sunshine as it sparkled off the water, my family and friends gathered nearby waving flags. Perfect summer days.

I love patriotic music because of the deep pride that wells up in my soul for so many family members, friends, and strangers who have served this amazing country, those who are currently serving, and all who will follow. Patriotic music has always tugged at my heartstrings, and I struggle to get through most of the songs without tears.

I love it because it reminds me of how great it is to live in America—the land of the free because of the brave. It helps me stand in awe of the sheer beauty of our spacious skies, amber waves of grain, purple mountains, and especially the lakes of Minnesota!

I love knowing our country started by asking for God's grace to be shed on it—where His good, brotherhood, and self-control were longed-for values. Where together we fought for freedom and pledged liberty and justice for all. Yet sometimes our nation's greatness seems on the verge of being lost—this love for our land and our neighbor. Like the heroes of the past, we can still fight for it, begging God to stand beside her and guide her, our home sweet home!

Prayer: God, we give You this wonderful country and thank You for the blessing to live here. Bless those who fight for our freedom. Help us remember that with liberty comes responsibility. Amen.

Respond to His Call: Today, listen deeply to a patriotic song such as "America the Beautiful" (all the verses!) and cherish what it means to be a proud American.

Heidi Harvey

Attentive and Grateful

For our boast is . . . that we have behaved in the world, and still more toward you, with holiness and godly sincerity, not by earthly wisdom but by the grace of God. 2 Corinthians 1:12

I have learned that to live a life of attentiveness and gratitude to God, we must choose to do so purposefully. I offer an example from my own life. When the odometer hit 100,000 miles and the children were young adults, my husband generously decided it was time to purchase me a new car. He surprised me with a sportier, higher-end, and definitely more attractive vehicle. Unfortunately, I became a little obsessed with comparing my new gift to cars other people were driving. In particular, I became preoccupied when I saw others driving this same make, model, and color. This little obsession of mine caused me to forget to be grateful.

God was showering His graces on me, allowing me to experience His abundance through the thoughtful act of my husband. I was missing those graces, failing to recognize His presence in all the good things in my life. When I realized what was happening, I intentionally turned this experience into an exercise of becoming more attentive to my blessings. I transformed my thoughts of envy and pride into praise. This spiritual aha! moment caused me to shift my thinking to a song of thanksgiving. Instead of allowing the negative to permeate my thoughts, I chose to see how everything in my life comes from God's goodness and mercy.

The scriptures always refocus my attention on the Lord. This time, St. Paul's second letter to the Corinthians gave me the guidance I needed. We may think it is by the world's standards and goods that we find joy, but my quick move to comparison taught me otherwise. Although I wasn't boasting to others, my actions revealed that my inward thoughts were indeed prideful. Truly, the only possession deserving my full attention, with a heart full of gratitude, is my faith and witness to Christ.

Prayer: Lord, may I see You in every blessing. May recognizing You in all things move my heart always to gratitude and thanksgiving. Amen.

Respond to His Call: Consider some ways you can be a blessing to someone today. Choose one, and do it!

Michelle Nash

On Road Trips and Relics

Therefore, since we are surrounded by so great a cloud of witnesses, let us also lay aside every weight, and sin which clings so closely. Hebrews 12:1

Take five children on a five-hour trip, stand in a two-hour line with 13,000 other people in hope of a 15-second encounter with a celebrity, and see what happens. Our trip to venerate St. Maria Goretti's relics was an adventure. Part of mothering is to guide children to role models who are worthy of their admiration. Thankfully, the Church has given us saints who point our children to Christ. St. Maria Goretti was martyred at age eleven, after being stabbed fourteen times for resisting a man's advances. She forgave her attacker and desired his repentance so that he could join her in heaven. Maria's forgiveness, when we might feel hatred, is nothing short of a miracle.

Before our visit, we talked together about Maria's story, her family, her murderer, her relics, and canonization. I wanted my children to understand the experience. During the trip, many questions raced through my mind. Did the kids grasp my teachings on forgiveness? Would they appreciate this opportunity to pray with this great but tiny saint? Were they prepared for their time of prayer in the church?

As we stood in line with thousands of others, I sighed, wondering when the line would ever move. At that moment, my ten-year-old son whispered to me, "This is great! I was worried the line would be short." I must have given him a confused look, because he explained, "Can you imagine St. Maria being brought here from Italy and having no lines of people to pray with her?"

It came full circle for me that day. There is so much I can learn from young children—the children that have been declared saints and also those living under my roof.

Prayer: St. Maria Goretti, pray for me to have the wisdom of ages and faith like a child. Amen.

Respond to His Call: Resolve to pray the next time you find yourself in a long line—even when in line for Holy Communion.

Andrea Gibbs

Sharing in the Glory

And he said to all, "If any man would come after me, let him deny himself and take up his cross daily and follow me." Luke 9:23

I slunk into the pew, put my head in my hands, and fell completely apart. "God, I am out doing your work," I sobbed. "How could you do this?" As the memories of the day washed over me, the sobbing intensified. Then in my heart, I felt a stirring to raise my head and gaze on the crucifix.

In my heart, I heard, *If you want to share in my glory, then you must be willing to share in the suffering.* The crucifix, just beyond the tabernacle, came into focus through my tear-swollen eyes. The voice in my heart continued. *If I did not spare my only-begotten Son from suffering, why, my beloved daughter, would you be any different?* Then I recalled Luke's gospel: "If any man would come after me, let him deny himself and take up his cross daily and follow me."

While Christ challenges us to pick up our cross if we want to follow Him, none of us will have to shoulder one as heavy as the Cross He carried to Calvary. Yes, I have experienced crosses, but none compare to the betrayal, the scourging, the crowning with thorns, and the jeering inflicted on Jesus. Every human being will face difficulties, and as Jesus reminds us in Luke's gospel, some crosses will present themselves daily. The beautiful gift of sensitivity empowers us to embrace those crosses and use them to help and heal.

Those powerful messages I received in the chapel penetrated my wounded heart. I wiped my tears and rose from the pew. Good Friday is about sacrifice, forgiveness, and redemption. Let us pick up our crosses daily and choose to follow Him.

Prayer: Lord, whenever I feel discouraged trying to live as a faithful Catholic, please fill my heart with all the graces I need to persevere in faith, hope, and love. Amen.

Respond to His Call: Today, contemplate all the ways you have already shared in not only Jesus' suffering but also His glory.

Allison Gingras

Say a Prayer

Likewise the Spirit helps us in our weakness; for we do not know how to pray as we ought, but the Spirit himself intercedes for us with sighs too deep for words. Romans 8:26

How often I have uttered the words "I'll pray for you" when someone shares a struggle. I've had those words said to me many times also. I want to share what those words really mean and how the Holy Spirit works through us every time we say those four simple words.

My father was in the hospital, and even with my early visits, I made sure I had enough time to start my day with the Rosary, as I've been doing for years. It was a Tuesday morning, and I received a very early phone call from a doctor to get to the hospital quickly. I flew out of the door without even washing my face, much less thinking about my Rosary. Through that day, as things looked grim, I thought about missing my Rosary, but I was talking with doctors, updating relatives, and holding his hand. I didn't have enough time or focus to engage in my daily routine.

Hours into the day, I received a text saying that several of my faithful friends were gathering to pray a Rosary for my dad. With everything going on, it was at least another hour before it hit me: They didn't just pray a Rosary for him; they prayed my Rosary—the one I couldn't pray—for me. I thought about the Holy Spirit. The Spirit prays for us when we can't. The Spirit worked through my friends in a particular way on the day that I missed my Rosary. It was a powerful reminder that whenever we follow the prompt of the Holy Spirit, we do the exact thing that needs to be done.

Prayer: Lord, help me to remember that when I say a prayer for others, it's not a gesture but a true offering to You. Help me to appreciate the importance of prayer in my daily life. Amen.

Respond to His Call: The next time you offer to pray for someone, remember that you are allowing the Spirit of God to work through you. Although you may never know the impact of that prayer, He knows, and He knows it is exactly what's needed.

Michelle Schroeder

There Are Days

Strength and dignity are her clothing, and she laughs at the time to come. She opens her mouth with wisdom, and the teaching of kindness is on her tongue. Proverbs 31:25–26

There are days so good that all you can do is marvel that God allowed you to experience them. I had such a day.

Let's start with some facts. Judy Cozzens is a hero of mine. She is the mother of Bishop Andrew Cozzens, the auxiliary bishop of the Archdiocese of St. Paul and Minneapolis. While pregnant with him, Judy was encouraged to have an abortion.

Kim and Henry Haverstock are converts. Their son, Fr. Paul Haverstock, was already in the seminary when they converted. Just one more fact—both Judy and Kim can sew.

Here is the story. On that day, I was walking through our parish offices when I heard women's voices in a small meeting room. When I stopped to see who was there, I witnessed something beautiful. Judy and Kim had yards of gorgeous material in front of them, and they were piecing together a chasuble. Judy was teaching Kim how to put it together. Judy had been making vestments for her son for years. She was showing another mom how to do the same for her son.

It was just the two of them, two moms, one helping the other. Knowing Judy, I suspect that she will offer more than just sewing help to Kim over the years. It seems being a mom of a priest carries both a special gift and a special cross; Judy is ready to help the new moms.

Perhaps you know that the word "chasuble" means love. Each piece of a priest's vestments has meaning, and over all of them, he puts on love. Some days, you realize that there is love in every single stitch of a chasuble, and those are the best days.

Prayer: St. John Vianney, join your prayers with mine, and those of all the sisters in Christ who will pray with us this day, in lifting up all parish priests, anointed and clothed in sacrificial love for God's people. Amen.

Respond to His Call: Find out your pastor's ordination date and arrange for a Mass to be said for his intentions. Attend that Mass if you are able.

Alyssa Bormes

Well-Fed by the Spirit

Trust in the LORD with all your heart, and do not rely on your own insight. In all your ways acknowledge him, and he will make straight your paths. Proverbs 3:5–6

At a retreat, when my turn came, I reached inside a basket to pick a rock inscribed with a word. We were to ponder this single word during the retreat. I hoped for a fruit of the Holy Spirit. I needed it. My life was filled with many blessings, but I still had feelings of sadness, anxiety, and unrest. I knelt to pray and turned my rock to reveal its message. I saw "Trust." What? How can this be my message? This must be someone else's rock. I wanted to return the rock or throw it into the pond beyond the chapel. I wanted straightforward answers. Trust had so many layers, like an onion; I wasn't for this.

I didn't have an epiphany at the retreat, but over the years, the rock kept resurfacing in odd places, such as my sock drawer or an old purse. I'd see "Trust" again, and each time its mystery unraveled further.

My rock of trust comes to mind when I gaze on the Divine Mercy image, with its simple message: "Jesus, I trust in you." I also think of Thomas, who openly doubted that Jesus had risen. When He appeared to Thomas, He said, "You have believed because you have seen me. Blessed are those who have not seen and yet believe" (Jn 20:29).

Faith, not sight, is what matters most. Faith requires trust in Jesus. He is our rock of trust; He returns no matter where we find ourselves. I am so grateful God gave me trust that day. Trust is a foundational piece for faith, joy, patience, and peace.

I now carry my rock in my purse. The polish is dull, the lettering faded; the word "Trust" is nearly gone. However, trust is engraved on my heart, as it should be. Jesus, we trust in You!

Prayer: St. Peter, the rock upon which Jesus built the Church, please pray for us to grow in the virtues and spiritual gifts. Amen.

Respond to His Call: Find a rock, write on it the virtue you most need *at this moment*. Put it where you'll see it often, prompting you to offer up a simple prayer for help.

Kerry McGuire

Are You Listening?

And a cloud overshadowed them, and a voice came out of the cloud, "This is my beloved Son; listen to him." Mark 9:7

"I can hear you," my mom said with a huge grin. "Although your voice sounds funny, I can hear!" Her radiating smile and excitement lit up the room. My mother had been losing her hearing over the span of decades. Although she is active and in excellent health, her hearing had diminished to a level of just 4 percent. At this audiology appointment following the cochlear implant surgery, my mom's face was aglow as she recognized that there was hope for her ability to hear.

My hearing has already begun to decrease like my mother's. However, of greater concern than my diminished ability to hear is my inability to listen.

The first word of the Prologue in *The Rule of St. Benedict* is "listen." Listening is not a passive activity. Listening is an action that requires effort, discipline, and practice. In a world of constant noise and distraction, I have learned that listening to God is, in fact, hard work.

Life is busy. Finding time and energy to pause, to still the external and internal noise, and to "listen with the ear of our heart" (as St. Benedict suggests) can be challenging. It is discouraging to admit that my mind still wanders when praying the Rosary, that I am still tempted to skip my daily prayers, and that my constant busyness can prevent me from listening to God. Oh, how I wish listening to God was easier! Fortunately, God can hear, and He does listen—even to those prayers that are not spoken. Thankfully, He knows our hearts and continually extends the grace we need to listen more closely to Him.

Prayer: Dear God, help me to make the effort to listen to You. Help me to recognize Your voice so that I can exclaim with joy, "I hear You!" Amen.

Respond to His Call: Practice listening to God and to others today. When another is speaking with you, turn your attention away from your task, look directly at the person, and listen with patience and charity. Next, practice listening to God—seeking His "still, small voice" throughout the day.

Dr. Pamela Patnode

Holy, Holy, Holy

And I heard every creature in heaven and on earth and under the earth and in the sea, and all therein, saying, "To him who sits upon the throne and to the Lamb be blessing and honor and glory and might for ever and ever!" Revelation 5:13

My friend has a radio show where she takes calls on spiritual matters. Recently I heard her lighthearted reply to a caller who was questioning certain types of prayer: "If you don't like repetitive prayer, you're not going to like heaven much, because we're going to be praising God over and over and over." It made me chuckle. I had never quite thought of it that way, but she was right.

Heaven is full of angels and saints who give glory to God and sing His praises constantly. In the book of Revelation, John tells us about four living creatures surrounding the throne of the Lord. Day and night, these four creatures never cease to sing, "Holy, holy, holy, is the Lord God Almighty, who was and is and is to come!" (4:8).

God draws us toward Him by giving us glimpses into the magnificent praises of heaven. Perhaps our glimpses aren't visions as vivid as John's were in the book of Revelation, but these brief encounters can show us the glory of God and ignite our hearts in such a way that we want to honor and worship God without ceasing.

On a warm July evening, I marveled at the perfectly choreographed dance of thousands of fireflies. With simple repetitive flickering, they transformed an Iowa cornfield into a stage for an exquisite fluorescent dance. It was as if these little lightning bugs were giving glory to God by doing what God created them to do.

Imagine if we no longer saw our repetitive actions as monotonous but delighted in them, using them to give God glory. What a show it would be if we all worked in our gifts, over and over, glorifying God!

Prayer: Lord, help me to find joy in the little repetitive things I do. May all I do give glory to You this day. Amen.

Respond to His Call: Today, take a moment to thank the Lord for the little things you get to do and pray for those for whom you do them.

Kelly M. Wahlquist

Lord, Guard My Speech

Set a guard over my mouth, O LORD, keep watch over the door of my lips! Psalm 141:3

When I gather with friends, many times our conversations revolve around the life events of shared acquaintances. We try to keep up with the lives of people we care about and discuss who has a new job or the location of a friend's new home. Sharing in one another's blessings can be a source of joy and help build our sense of community. However, in times when we're struggling, it can be difficult to witness blessings in the lives of others. Envy can gain a foothold in our hearts, leading us astray. Thomas Aquinas defines envy as "the self-indulged sorrow at beholding the good of others."

Have you ever had a friend ask, "Can I just vent for a minute?" We all need a safe space and person in whom we can confide, yet often this question leads to an uncharitable conversation about another person, or outright gossip. This is detrimental to our spiritual health. When listening, be alert to the conversation taking a wrong turn. If your friend is trying to address something, or to decide how to respond to an issue, she may be sincerely seeking your good counsel before making a decision. But if the venting turns into a complaint session, disparaging the character of another, it is time to redirect or end the conversation.

Gossip does damage to the souls of all involved. It can enter subtly and gain traction if indulged. We must exercise restraint in our speech in order to maintain our virtue and the reputation of others.

Prayer: Lord, I thank You for the people You have placed in my life as friends and family. Help me to speak charitably and simply at all times, and to say nothing that will disparage another or lead to regret. Amen.

Respond to His Call: Today, exercise the virtue of prudence in what you say and in what you choose to leave unsaid. Speak sincerely yet sparingly, promoting only what is good and true in your words to others.

Jennifer Beutz

Eyes to See, Ears to Hear

Return, O Israel, to the LORD your God, for you have stumbled because of your iniquity. Hosea 14:1

In his book *The Gulag Archipelago*, Aleksandr Solzhenitsyn says, "One thing is absolutely definite: not everything that enters our ears penetrates our consciousness. Anything too far out of tune with our attitude is lost, either in the ears themselves or somewhere beyond, but it is lost." Isn't it true that when we view the world through a certain lens, it's difficult to perceive how others might see it? How often have I debated with my spouse on what he "heard" me say versus what I intended to say!

Lately, it seems our world is in turmoil. We can't hear beyond the noise. Could it be that the world is in need of repentance? When we don't repent, it's difficult to see clearly; it's as if our souls are blurry.

Through the prophet Hosea, our Lord calls to the Israelites: "Return, O Israel, to the LORD your God, for you have stumbled because of your iniquity. Take with you words and return to the LORD; say to him, 'Take away all iniquity'" (Hos 14:1–2). Our Lord continues, "I will heal their faithlessness; I will love them freely, for my anger has turned from them" (v. 4). Our Lord continually calls us to Himself: "Whoever is wise, let him understand these things; whoever is discerning, let him know them; for the ways of the LORD are right, and the upright walk in them, but transgressors stumble in them" (v. 9).

God has given us the beautiful gift of grace. Grace gives us clarity of vision, peace of mind, and sincere love of God and neighbor. Grace is sustained through the Sacrament of Reconciliation, where all burdens are lifted. It continues with the Sacrament of the Eucharist, where all divine life is given. Grace helps us hear God clearly and keeps us in tune!

Prayer: Lord, help me to see as You see and to hear as You hear. Pour out Your grace. Help me to repent often, so that I may be free to live in union with You. Amen.

Respond to His Call: Receive the Sacrament of Confession more frequently as a way of growing in self-awareness.

Margie Mandli

Only You Can Prevent . . .

For lack of wood the fire goes out; and where there is no whisper-er, quarreling ceases. Proverbs 26:20

Anyone who knows me will tell you I am the least outdoorsy person in the world. I don't hike in the summer, I don't ski in the winter, and if you ever catch me camping, it can only mean I'm on the run from the law, so maybe you'd better call the police (unless you're into abetting, which I'm sure in the circumstances I would appreciate). That being said, I freely confess that I was once a Girl Scout.

Yes, I wore the green sash. Yes, it had some merit badges on it. No, I don't remember what a single one of them was for. But I can tell you this: not one of them was for building a fire. When it came to fire building, I was the one who collected the kindling. The other girls in my troop were proud of their fire-building skills. They built log-cabin fires, teepee fires—you name it. And every one of those fires required wood, lots of it. If you ran out of wood, you ran out of fire, plain and simple.

Strife happens. It happens among coworkers, among friends, in families. The fact that we can use words to resolve our problems with each other is a wonderful gift. Unfortunately, sometimes people opt to use their words to keep the fire burning. They may do it out of anger, or they may do it out of boredom. They may do it just to keep everyone "caught up" on the topic.

Talking about our grievances to people who aren't involved just keeps the memory of the cause of the strife alive. When we gossip about a problem—a slight, a grudge, someone's less-than-perfect behavior—we may even be reminding someone who had almost forgotten it. And it lives to annoy us again!

Take the book of Proverbs' advice and stop fueling the fire. Change the subject. Or just smile and say nothing. The other person will get the message, and you will have dampened the fire.

Prayer: Lord, help me put out the little fires of strife. Amen.

Respond to His Call: The book of Proverbs talks a lot about gossip. Read 10:19, 11:9, and 11:13.

Susan Vigilante

Paddling Upstream

I will meditate on your precepts, and fix my eyes on your ways. . .
. I will not forget your word. Psalm 119:15–16

My son and I planned a special outing kayaking on a nearby river. To my initial dismay, we learned at the kayak rental shop that we would be paddling upstream. It was my son's first time kayaking, and I was excited to share my newfound love for this sport, but I was concerned that he might get discouraged paddling against a current.

As we began to paddle against the flow of water, I quickly realized how easy it was to get off course. We appeared to go a little to the left, then a little to the right, as we slowly zigzagged forward. Occasionally, we backtracked. A few times, we got stuck in the muck. When the water was too shallow, we used our paddles as leverage while we pushed down on the bottom to escape and move forward.

My son and I chatted about our two-hour kayaking adventure over pizza that night. We discussed the commonalities between kayaking against a current and living a virtuous Christian life. Often doing what is right feels like paddling upstream. Living with Christ requires perseverance and determination to stay on course. A distraction here, a lure there. If we are not purposeful and passionate about reaching our destination, we may find ourselves going off course.

In kayaking, I had to stay engaged, because even a subtle current altered my direction when I was not paddling. It is the same in my walk with God. I cannot float through life, expecting Him to lead me and strengthen me for the journey. I have to purposefully and continuously engage my heart and soul. I go to adoration to nurture my interior life, and I go to Confession to clean my soul. When I get stuck in the muck of life, I ask God in His mercy to set me back on course.

Prayer: Lord, when I am stuck in the muck or drifting off course, may Your mercy guide me back to the path You have set for me. Amen.

Respond to His Call: Invite a friend out for coffee or a special treat. Use your time together to encourage each other in living your journey of Christian faith.

Kathleen Billings

Are You Mary or Martha?

He entered a village; and a woman named Martha received him into her house. And she had a sister called Mary, who sat at the Lord's feet and listened to his teaching. But Martha was distracted with much serving. Luke 10:38–40

Our neighborhood church, St. Joseph's, was the center of my life as a child. It stood near my friends' houses, my grade school, and our home. My mother was active in the Altar and Rosary Society and never hesitated to volunteer any of her six daughters for church functions.

When I moved out of my childhood home, I became a member of St. James Catholic Church and immediately joined the Council of Catholic Women. I identified with the "church ladies," as they reminded me of my mother, six hours away. Through the years, I, like my mother before me, also volunteered my children for church activities.

All that to say, I identify with Martha and feel that she often gets a bad rap! Someone has to make the coffee and serve the food, right?

The Catholic Church needs both Marthas and Marys—both hospitality and spirituality. When you've visited a Catholic church outside of your parish, how were you welcomed? Did anyone smile and greet you, introducing themselves and asking your name? How about at your church? Do you try to identify and speak to someone new at Mass? Asking a simple question, such as "Are you visiting?" or "Do you live around here?" shows interest and can make a real difference to people.

Perhaps it is the Mary part of your life that needs cultivating. Do you feel a desire to grow closer to Jesus, to listen to His every word? Meditating on the day's gospel or making time for spiritual reading will enhance your faith. Are you Mary or Martha? My answer is yes!

Prayer: "Let everyone that comes be received as Christ" (from *The Rule of St. Benedict*). Lord, help me to be as both Mary and Martha, in service to You and to others. Amen.

Respond to His Call: Look into ways to volunteer in your community. Ask God if He's calling you to be Martha in any of these opportunities.

Lucy H. Johnson

I Forgive

Then Peter came up and said to him, "Lord, how often shall my brother sin against me, and I forgive him? As many as seven times?" Jesus said to him, "I do not say to you seven times, but seventy times seven." Matthew 18:21–22

After my presentations, audience members frequently whisper to me, "Thank you for sharing the power of forgiveness." Forgiveness seems to strike a universal chord in the hearts of people. There is an innate hunger and desire to let go of suffering. Those who do so say they experience a rebirth—in some cases, a new life. When we choose to hold on to anger, we continue to bear the weight and suffering, not realizing that we're hurting only ourselves, not the offender. We give power to the one who caused us so much pain, allowing them to continue to hurt us with sleepless nights, an upset stomach, high blood pressure, or headaches. For our own health, we must forgive them whether they deserve it or not.

Forgiveness brings healing. Some people go to Confession to have their sins forgiven but haven't forgiven themselves. We can't extend mercy to others until we have mercy on ourselves. So let's begin today by forgiving, first of all, ourselves for past mistakes. What we did then was done by who we were then, based on what we knew then.

Today, by the grace of God, we are different. And today, we begin to forgive others, no matter how horrific the offense. Jesus already did this for us. At the Last Supper He told the disciples to drink His blood, "my blood of the covenant, which is poured out for many for the forgiveness of sins" (Mt 26:28). Period. Done deal. In His dying breath, Jesus said, "Father, forgive them; for they know not what they do" (Lk 23:34). Jesus came to show us the way, the truth, and the light. Let's follow His way. Forgive ourselves and others.

Prayer: My benevolent God, thank You for forgiving all my mistakes and missteps. Help me to forgive myself as You have forgiven me. Amen.

Respond to His Call: Today, write on a slip of paper the name of someone you will now forgive. Place the paper in a nonflammable container and burn it, watching the smoke and your release rise to heaven.

LeeAnn Thieman

Baptized in the Name of the Holy Trinity

. . . which is his body, the fulness of him who fills all in all. Ephesians 1:23

We are to evangelize all the world, make disciples of the nations, and baptize in the name of the Holy Trinity. The last few months have included times of fear, doubt, and sadness. More often than not, I felt that I didn't understand what was happening around me. But my faith has anchored me. Each person of the Trinity calls me differently.

In recent years, I've come to appreciate God's Fatherly love for me better. I know I am His daughter and that I am not alone. I'm not in charge. When I let go, I experience peace and true freedom. I also trust that Christ the Son is with me in all things. In His life on earth, He promised to always be near me, to love and redeem me. There's nothing to fear when I abandon myself to Him. Finally, I call daily on the Holy Spirit for inspiration and guidance, feeling the reality of His presence.

It's in living these certainties that I can begin to make disciples. When Jesus ascended into heaven, He told His disciples to stay because He had a gift for them. That gift was the Holy Spirit, and many were baptized the day the Spirit descended. Many of us can relate to the sadness and ache that Jesus' disciples must have felt when He left them to go to the Father. But we are never alone. Jesus' presence in our hearts and our lives is a gift. Today, we are called through the Holy Spirit's guidance and the grace of the Father to share that presence with the whole world.

Prayer: Come, Holy Spirit, inspire, guide, and be near me always. Never allow my belief in the true presence of Christ in the Eucharist to waver. Amen.

Respond to His Call: Invite someone you know to attend daily Mass and breakfast with you. Enjoy the conversation!

Lindsay Schlegel

God Makes Mosaics
out of Brokenness

Jesus wept. John 11:35

When I was working on my latest album, my dad had a business trip in North Carolina, so we took his perfectly clean Honda CR-V (as opposed to my less than perfectly clean CR-V) and drove down to Burlington together to record my last four songs. I always feel fifteen when I'm riding shotgun with my dad—like I should be wearing soccer cleats.

The road to Burlington begins as one of the most beautiful drives I know. It leads through Charlottesville, Virginia, a place I especially love. As I looked out my window at the bare and brown world, it looked very similar to when I began my musical journey. I was in a fragile place, tired and worn and afraid and not much of a believer even in my little dream. So I wrote songs through it and hoped that I could make some sense of it all.

Maybe I am still trying to make sense of it all. But I am learning that the artist and the saint have one thing in common. They can enter into the mystery of suffering and make something beautiful. And if that is the case, think how much more the Divine Artist can make beauty out of the mess of this suffering world!

The fullness of beauty that is God enters into our unspeakable sadness and creates color, light, and music like a host of angels breaking into the cold and darkness to light an entire sky with the best news we've ever heard—God has become one of us. What could ever be more beautiful? And no matter where we go, no matter how drab our life appears, Beauty Himself will always color our lives to draw us back to Him.

Prayer: Dear Lord, I know You see me in my suffering. You love me, and You will make these broken pieces into a beautiful mosaic for Your glory. Amen.

Respond to His Call: If your heart feels broken today, give it away in a small act of kindness toward a neighbor, friend, family member, or coworker.

Marie Miller

God Knows

Search me, O God, and know my heart! Try me and know my thoughts! Psalm 139:23

In my first virtual session with a new spiritual director, I confessed to the beautiful religious sister on the computer screen that my prayer life felt like a disaster. With gentleness and grace, she asked me to speak first about my relationship with God. I began to fill the space between us with words and notions, explaining to Sister that I am a lifelong practicing Catholic. I listed my bona fides and described my personal rituals for daily devotional time and scripture study. I described my efforts to grow my faith so that I can share it with others.

As she sat silently, listening to my ramblings, I realized for myself the words that Sister left unspoken. Rather than describing a relationship, I had listed my own credentials, completely neglecting God's role in the equation. I began to ponder in that instant how I'd fallen into a prayer routine that was dry and unfulfilling. Without being prompted, I began to discuss how a healthy relationship with God could perhaps look in small ways like the type of marriage I desire: a mutual love affair sometimes carried forward through words but often nourished by the silent accompaniment of two lovers cherishing life's journey together.

God knows every ounce of our being and every need of our hearts. Since that first session, I have found great solace in coming into God's presence wordless and simply sitting in the warmth of His embrace. The saints walk alongside me toward God's company, shining the light of their own experiences. My brokenness is not an obstacle that prevents my Father from loving me. The Spirit translates my unutterable intentions. My words do not need to fill this sacred space. God knows.

Prayer: Holy Spirit, help me to sit quietly and trust that my Father knows every need and desire of my heart. Make of my silence a perfect prayer, crafted with love, gratitude, and trust. Amen.

Respond to His Call: Instead of your normal prayer ritual today, simply sit in God's presence. Allow your heart to brim with love and gratitude.

Lisa M. Hendey

Go to Where You Know Jesus to Be

Now on the first day of the week, Mary Magdalene came to the tomb early, while it was still dark, and saw that the stone had been taken away from the tomb. John 20:1

We all have our go-to saints, those who have run the good race and won the eternal reward. I have a group that I rely on regularly for various reasons. Sts. John Paul II, Clare of Assisi, Catherine of Siena, Teresa of Calcutta, and Blessed Jordan of Saxony are often nearby, but there is one saint who is with me always. That's my friend Mary Mag. A tower of courage inspired by an immeasurable depth of love, St. Mary Magdalene is an excellent example of what it means to be a disciple of Jesus.

On Holy Saturday, when Mary Magdalene faced her darkest hour—her Lord, her Hope, her Love, her Savior was dead and buried—she went to the tomb. She went to where she knew the Lord to be. We can learn a great lesson from Mary Magdalene's actions in her time of great suffering.

When we face our darkest hour, we can go to where we know the Lord to be. We can go to scripture, to prayer, to adoration, to Mass, to the Eucharist. It is there where we will find Him. Even if we still feel empty and alone, we can take comfort knowing He is there with us.

Scripture says that Mary Magdalene stood at the tomb weeping, but it also tells us that her faith, love, courage, and devotion to Jesus were greatly rewarded. She was the first (besides our Blessed Mother, as the Church Fathers teach) to see the risen Lord. And she was the one to proclaim it to the world: "I have seen the Lord!"

On any dark days you face in the future, go to where you know Jesus to be.

Prayer: Jesus, give me the courage to follow You each day and the grace to be a witness of the power of Your merciful love. Amen.

Respond to His Call: Today, go to where you know Jesus to be. Close your eyes and listen with your heart to the message He has for you.

Kelly M. Wahlquist

Don't Worry, Be Hopeful

Therefore do not be anxious, saying, "What shall we eat?" or "What shall we drink?" or "What shall we wear?" For the Gentiles seek all these things; and your heavenly Father knows that you need them all. But seek first his kingdom and his righteousness, and all these things shall be yours as well. Matthew 6:31–33

I spent hours fretting over what I would wear and serve at a recent dinner party. What a waste! I can't believe the anxiety I nurture sometimes. Opening my Bible to Matthew 6:24–34, I heard Jesus speaking directly to me. Why spend time and energy worrying about what you'll wear or eat? There's so much more to life! Jesus isn't saying don't plan or don't be concerned if you're in need; He is saying don't stress over it.

He goes on to point out that the birds don't plant or reap and stockpile food, yet God provides for them. God, who cares for the birds, cares far more for us. Do you know how very much God loves you? He didn't make you His child to abandon you. Worry is worthless. Like a rocking chair, it gives you something to do, but it doesn't get you far. Do what you can, then leave it with God.

Are you giving worry control of your heart, as though it might solve your problems? As Jesus says in verse 32, those who do not know God seek "all these things." Food and clothing are first on their minds. Why? Because they don't know God as a loving, caring Father. Instead, their future hangs in the hands of fate and fortune, and it's every man for himself. No wonder they worry. Jesus proposes a different way to His followers: "Seek first his kingdom and his righteousness, and all these things shall be yours as well" (v. 33). What do you seek above all else? Does your thought-life reflect trust in God or dependence on yourself and fortune? Only in God do we find rest; He is our rock and salvation.

Prayer: In every need, Lord, I will seek You. How grateful I am for Your divine providence. Amen.

Respond to His Call: Meditate on Psalm 62 and notice the subtle shift in wording at the start of the first two stanzas. Make this psalm your prayer today.

Sarah Christmyer

Mind, Body, Heart

Trust in the LORD with all your heart, and do not rely on your own insight. Proverbs 3:5

We are many parts—mind, body, and heart. Yet, all too often, we let our minds control our bodies and our hearts.

Our bodies are stronger than we think. When I'm trying something physical such as a plank exercise, my mind says, "I can't do this; it's too hard," but my body comes through. The mind tells the body stories, but the body knows the truth. We need to listen to our bodies, but we need to lead with our hearts.

In India, the Catholic Church offers counseling, or guidance, sessions. People wait in line for it as we do for Confession. I asked my friend, Fr. Joses, to describe a typical session. He showed me a small, heart-shaped rock. He tells someone he is counseling to hold the rock, close their eyes, and imagine that it is the heart of Jesus. He instructs them to place the rock on their chest and allow their heart to talk to the heart of Jesus.

I love this imagery. I often think of the Sacred Heart of Jesus or the Immaculate Heart of Mary. When my mind can't find the right words to say, I let my heart talk to theirs. Placing my worries in the hearts of Jesus and Mary gives me peace.

As a child, I used to hear my mother say her prayers out loud as she worked around the house. One of those prayers was the Novena of Confidence to the Sacred Heart of Jesus. My mother prayed: "O Most Sacred Heart of Jesus, I have asked for many favors, but I earnestly implore this one. Take it, place it in Thy Sacred Heart. When the Eternal Father sees it covered with Thy Most Precious Blood, He will not refuse it. It will no longer be my prayer, but Thine."

Prayer: O most Sacred Heart of Jesus, teach us to listen to our bodies but lead with our hearts. Amen.

Respond to His Call: Challenge your body over your mind by walking one block more or holding a plank ten seconds longer.

Lucy H. Johnson

Grace for the Asking

Let us then with confidence draw near to the throne of grace, that we may receive mercy and find grace to help in time of need. Hebrews 4:16

I thought all parking spaces were alike—until my sister and I bought a condo and I drove my Honda Accord, named Grace, into the garage for the first time. Grace didn't come close to fitting into my space, which was against a concrete wall. A friend's Honda Fit wouldn't, well, fit either. We quickly learned we had no remedy with the condo association or the local government, and an attorney advised against legal action.

The nearby apartment building where we'd previously lived agreed to rent us a space temporarily. For the next month, the situation consumed me. Did I pray about it? Not really. I figured God had more important things to focus on than my stupidity. At the end of the month, I drove home at about 10 p.m., still without a plan. I said out loud, "Jesus, help me. I don't know if I should sell the car, rent some parking, sue the condo association, or what. I feel like whatever I do will be wrong." Within seconds, a voice spoke straight into my soul: "Don't sell Grace." I slept well for the first time that month.

The next day, I asked the apartment building manager if I could rent a space indefinitely. She said sure. The parking space turned out to be only one of many issues with the condo. After two years, my sister and I sold it and moved back into the apartment building. As I write this, Grace is parked in the same place she's had for nearly seven years. Some people would say the lesson is to check out the parking space before buying a townhouse or condo. For me, the lesson is that grace is there for the asking—even if it's something as seemingly small as what to do with a car named Grace.

Prayer: Jesus, may I come to You at the first sign of trouble, confident in Your wise counsel. Amen.

Respond to His Call: Think of a situation you're trying to manage yourself. What is keeping you from seeking Jesus' help?

Melanie Rigney

A Divine Love Song

O that you would kiss me with the kisses of your mouth! For your love is better than wine. Song of Solomon 1:2

The Song of Solomon is also known as the Song of Songs. That title, translated from Hebrew, means "the greatest of songs." The poems in this book of the Bible are great indeed, expressing mutual love between the Lord and His people. When I first read the scripture above, I thought of a baby learning to kiss—mouth wide open. The infant seems to inhale you and expresses such joy experimenting with kisses. Babies indeed are a gift from God, and none are more precious than grandchildren. Today, July 26, is Grandparents Day. Although not a secular holiday, it is the Feast of Sts. Joachim and Anne, grandparents of Jesus.

In lieu of presents, my husband and I have begun a tradition of spending the day with each grandchild on their birthday, allowing them to choose the activities. Whether exploring the zoo or going to the park, these adventures have awakened in us a new appreciation as we view the world through a child's eyes. Spending time with grandchildren is different from raising your own children. Grandchildren can do no wrong. Even when naughty, they are lovely. The love I feel for my grandchildren helps me to understand God's love for me better. Our grandchildren love us, and we love them—unconditionally. This mutual love mirrors the mutual love of the Lord and His people. Grandbabies' kisses are sweeter than wine, as are God's kisses.

If you have the joy of being a grandparent, think about what you are learning from your grandchildren and what memories you'd like them to have. Do you reflect God's love to them?

Prayer: O Lord, we can create a legacy of faith. May my life and the testimony I leave be a comfort and an example for generations to come. Amen.

Respond to His Call: Take a moment today to reflect on your relationship with your grandparents. What lessons did they teach you? Can you feel God's love through their love?

Lucy H. Johnson

Growing Up

> In those days Mary arose and went with haste into the hill country, to a city of Judah, and she entered the house of Zechariah and greeted Elizabeth. Luke 1:39

When the angel tells Mary that she will conceive by the Holy Spirit, Mary agrees, issuing the fiat that upended the universe. The next thing we read in Luke's account is that Mary has set out to see her cousin Elizabeth, who in her old age is pregnant with the Baptist.

Whenever I read this passage, I'm struck by one thing: where is St. Anne, Mary's mother, in all this? Did Mary tell her about her pregnancy? Or did she hurry off to see Elizabeth first? And when Mary returned three months later, clearly pregnant, how did St. Anne feel? Did she wonder why her daughter ran off to her cousin, instead of letting her mother help? Did she think, "You are the darling of my soul, Mary—why didn't you come to me?"

I think Mary would have answered that question, "Because the angel didn't tell me to do that." When Mary rushes to see Elizabeth, she is doing the will of the Lord. She is, as a more modern interpreter might put it, following her destiny. She is, in other words, growing up.

Humans have their own destiny, even our children. It may not be exactly what we wanted for them; it may not be even close. This can be hard to take. "But I had such a great plan for him!" Well, okay. But it was your plan, not his. And it is his life—not yours.

We glow with pride when our adult children forge their paths in the world, but it can be so tough letting them go. Even though we know it's essential, it's still difficult. But it's part of God's plan.

Prayer: St. Anne, pray for me as I watch my children go off to school or a job far away. Help me remember that you understand what I'm going through. I know with your help I can be brave. Amen.

Respond to His Call: Pray to St. Anne. Ask her to look after your children who have left home.

Susan Vigilante

Life, Liberty, and the Pursuit of Holiness

For you did not receive the spirit of slavery to fall back into fear, but you have received the spirit of sonship. Romans 8:15

Like St. Paul, I often do not do the good I want to do, but the evil I do not want to do (Rom 7:19). At one time in my life, as I struggled in a trial of my faith, that freedom to choose a lesser good or even an evil made me question God's goodness. Why is it so hard to be good? Why do we struggle to choose God? During this period of despair, someone advised me to fall in love with God. Free will entails not just avoiding what I shouldn't do but choosing to love God and also others.

We are not slaves; scripture tells us that slavery is not the reason God made us. Love's choice is freely made. Our Savior tells us, "The thief comes only to steal and kill and destroy; I came that they might have life, and have it abundantly" (Jn 10:10). He came to give us life, and with life, liberty to choose right over wrong, love over hate. We have the freedom to accept or reject the graces the Father wishes to bestow on us.

Christ within us and our free will call us to say yes to the pursuit of holiness and eternal life. Let us send our praise to God for the freedoms He has granted us. Ask Him for the grace to always give Him our yes. Pray also for all those who are not blessed with the freedoms we have in our nation. Ask our risen Lord, who has broken the chains of sin and death, to lead all of humanity to love one another, as our Father freely loves us.

Prayer: O Lord, like St. Paul, my choice to love is weak; I do not do the good I want. Increase my strength of will toward Your path of love and mercy. Send Your love through me to others, that I may be Your loving disciple from now until life eternal. Amen.

Respond to His Call: Volunteer at your parish office, offering to spend a day on tasks your parish needs completing. Consider doing this more than once.

Angela Koenig

Martha the Believer

Martha said to Jesus, "Lord, if you had been here, my brother would not have died. And even now I know that whatever you ask from God, God will give you." John 11:21–22

Sometime after the dinner in Bethany—the visit when Jesus tells Martha she is "anxious and worried about many things," her brother Lazarus falls ill and dies. Martha and her sister Mary send for Jesus to heal him. But Jesus doesn't come. He knows His friend Lazarus is sick and dying, yet He doesn't heal him, as they know He can. How do you think that makes Martha feel? Her friend—the one who had eaten at her table—had abandoned her family in their time of need. And yet, Martha does not dwell on the fact that Jesus did not come when she sent for Him.

Sometime between the dinner party and Lazarus's illness, Martha has changed. Perhaps she took the words of Jesus into her heart, pondered them, and put into practice "the better part" as He had instructed. Martha went out to meet Jesus on the road as He came to Bethany and conveyed her trust in Him. "If you had been here, my brother would not have died," she says in greeting, "and even now I know that whatever you ask from God, God will give you." Astonishingly, she professes her faith: "Yes, Lord; I believe that you are the Christ, the Son of God, he who is coming into the world" (v. 27).

What a transformation! Martha proclaims that Jesus is the Son of God, even after He has seemingly let her brother Lazarus die. If Martha can change so dramatically, so can we. There will be days when we are worried and anxious, when the demands of life seem to leave us little time to sit at the feet of Jesus. Instead of asking, "Where were you when I needed you?" let us trust like Martha and say, "Yes, Lord; I believe."

Prayer: Lord, let my prayers of doubt be transformed into words that speak to who You truly are. May I, like St. Martha, proclaim with confidence, I have come to believe You are the Son of God! Amen.

Respond to His Call: Recall a miracle Jesus provided in your own life. Share that miracle with someone who does not know about it.

Stephanie Landsem

What's Your Perfume?

Now when the turn came for each maiden to go in to King Aha-
suerus, after being twelve months under the regulations for the
women, since this was the regular period of their beautifying, six
months with oil of myrrh and six months with spices and oint-
ments for women . . . Esther 2:12

My friend's son had some medical conditions that required a special diet.
When our kids were young, she spent lots of time researching farms in
our area where she could buy the most wholesome foods for her son.
Then she would get up early each morning to cook every meal and every
snack for him. Sometimes we would get our kids together for playdates,
and as she greeted me with a hug, she would say, "I'm sorry I smell like
food, but I could never spray enough perfume over me to cover the
smell." We would laugh about that!

When I started reading the book of Esther, I realized there was spiritual wisdom in what my friend said. When Esther was chosen to be
part of the king's harem, she and the other girls had to go through a
lengthy beautification process mandated by the culture of the time. For
six months the young women used oil of myrrh, which comes from the
Hebrew word for "bitterness." As I reflected on this passage, I thought of
the times bitterness can creep into our lives. We could all benefit from
a purification process when things don't go our way, when our prayers
are not answered as we thought best, when we face disappointments in
relationships, unforgiveness, or illness. We each have a choice to make: we
can become bitter, or we can be purified by surrendering all to the Lord
and trusting Him. Only then will we be ready for the beautiful fragrance
God has for us: "For we are the aroma of Christ to God among those
who are being saved and among those who are perishing" (2 Cor 2:15).

Prayer: Lord, take away any bitterness that has crept into my heart. Replace
it with Your sweet-smelling aroma, so that I can lead others to You. Amen.

Respond to His Call: Take some time to reflect on any areas of your life
where bitterness may have creeped in, and give them to your heavenly
Father to purify.

Dianne Davis

10:30ish

No greater joy can I have than this, to hear that my children follow the truth. 3 John 1:4

It was 10:30ish at night. My phone rang, and when I answered, I heard my mother's voice say, "Happy birthday! I almost forgot." Stunned, and with a little laugh, I replied, "It's not my birthday."

"Well, of course it is," she replied. "I was there; I ought to know."

Laughing harder now, I said, "Mom, my birthday is August 31."

"Well, I know that. That's why I'm calling." Now *she* was giggling, convinced I'd forgotten my birthday.

"But it's not August!"

We were both laughing hysterically now. She said, "It is too. I'm looking at my calendar right now."

"You must be looking at the wrong month!"

"No, I'm not," she said (but I could hear pages turning). In her calendar, the last few days of July were on the August page. When she turned the page, seeing August and the 31st, my birthday jumped to her mind.

Finally, as our laughter subsided, she said, "Oh well, then . . . I'm early." Somehow this got us both laughing again.

Many holy people talk about laughter. Padre Pio said, "Serve the Lord with laughter." Mother Angelica advised, "Try to laugh a lot, because life is funny, and everybody today is too serious." St. Thomas Aquinas said, "It is requisite for the human mind that we make use, from time to time, of playful deeds and jokes." The crazy phone call with my mom is one of my favorite birthday greetings. My absentmindedness seems to have been a gift from her. Do you know what else she gave me? Her laugh, not just on that night at 10:30ish, but for my whole life. And it is a great gift.

Prayer: Help me be grounded in You, Lord, for there are good times and times of trial in my life. With joy, let me always give thanks to You for everything. Amen.

Respond to His Call: When's the last time you laughed with a friend? Call that friend and relive that moment, telling them how they bring the joy of the Lord into your life.

Alyssa Bormes

Just the Way I Am

You have been going about this mountain country long enough; turn northward. Deuteronomy 2:3

I have crazy curly hair. When it's humid, it gets bigger. As it gets longer, at some point it quits growing south and changes to east/west. I spent a good portion of my younger years trying *not* to have curly hair. I came of age at a time when feathered hair was the rage. Think Farrah Fawcett. You can imagine the torture as I tried to achieve this look by straightening my hair. Many people didn't know what I "really" looked like.

One friend with straw-straight hair was horrified when she learned about my efforts to change my hair. She suggested that it was at least a venial sin to maim myself that way. One morning I was running late for Mass and didn't have time for my usual process. I called my friend to see if she was going. When she asked why, I told her I would be there with my hair as God gave it to me. She beat me to church!

Now that I am, well, older, I have come to appreciate what used to seem such a tragedy. My hair has thinned a bit, but it doesn't seem to be the problem that it is for other "mature" women. It's my own little game of rock-paper-scissors. Curly covers thin. You might say that I have come to be thankful for a gift I didn't realize I had.

Have you ever spent your time trying to be more like someone else and less like yourself? Looking at that weed-free garden over at the neighbor's house? Or the perfect life of that Facebook "friend"?

Prayer: Jesus, help me find a gift in all circumstances. Make my words a blessing to those around me. Amen.

Respond to His Call: Contact a friend who is struggling and tell them something you admire about them.

Teresa McCarthy

Do Whatever He Tells You

And Jesus said to her, "O woman, what have you to do with me? My hour has not yet come." His mother said to the servants, "Do whatever he tells you." John 2:4–5

The mother of Jesus says to the servants at the wedding feast at Cana, "Do whatever he tells you." And she has said those same words up and down the ages to every one of us who believes her Son is true God and true man.

Of course, what Jesus tells us to do can be found in scripture. But we can also hear Jesus speak to our hearts through the power of the Holy Spirit dwelling within us. St. Ignatius offers a beautiful way to discern what God wills for us in specific situations. There are some wonderful online resources to help you with the steps of discernment using the Ignatian method. Discernment retreats are offered, as well.

Sometimes Jesus tells us what to do through the voice of a loved one or maybe even a stranger. Jesus may also tell us what to do while we're reading something other than the Bible. God can speak to us through all of His creation. The crucial thing we must do is pay attention. Many of us are distracted by our thoughts or by the cacophony that is our modern world, and we miss His messages.

The Blessed Mother is our model for doing whatever He tells us. Mary displays responsiveness to the Holy Spirit through her humility. Humility enables us to be receptive to what God wants to do through us. It will be God's work, and it will be for His glory. But we have the honor of participating in whatever it is that He wants accomplished. That's why we must pray before we do anything. Pray for wisdom, pray for the ability to discern God's will, and then listen. Watch what happens and be amazed!

Prayer: Jesus, we expect an answer when we ask for Your divine assistance! Help us to hear and to respond in ways that are pleasing to You. Amen.

Respond to His Call: Pray with certainty that Jesus will respond to you, just as the Blessed Mother displays in her directive to the wedding servants. Be ready to "do whatever He tells you."

Lynda MacFarland

Jesus Meets Us

Thomas answered him, "My Lord and my God!" Jesus said to him, "You have believed because you have seen me. Blessed are those who have not seen and yet believe." John 20:28–29

Jesus meets us where we are—physically, mentally, spiritually. He longs for each of us to recognize Him and say, as St. Thomas did in the Upper Room, "My Lord and my God!" Through this bold and straightforward proclamation, we open our hearts to Christ and, through the power of the Holy Spirit, participate in the eternal life of the Triune God. This participation in the life of Christ is the good news proclaimed by John the Evangelizer in the book of Revelation (1:9), which we continue to proclaim as Christians and Women In the New Evangelization.

But, how do we gain eyes to see and hearts to recognize the risen Lord? The circumstances of individual conversion vary greatly. Some come to know the Lord through the gift of faith; others are drawn to Christ through personal testimony, the words of sacred scripture, or observance of signs and wonders. Jesus meets us where we are, whether through a tangible personal encounter, like that of Thomas, or an experience felt deep within the heart. No matter what the means, we come to know Christ through the unmerited gift of grace. Through grace we are saved, and through grace we grow in holiness and intimacy with Christ.

Jesus came that we may know the boundless love and mercy of His Father. He continues to inspire, heal, forgive, and call each of us into a deeper relationship. Thank you, Jesus, for your self-sacrificial love, and for your Passion, Death, and Resurrection. Thank you, Jesus, for meeting us where we are and giving us visible signs and quiet movements of the heart that inspire us to say, "My Lord and my God!" Jesus, I trust in You.

Prayer: Lord, come to me, here, where I am. Open wide before me the floodgates of Your tender mercy. Amen.

Respond to His Call: Today, seek Jesus in your everyday moments.

Karen Schwaner Sheehy

The Rosary in Real Life

Jesus took with him Peter and James and John his brother, and led them up a high mountain apart. And he was transfigured before them, and his face shone like the sun, and his garments became white as light. Matthew 17:1–2

The mysteries of the Rosary have intentions built in. For example, I pray for the sanctity of marriage while meditating on the Wedding at Cana. I pray for expectant mothers, newborn babies, and an end to abortion while contemplating the Nativity. I pray for all of us to know and accept God's will while reflecting on the annunciation.

In the past, when I thought about the Transfiguration, I focused on Moses and Elijah and Jesus, revealing God's divine nature. Moses represents the Law, Elijah the prophets, and Jesus the fulfillment of both. Now when I meditate on this mystery, I think about the apostles that accompanied Jesus: Peter, James, and John. These three men formed Jesus' inner circle of confidants. They were also the ones Jesus chose to accompany Him to the house of Jairus (Mk 5:37) and the Garden of Gethsemane (Mt 26:37). Why were they chosen? James and John were brothers, and Peter had a brother, Andrew. These four men were fishermen and good friends. So what about poor Andrew? Did he feel slighted when Jesus took the other three with Him on these special occasions?

A priest once said in a homily that he thought of Andrew as the sort of stable individual that Jesus could trust to keep the rest of the group together when Peter, James, and John were gone. Andrew served wherever needed and didn't envy his brother and friends.

Thinking about how the disciples responded to Jesus makes the lessons held within each mystery of the Rosary more concrete and applicable to my life. I hope to imitate the apostles and learn to love the Lord with my whole heart, mind, and soul.

Prayer: It is good, Lord, that You are here with me. Guide my heart to love, in imitation of You. Amen.

Respond to His Call: Today, pray the Rosary for your WINE group. If you don't have one, pray about starting one.

Lucy H. Johnson

What in Your Life Needs Pruning?

For there shall be a sowing of peace; the vine shall yield its fruit . . . and I will cause the remnant of this people to possess all these things. Zechariah 8:12

In the dead of winter, my husband pruned the fifty-three vines in our vineyard. I watched through the kitchen window as Troy chopped, cut, and made a gnarled mess of grapevines, and I reflected on the spiritual significance of what his labor of love brought to mind. His aggressive pruning was a vision set before me of what God, the gardener and keeper of my soul, desires to do to me—prune the vines in my life.

When Troy prunes the vines, he cuts off not only diseased branches but some perfectly healthy branches as well. Why cut the healthy ones? Too many branches growing on the vine prevents optimal sunlight from hitting the budding grapes, thereby yielding a smaller harvest. The vine's energy is also divided among all the healthy branches, resulting in less energy being available to each.

Everyone's soul has healthy and unhealthy branches that need pruning in order to produce abundant godly fruit. A diseased branch might be an unhealthy relationship or an attachment that pulls you away from God rather than inspiring a godly life. What about those healthy branches that may be removed? Healthy branches are the good activities and relationships that pull away energy you could otherwise invest in developing your interior life and relationship with God.

If Troy had not pruned our vineyard last winter, our crop of grapes would be small this upcoming summer. Proper pruning during a particular window of time determines the outcome of fruit. God knows when your branches need pruning. Don't miss the abundance of fruit that He yearns to give!

Prayer: Lord, open my heart to recognize which branches in my life need pruning. Amen.

Respond to His Call: Make a list of the healthy and unhealthy branches in your life that can be pruned, either a little or completely, to help you produce better fruit.

Kathleen Billings

Superhero

Ever since the creation of the world his invisible nature, namely, his eternal power and deity, has been clearly perceived in the things that have been made. Romans 1:20

Benjamin was a quiet boy who always chose a seat in the back of class. He was good, sociable, and compliant—sort of. I could see the top of the comic books hidden inside his textbook during my scripture classes. The inspiration came as I prepared a lesson on the Transfiguration. There it was right in front of me. The making of a superhero!

I began the next class with Superman: His father was from another world. He lived at home until the age of thirty and then went out, not revealing his superpowers to those around him, and saved the world. I asked the class, "Does this remind you of anyone in scripture?" Benjamin closed his book and sat forward. I went on.

Peter Parker was a weakling nerd who was given superpowers when a spider bit him. He had a new identity. He became a new man. Hiding his true identity from his friends, he too went out to save the forsaken. I asked, How do we receive a new identity? Benjamin's eyes lit up at the prospect of receiving Confirmation.

I continued. Thor loved the people of earth because his father did. But Loki, his brother, was jealous and went to destroy the earthlings. Fueled by his love for his father, Thor helped the earthlings fight back.

When we discussed our favorite movies, student after student readily pointed to the symbols of Christ coming out in the stories. The class was hooked! I watched gratefully as Bible stories came alive for them. Scripture suddenly made sense to them. Amazing. Humanity celebrates salvation history! I could not help but notice that Benjamin was first in line when I asked if anyone wanted to go to the Sacrament of Reconciliation.

Prayer: O Lord, help me to know myself as You know me. Remind me of the new identity you have given me through Christ. Amen.

Respond to His Call: Give the Lord permission to let you see yourself through His eyes. The result will amaze you.

Lynne Keating

Stepping Forward with Humble Faith

The people who walked in darkness have seen a great light; those who dwelt in a land of deep darkness, on them has light shined.
Isaiah 9:2

I left for college for a degree in literature, hoping to study in London and visit the homes of literary giants. My dreams were short-lived. England was not for me. The farmlands of home seemed a world away, and I wept, a lonely freshman missing my family. This is why the story of James and John following Jesus strikes me.

The brothers were mending nets with their father when they heard Jesus' call. They left without hesitation to follow Him. That detail catches my attention. Scripture never tells us that the brothers longed for home. Maybe there is more to this story of the disciples. Perhaps life on the sea wasn't everything James and John had envisioned. Did their hearts long for more? Had they passed opportunities to pursue holiness elsewhere? No matter why, their yes is a lesson of humble faith.

It can be tempting to stay in the familiarity of relationships, careers, or situations that have grown comfortable. It takes courage to step into the unfamiliar light of Jesus' invitation. Change can be terrifying! However, in Christ, we needn't fear.

I have grown in many ways since that fateful voyage to England. Now when times appear dark or change comes my way, I picture Jesus before me, tenderly stretching out His hand and saying, "Follow me." And I find comfort in the words of Isaiah—for I know the love of God is lighting the path to my heavenly home. I just need to follow without hesitation.

Prayer: Lord, may my heart be filled with faith and courage as I take whatever steps You ask of me today with great trust. Amen.

Respond to His Call: How is Jesus calling you to follow Him today? What do you need to leave behind to pursue His love and mercy more deeply?

Katie Anderson

The Tablet of Your Heart

You yourselves are our letter of recommendation, written on your hearts, to be known and read by all men; and you show that you are a letter from Christ delivered by us, written not with ink but with the Spirit of the living God, not on tablets of stone but on tablets of human hearts. 2 Corinthians 3:2–3

You play such a beautiful role in this world. Your very existence signifies just how wanted you are. The Father doesn't make mistakes; He creates saints. Every one of us is called to sainthood, that remarkable moment when the veil is lifted and we see our Lover face-to-face. Until that sweet moment of divine judgment, we have work to do.

St. Paul tells us in his second letter to the Corinthians, "You are a letter from Christ delivered by us, written . . . on tablets of human hearts." As beloved daughters of the Almighty, we are called to use the gifts of our feminine nature to be love letters to the world. Our God has such a romantic heart! That same heart is filled with a tenderness that we cannot fully comprehend, and in His generosity He has passed that gift on to us.

It is not always an easy task to love as we should, selflessly, without counting costs, but it is a greatness we are called to. By God's grace alone can the ink of Love's humility permeate our souls and be visible to all men.

Let us pray for the grace to surrender ourselves to the will of the Father, to allow Him to fill the tablets of our hearts with the image of His beautiful face—a face radiating compassion, attentiveness, and the Spirit of the living God.

Prayer: Holy Spirit, come and rest in my heart. Fill it with Your divine words, that all my actions today may be a worthy part of Your love letter to the world. Amen.

Respond to His Call: Share the Spirit's love by sending an encouraging message to anyone the Father puts on your heart today.

Angela Koenig

Only Say the Word

But the centurion answered him, "Lord, I am not worthy to have you come under my roof; but only say the word, and my servant will be healed." Matthew 8:8

Those of us who grew up in Minnesota know two seasons: road construction and hockey. As a child, I spent many hours at my brother's hockey games, standing frozen-toed in ice rinks and cringing at the fumes wafting from the hockey bag on the ride home. One weekend, my friend Molly and I were dragged to her brother's hockey tournament. This meant Mass in a different church. As Molly and I sat next to her mom in church, we got to the part in the Mass where the congregation responds, "Only say the word, and I shall be healed." I looked at Molly and whispered, "What is the word?"

Molly looked at me and seriously pondered the question. She said, "I don't know." She elbowed her mom and said, "Mom, what is the word?"

With her eyebrows crinkled, Molly's mom looked down at her and said, "What are you talking about?"

"You know. The word! 'Only say the word, and I shall be healed.' What is the word?" Molly said.

Molly's mom looked at us for a moment and with a straight face answered, "Shazam."

We thought about it for a while before we realized she was joking. What naive twelve-year-olds we were, believing that our salvation rested on the recital of just one word! But looking back, I realize we weren't too far from the truth when we posed our innocent question, "What is the word?" Christ tells us that we must accept the kingdom of God like a child, and there is but one word that leads us to salvation, and that Word has been since the beginning, and "the Word was with God, and the Word was God" (Jn 1:1).

Prayer: Lord, help me have a childlike faith, always seeking, always asking questions that help me know and love You more. Amen.

Respond to His Call: Today, using reliable Catholic resources, take time to research a question you have about the faith.

Kelly M. Wahlquist

The Power of Grace

For the sake of Christ, then, I am content with weaknesses, insults, hardships, persecutions, and calamities; for when I am weak, then I am strong. 2 Corinthians 12:10

As a mother, I make a lot of mistakes. I consider that a fair and accurate evaluation—one that keeps me humble, honest, and always trying to improve. Most of all, it makes me reliant on the grace of God! The truth is, I can say the same thing about many aspects of my life, including my spiritual growth. I experienced a period of feeling inadequate in my faith, and instead of choosing to do the work needed to go deeper, I decided not to include the Catholic faith in my life. I made excuses about why I wasn't attending Mass regularly and was avoiding Confession, even why I'd given up on praying.

Just as I have accepted my limitations as a mother, sought guidance, and educated myself on how to improve, I've taken steps to get back on track spiritually as well. There are so many fantastic options to help us grow in faith. First and foremost, I can turn to God, for He has no limitations. Humbling myself before Him, I open my heart to receive the abundant graces to fill where I lack, especially in knowledge and understanding of Him and His Church. St. Paul explains the beautiful power of grace in his second letter to the Corinthians: "But he said to me, 'My grace is sufficient for you, for my power is made perfect in weakness.' I will all the more gladly boast of my weaknesses, that the power of Christ may rest upon me" (12:9).

With grace, every weakness in my life genuinely becomes my strength. When I set aside my pride and joyfully leave behind all the excuses, I can seek to learn all God desires to teach me.

Prayer: Lord, humbling myself before You, I come as a grace beggar. Please take pity and fill me with Your Holy Spirit. In every circumstance, I believe Your grace will be sufficient for me. Amen.

Respond to His Call: Write down three ways you will grow in faith this year.

Allison Gingras

Of All the Ways to Waste Time . . .

Fine speech is not becoming to a fool; still less is false speech to a prince. Proverbs 17:7

Anybody grow up watching *All in the Family*? It's okay, you can admit it. You're among friends. There's a wonderful episode in season 2 where Archie Bunker encounters his first Catholic priest, brilliantly played by Barnard Hughes. Archie's wife, Edith, has accidentally damaged the priest's car, and she left him a note saying that she wants to pay for the damage. Archie, who is convinced the Catholic Church owns half the real estate in New York and "has more money than God," is not thrilled about this. He gets into a shouting match with the priest and the priest gives up, quoting the passage from Proverbs above. A bewildered Archie asks, "What's that mean?" The priest snaps, "It means don't waste your time arguing with an idiot."

That may not be the most charitable interpretation of the passage, but it is definitely the clearest. I think of it every time I see people getting into arguments online or in the comments section of the newspapers. You see everything from name-calling to death threats these days. More and more, you see people at their worst.

Most of these people are not "idiots," as Archie's priest friend put it. Most of them are pretty much like you and me. But they get carried away in the moment, and they type fast. I wonder how many of them regret their outbursts later. I know I certainly have regretted mine!

How much time and energy are wasted in useless online arguments these days? Is this really what God had in mind when He gave us the gift of the intellect?

Prayer: Lord, help me stay out of foolish arguments this week. Help me remember why You gave us the gift of the intellect—not to win petty victories but to glorify You. Amen.

Respond to His Call: Pray for the angry people you encounter online.

Susan Vigilante

Out of Wine?

When the wine failed, the mother of Jesus said to him, "They have no wine." John 2:3

When I was eleven years old, my parents sent me to a summer horse-back-riding camp in the mountains of North Carolina for four weeks. Upon arrival, I learned that all of the girls in my cabin already knew each other and had brought their horses, plus trunks filled with designer clothing and English riding gear. Not only did I not have a horse but also my no-name jeans and Le Tigre polo shirts from Kmart—which my mother assured me were just as good as Izod polo shirts—were enough to quickly brand me as the nerdy outsider. Sadly, in true mean-girl fashion, some of the girls embarrassed me, leaving me longing for home.

It isn't difficult for me to imagine the embarrassment of the groom and his family at the wedding feast of Cana when they realized they were running out of wine. In the ancient Jewish custom, the groom's family hosted the reception in their home. Running out of wine would have negative social repercussions that would last for years. So Mary quietly takes the matter to Jesus before any of the guests notice, trusting that He can remedy the problem.

In some ways, it seems like a small matter to prompt Jesus' first public miracle and pave the first step on His road to Calvary. But the Holy Spirit is conveying an important message here: our smallest needs—the details of our daily lives—matter to God. They matter to Mary, too.

Where have you run out of wine? Are there old painful memories or current concerns—especially regarding humiliation—that seem too small to take to Jesus? He understands, and He longs to console your trembling heart. Let's humbly bring our poverty to the Lord, asking Him, through Mary's intercession, to work miracles of healing and transformation in us.

Prayer: O Jesus, like the water turned to wine, may You glorify our wounds so that they might become a source of blessing to others. Amen.

Respond to His Call: Bring a past hurt or embarrassment to the Lord, asking for healing, regardless of how insignificant you considered the situation.

Kitty Cleveland

Surrendering Our Burdens

Take my yoke upon you, and learn from me; for I am gentle and lowly in heart, and you will find rest for your souls. For my yoke is easy, and my burden is light. Matthew 11:29–30

Sometimes life can feel like an uphill battle on a steep mountain. Are you trying to climb but running out of steam? Do your burdens seem too heavy to carry any further?

On our own, we won't be able to make it over to the other side of the mountains in life, but God is our power and strength. He is with us in our battles and never abandons us. While we can't see what is on the other side, He knows what is ahead and promises to make all things work together for good.

In our human nature, we often want to know every little detail about what the future holds, but God asks us to trust. We need to believe with eyes of faith that whatever He has planned on the other side of our trials is more glorious and beautiful than we can imagine.

Our desire to know everything can become burdensome and even lead to sin and despair. In the garden, the enemy tempted Eve not to trust in the goodness of our Father. We need to be careful in moments of trial and remember we have a good Father who wants us to be happy. He doesn't want us to grow weary and distrustful. He will lighten the burdens of life.

Let us unite our will with His and learn to enjoy the moment. Remember that with every battle won, our faith becomes stronger. Let us not give up but, with eyes of faith and a heart full of hope and love, trust that the best is yet to come. It will be so much sweeter and lighter than we ever thought it could be.

Prayer: Jesus, I surrender my present burdens to You and trust that You have amazing plans for my life. Please strengthen me through this difficult time and help me to know and do Your will. Amen.

Respond to His Call: Ask the Holy Spirit to reveal what burden is holding you down or back today and choose to give it to Jesus.

Joelle Maryn

To Amaze Jesus

When Jesus heard him, he marveled, and said . . . "Truly, I say to you, not even in Israel have I found such faith." Matthew 8:10

The centurion in Matthew's gospel comes to Jesus with a problem. His servant is ill and suffering greatly. When Jesus offers to come with him to cure the servant, the centurion responds humbly with words we repeat at every Mass: "I am not worthy to have you come under my roof" (Mt 8:8). Although the words are so familiar, I hadn't reflected on them until I noticed Jesus' reaction to the centurion. Jesus "marveled." The Greek word for marvel (*thauma*) also translates as "amazement."

Can you imagine what it must be like to amaze Jesus? The centurion, although a Gentile and an officer in the enemy army, amazed Jesus with his great faith. I think the centurion models for us how to approach Jesus. He humbly petitions Him, and then has full faith and confidence that Christ will respond to his need in the way that Jesus knows is best.

How often do we approach Jesus in prayer with both a problem and a solution? We tell Jesus what we think should happen to resolve the situation. But a faithful, humble servant will present a situation to Jesus and then remain open to His will, His solution. That's exactly what the centurion does; that kind of faith amazes Jesus.

At Mass, before we receive Jesus under our own "roof," we repeat the centurion's beautiful words. In those moments before we receive Communion we stand face-to-face with God, as the centurion did. We, too, have an opportunity to place our petitions before Him and await His answer to our needs. We also have the opportunity to pray, "Just say the word, Jesus." To possess unshakable faith in Christ's ability to address all of our needs can have amazing results—it can amaze God!

Prayer: Jesus, I desire to amaze You. Give me an unshakable faith, the kind of faith the centurion had, which rests in total confidence in Your holy will. Amen.

Respond to His Call: Think of an intention that weighs deeply on your heart. In prayer, give that intention to our Lord to take care of in whatever way He sees fit. Then rest in His care for you.

Katie Warner

The Assumption

But Mary kept all these things, pondering them in her heart. Luke 2:19

Sometimes I ponder in my heart what it was like for Mary to ponder "all these things" in her heart. What a rich life she had, even though it was hidden from the eyes of the world.

Today we celebrate Mary being lifted body and soul to heaven. When I reflect on the assumption, I imagine Mary uttering another fiat. Her earthly life had ended; she was to be taken to paradise to see Jesus. Imagine the yes in her heart on that day! Mary's heart, which had been pierced so often by sorrow, was full of trust, as it had been her whole life. Now she would take that wounded heart to her Son, who makes all things new. The seven wounds of Mary would become settings for the jewels of love.

Mary must have pondered all that had brought her to this point. She was a faithful Jewish girl visited by an angel, who told her that she was chosen to bear the Redeemer. The vision of the annunciation must have been as vivid at the assumption as it was on that first day.

The same must have been true of the other joyful events of Mary's life: the Visitation, the Nativity, and the Presentation. Surely she reflected on the joys the Christ child had brought her. Perhaps she pondered anew the sorrows as well—the piercing sadness that Simeon foretold, the flight to Egypt, the loss of the Child Jesus in the Temple, the encounter with her Son as He carried the Cross, His Crucifixion, her embrace of His lifeless body taken down from the Cross, and His burial.

At the assumption, Mary could look back at that young woman who faithfully trusted God's Word to her, in joy and in sorrow. She was the first to receive the Christ, holding Him in her womb and then in her arms. Now she would receive what we all hope to receive—the ability to gaze on Jesus for eternity.

Prayer: Hail Mary, assumed body and soul into heaven, pray for me, who has recourse to thee. Amen.

Respond to His Call: Meditate for a few moments on the joy of spending eternity with Jesus.

Alyssa Bormes

Called to Rebuild

But many . . . , old men who had seen the first house, wept with a loud voice when they saw the foundation of this house being laid, though many shouted aloud for joy. Ezra 3:12–13

Rebuilding is joyful, but it can also be sorrowful. The book of Ezra is about rebuilding the house of the Lord in Jerusalem. As they lay the foundation, the priests rejoice, blowing trumpets and singing praise to the Lord for His steadfast love. The anticipation is palpable, and excitement fills the crowd. At the same time, the older men, who had been there when the foundation of the old Temple was laid, weep. They feel such sorrow in what was lost. The joy and weeping intertwine in an emotional mix.

As I prayed these verses, I was in a time of total rebuilding. We had moved multiple times. I had left my job of ten years and transitioned into being a mom of two while starting new ministries. These changes deserved celebration and brought blessings, potential, and fruitfulness. Rebuilding can force us to let His will be done and see our purpose as His purpose. However, sometimes we focus on the joy and excitement of imminent changes to the point that we lose touch with the sorrow we may also be experiencing in a time of change. We need to acknowledge that there are losses we mourn. Growth may require re-laying some of our foundations, which is hard work and involves leaving certain things behind. Recognizing these heartaches can lead to a deeper union and authenticity with God. It does not undermine our relationship.

We are dynamic beings; we can experience joy and sorrow simultaneously. The struggle means not that we are failing but that we are experiencing the sanctifying process of surrendering more of ourselves to God.

Prayer: Lord, I surrender to You the heartache I long to bury, knowing You are beside and within me, rebuilding. I know the result will be worth it. Glorified and exalted, my "sorrow will turn into joy" (Jn 16:20). Amen.

Respond to His Call: Reflect on where you are being called to rebuild. Plan a way to celebrate the newness arising and to mourn the losses.

Katie Lee Taylor

Responding to His Call

Harden not your hearts, as at Meribah, as on the day at Massah in the wilderness. Psalm 95:8

Remember when the doors to our churches closed? I attended the last public Mass before my parish closed on March 16, 2020, due to COVID-19. Devastated to be kept from Mass and the Eucharist, I turned to the Liturgy of the Hours and was drawn to Psalm 95 and the antiphon taken from that same passage: "Today, when you hear his voice, do not harden your hearts." The verse reverberated through my mind, like the repetitive ticking of a clock.

Convinced the Lord was calling me to action, I questioned how I could minister to others while sequestered at home. As I prayed for discernment, an idea took hold. I opened my cell phone, hit video, and started to talk about God's mercy and my trust in the Lord to keep us safe.

More than one thousand people viewed that first message on Facebook. The following morning, I made another video and continued posting videos of encouragement each day for three and a half months. When so many were isolated and alone, the videos were a way to bring us together, and almost immediately, a virtual community formed to pray for our country, our medical personnel, and especially the sick and dying. People left prayer intentions in the comments and often messaged me, saying they were comforted by the videos and grateful for the prayers.

Knowing so many folks—most of whom I had never met—were praying for the good of all bolstered my spirits and gave purpose to that time of isolation. I had heard the Lord's voice, and in the midst of a pandemic, He revealed how the smallest response to His prompting, even short videos, can shed light in the dark and lonely places of the world.

Prayer: Lord, allow me to hear Your voice, discern what You are asking of me, and respond in faith to do Your holy will. Jesus, I trust in You. Amen.

Respond to His Call: If there is something the Lord is asking you to do, step out in faith, and be assured that not only will your response bless others but God will bless you as well.

Debby Giusti

Mommy Metaphors for God's Love

As one whom his mother comforts, so I will comfort you; you shall be comforted in Jerusalem. Isaiah 66:13

When I explain my spirituality to other people, I tend to use mommy metaphors. It makes perfect sense that my vocation as a mother is the lens through which I understand God's presence and action.

For instance, I have learned to trust in our Lord's tender and faithful affection for me. He never stops wooing my soul, calling softly to me and reminding me of His presence. This brings to mind reading to my daughter when she was tiny. We started with board books and picture books, and I held her snugly on my lap and cuddled her while I read. My voice was gentle and singsongy, and it didn't matter that she comprehended so little; she felt loved, and she learned to respond to the sound of my voice. Over time, she recognized the images and started to grasp the simple plots. Eventually, she learned to anticipate the events of the story and ask questions, to probe for deeper understanding.

God tells us the story of His love in a similar way. We don't understand most of what He is saying, but we learn to love His voice and respond to Him, moment by moment and day by day. Our prayer lives start to take hold, as we begin the most important conversation of our lives. And God is so generous that, when we make even the slightest movement toward Him, He is delighted, like a mother crouching and joyfully opening her arms wide to embrace a toddler taking her first step.

God is our loving Father, but He encompasses and expresses the maternal love that He created, giving it great dignity. We can look to the scriptures to see these consoling images of God's "maternal" love.

Prayer: Loving Father, may I hear deep in my soul the story of my life You have written there. May I respond with trust to the gentle love You shower on me. Amen.

Respond to His Call: Today, make a conscious effort to respond with great love to God's movement in your life.

Lisa Mladinich

What Do You Want Me to Do for You?

And Jesus said to him, "What do you want me to do for you?"
And the blind man said to him, "Master, let me receive my sight."
Mark 10:51

As Jesus is leaving Jericho with his disciples, a blind beggar on the side of the road named Bartimaeus calls out to Jesus to have mercy on him. Jesus summons Bartimaeus, who immediately throws aside his cloak, jumps up, and goes to Jesus. When Jesus asks, "What do you want me to do for you?" Bartimaeus responds that he wants to see again.

Bartimaeus had learned from the crowd that it was Jesus walking along the road. Had he heard of Jesus and did he know Jesus could heal him? Why did Bartimaeus so readily discard his cloak, which may have been his one and only possession? By throwing it aside, he was testifying to his trust that Jesus would provide everything he needed, as long as he followed our Lord and Savior. By telling Jesus that he wanted to see, he was acknowledging not only his physical blindness but also his spiritual blindness. He wanted to be a follower of Christ.

Do you want to be healed of your spiritual blindness?

Two days after being diagnosed with breast cancer, I was sitting in church when Jesus literally shined down light upon women who had gone through breast cancer before me. It opened my eyes to the mercy of Jesus, who was giving me other women to reach out to on my journey.

What is holding you back from following Christ? What are you blind to? What obstacles are preventing you from believing that God has great plans for you? Let His love break through those barriers, and run to Jesus. He is waiting with open arms to hold you tight and ask you, "What do you want me to do for you?"

Prayer: Dear Jesus, please help me to see what is keeping me from following You. Amen.

Respond to His Call: Identify an obstacle that is preventing you from running to Jesus.

Rhonda Zweber

Doing His Will

Teach me to do your will, for you are my God! Let your good spirit lead me on a level path! Psalm 143:10

Do you ever wonder what your life purpose is? Often I try to make sense of life, asking what God is calling me to do or to be. Growing up in a small town, I felt limited by narrow life experiences. I played sports, sang in the church choir, and attended retreats. Involved in our local youth group, I experienced peace and joy.

But I was restless. I moved to a bigger city to see what waited there. I waited . . . desperately missing the former peace and joy I had known. What exactly was I searching for? I drifted, not knowing that God would soon show me an opportunity to renew my sense of purpose and give me both peace and joy.

I attended several large, beautiful churches in my new city. Whatever I wanted wasn't there. I felt at home finally at a small, older church with limited ministries. Soon, with the priest's blessing and tremendous trust, I started a women's organization that focused on prayer, service, and community. Women prayed together, performed service projects, and hosted game nights for the parish. From this group, the Lord called women to create a bereavement committee and Rosary groups. Other women hosted Lenten events, back-to-school activities for the kids, and more.

Each of us has an individual spiritual journey; however, we all yearn to belong together in Christ. We are all "Drawn by Love—Sent on Fire," as expressed in the National WINE Conference theme of 2017. Our women's group became a chapter in this remarkable national apostolate.

Never wonder whether God has a plan for your life. God will show you His purpose. Allow Him to tell you what He wants you to do to bring others closer to Him.

Prayer: Lord Jesus, I want to follow You; give me the grace. Help me to discern where I can best use the gifts and talents you have given me. Amen.

Respond to His Call: Find out what ministries are in need of volunteers in your parish. Select one to try, and if it isn't a fit for you, try another.

Donna Luna Hernandez

Time Travel

He has made everything beautiful in its time; also he has put eternity into man's mind, yet so that he cannot find out what God has done from the beginning to the end. Ecclesiastes 3:11

I ask God a lot of questions. What does that scripture mean? Where are You? What do I do now? Paragraph 600 in the *Catechism of the Catholic Church* states, "To God, all moments of time are present in their immediacy." In essence, that means all time—past, present, and future—is available to God simultaneously. Okay, Lord, I know it's true. But is there proof in creation?

Over the last twenty years, science has finally begun to catch up to the truths in the Bible. Scientists have proved mathematically that there is an Intellect that created the world (God). They have also proved scientifically that we have a "trans-physical self" (soul), and that divided cells continue to affect one another even when years and miles apart (change yourself, change the world!). But back and forth in time? I don't know why I was surprised when a person I hardly know shoved a paper from an astrophysicist into my hands saying, "You'll like this."

The author, a Catholic with ten kids, published in impressive journals and newspapers. His paper asks, "How can we fix something in the past if it no longer exists?" It addresses Catholic teachings on sin, sacrifice, and Lent, referencing what astrophysicists call "space-time." Incorporating scripture and sound Catholic theological writings, he concludes that everything we have ever done is still available "somewhere."

Through the generosity of God, we can perform acts of sacrifice to fix the damage we introduced into His plan of salvation. But until we perform such acts, the damage of the past remains. His paper ends, "Thank God for Lent!" How amazing is God! He allows me to fix my past so that I can change the future. Okay, Lord, I can do that!

Prayer: Heavenly Father, help me to live in the light of eternity, ordering all my actions and choices in its clarity. Amen.

Respond to His Call: Is there something in the past, present, or future that you are finding difficult to entrust to Christ? Give it to Him today.

Lynne Keating

Let All That You Do Be Done in Love

Be watchful, stand firm in your faith, be courageous, be strong. Let all that you do be done in love. 1 Corinthians 16:13–14

When Paul was in Ephesus, he received a letter and visitors from Corinth, an important seaport in what is now southern Greece. Paul had spent eighteen months there, establishing a new Christian community. The visitors, however, had bad news for Paul. The church in Corinth had become divided between the Jewish Christians and the Gentile converts, with each group attached to a different leader. They disagreed about how to worship properly, whether to eat meat that had been sacrificed to pagan idols, which spiritual gifts were more important, and how to care for the poor. Paul responds to this dilemma with solid, practical advice and with a reminder of what's truly important—the Resurrection and the unity of the Body of Christ.

In the closing of his first letter to this nascent community, Paul warns the Corinthians to be on their guard, always looking toward the truth of the Resurrection. "Be watchful, stand firm in your faith, be courageous, be strong. Let all that you do be done in love," he wrote. He wants them to be careful of those who might try to twist their faith or instigate division among them. Vigilance, steadfastness, courage, strength, and love are the weapons with which they must arm themselves in the battle against the wiles of the devil.

St. Paul's advice to the Corinthians is good advice for us as well. We must be wary of those who misrepresent the faith and thus sow division. We must be resolute in our faith, drawing on Christ for strength and courage in temptation and trial. Above all, everything we think, say, and do must be motivated by the love of Christ.

Prayer: Jesus, I want to truly live St. Paul's advice in my own life. Bestow on me the armor of watchfulness, firmness, courage, and strength and the grace to do all that I do in love. Amen.

Respond to His Call: Resolve to do one act of love today for someone who needs to see Christ's love. Offer it as a gift of love to our Lord.

Marge Steinhage Fenelon

St. Rose of Lima

Blessed are you when men revile you and persecute you and utter all kinds of evil against you falsely on my account. Matthew 5:11

St. Rose of Lima is the patroness of gardeners and florists, embroiderers, and people who suffer from ridicule because of their faith. Four years ago, I had a barely passing knowledge of St. Rose, namely, that she was a saint from Lima, Peru. Three years ago, I started reading about her in earnest.

At that time, I often prayed a self-styled litany of saints to holy women. I came to think of them as my friends. These women surrounded me and lifted me in prayer as I was going through a difficult period, both personally and professionally. The experience taught me a great lesson: the saints are regular people like you and me. Oh sure, we might get caught up in their martyrdom or exemplary piety and feel we could never emulate them, but really, we're made for this holiness, too. Like them, we are called by Christ. And through their example, we can learn how to better answer the call.

St. Rose fascinated me because of her fortitude in the face of her parents' desire to marry her to a wealthy suitor. She had already given her life to Christ and so rejected marriage offers. Her parents denied her when she asked to become a nun. Her father, frustrated with Rose's decision to pursue a life of chastity, finally let her have a room to herself and allowed her to join the Third Order of St. Dominic. She spent her life in prayer, fasting, and caring for the sick in her community.

I've learned a great deal about fortitude through St. Rose. She is my friend in heaven, and I am her friend on earth. This is the beauty of the Communion of Saints. Though Rose is no longer here on earth, we are still together.

Prayer: St. Rose of Lima, pray for me for an increase in the virtue of fortitude. Amen.

Respond to His Call: Recall times when you have responded to the grace of fortitude in your life. Whisper aloud your thanksgiving to Jesus during your prayers today.

Maria Morera Johnson

Sunset Moment

But immediately he spoke to them, saying, "Take heart, it is I; have no fear." Matthew 14:27

The days blur together. At the end of a long week, emotions well up within me as questions still arise. I move slowly to the kitchen sink to do the dishes. My daughter runs into the house, enthusiastically inviting me to step outside and observe the sunset. A negative thought pops into my mind: *If I've seen one sunset, I've seen them all.* I know this is untrue, but I am emotionally fatigued, and discouragement takes over.

I see the look on her face. How can I refuse this precious child of mine? How can I crush her joy with my melancholy? As I walk out of the front door onto the porch, I behold a marvelous spectacle in the sky. Red and orange and pink. Bright and vibrant and glorious. Hope bubbles from deep within me. It wells up and dispels the darkness trying to make a home within my heart. Then I hear a still, small voice that was muffled when negative emotions were dampening my spirit.

"Why are you afraid, Sarah? Take heart, it is I; have no fear."

In that sunset moment, I lean into Jesus' compassion and assurance. As my family stands around me, marveling at God's incredible artistry, I entrust all of the unknowns to the One who knows it all and, most importantly, knows me.

That night, God reminded me of His love, His mercy, His desire to come close and minister to His suffering children. He wrote it clearly in glowing yellow and orange. The beauty of His majestic sunset warmed my heart as He enveloped me in His embrace. I felt safe and secure, knowing He cares for me.

Prayer: Thank You, Lord, for the loving reminder that You are always near, especially in my suffering. Thank You for calming my fear and anxiety, so I can clearly hear Your words of consolation and peace. Amen.

Respond to His Call: Today, take notice of the ways God is trying to get your attention, so He can speak truth into your heart.

Sarah Damm

Rest

And on the seventh day God finished his work which he had done, and he rested on the seventh day from all his work which he had done. So God blessed the seventh day and hallowed it, because on it God rested from all his work which he had done in creation. Genesis 2:2–3

Sundays are a gift to shore up our wearied lives. Rest is one of four priorities for the Lord's Day. That's not my idea; it's from paragraph 1193 of the *Catechism of the Catholic Church*: "Sunday, the 'Lord's Day,' is the principal day for the celebration of the Eucharist because it is the day of the Resurrection. It is the pre-eminent day of the liturgical assembly, the day of the Christian family, and the day of joy and *rest* from work" (emphasis mine).

According to the *Catechism*, Sundays should focus on Mass, the family, celebration of joy, and rest from work. Many of us don't get enough rest because we fail to see it as a priority. And this is where we err.

Unfortunately, acute pressures exist to make Sunday just another day of the week. Don't fall for that lie. If we want to fill the depleted energy in our souls and bodies, we need to learn or relearn to rest. The past year has made this abundantly clear. Amid pandemic fatigue, schedule disruptions, staggering unemployment and financial fears, closed churches and schools, social and civil unrest, prolonged sorrow, unmitigated suffering, and wearying grief—we need rest.

"Come to me, all you who labor and are heavy laden" (Mt 11:28). Jesus is giving us His permission to come to Him for the rest we seek. Let's start anew.

Prayer: Lord Jesus, may I find true rest in You. Amen.

Respond to His Call: Look at your calendar and make a plan for rest on Sunday. Start with just one thing that will help. Pray about how to make rest a regular gift in your life.

Pat Gohn

When the Waves Come

And he said to them, "Why are you afraid, O men of little faith?" Then he rose and rebuked the winds and the sea; and there was a great calm. Matthew 8:26

Rushing to the car with a cart full of groceries, I hit a pothole. Not a big one, just deep enough to grab the front wheel of the cart. The cart flipped forward, and I flipped with it. It all happened in slow motion: the bar hitting my shin, me recoiling in pain, the coffee flying, me pulling back, the sideways lurch, the catapult, the unforgiving pavement. I lay there stunned, watching people walk into the store, eyes on their cell phones, oblivious or determined not to see.

Life hits like that sometimes. One year, we moved across the country and couldn't sell our house. Not long after, my husband was laid off, we lost our savings, my grandpa died, and my mom received a cancer diagnosis. "It never rains but it pours," they say, but that doesn't capture the pummeling we feel when bad things won't stop coming. I think of the disciples in the storm in Matthew's gospel. Wave after wave came across the bow of their fishing boat until it seemed they would sink, and Jesus slept.

They woke Him up. I imagine them wild-eyed, shaking Him, begging for help. He did, of course, but it's what He says that grabs my attention: "Why are you afraid, O men of little faith?" Why indeed? Why am I afraid when storms rock my boat, when Jesus is beside me? Even if He seems to sleep—why am I afraid? Do I not have faith that He will help? Jesus calmed the sea for the disciples, but I wonder if there was some greater good that might have come about had they had faith to wait.

Prayer: Jesus, I often struggle with doubt and long to jump from the boat in the midst of the storm. Restore my peace and calm my anxious heart. Amen.

Respond to His Call: Consider this advice from Padre Pio and take hope from it today: "Stay in the boat in which he has placed you, and let the storm come. Long live Jesus! You will not perish. He may sleep, but at the opportune time he will awake to restore your calm."

Sarah Christmyer

Carrying Our Cross, Sharing It with Others

Then Jesus told his disciples, "If any man would come after me, let him deny himself and take up his cross and follow me. For whoever would save his life will lose it, and whoever loses his life for my sake will find it." Matthew 16:24–25

Recently I traveled to Italy. The wine country, the basilica in Assisi, St. Monica's tomb—all were amazing. However, my favorite experience came unexpectedly, in heat and humidity. Our group of thirty women carried a heavy, six-foot wooden cross through Rome to St. Peter's Basilica, straight to the rock, Peter, upon which our Church was built.

At times in the past, I felt ashamed to share my faith. I reasoned, *It's a personal journey; I have every right to keep it to myself.* However, I admired those who publicly expressed their faith. I wondered, *What is my problem?* As we carried the cross through Rome, people stopped and took pictures. We prayed our way to St. Peter's tomb. It felt as if the weight of the world was on our shoulders. We carried the cross for our sins and those of the world. We thanked Jesus for carrying His Cross.

During our prayerful journey, people respected our passage. I realized the world needs God—right in the open, for all to see. When we neglect grace before meals in public, or hesitate to be truthful with others about our pro-life stance or our belief in a unified, traditional family structure, we are doing the world—and God—a disservice.

The world is crying out for God, and no one else will evangelize for us. Carrying the cross in Rome hammered this point home to me. We must carry our cross, share it with the world, and allow the crazy flow of traffic to stop and take notice.

Prayer: Lord, help me to share my faith with the world, so that others may know You are an ever-present, faithful, and loving God. Amen.

Respond to His Call: Choose a church, shrine, or other holy location and plan a pilgrimage there. It can be nearby, in your own town or state. Bring with you prayer petitions of your friends, family, and the world.

Julie E. Kenney

Daily Wonder Bread

Give us this day our daily bread. Matthew 6:11

Daily Mass was a lovely aspiration for me even before I came into the Church, but my duties and station in life prevented it. I homeschooled two kids through high school and could not justify a two-hour inter-ruption of every school day. And for years we simply could not afford the gas for a fifty-mile round trip to church every day, even if time had not been an issue.

Furthermore, I am not an early bird, so rising at dawn was onerous, even for things I was enthusiastic about. Add to that, my husband and I had coffee and morning prayer together. How could I abandon that wonderful practice to go to church? And anyway, God met me every day in the scriptures.

About a year ago, I felt the Holy Spirit stirring my heart to reconsider daily Mass. I did, and then remembered how early I would have to rise to get there. I promptly determined I would decide later. But I pondered it.

My prayer life was languishing in semi-dryness. Not terrible, just "meh." I started to pray my Rosary by rote each morning, for focus, and then turned to the daily Mass readings. I received insights regularly—subtle, but enough to tell me He was there. I kept muddling along like this for about a week, showing up to prayer each morning with a sigh and a bit of a spiritual eye roll. The only thing I could muster to say was, "Here I am, Lord."

That Sunday I received Communion, and as I knelt in my pew to pray, I heard the Lord say clearly, maybe with a smile, "Here I am, Sonja." I bit my tongue, trying not to laugh out loud! Well played, Lord. Well played. I began daily Mass attendance the very next day.

Prayer: Lord, help me to be truly present to someone today, as You are to me at all times. Amen.

Respond to His Call: Watch for the moment today when someone calls you to be present to them. Ask your guardian angel to alert you to that moment so you can truly participate in it with the Lord.

Sonja Corbitt

Becoming More

They still bring forth fruit in old age, they are ever full of sap and green. Psalm 92:14

Wrinkles and age spots have recently been on my mind, or should I say, on my skin. Even as a teenager, I remember starting a night cream routine and lying on the couch with my head upside down to ward off saggy skin and a double chin. Happily, though, as I age, I have become much less focused on the superficial signs of aging and more focused on growing deeper in Christ.

Each season of my life has brought different challenges. Raising young children presented a time squeeze, building a career required balance, and as I approach the golden years, I wonder if the energy to evangelize will be there. God's timing is always perfect. As career and child-rearing duties subside, life slows down a bit. This movement lets me make room for more prayer. But will it bear fruit?

When I was a teenager, my mother worked at a nursing home. Having just one car at our disposal, I sometimes went to pick her up and visited with the residents as I waited for her shift to end. The old people sort of scared me, and I asked my mom why some were so mean while others were so sweet. She replied, "I think that as we get older, we become more of what we always were." Wise woman.

We are called to live the life that we are living right now. Whether it is changing diapers or choosing bladder-control products, we can attend to our daily tasks in a mean and begrudging way or embrace them with love. As we age, we can look forward to becoming even more of what we are now. How do you choose to be?

Prayer: Lord, help me to reflect Your love to those I meet. Help me to face each season of life with joy in anticipation of growing closer to You. Amen.

Respond to His Call: Journal about how you would like others to describe you when you are ninety-two years old. Strive every day to become that person.

Sharon Agnes Wilson

Unplug and Let Go

And he went about all Galilee, teaching in their synagogues and preaching the gospel of the kingdom and healing every disease and every infirmity among the people. So his fame spread throughout all Syria, and they brought him all the sick, those afflicted with various diseases and pains, demoniacs, epileptics, and paralytics, and he healed them. Matthew 4:23–24

Last month I suffered a concussion. The doctor prescribed bed rest and no screens for a week. Ordinarily, that would be impossible. How could I communicate? How could I get my work done? How could I even live in the modern world? But my brain was injured, and sleep was the only thing I could do.

As I began to heal, I slept less but still lay quietly in a dark room with no sound, no screens, no distractions. That's when the graces began to flow.

Removing myself from the constant daily stimuli that we all experience allowed me to slip into a meditative state. In those deep recesses of my mind Jesus met me, flooding me with His love and mercy. He came to me as Divine Physician, healing my injury and also healing me of other things that had been building. I had been working too much, and the stress was taking an emotional and physical toll. I had been trying to grow in holiness, but my diet was terrible, there was no time for exercise, and I got virtually no rest. My spiritual efforts were not bearing much fruit, and I did not allow God to direct my life.

As I drew close to Him in the quiet dark, I felt the warmth of His Love envelop me. The word "rest" settled into my soul. I let go of everything I'd been clutching tightly, and peace replaced it like water rushing from an opened dam. God needed to whack me upside the head to give me the gift of His love and care. Don't wait for something drastic to happen in your life. Let God fill you with something much better.

Prayer: Jesus, You are my compass. Help me see how You are leading me toward the ultimate good—communion with You. Amen.

Respond to His Call: Spend some time resting today.

Sherry Kennedy Brownrigg

The Pink Chairs

When the Lord restored the fortunes of Zion, we were like those who dream. Then our mouth was filled with laughter, and our tongue with shouts of joy; then they said among the nations, "The Lord has done great things for them." Psalm 126:1–2

You know that funny state between sleeping and not sleeping—when it feels as if you are awake, but you are dreaming?

At the end of my bed are two pink chairs. In that lovely dream spot between sleeping and not sleeping, I had a nightmare. Sitting in one of the chairs was a man who was berating me. I knew him immediately, by sight and by the insults. In the haze of the dream, I closed my eyes but could still hear him. I said to him, "I refuse to believe you this time."

I forced myself from the dream and awoke. The chair was now empty. What came next was a mix of rebuke and morning offering. I said firmly, "Don't come back to this house. Your scorn has nothing to do with me, and you may never again sit in my pink chairs." In the next breath, I said fervently, "Jesus, I will serve You. What will You have me do?"

Thinking about it in the shower, I was amazed—not only that it had happened but also that it was handled. What a victory! In the past, I always gave credence to visitors in dreams, or real life, who berated me. My day, week, or month was finished. I sank. I wouldn't reach for Christ, but now I have a trick—I reach for Jesus every day. I offer my day to Him. When someone tries to interrupt my life, I will no longer listen to their lies. They cannot destroy my soul.

I now reserve that dream space for the angels—or, Lord, if You and Mary want to swing by and take a seat in the pink chairs, I'd love to have You visit!

Prayer: Jesus, I dig You! Thank You for allowing me to offer my day to You every morning. Amen.

Respond to His Call: Today in prayer, ask Jesus to sit next to you tonight, reminding you of His Sacred Heart's special love for you. Promise your fervent, faithful, loving response.

Alyssa Bormes

Judge Ye Not Thy Teenager, That Ye Not Be Judged

He saved us, not because of deeds done by us in righteousness, but in virtue of his own mercy, by the washing of regeneration and renewal in the Holy Spirit. Titus 3:5

Sometimes, I think God gets a kick out of situations that test our parenting skills, maybe because we challenge His parenting of us all too often. One Easter Sunday, I learned not to be too quick to judge what appeared to be a teenager's lack of interest.

The priest presiding over Mass did a fabulous job explaining why we renew our baptismal promises on this day of the Resurrection, noting that when we make the Sign of the Cross, we say yes to being created anew in the Father, Son, and Holy Spirit. Hence, I was mortified when my teenage daughter refused to cross herself as the priest sprinkled our section of pews with holy water. How could she blatantly go against what Father just explained?

As we walked to the car, I did my best to address the situation calmly. I said, "You know, that was very disrespectful, what you did in Mass." She looked at me dumbfounded and said, "What did I do?" "You didn't make the Sign of the Cross when the priest was sprinkling us with holy water," I replied. My daughter's face instantly lost fourteen years, and with the eyes of a three-year-old, she looked at me and said, "But the water didn't hit me." Instantly, I burst into laughter, and I realized things aren't always what they seem. I learned a lesson about judging others, particularly teenagers. I'm sure God was smiling as I explained to my daughter that you don't need to be drenched by holy water to renew your baptismal promises.

Prayer: Lord, increase in me the heavenly virtues of faith, hope, and charity, which I received at baptism. Grant me the grace to live out my baptismal promises. Amen.

Respond to His Call: Today, when someone does something you don't understand, don't be too quick to judge the reason for their actions.

Kelly M. Wahlquist

Trust You Did Enough

Train up a child in the way he should go, and when he is old he will not depart from it. Proverbs 22:6

My dearest Gemma Marie,

The day has finally come to load the car and drive you to your new home. Today is the beginning of an incredible journey for you as you enter into the next season of your life. Your father and I also embark on a new journey, of letting go. I cannot reflect on my millions of memories too long before tears well in my eyes. I have a limitless supply of memories to cherish and keep close to my heart as you leave the nest and soar.

You are a smart young lady with a solid faith. I hope college will stimulate your mind and tone your spiritual muscles. Never lose sight of the compass you have in Christ. He will lead you to new destinations, stretch you in ways you never knew possible, and open your eyes in wonder. May your life reflect our Lord as you seek His will and follow His path.

I am proud of the woman you have grown into and confident your faith will guide you when life presents difficult choices. As you form new friendships and discover your niche, remember—you were made for mission. God has a specific purpose and plan for your life. Enjoy the adventure as you discover both a little more each day. Absorb it all during this new, exciting season of your life.

Your grandmother had a plaque hanging on her living room wall when I was young. It read, "You give a child two things—you give them roots and you give them wings." Gemma, your roots are deep and strong; now go fly, honey!

I love you,
Mom

Prayer: Lord, give me the strength and wisdom to train my children in the way they should go, and the peace and trust to let them navigate that way on their own, when the time comes. Amen.

Respond to His Call: Write a letter to someone who inspired and supported your desire to grow deep, strong roots of faith. Be sure to share a few special memories.

Kathleen Billings

Exuberant Faith

That disciple whom Jesus loved said to Peter, "It is the Lord!" When Simon Peter heard that it was the Lord, he put on his clothes, for he was stripped for work, and sprang into the sea. But the other disciples came in the boat, dragging the net full of fish, for they were not far from the land, but about a hundred yards off. John 21:7–8

I love envisioning the scene in the passage above—Peter, jumping into the sea to swim to shore, full of anticipation and joy. The disciples following in the boat, hauling in a huge catch of fish after trying all night with no success. John notes in the account that the disciples were close to shore, but Peter can't wait. He throws all caution and good sense to the wind and jumps into the water to meet his Lord.

Now, Peter is known for being impetuous. He is often described as running into a situation without much preparation (in thought or prayer), with the result that Jesus has to save his life (see John 6:18–21), correct him (see John 18:9–11), or chastise him (see Matthew 16:22–24).

And once again, even after the Resurrection of Jesus, Peter acts before he thinks. Traveling a hundred yards to shore in the boat could not take much longer than jumping in and swimming. And, even funnier, Peter puts *on* his clothes to swim! Gotta love him. And Jesus does. Despite his flaws—one could argue rather serious flaws—Peter is beloved by Jesus, and Jesus makes him the foundational rock of the Church.

Despite all his rash behavior and mistakes, Peter shows great faith. He is teachable and open to the workings of the Holy Spirit. Shouldn't we all be a little more like Peter?

Prayer: Lord, help me to be teachable. Holy Spirit that dwells within me, let me always be open to Your will for me. Amen.

Respond to His Call: Before you act in any situation, pray. Once you have discerned, through the guidance of the Holy Spirit, that it is time to act, jump in with all of your strength, all of your enthusiasm, and all of the joy and love you have for the Lord.

Lynda MacFarland

Our Labor, God's Banquet

It is in vain that you rise up early and go late to rest, eating the bread of anxious toil; for he gives to his beloved sleep. Psalm 127:2

Labor Day weekend is a time to relax, or maybe not. If we've scheduled many projects and activities, it can seem as if the weekend is a special time of labor, rather than a national celebration of work. Whether it's taking the last camping trip of the summer, hosting a family gathering, or starting on house-winterizing projects, it seems there's always more to be done. And maybe, after getting the kids ready for school and finishing up the work that couldn't wait until Tuesday, we're wiped out at the end of the long, "restful" weekend.

It makes sense that our country should have a holiday celebrating labor. Work is a gift if we don't take it to the extreme. But don't we sometimes take our work ethic into our spiritual life? On busy days it can be a challenge to fit in prayer time. Some days I'm working hard to make it to Mass or go to Confession, and I find myself approaching these sacramental opportunities like tasks on my to-do list. It can be tempting to think that if I check off these "tasks," I've stored up enough spiritual capital for the rest of the day. No more prayer needed.

The key to daily intimacy with God is to take time out from what we're doing—even if we're busy—to be present to Him throughout our day. I believe God wants us to spend time with Him and become accustomed to His voice. If we make that effort, He will give us good things money can't buy, like a beautiful sunset we might have missed, a pleasant surprise, or a gentle reminder to call a friend.

Prayer: Lord, I know that I need to give time to daily prayer. Help me to remember that it's when I'm busiest that I need to pray extra. Amen.

Respond to His Call: Sit and do nothing other than to listen and praise God as thoughts drift through your mind. For example, if the thought *I have to do the dishes* pops into your head, pray, "Praise be to God, I have dishes to wash."

Susan Klemond

The Moments You Choose to Share Matter

But he said to me, "My grace is sufficient for you, for my power is made perfect in weakness." I will all the more gladly boast of my weaknesses, that the power of Christ may rest upon me. 2 Corinthians 12:9

Is checking social media built into your routine? Social media is a sharp, double-edged sword, showing only highlights—not trials. We critique our lives against it. Yet in this world of broadcasting perfect moments, I've used my blog to describe my healing from a severe case of anorexia that almost took my life. You may think I'm brave, but I am weak. It all comes down to Paul's writing from 2 Corinthians.

I've been in recovery for ten years now. No matter the addiction, recovery is a daily choice. It's not my doing. It's His. Jesus *is* my recovery. I would fail on my own. Sustained recovery came when I fully surrendered to Christ. I gave Him my broken heart, fears about my body, meal plans, plans for the future—everything. What did He give me? Grace. "My grace is sufficient for you, for my power is made perfect in weakness."

My weakness is astounding, ugly, sneaky—not something generally displayed for all to see on social media. When my mind is haranguing me about my worth, or I sense a slippery path, God showers me with the grace to persevere. He strengthens me through my weakness. Being healthy and thriving is a testimony to God's grace. My weaknesses have been His access points to my heart. This is why I share all the non-Instagram-worthy parts of myself. God shines brightest in my weakness.

I will boast about it, as Paul encouraged. Being real about our struggles, allowing God's grace to radiate, encourages others to see His grace in their lives, too, which, if you ask me, are the moments that deserve to be on social media.

Prayer: Lord, let me boast in my weakness, secure in the knowledge that Your grace is sufficient for me. Amen.

Respond to His Call: Note a few weaknesses that bring you frustration. Thank God for them, knowing they draw you to rely on Him.

Caralyn Collar

Jesus Asks Only for What We Have

Jesus said to them, "Fill the jars with water." And they filled them up to the brim. He said to them, "Now draw some out, and take it to the steward of the feast." John 2:7–8

I remember when I first learned the concept of our Christian baptismal identity: priest, prophet, and king. "That's just not me," I thought, especially the idea of sharing in the redemptive mission of our Lord. I mean, isn't that sort of blasphemous? Anyway, surely I must be the least qualified and most unworthy. What good would my offering be, even if I had something to offer? My life is small, confined.

When I finally allowed myself to entertain the possibility of participating with Jesus in the salvation of mankind, I began a sort of argument with Him. "All I have to offer You is my sinfulness," I whined, trying to pray. I closed my eyes, frowning. When I did, I glimpsed a quick image of myself holding a heavy, jagged rock, standing before Jesus. "No, You can't have this; You are sinless! This belongs to me," I said. "I came to take away sin," Jesus replied, smiling and taking the heavy rock from my arms.

A frightening feeling of emptiness came over me when Jesus took the rock. "That's all I have to give that is really mine," I said. Tears rolled down my face. "Yes," He said softly, "And now it is Mine."

I opened my eyes and realized that, up until that moment, I had professed that Jesus came to take away my sins, but I had not fully understood or believed it. I realized that He only asks for what we have—things as simple and ordinary as water poured into stone jars. When we surrender what we have, He does marvelous deeds. He produces wine—the Precious Blood of salvation. In our simple offering, we fulfill our baptismal identity as prophet, our meager actions magnifying God's glory.

Prayer: Jesus, today I bring You myself, just as I am. Change me into Your blessing for the world I encounter today. I trust in Your mercy and grace. Amen.

Respond to His Call: Review your calendar. Choose a time and day to offer to Jesus in a special way, to transform into a gift for His chalice for the world's salvation.

Lynne Keating

Knitted out of Love

Because you are precious in my eyes, and honored, and I love you, I give men in return for you, peoples in exchange for your life. Isaiah 43:4

When I begin a knitting project, like a new scarf, there is a time when that scarf does not exist. There is only a skein of yarn, some needles, and my desire to create. At first, it doesn't look like much, just some little stitches. But over time, those stitches come together to form the scarf. As the scarf grows, I delight in the pretty pattern and color variation. It continues to come together, becoming a unique work of beauty with a special purpose.

There are moments in the creative process when I notice a stitch out of place. At that point, I pause, go back to fix the stitch, and make it right. When the scarf is finally complete, that skein of yarn has become what it was always meant to be: a delightful, cozy scarf—and I love it. Whether I give it away or keep it for myself, it serves an important purpose. It promises warmth and brightens up the dark world with its beauty.

Isn't it even more incredible that God does the same with us? He created us out of absolutely nothing; He didn't even need yarn and needles. He simply desired us. He created us because He loved us and wanted to delight in us.

There are times when one of our stitches is misplaced, and we become flawed. And in those moments, He pauses to fix what went wrong. He fills in what is missing. He redeems us back to Himself, back to wholeness. God has a unique purpose for us to live out, so we can brighten this dark world with our beauty. We don't have to be anything more or anything less, just who God created us to be. Oh, how He loves us!

Prayer: Heavenly Father, thank You for loving us into existence and for redeeming us to live our purpose to the fullest. May we always trust in Your great design of who we are—right here and now—and may we always love You wholly in return. Amen.

Respond to His Call: Today, take some time to create something. Offer it as a prayer of gratitude to the Lord, for His complete love for you.

Sarah Damm

Sometimes Evangelization Is Messy

For my thoughts are not your thoughts, neither are your ways my ways, says the LORD. Isaiah 55:8

Our ways are not the Lord's ways. Thank God! Because God's ways are so far beyond ours, and let's face it, they are much neater.

Today we recognize the Blessed Mother's birthday. With that bit of knowledge, my friend Rita planned a birthday party for 4,500 families for the Mother of God—not a small undertaking. Rita delegated responsibilities to various committees, but God showed us He had a bigger plan in all the little details. Though we never saw picking up cupcakes as an opportunity to evangelize, the Lord did. Three times on the cupcake excursion, workers asked if the five hundred cupcakes were for a wedding. Each time, Rita joyfully responded, "No, they are for the Blessed Mother's birthday." You should have seen the looks on their faces!

As if being an outlet to share the Good News at the store wasn't enough, Our Lady used her birthday celebration to teach the littlest among us how to live the Gospel. As the children went to hear the day's scripture, they had to walk past a table of beautifully decorated, scrumptious cupcakes and not touch one! Ironically, the gospel was about carrying your cross. You'd be hard-pressed to find a more significant cross for a wide-eyed, hungry five-year-old than a tower of untouchable cupcakes.

Afterward, crosses endured became blessings as chocolate crumbs littered the floor and blue frosting stained little teeth. Various committees got to be of service to their parish family, and grocery-store workers found themselves pondering the birth of the Mother of God—a thought that hopefully did what our perfect mother always does: point to the greatest birth of all, the birth of our Lord. Happy birthday, Theotokos!

Prayer: Lord, help me to trust in Your ways, especially in moments when sharing the Gospel takes me out of my comfort zone. Amen.

Respond to His Call: Today, buy yourself a cupcake, or a cake, or your favorite dessert, and tell others you're celebrating the birthday of the mother of Jesus. Then, enjoy it!

Kelly M. Wahlquist

The Early Bird and Later Types

He who blesses his neighbor with a loud voice, rising early in the morning, will be counted as cursing. Proverbs 27:14

Some years ago, my husband and I went to daily Mass at a small Franciscan church in Queens. It wasn't our home parish, but our parish didn't have daily Mass at a time that worked for us, so we went to this one.

Probably because we didn't go there on Sundays and never laid eyes on the parish bulletin, we never learned the names of the priests there. But we had to call them something, so we used nicknames.

My favorite was Zoomer, so-called because he celebrated Mass in record time. Not because he was in a hurry, but because (a) like me, he was a native New Yorker, and fast is just how we roll, and (b) he knew the bus schedule. Zoomer's pace made it possible for his parishioners to attend early Mass and still get to work on time. Win-win.

Then there was the priest we called the Young One: Not a Morning Person. This poor guy stumbled into church minutes before Mass was supposed to start, still tucking in his shirt and looking as if he would kill for a cup of coffee. Once at the altar, he came to life just fine, but you could see from a mile away that 6:30 a.m. was tough on him, and probably always had been.

Not everyone is a morning person. Morning people may find this difficult to understand, but it is a fact. Booming a cheery "Sun's up, Buttercup!" to a non-morning person is likely to get you some choice replies. And if the proverb above is anything to go by, you'll deserve every one of them.

It's straight from the wisdom of Solomon: keep it low in the a.m. At least until the coffee's ready.

Prayer: Lord, every morning You give us is glorious and worthy of praise. Please remind me to keep my praise on the quiet side. Amen.

Respond to His Call: Get the coffeepot ready tonight. Don't take chances!

Susan Vigilante

Discovering the Prodigal Brother

Now his elder son was in the field; and . . . heard music and dancing. And he called one of the servants and asked what this meant. And he said to him, "Your brother has come, and your father has killed the fatted calf, because he has received him safe and sound." But he was angry and refused to go in. Luke 15:25–28

In the story of the prodigal son, we can easily overlook the responsible and obedient older brother. Scholars tell us this brother represents the Pharisees, with whom Jesus is sharing this parable. When I first joined the Church, I, like the Pharisees, was concerned about who was not following the rules. Entering church for Mass, I would quickly find my seat and kneel until Mass began—head bowed but eyes darting around and mind filled with anything but prayer.

I was intensely envious of some fellow parishioners who seemed so fortunate but, in my opinion, didn't deserve any of it. This attitude continued until I read, "Judge not, that you be not judged. For with the judgment you pronounce you will be judged, and the measure you give will be the measure you get" (Mt 7:1–2). Those verses stopped me in my tracks, convicted me, and cured me of my Pharisaism. Like the brother brooding in the field, I thought my only way to God's heart was to be perfect. It made me crazy that people who seemed not to be trying as hard were receiving the same reward.

The father meets the prodigal brother where he is and pleads with him to come rejoice with the lost being found, the sinner being forgiven—mercy being shown. This beautiful gesture of reassuring the brother who feels slighted shows the depth of the father's love, compassion, and generosity. God's mercy toward others never takes away from the blessings waiting for the rest of His children. Instead of being jealous, we should beg that He bestow the same loving mercy on each of us!

Prayer: Lord, when I am the prodigal brother, standing at the door of the Father's love, may Your wisdom always push me through. Amen.

Respond to His Call: Before bed, examine your conscience. Ask Jesus for His mercy and forgiveness.

Allison Gingras

September 11

Change the Narrative

> Know this, my beloved brethren. Let every man be quick to hear, slow to speak, slow to anger, for the anger of man does not work the righteousness of God. James 1:19

I left work fuming. Once home, I asked my husband if I could vent. He delivered a gentle correction; we needed to have a holy and constructive conversation, calling on the Holy Spirit and looking for practical ways to make a positive difference. As we took a calming walk, there was space to stop, breathe, and respond to my anger. In changing the narrative, we found tangible solutions that eventually made a difference.

St. James reminds us to be "quick to hear, slow to speak, slow to anger, for the anger of man does not work the righteousness of God." Pride can build into unrighteous anger, becoming an uncontrolled outpouring of words. How often as women do we enter into venting dialogue? Does it solve the problem, or do I brood in anger? These negative conversations can take many forms, but far too often, they focus on belittling others. Even our husbands may become targets, which acts against marriage. We diminish others to elevate ourselves.

Sometimes the narrative we tell ourselves becomes our reality. Perhaps seeing a flaw in myself, I fear judgment, which causes me to be guarded, setting me apart from my loved one, friend, or coworker. This distance becomes my reality. However, when I acknowledge this guardedness, an opportunity to love becomes my reality.

What narratives am I creating in my marriage, in my life? Do I speak to my husband and others with the respect and love that I would want of them? By controlling anger and bridling my tongue and thoughts, I cultivate patience and understanding within myself. Life is enriched.

Prayer: Holy Spirit, change the narrative of my heart to one embedded in truth, surrender, and life-giving love. Amen.

Respond to His Call: The next time you face the temptation of venting, belittling, or engaging in negative self-talk—stop, breathe, and respond. Change the narrative to one of life-giving truth, and surrender to the Holy Spirit.

Katie Lee Taylor

September 12

The Gift of Tears

He will wipe away every tear from their eyes, and death shall be no more, neither shall there be mourning nor crying nor pain any more, for the former things have passed away. Revelation 21:4

I remember around the age of eight thinking to myself one afternoon on the playground that I had not cried once that day! My overactive tear ducts have not always been convenient, but more and more, I've come to see these salty droplets of water as a gift, and perhaps the most powerful prayer I can offer to God—even when no words accompany them.

In my visits to the Carmel of Mary Monastery in Wahpeton, North Dakota, I received further insight regarding tears in time spent with Sr. Theresa Nguyen and her superior. After four years in formation with a Dominican religious order in Texas, Sr. Theresa was ultimately turned away from the community. Asked how she handled the rejection, she admitted to a torrent of tears that lasted several days. "God, I have tried to follow you, so why is this happening?" she asked. But ultimately, her tears dried up, and she began to see God's plan in a new and beautiful light.

Meanwhile, hundreds of miles to the north, a small Carmelite community had been praying for another member. Within weeks of her inquiry, Sr. Theresa arrived at their doors, ready to give her life to God as a contemplative. Mother Madonna, the prioress, shared that it was as if Sr. Theresa had said, "Okay, God, I've had all my tears. Now I know I'm in your hands." Reflecting further, Mother Madonna shared, "I often think that tears are watering something; that they are seeds of the next step." Mother believed that through her tears, Sr. Theresa's vocation deepened. "Now, her rejoicing can begin in this community, with all her gifts and the talents she brings."

Prayer: Dear Lord, I offer you any tears I might shed today, or anytime this week, as my purest and most heartfelt prayer, for Your glory. Please accept my lamentation, and in turn, I will try to remember Your promise that in time all our tears will be turned into dancing. Amen.

Respond to His Call: Whose tears can you dry today, or to whom can you safely bring your tears, that you might be heard and healed?

Roxane B. Salonen

"Great" Grandparents

And Mary said, "Behold, I am the handmaid of the Lord; let it be to me according to your word." Luke 1:38

September 13 is National Grandparents Day, a good day to recall the best grandparents ever: Jesus' grandparents. Very little is known about Mary's childhood, but we can tell by details of her life mentioned in the Bible that she must have come from a close-knit family with a strong devotion to prayer. Her parents most likely instilled in her the importance of being open to God's plan for her life, which resulted in her yes to the Incarnation. Mary exhibited incredible courage and grace in Her total commitment to Jesus. Her steadfast faith enabled her to remain true to her word, all the way to her Son's Cross and beyond.

How many generations before Mary reflected those same character-building qualities and a firm faith in the Lord? Many, I'm sure. Parents tend to pass down to their children what is most important to them. Do you know what aspects of your faith were instilled in your parents before being passed on to you? Maybe you witnessed your grandparents' example of living their faith. Perhaps you saw both your parents and your grandparents living out their faith with steadfast love.

If you are blessed to have living grandparents, ask them questions about their life of faith. Practicing their faith may have been a very different experience in comparison to how you live your faith today. Grandparents have so much wisdom gleaned from long life experience; God has been working on them longer. They want to share that wisdom with you.

Someday, you may be a grandparent. What will you want to instill in your grandchildren? When my granddaughter was born, I used every opportunity to tell her about Jesus and Mary. She won't remember all of what I taught her, but she recognizes Jesus and Mary, and on this feast of grandparents, that is quite a gift.

Prayer: Dear Jesus, please help me to say yes to Your plan for me, just as Mary did. Amen.

Respond to His Call: Identify how many times a day you give your yes to your family, your friends, and to Jesus.

Rhonda Zweber

Giving Up My To-Do List

Have you listened in the council of God? And do you limit wisdom to yourself? Job 15:8

I'm a to-do-list girl. When I start on a new project, I create a list of tasks. I take great joy in crossing off items as I complete them. God designed my brain to work this way, so He knows that certain things about my faith life are challenging for me. Particularly the part about not knowing His exact plans for me so I can create a to-do list. I have learned that His plans are usually given to me piecemeal. I cannot merely list the steps, and then go along my merry way. Each new development requires checking in with God if I want to stay on the path.

Fortunately, God gave us a perfect example to follow. Mary's yes didn't begin and end at the annunciation. She certainly didn't wake up and say yes to God for the first time at the angel's appearance. Mary had been following God's direction her whole life. Mary had to wait for God and keep saying yes. She had no idea what the entire project would entail, so she certainly couldn't make a list and check things off as she did them. Her beautiful example of faith and trust blows my mind. Given my weakness in this area, she gives me hope.

Whenever I feel like God is leading me somewhere, I set about making a different kind of to-do list. First, I actively seek Mary's help to continually reshape my approach to remain more like her. Then I submit myself to God's will every step of the way. It's a work in progress and some days are better than others, but I'll continue to try. I'm hopeful that with enough practice, I may eventually let go of trying to reduce my faith life to a checklist. Then I'll finally be able to check that off!

Prayer: Lord, help me to practice listening for Your counsel today. May my every step be guided by Your wisdom. Amen.

Respond to His Call: Retrieve the last to-do list you completed. Consider how the tasks related to the *actual* outcome. Then sit quietly for a few moments, giving over to God your plans, your questions, and all of the moments in the coming day.

Michelle Schroeder

The Most Beautiful Question in the Bible

The word of the LORD came to Jeremiah: "Behold, I am the LORD, the God of all flesh; is anything too hard for me?" Jeremiah 32:26–27

The first time I remember hearing this verse, the translation was, "Is there anything I can't do?" Talk about a conversation stopper. Game, set, and match, right? Jeremiah reminds us in the simplest possible terms, first, who God is and, second, what He is capable of—which is, of course, anything and everything.

The calming effect of this knowledge is remarkable. There is nothing God cannot do, because of who He is. That's it. That's the whole ball game.

(Of course, there's always the question of does He want to do whatever it is you're asking. What God wills is different from what He can do.)

Can Jesus cure the sick, heal the blind, restore the dead to life? Check, check, and check. Can He dispel your despair, clear your confusion, give you all the hope you need? Again, that's a triple check. God took Jeremiah ("But I don't know how to speak! Besides, I'm just a kid!"—see Jeremiah 1:6) and made him a prophet to the nations.

God took Joan of Arc, an illiterate peasant girl, and made her a victorious commander of armies. And He took Peter—impetuous, weak-kneed, foot-in-mouth Peter—and made him the Vicar of Christ.

Those three examples are enough to demonstrate that nothing is too hard for God. But there are countless others. I'm sure you can think of a few right now.

Yeah. I'd say there's nothing too hard for God.

Prayer: Lord, today let me remember to lean on You, for You can do all things. Amen.

Respond to His Call: The opening passage is one of those verses worth writing down on a handful of index cards and leaving all over your home—in a kitchen drawer, in the laundry room, and anywhere else you sometimes find yourself feeling overwhelmed. Take a few deep breaths from time to time and read it. You'll be glad you did.

Susan Vigilante

Seeking the Face of God

You have said, "Seek my face." My heart says to you, "Your face, LORD, do I seek." Psalm 27:8

In the Old Testament, the desire to see God's face is expressed more than one hundred times. The Incarnation of Jesus gave a face to the God of the universe. As Pope emeritus Benedict XVI says, "God can be seen, God has shown his face, he is visible in Jesus Christ." Where can we find the face of Jesus and, in Him, the face of His Father?

When we read the scriptures, we learn to know and love the Son, who did His Father's works. By reading and meditating on the written Word, we draw closer to seeing the Word Made Flesh in His humanity and divinity. Likewise, prayer, even a few minutes a day, brings us closer to Jesus. When we sit in front of the Blessed Sacrament, we are sitting face-to-face with Jesus. Adoration is a time to talk to Him, listen, and be in His presence, as we would be in a beloved friend's presence.

We can see the face of Jesus in the poor, the hungry, strangers, and those in need. "'Lord, when did we see you hungry and feed you, and thirsty and give you drink? And when did we see you a stranger and welcome you, or naked and clothe you? And when did we see you sick or in prison and visit you?' And the King will answer them, 'Truly, I say to you, as you did it to one of these the least of my brethren, you did it to me'" (Mt 25:37–40).

As we look at those we love, let's remember that the joy we feel gazing on the faces of our spouse, family members, and friends is a small reflection of what we will encounter when we reach our heavenly home and behold the face of God. Where will you seek the Lord's face?

Prayer: Lord, help me to see Your face in the poor, hungry, oppressed, and wherever there is need. Amen.

Respond to His Call: Select four or five photos of your family, and ponder them in your prayer time today. Ask Jesus what He wants you to see of Himself in each photo. Pray with each photo for several minutes and wait for His response.

Stephanie Landsem

You Are Beautiful

For you formed my inward parts, you knitted me together in my mother's womb. I praise you, for I am wondrously made. Wonderful are your works! You know me right well. Psalm 139:13–14

"Women are self-deprecating," I tell the writing class I host at my church. "Add a negative slant to your heroine's introspection when referring to her physical attributes." Fiction mirrors life, and regrettably, many women have a poor self-image. We see ourselves as too fat, too thin, too flat, too curvy. The truth is we're our own worst enemies. We compare ourselves to others and invariably come up short. In reality, we need to see ourselves through God's eyes. He created us in His image and likeness and looks at us with love and affirmation. Instead of dwelling on what we lack, we should recognize the qualities that make us unique.

Yet changing long-standing misperceptions about ourselves is difficult. Usually, the lie we've accepted as truth stems from something in our youth, like a parent's offhanded remark that we aren't as pretty as our sister—or as smart. Jeers from bullies on the playground who called us Fatso or Four Eyes or Dummy cut us to the quick in our youth, fester into adulthood, and impact not only how we see ourselves but also how we interact with the Lord.

I write Christian fiction. My heroines are flawed. Their relationships with the Lord are as well. In the course of my stories, as they tackle seemingly insurmountable odds to achieve their goals, these women gain a clearer vision of their own self-worth. In the end, they reconcile with God and begin to regard themselves as a new creation.

Like my fictional heroines, we need to weed out the lies we've lived for too long and accept ourselves as God's beautiful creation. Only then can we embrace the Psalmist's words, "I praise you, for I am wondrously made. Wonderful are your works!"

Prayer: Lord, heal my brokenness. Help me overcome the lies that hold me back from loving myself and loving You more completely. Amen.

Respond to His Call: Counter any negative self-talk with positive affirmations until you can see yourself clearly as an amazing child of God.

Debby Giusti

A Different Kind of Strength

But they who wait for the LORD shall renew their strength, they shall mount up with wings like eagles, they shall run and not be weary, they shall walk and not faint. Isaiah 40:31

Three times in my life, I've dragged my oversized body across the finish lines of marathon races. I have hiked numerous mountains around the globe. A few years ago, I completed a 320-mile walking and biking pilgrimage in less than two weeks. Along many of these "races," the words of Isaiah 40:31 passed my lips. I often recited this, my dad's favorite scripture passage, as my personal pep talk when the physical challenges felt too great. If I was really feeling in need of strength, I would hear them in the Scottish brogue of Eric Liddell, the Olympian who recited them in the classic film *Chariots of Fire.*

My framework for understanding Isaiah's wisdom was fundamentally rewritten when my mother's battle with Parkinson's-related dementia became intense. Suddenly my best friend and lifelong hero was not only unable to walk independently but also robbed of her ability to control most of her life's choices. Striding with Mom along this particular course has been harder than anything I've ever done in life.

Read in its entirety, Isaiah 40 is a love song of consolation destined to comfort the Chosen People as they wander in exile. I often whisper these words to Mom in my heart as I pray for the courage to walk each step of this journey with her. When I feel unable to continue the race and want to quit or beg God to end Mom's suffering, Isaiah reminds me that it is in the mounting up and running and walking that we prepare ourselves for what lies ahead. Together, Mom and I wait for the Lord. Together, we are renewed in the strength needed to cross the most beautiful finish line ever. Together, though separately, we will win the race.

Prayer: Creator God, instill in me the strength of spirit, mind, and body to fulfill Your chosen mission for my life. In You, I find courage and rest. Amen.

Respond to His Call: Consider your greatest problem today as a race and pray that God will give you the strength to run well, regardless of what place you earn when you cross the finish line.

Lisa M. Hendey

Find Me Ready, Lord

Pray for the peace of Jerusalem! "May they prosper who love you!" Psalm 122:6

I was pregnant with my second child, a girl, when we moved cross-country. With no family around and only a few brand-new friends, I was unnerved by the thought of possibly giving birth before my mom arrived to take care of our toddler son.

My husband and I played the guessing game as to when she would arrive. If she was delivered late like our son, we would be fine. If she was born no earlier than when my mom arrived, there was no reason to worry. For weeks we tried to predict the day and the hour. Of course, this was futile. We couldn't predict her arrival; we could only prepare for it.

Jesus says that no one knows the day He will return. Just as the people in Noah's time had no idea when the flood would begin, so too will Christ come unexpectedly. We can, in imitation of Noah, prepare, so we will not be caught off guard. Noah was diligent in preparing for that unpredictable moment when God poured His judgment upon the earth.

God doesn't want us to spend our time speculating about when the end times will come. Rather, He wants us to devote our energy to preparing for those times, whenever they may arrive. That preparation entails prayerfulness, repentance, obedience, trust, courage—diligence in making our hearts and lives ready to meet Christ when He comes again.

Ultimately, we must prepare for Christ's coming by growing in charity, by expanding our love for others and for the Lord. Let us not be found sleeping when He comes like a "thief in the night" (1 Thes 5:2), but instead be ready and waiting with eager hearts. The Psalmist assures us that God will bless us if we live this way: "May they prosper who love you!"

Prayer: Lord, heighten my awareness of the many things I must tend to in advance of Your coming. Let me not be caught unaware, but instead let me be devoted to You in every way. Amen.

Respond to His Call: What is one thing you can do today to prepare for Christ's coming?

Katie Warner

Playing the Long Game

So faith, hope, love abide, these three; but the greatest of these is love. 1 Corinthians 13:13

My husband and I recently celebrated our twenty-eighth wedding anniversary. It was in the time of COVID, so instead of going to a fancy restaurant, we ordered takeout at the African grill down the street. We rode bikes, watched a movie, and celebrated the whole weekend. It was one of the best anniversaries we've ever had.

Our celebrations weren't always this good. For many years, I focused on my husband's shortcomings, the comments that hurt me, and his view of married life, which is different from mine. Then, one day, God helped me move past all of that. I was visiting with a friend while our large golden retriever played with another dog. I took my eyes off them momentarily, and sure enough, they barreled into me, knocking me down and spraining my ankle. Our house was more than a mile away, so I hobbled back as best I could.

When I walked in the door and told my husband what had happened, he immediately snapped at me for my carelessness. I stared at him, ready to snap back about how ridiculous he was. Then God whispered in my ear, "Play the long game." I walked away without saying anything and immediately went into prayer.

Play the long game. What God was telling me is that minor slights mean nothing compared to the goal of getting my spouse to heaven. Our vocation as husband and wife is to help each other to eternal life, but it can be easy to lose sight of that truth in the nitty-gritty of daily life. When you play the long game, you focus on the goal, not the injuries that happen along the way.

Prayer: Lord, help me to see beyond the temporary hurts and the slights and focus on the ultimate goal of heaven. Amen.

Respond to His Call: Satan seeks to divide us while God brings peace. In what relationship is God asking you to play the long game?

Sherry Kennedy Brownrigg

Suitcases in a Small World

The glory which you have given me I have given to them, that they may be one even as we are one. John 17:22

They said Jesus could handle my baggage, so I brought my suitcase to Mass. Seriously. Our group of young American professionals hopped off the bus, luggage and all, and trudged over to the Bayeux Cathedral for Mass on day 7 of our France pilgrimage. Amid many visitors to the cathedral that evening, one older gentleman particularly grabbed my attention (and heart).

I sensed agitation growing behind me throughout Father's homily. The cries grew louder until he suddenly shouted three distinct questions: "*Parlez-vous français? Sprechen sie Deutsch?* Do you speak English?" His dear wife soon calmed the gentleman down. Mass concluded. Pilgrims departed. I never saw the man again, but he left me forever changed. Jesus prayed that we would all be one. Holy Mother Church too desires the unity of her children. The word "Catholic" literally means universal. My small Minnesota church is the Body of Christ, alongside the Church in France and the Church everywhere. How beautiful that we can celebrate Mass anyplace in the world and gather around the table as family! We need no common language, for our faith makes us one.

In the innocence of his spirit, my new French friend was onto something profound. We are all pilgrims in a foreign land. We are all on this journey together. And life is so much better when we receive each other as a gift. St. Teresa of Calcutta cautioned us, "If we have no peace, it is because we have forgotten that we belong to each other." Mass is only a microcosm. Come sit down at the table with me. Bring your baggage too. You are loved. You are valuable. You belong here.

Prayer: Father, Son, and Holy Spirit, You perfectly show us what it means to make our community of one heart and mind. Consecrate us in Your truth and bring us all to deeper unity as Your body on earth. Amen.

Respond to His Call: Stop at a parish you have never visited for Mass, adoration, or quiet prayer. Notice how the unique charisms of this community expand your own appreciation for the universal Church.

Katie Anderson

The Recording

But Moses said to the LORD, "Oh, my Lord, I am not eloquent . . .
I am slow of speech and of tongue." Exodus 4:10

My brothers used to tease me about my terrible singing. I thought they were jealous; singing was my life! I decided to record a little something to prove my prowess. We had a tape player with a handheld microphone; my song selection was "The Twelve Days of Christmas." I began what would surely be historical documentation of the prodigy at her craft.

Admittedly, there were points where I had to clear my throat or a note was out of range, but I sang on. Excitedly, I began the playback. Soon my brothers would eat crow.

To some, what followed would have been dream crushing. It was awful! My voice was cracking. Where was the melody? However, I was certain I was a songstress; therefore, the metallic scratching sounds could only mean one thing . . . the recorder was broken! Unfortunately, my brothers found the tape. The mocking began. I retorted, "The recorder is broken!" They laughed harder.

That was nearly five decades ago. Oddly, I never became a professional singer. My brothers were right, but I still love singing. If I can't hit the notes, I skip them, turn up the volume, or laugh and keep going.

G. K. Chesterton said that anything worth doing is worth doing badly. Thinking we have to be good at what we like to do may leave us paralyzed. Don't be hindered by not being the best, or even by being the worst. Greatness is only bestowed now and again. So much joy and so many good works are found right in the midst of mediocrity. So, go on—do something badly, but with all the joy you can muster!

Prayer: Lord, what joy do You have for me today? Lead me to it through the laughter and love of others. Help me to find it in the mediocre, where love shines brightly. Amen.

Respond to His Call: Do something today for which you have only average talent. Thank God for the courage it took to praise Him with that choice.

Alyssa Bormes

A Grateful Reminder

O give thanks to the LORD, for he is good; for his mercy endures for ever! 1 Chronicles 16:34

I opened the envelope that had arrived in the mail and was surprised to see a thank-you card. The note was from a young couple expressing their appreciation for the wedding gift our family had given them. I paused in dismay. The wedding had taken place eleven months earlier. Although I had read that a bride and groom can take a full year to send out their thank-you cards, waiting that length of time, to me, felt tacky, even ungrateful.

When I was growing up, my parents were sticklers for prompt and consistent gratitude. Together we would sit at the kitchen table to write thank-you cards to grandparents, other relatives, and friends who had blessed us with gifts for special occasions. We wrote out the cards within the first few days of receiving the gifts. As I reflected on those days sitting at the kitchen table with my parents helping me spell words of gratitude, an unsettling thought entered my mind. Although I have maintained the practice of sending timely thank-you notes, I've been much less consistent in expressing prompt gratitude toward God. I thought about the many times I had called out to Him with a plea, big or small, which He had answered in love. How often I had forgotten to thank Him or was slow in expressing my gratitude. Too many times, I had to admit humbly.

A priest I know once said, "Imagine if God gave us only those things for which we had expressed gratitude." That statement, like this overdue thank-you note, arrested my attention. Loving both God and others demands prompt and consistent gratitude. What a compelling reminder of this I received in the mail today. Thanks be to God!

Prayer: Dear Lord, help me to become a person of gratitude. May I ever recognize the blessings I have received, and never miss an opportunity to thank You and others. Amen.

Respond to His Call: Consider starting a gratitude journal, and give thanks to God for each blessing you record in it. Also, send a note of thanksgiving to someone who has blessed you.

Dr. Pamela Patnode

On This Mountain

On this mountain the LORD of hosts will make for all peoples a feast of fat things, a feast of choice wines. Isaiah 25:6

The mountain on which the Lord of hosts will provide a banquet for all peoples is Mount Zion, a symbol of the heavenly Jerusalem, and the banquet he offers is the promise that awaits us at the end of time. Throughout the Bible, mountains play an essential role—Moses received the Ten Commandments on Mount Sinai, Abraham sacrificed Isaac on the mountains of Moriah, and, of course, Jesus died on Mount Calvary.

Climbing mountains, or in my case hills, is an exciting and sometimes scary feat. Have you ever noticed that it's easier going uphill than down? As we ascend, our eyes are fixed on what's ahead. As we descend, we watch our feet so that we don't trip or fall.

I usually walk home from work. Recently I've challenged myself to take the hilly route. Halfway up the first, steepest hill, I find myself stopping to catch my breath and enjoy the view of downtown. When I reach the top, I feel close to God. I feel accomplished, and the smaller hills the rest of the way home seem insignificant.

Every day we encounter mountains. Some of them can seem overwhelming, but bit by bit we can conquer them. When we stop halfway, we can feel a sense of accomplishment in how far we've come. We can also reflect on the best way to get to our destination. We may need to change paths, go around obstacles, or simply forge straight ahead.

Take time today to reflect on your journey. Are you going uphill or down? Do you need to adjust the route or perhaps rest a little more along the way? When we reach our final destination, the top of the heavenly mountain, we will feel exhilaration and a sense of accomplishment as we feast on God's banquet of rich food and choice wines.

Prayer: Lord, transform my mountains into molehills by accompanying me every step of the way. Amen.

Respond to His Call: Identify a situation that is slowing your ascent of the spiritual mountaintops. What can you do today to move beyond that situation?

Lucy H. Johnson

Live Life Chronologically

Be strong and of good courage . . . the LORD your God . . . will not fail you or forsake you. Deuteronomy 31:6

I've always been a planner and organizer. From my youth, I coordinated the whole family. In hindsight, I realize someone should have staged an intervention by the time I was ten. As an adult, I've enjoyed the luxury of a Google calendar with color-coded categories. However, one day my attention to detail instantly ceased to matter. Category 5 Hurricane Michael leveled our community.

The ramifications of a serious storm like this go beyond the loss of physical property. We lost neighbors, jobs, schools, churches, a sense of stability, and our ability to cope with everyday things. In the aftermath, I found myself feeling incredibly lost. There was no planning to be done. We didn't have power, water, food, or a bathroom.

We were unsure if our insurance company would agree with our needs, or if we could find an honest contractor. My Google calendar became insignificant. In my dazed existence, I sometimes disappointed others as a detail fell through the cracks; my response was, "I'm just dealing with life chronologically right now." I was living moment to moment. I could only deal with the immediate. In His infinite wisdom, God was teaching me valuable lessons—I won't always have it all together, and the Body of Christ is genuinely compassionate when a member is suffering.

Don't feel ashamed to say, "It's just too much." We need to lean on the faith of others, especially when God seems far away. Cry out to God and those around you in your times of suffering. Be blessed by the Body of Christ that seeks to help. Finally, know that you are beautiful and worthy even if all you can do is live life chronologically.

Prayer: Lord, I cry out in my suffering. However, blessed by the Body of Christ, I know I am never alone. May Your compassion, shown through others, see me through. Amen.

Respond to His Call: Identify friends who can pray with you and for you when you need spiritual support. Call one of these friends and pray together for anyone you know who is in need of prayer.

Lori Ubowski

God's People

Take good care to observe the commandment and the law which Moses the servant of the LORD commanded you, to love the LORD your God, and to walk in all his ways, and to keep his commandments, and to cling to him, and to serve him with all your heart and with all your soul. Joshua 22:5

A priest friend of mine was moved from his beloved parish of fifteen years to a new parish. I went to visit him shortly after the move. He was still visibly grieving the move and the separation from his previous congregation. As I drove him back from the coffee shop where we visited to his new parish, we saw schoolchildren playing on the playground. He made a loving remark about the children and the parishioners. I can't remember it exactly, but he said it with the utmost kindness and love.

While grieving the loss of people he cared for deeply, he responded to his new parishioners with love. I turned to him with a smile and said, "You love them, don't you?" His reply was, "Of course, they are God's people."

What a beautiful lesson of service! As I work through the challenges of serving people, especially difficult people in difficult situations, I try to remember Father's words—they are God's people. Christ calls us to see Him in others, and in each moment we are to serve others with love.

Prayer: Lord, give me the eyes to see Your people, Your beloved creations, just as You do. Amen.

Respond to His Call: If your church parish has a school, pray for it today. Intercede, by name where possible, for the teachers, students, parents, support staff, and those who care for the buildings and grounds. If you can, make plans to serve God's people there by volunteering your time in the cafeteria or wherever needed.

Sharon Agnes Wilson

The Real Presence

The cup of blessing which we bless, is it not a participation in the blood of Christ? The bread which we break, is it not a participation in the body of Christ? 1 Corinthians 10:16

I awakened slowly to the truth of the Real Presence in the Eucharist. As a Protestant preparing for confirmation in my church, I memorized creeds, commandments, prayers, and scriptures. I hoped God would show me He was really there in the ceremony. But I experienced only hollowness. I asked, *Isn't something meaningful supposed to happen?*

Years later, I received the baptism of the Holy Spirit and entered into a life of ministry. My husband and I were privileged to live in France, Israel, and England and to spend extended time in North Africa. We witnessed miracles, signs, and wonders. Nevertheless, on certain Sunday mornings the emptiness of my confirmation would again visit me, causing me to question, *Isn't something meaningful supposed to happen?*

Then, one day during meditation, Jesus presented Himself, extending His arm toward me. I quickly said, "We are the works of Your hands." Immediately, a loaf of bread appeared in His hand. Jesus replied, "You are also the work of My heart." Instantly, I understood that eating that Bread surrendered me into His hands. I knew Jesus was truly present as flesh and blood in bread and wine; however, I did not yet know that this Presence was the core of the faith of the Catholic Church and "the source and summit of the Christian life" (*CCC* 1324).

A few years later, in France, God opened my eyes, ears, mind, and heart to the Catholic Church through His Mystical Body present on the earth: the French Catholics who loved Jesus so passionately and loved me unconditionally. They nourished me with their love, which in turn led me to the Eucharist, where I found what I was missing: the nourishment of Jesus' Body and Blood.

Prayer: Jesus, we wait to hear Your voice, to feel Your touch, and to see You with our own eyes. We are only alive in You. Amen.

Respond to His Call: Spend an hour in adoration. Give thanks for the gift of experiencing the presence of Jesus Christ, your Redeemer.

Deborah Kendrick

The Whole Armor of God

> Finally, be strong in the Lord and in the strength of his might. Put on the whole armor of God, that you may be able to stand against the wiles of the devil. For we are not contending against flesh and blood, but against the principalities, against the powers, against the world rulers of this present darkness, against the spiritual hosts of wickedness in the heavenly places. Ephesians 6:10–12

If you are Catholic, people might not like you. They may dislike you precisely because you are Catholic. But why? When Christ established the Church, He knew what her followers would face. We Catholics are in active opposition to everything the evil one represents, or we should be.

Prayer, faithful participation in the Mass, public witness to our beliefs, frequent use of the Sacrament of Confession, and baptism of our infants—all of this drives the devil insane. How does he retaliate? The thinly veiled cracks about our faith passed off as a joke, the stripping away of freedoms with unjust laws, teasing about praying before a meal in public. The important thing is how we, as Catholics, respond.

The things for which we are often ridiculed serve a purpose. Wearing a crucifix, crossing ourselves when passing a church, praying the Rosary, fasting—all are ways to spiritually gird our loins, but we have unfortunately gotten away from some of these practices.

So, what do we do? In Ephesians 6:10–18, St. Paul tells us to be strong in the might of the Lord. We are to clothe ourselves with the whole armor of God, that is, we are to use all of the spiritual means at our disposal to safeguard ourselves against the devil's tricks. St. Paul reminds us that our fight is an invisible one against the powers of darkness.

God is with us. We needn't be afraid, but we must be vigilant. We have our armor—prayer, the Eucharist, the Sacrament of Confession—but armor must be worn to be effective.

Prayer: St. Michael the Archangel, defend us in battle against the malice and snares of the devil. Amen.

Respond to His Call: Reflect on how you can put on the whole armor of God in your life.

Elizabeth Westhoff

Keep Trying

Love is patient and kind; love is not jealous or boastful; it is not arrogant or rude. Love does not insist on its own way; it is not irritable or resentful; it does not rejoice at wrong, but rejoices in the right. Love bears all things, believes all things, hopes all things, endures all things. 1 Corinthians 13:4–7

Jesus faced rejection in His hometown of Nazareth. His words "a prophet is not without honor except in his own country and in his own house" (Mt 13:57) still ring true today. We must continue to speak the truth even when others reject our message. We must continue to speak out against injustice, sin, and falsehood, even when it is not appreciated. The charism of a prophet is to not back down from the truth.

No one likes to be rejected. Reading 1 Corinthians 13, known as the "love chapter," is very helpful in combatting rejection. Here's an exercise to try. Read the chapter aloud, but substitute the word "I" for the word "love." At first, it may seem strange to say, "I am patient, I am kind, I am not jealous . . . I do not brood over injury, I bear all things," but after a while, you'll understand how to act in love, even if you're hurt.

The people of Nazareth rejected Jesus even as the scripture was being fulfilled before their eyes. They saw Jesus as a man who grew up nearby, working as a carpenter alongside His father. Often the hardest place to speak the truth is with our own family members and friends who have strayed from Jesus' teachings. But as with Jesus in his hometown, one must still speak the truth. There are several messages that we, as Christians, must continue to proclaim today, although they are unpopular. Life is sacred from conception to natural death. Jesus is truly the Son of God. Jesus died for the sins of the world. Love God and neighbor. Flee from sin. Let us remember to speak the truth in love.

Prayer: Dear Lord, Give me the courage to speak the truth in love even though I may be opposed. Amen.

Respond to His Call: Write the scripture above in your journal, substituting the word "I" for the word "love." Now think of a situation you recently faced where you could have used these attributes of love.

Emily Cavins

Fall Down Seven Times, Stand Up Eight

For a righteous man falls seven times, and rises again; but the wicked are overthrown by calamity. Proverbs 24:16

These words from Proverbs give me strength; they remind me of Jesus and His Cross. Laboring under a heavy wooden cross, Jesus fell three times along the path to the Place of the Skull for His Crucifixion. If Jesus fell, even under that heavy burden, and managed to stand again, why am I so hard on myself each time I fall?

When I fall—that is, when I choose to do wrong, choose to sin—I feel terrible. At times I feel like Adam and Eve hiding from God in the garden, which makes no sense at all—He knows what I did and where I am. What's the point of hiding? However, sometimes I stay away from Mass, or it takes me weeks to confess my sins, even though my heart is aching for forgiveness.

Instead, I listen to misleading whispers that tell me I'm not good enough, that God won't love me. I fear that He couldn't possibly forgive me, that I squandered His loving forgiveness the last time He absolved me from my sin. How could I be so stupid again?

I know I struggle with sin. It is in that verb, struggle, that I should take delight! The fact that I fight against sin is beautiful in God's eyes. I remember a homily in which the priest explained that God takes delight in forgiving us. That thought gives me courage. Somehow, in the darkest depth of the night that is my sin, a glimmer of hope emerges; the words from Proverbs echo in my mind, fueling my strength. Renewed with a bit of peace, I rise early and get dressed, determined to find my way to the Sacrament of Reconciliation.

Prayer: O Lord, although I fall again and again, renewed in Your love and peace, I will arise every time. Amen.

Respond to His Call: Make time today for a thorough examination of conscience and add the Sacrament of Reconciliation to your to-do list.

Julie E. Kenney

Perfection Is God's

You, therefore, must be perfect, as your heavenly Father is perfect. Matthew 5:48

St. Thérèse of Lisieux, a little saint who lived a little life from 1873 to 1897, is a Doctor of the Church for good reason. Although she spoke in simple ways of her littleness and weakness, she reflected a profound spirituality that we can all strive for. She announced, "I can, in spite of my littleness, aspire to holiness." She spoke of the path to heaven as a rough staircase, one with steps far too big for someone as little as she to climb. She was too small even to climb the first step! But she did not despair. Instead, she turned to Jesus and said, "The elevator which must raise me to heaven is Your arms, O Jesus!"

St. Thérèse says that for Jesus to stoop down and lift us to heaven—for Him to make us holy—we must do three things: acknowledge our littleness, "raise your little foot to scale the stairway of holiness," and trust in Jesus to do the rest. The Church builds into the liturgical calendar a singular opportunity for us to acknowledge our littleness. At the beginning of Lent, we receive ashes on our foreheads to remind us that we are not perfect as our heavenly Father is perfect, and that we are sinful and weak. That season of repentance is a good time to take that first step. Then, like St. Thérèse, we can raise our little foot to the stairway. This will take different forms, depending on our own spirituality and season of life. It might be by committing to a daily prayer time or a weekly holy hour. It might be by going to Confession or reading scripture.

We must make that small step, and then trust in Jesus to work in us, carrying us up that rough staircase to the heights of heaven. On our own, we can't be perfect as our heavenly Father is perfect. But with Jesus, all things are possible. Take that first step and trust in Jesus' mercy.

Prayer: St. Thérèse, pray for me to humble myself and so to trust my heavenly Father that I too may be lifted to heaven. Amen.

Respond to His Call: Ask St. Thérèse to send you a rose to encourage you in seeking the path to holiness—and believe that she will do so!

Stephanie Landsem

Motherhood and the Call to Welcome Others toward God

I made known to them your name . . . that the love with which you have loved me may be in them, and I in them. John 17:26

Gail built a house, lives in it, and opens its doors to anyone; it's God's place. Her doors are unlocked; her kitchen is often full of strangers. Entering the Blessing House, I felt a sense of peace. Gail rushed to hug me. Joyfully, she spoke about how blankets and pillows provide comfort to those who enter. "We have to hold on to something when we are healing," she said. The Blessing House facilitates an outpouring of God's love; people find healing and peace, celebrate life, and mourn lives lost.

Gail's home is that of any mother. Although not as radically as hers, our doors are open by virtue of our motherhood, and we don't know who God will invite to wander into our lives. Through the gift of motherhood, God's love resides within us and may transform those around us. Motherhood is selflessness, the constant pouring forth of love from God unto others, but it can be challenging. Sometimes our grown children choose to isolate themselves in moments of pain. Yet, God has blessed mothers with gifts to welcome children back into love and joy.

I know a mother who speaks so quietly that her children lean in to hear her joyful prayer, another so ebullient that her kids laugh and skip with her, and one more whose baking welcomes the whole small town for comfort and socializing. They love others through their gifts. Memories of my mother flood my mind. She was there consistently, quietly, welcoming me back, nourishing me with food and words of encouragement.

The journey of life is long, but we mothers are in it together. We are so blessed that God fashioned and prepared us for this great work.

Prayer: O Lord, today assist in a special way women who are spiritually mothering those in need. Amen.

Respond to His Call: How can you expand your scope as a mother by radically welcoming those around you? Or, in a daily sense, how can you cultivate your gifts of the Holy Spirit to bring your children peace and welcome in their difficult moments?

Anne Carraux

Dying to Be Healed

And take the helmet of salvation, and the sword of the Spirit, which is the word of God. Ephesians 6:17

First of all, it wasn't Naaman's idea to seek out a holy man—a prophet—to ask for healing. A military commander held in high esteem by the king, he no doubt had tried all the experts already—medical, spiritual, nutritional. When he does see Elisha at the suggestion of a servant girl, the cure that the prophet suggests angers him (2 Kgs 5:11).

Bathe in a river? I've done that thousands of times! Nothing more original or at least more mysterious than that? Naaman sneers at the suggestion and turns to go home. However, at his servants' pleading, Naaman turns his entourage around and heads for the Jordan, plunging himself into the water seven times. Healing takes place. Scripture tells us that his skin was made new, like the skin of a baby.

Sometimes my feeling of unworthiness makes me reluctant to approach God; sometimes, my needs seem too small compared to the needs of the world. I stop at a distance from Him. Like Naaman, I allow my intellect and logic to wage war with the Word of God.

It is precisely here, at the intersection of my will and the Word of God, that the battle and my healing begin. How is such a battle won? St. Paul tells us to pick up "the sword of the Spirit, which is the word of God," the weapon that puts to death anything that threatens to separate me from God, and from my most authentic and most profound healing.

So often I have looked back over a particularly dark or difficult time through which I have come and wondered, "How did I do that?" In the midst of the struggle between vice and virtue, the healing sometimes comes softly and almost unnoticed. And I find, to my surprise, that I have been made new.

Prayer: O my Jesus, have mercy on me as You had mercy on the leper Naaman. Take away the obstacles in my mind; show me where I need Your healing touch and grace. Strengthen my obedience to Your Word. Amen.

Respond to His Call: Make a list of all the ways you long for Jesus to heal you. What do you need to surrender before that healing can begin?

Lynne Keating

And the Word Became Flesh

And the Word became flesh and dwelt among us, full of grace and truth; we have beheld his glory, glory as of the only-begotten Son from the Father. John 1:14

On an Italian pilgrimage in 2006, our parish journeyed to the Holy House of Loreto, which tradition holds to be where Mary encountered the archangel Gabriel. We entered the massive basilica that houses the shrine and walked to a small building whose exterior was adorned with religious carvings and sculptures. Our guide explained that this was the site of the annunciation and the Incarnation. As I entered the Holy House, the magnitude of where I was standing overcame me. I knelt. For the first time, I grasped with my heart that God "really" became man. I rested my head on the wall of the house and wept.

The tour continued, and my fellow pilgrims followed as the guide headed out to our lunch destination, as it was almost noon. But I could not leave. Suddenly, the doors to the Holy House closed. I was trapped! Then, bells began to ring, the doors behind the altar opened, and Capuchin priests walked into the shrine, took their place, and led the Angelus. I was in heaven, surrounded by angels and saints. I was in an altered state, a spiritual ecstasy. The prayer ended, the priests left, and the doors to the Holy House reopened. I reentered the world—convicted like never before.

Ten years later, on another pilgrimage to Loreto, I was hoping to have another ecstatic experience. But the Lord had other plans. This time I encountered suffering. I arrived in Loreto in excruciating pain. I somehow made it to the Holy House and offered up my agony to God. Five hours later, in the Assisi hospital, I was diagnosed with a kidney stone. To this day, I thank Our Lady and St. Francis for showing me that heaven requires the Cross and embracing the Cross is part of the ecstasy.

Prayer: Blessed Mother and St. Francis of Assisi, pray for all those who suffer, that one day their pain may lead to everlasting joy. Amen.

Respond to His Call: Today, pray the Angelus.

Patti Jannuzzi

The Trail of Hidden Treasures

For truly, I say to you, till heaven and earth pass away, not an iota, not a dot, will pass from the law until all is accomplished. Matthew 5:18

Jesus' authoritative statement from Matthew's gospel can give us pause. However, we are reassured by the truth that God's rules are our ticket to freedom. We discover the treasure tucked inside them by obeying the law in ordinary moments of our days. God honors, blesses, and makes fruitful all our efforts—despite our imperfections. Our weak attempts to follow the trail of treasures hidden in His commandments lead to more life, freedom, and joy. We find abundance in obeying His laws. On the other hand, being "free" of God's rules is to spiral into darkness.

I lived this. At thirty-three, I hit rock bottom. Wounded by a sexual assault in my twenties, struggling as an actress, and enduring the devastation of infertility—I felt like all the beauty was bleeding from my life. I was angry with God. He was missing just when I needed Him most. Nothing was working, my relationships were in shambles, and I hated God with a red-hot rage that I thought nothing could quench or heal. In an agony of emptiness, I embarked on a spiritual journey that was not intended to bring me closer to God. I was escaping my life, rejecting religion as a meaningless burden, and running into darkness.

But He met me there, first sending His mother through a string of women, like the beads of a rosary, who ministered to me. Mary drew me to the Sacrament of Reconciliation, which I had avoided for years. The healing in the confessional unchained my soul and brought a flood of beauty, creativity, and joy. I hungered for God's laws. Clearing the ugly cacophony of years of unconfessed sin allowed me to hear His gentle voice and rest in His love. His laws were no longer an empty set of rules, but a treasure map, and zeal for His ways set my heart on fire.

Prayer: For those away from the Church, angry with God, in a battle with themselves against believing, we pray, *Hail Mary, full of grace . . . Amen.*

Respond to His Call: Recite a decade of the Rosary for someone who is rejecting God in their life.

Lisa Mladinich

Praying with Mary

But Mary kept all these things, pondering them in her heart. Luke 2:19

Is it possible to incorporate the Blessed Mother's prayer life, on a practical level, into our crazy lives? The idea of forming a diligent and profound prayer life like Mary's can be a daunting task, especially when our days often flit past in a harried, hectic blur. How can we reconcile the desire to pray like Mary with the reality of projects, deadlines, communications, chores, and errands? Here are some possibilities for praying with Mary and responding with full availability to God's activity in our lives.

We can foster a climate of recollection—of pondering, like Mary—by making good use of our morning coffee (or tea) time. Instead of complacently letting the day creep up on you as you struggle for wakefulness, why not have your elixir of wakefulness with Mary? Invite her to join you for a minutes as you think about yesterday and the day ahead.

Ask yourself: What happened yesterday? How did it affect me? How did I respond to the people and happenings around me? What can I do better today? Know that Mary stands near you in silent prayer. Mary stayed close to Jesus throughout His public ministry, even to the foot of the Cross. She continues to stay close to Him, and she also remains close to us, especially if we invite her into our prayer life.

We can also use our morning drive—or chore time if we work at home—to be silent and reflective. Rather than listen to talk radio or mindless tunes, we can intentionally listen for God's word to us today. We can think about how our Lord loves us—so much that He gave His life for us! Starting the day this way will help us remain calmer and more focused as we go about our daily duty—more open to God's inspiration, like Mary.

Prayer: Join me this morning, Blessed Mother, as I ponder the day ahead. Help me to remain close to your Son in imitation of you. Amen.

Respond to His Call: Today, when faced with a decision, ask yourself, "How would the Blessed Mother respond?" Imagine she is cc'd on each email you write or in your group text, and respond that way.

Marge Steinhage Fenelon

These Are My People

Then he said to them, "Go your way, eat the fat and drink sweet wine and send portions to him for whom nothing is prepared; for this day is holy to our LORD; and do not be grieved, for the joy of the LORD is your strength." Nehemiah 8:10

Our Church honors a plethora of heroes today: St. Adalgis, St. Apuleius, St. Augustus of Bourges, St. Canog, St. Dubtac, St. Gerold of Cologne, St. Helanus, St. Julia the Martyr, St. Justina of Padua, St. Marcellus of Capua, St. Osyth, St. Palladius, and Blessed Chiara Badano.

These saints are some of my favorites because most of them are unknown. They don't have Caribbean islands named after them, as some of their buddies do. They don't have cartoon versions of themselves pasted on flashy greeting cards or an overcommercialized holiday. These saints may not have led vast armies, converted entire cities, or founded popular religious orders. Nonetheless, they are beautiful models of faith for us.

Blessed Chiara Badano was an Italian teenager who dreamed of becoming a flight attendant and a missionary. Her plans came to a halt with her bone cancer diagnosis, which ended her life at just nineteen years of age. She witnessed to her family and friends, as well as doctors and other patients in the hospital. She was an ordinary teenager who drew deep into Christ's heart and gained strength to fight her battle with cancer. She used her pain to bring strangers into the Catholic faith.

The unknown saints are my people. They are ordinary people with extraordinary faith. God has called all of us to desire and strive for that coveted title of saint. To doubt that we can attain sainthood is to question the forgiveness and life renewal that Christ offers in the Eucharist. Let's all continue to work toward sainthood, even if it means being an unknown saint. Blessed Chiara, pray for us!

Prayer: All holy men and women of heaven, pray for us. Amen.

Respond to His Call: Research a saint completely unknown to you, and spend a little time getting to know your new friend in holiness.

Andrea Gibbs

Daughter of a King

But you are a chosen race, a royal priesthood, a holy nation, God's own people, that you may declare the wonderful deeds of him who called you out of darkness into his marvelous light. 1 Peter 2:9

When we think of royalty, childhood visions of storybook characters may dance through our minds, or we may recall the latest scoop on our favorite modern royals. We tend to forget that we are, in fact, royalty.

That's right! By virtue of our baptism, we are brought one by one into God's royal family, anointed as priest, prophet, and king. Despite the messiness of life that surrounds us, every one of us is adopted into a family that encourages us in love to become radiant daughters of God, the King of the Universe. God loves each of us enough to send His Son to redeem us of our sins, precisely so that we can share in His royal inheritance. God loves us so much that He calls each of us by name, putting in our hearts and lives the tools we need to live as brave warriors in His royal family.

Life is not easy, but we must pick up the tools we've been given—including the sacraments and God's Word—and use them to answer His call to live as daughters of a King. Princesses come in all shapes, sizes, and personalities. Some are born into royal life, while others have found their way into the royal fold. Each princess has her talents, gifts, and abilities to serve the King, and is hand-selected to serve others as the King's representative. We are called by name to be princesses, to be royalty, and to serve our most loving King! How will you respond to the call?

Prayer: Dear Lord, thank You for calling me into Your family. Grant me the courage to live as Your daughter, serving You above all others. Amen.

Respond to His Call: Today, ask St. Elizabeth of Hungary, a real-life princess who served our heavenly King, to pray for you and your intentions.

Ann Aliese Harry

Leaving Our Comfort Zone

And when they had brought their boats to land, they left everything and followed him. Luke 5:11

I clearly remember my heart rate accelerating as I first approached the Grand Canyon. I was in awe of the profound depth of natural beauty I observed, and my heart was drawn into the spiritual significance before me.

Creating depth takes time, perseverance, and courage. Just as natural forces created attractive layers of sediment in the canyon over time, so too will God gradually transform our interior life, and develop our spiritual muscles, when we rely on Him. Each prayer, sacrifice, temptation resisted, and act of love deepens our soul. If we stay at the surface for fear of the unknown, we never tap into our God-given potential to create beauty in our soul's depth. The depth of our interior life depends on our willingness to leave our comfort zone.

In Luke, we catch a glimpse of some of the disciples leaving their comfort zone. We are told, "When they had brought their boats to land, they left everything and followed him." Just like that, they left everything to do what they believed would fulfill them.

Immediately prior to the disciples leaving everything to follow Our Lord, they were fishing from their boats. After not catching anything all night, they obey Jesus when He directs them to put into the deep, and there they catch many fish. This story provides a tangible example of the unbelievable bounty we will discover in the deep.

If we want to grow in our interior life, we need to leave the comfortable and familiar behind and set out with Jesus into the deep. Like the excitement I felt as I walked the road to view the canyon, spiritual excitement builds in us as we glimpse the profound beauty we can experience when we journey out of our comfort zone with Jesus by our side.

Prayer: Jesus, I long to put into the deep with You. Let nothing upset my steadfast faith in You. Amen.

Respond to His Call: Take a walk and wonder at the world God has made.

Kathleen Billings

Seasons

And let us not grow weary in well-doing, for in due season we shall reap, if we do not lose heart. Galatians 6:9

I love the word "season." Growing up in Michigan with its stunning fall colors, I've always associated the word with beauty and change. But when I was a young mom with three small children, a full-time parish music career, and a growing itinerant music ministry, the word took on a more profound meaning.

The word "season" still represented beauty, change, the reassurance that God is in control, and that some things will get ugly before they become beautiful again. But it took on a deeper meaning for me in times of restlessness. I don't recall the specific occasion, but I was most likely worried about the future. It could have been parenting, career, ministry, or financial concerns. Whatever it was, I experienced a transformative moment when one of my mentors said kindly, "This is a season. You may be worried or unsure about what you're supposed to do now, but it's part of this season of your life, and you won't be here forever."

I now find myself sharing this personal revelation with other women in hope of relieving their worries about their present circumstances. Looking back, I wish I had approached each season with the confidence of knowing God had me right where I was supposed to be. With time and experience, I eventually came to trust that even in the ups and downs, uncomfortable moments, and moments of rejoicing, I served God's purpose for my life. He was always preparing me to fulfill His purpose in the next season. I pray that I remain in this place of calm and prayerful anticipation of what's to come while also enjoying what He has given me right now.

Prayer: Heavenly Father, help me to see You and Your will for me in every season. Amen.

Respond to His Call: Take a moment to reflect on past seasons and identify how God has prepared you for right now.

Lori Ulbowski

He's There Loving Me

Have no anxiety about anything, but in everything by prayer and supplication with thanksgiving let your requests be made known to God. And the peace of God, which passes all understanding, will keep your hearts and your minds in Christ Jesus. Philippians 4:6–7

Sure, I get what Paul is saying to the Philippians. I cannot experience the peace of Christ, which surpasses all understanding, if I continue to hold tightly to my anxiety. This vise grip to control my surroundings and life reveals a lack of trust in God and His will for my life.

I was told by a friend that, if we are worried about our children, we should just keep bringing them back to God until the worry lessens. Indeed, it will diminish even if you find you're lifting them up to Him every hour all day long. When we hold tightly to our fears, our grasping embrace leaves no room for light and peace. We should instead strive to embrace gratitude and give thanks for God's love for us.

Ultimately, our prayers to let go of fear and worry will bring us closer to God and help us to trust Him. We can be grateful to God even for our anxiety, because it pushes us on toward Him and reminds us of our dependence on Him for everything. Even when I doubt, even when I'm fearful, I really do know, deep down, that He loves me.

Prayer: Dear God, help me to let go of my fears and worries. Help me to accept my crosses knowing that when I carry them with Your grace, they will always bring me closer to You. Amen.

Respond to His Call: Get the attention off your worries by serving someone else. Volunteer at the parish office, put together some books to donate to a public library, or give your time to any charity serving others' needs.

Lynda MacFarland

Advocacy Is for Each of Us

So we are ambassadors for Christ, God making his appeal through us. 2 Corinthians 5:20

For sixteen months, my dad plumped hospital pillows, formed alliances with nurses, and asked doctors hard questions. He never tallied the hours spent or miles driven. Grandpa was the "cause" of my devoted "dadvocate," who unceasingly supported his father. Even when Grandpa's care plan finally turned to heartbreaking hospice, Dad never stopped seeking the utmost for his best friend. These intimate moments I witnessed between Dad and Grandpa taught me true advocacy, which is a pure and selfless gift of love. The greatest advocates never stop fighting for what is true, good, and beautiful because they desire the best for the other.

Advocacy on this side of heaven is only a glimpse of the spiritual reality we are invited into daily. Jesus speaks these peace-infused words about His heavenly Father: "He will give you another Advocate to be with you always" (Jn 14:16, NABRE). Jesus knew we would struggle without His presence and offers us the Holy Spirit to be our Advocate and Comforter. Our Advocate is near in the crushing news, the impossible tasks, and the unbearable crosses of our lives. He desires our best and will remain with us until the end, as the best advocates do.

The Advocate upholds us through the Eucharist and other sacramental graces, and bolsters our weary spirits. Heartened by this divine gift, we must advocate, with the gifts of time and talent, for that special person or cause that touches our heart. Advocacy is for each of us—not just my father. Whether you lean into the support of the Spirit today or bravely go forth to bolster others, know that you are accompanied by the divine, He in us, and we in Him.

Prayer: Holy Spirit, my Advocate and guide, be always with me. Amen.

Respond to His Call: Ask yourself who needs you as an advocate. Is it an RCIA inquirer, the elderly woman next door to you, a young person in need of tutoring? Spend a day serving as that advocate. Or commit to an hour of prayer before the Blessed Sacrament to advocate for the souls in purgatory.

Katie Anderson

No One but Thee

But save us from the hand of our enemies; turn our mourning into gladness and our affliction into well-being. Esther 14:14

You, my dear sister, are a masterpiece. As a beloved daughter of the Almighty, you are created to do amazing things.

One of the greatest gifts our Father has bestowed on you is bearing His image to a lonely world. How beautifully humbling is that? The Father knows the world is in desperate need of love, and He created you to witness to His charity.

Perhaps instead of being humbled by this gift, you find yourself burdened by it. It can be difficult to carry out a mission when you feel ill-equipped, even unworthy. Do not fear, and do not let your insecurities and past stumbles prevent you from seeing your beauty and purpose; your Father doesn't. It is a treasure to be loved by a God who knows your littleness, yet calls you to His greatness.

When you humble yourself, when you admit that you can do nothing on your own, it is then that the created is united with her Creator, and He can move in the heart of His masterpiece.

God is always waiting to be invited into your heart. Cry out to Him, just as Esther cried out in her moment of need, "Help me, who am alone and have no helper but you" (14:3). Not only in times of despair but also in times of triumph, look to the Lord. Allow the One who is all things good and true and beautiful to be all things to you. When united to the heart of the Father, you too can say, "For no one but Thee do I live, O Lord, no one but Thee do I need."

Prayer: Father, help me to recognize my littleness and submit all I have to You. May Your will be my will, Your joy my joy, Your love my love. Amen.

Respond to His Call: If you are tempted today to do it all on your own, stop for a minute, close your eyes, and look to your Creator. Let Him be your help; He is all you need.

Angela Koenig

Ten Wise Virgins

> Then the kingdom of heaven shall be compared to ten maidens who took their lamps and went to meet the bridegroom. Five of them were foolish, and five were wise. For when the foolish took their lamps, they took no oil with them; but the wise took flasks of oil with their lamps. Matthew 25:1–4

As a teenager, I was confused by my parents attending Mass daily. Despite always having a lot to do, my mother assured me that she got more accomplished when she started her day with Mass. I have grown to understand this idea, and I love attending Mass and hearing the Gospel often. One day, my sister, my husband, and I met for lunch. We had all gone to Mass earlier but at different churches, and we each heard a homily that reflected a different point of view on the same gospel.

My husband had attended Mass with our son at his all-male high school. The priest focused on the theme of preparation. He described a local man, now playing in the NFL, who had a "passion to prepare" and approached each practice with intensity. The priest instructed the high school students to begin the school year prepared like the wise virgins. The homily at my sister's parish focused on the foolish virgins and how they desired what truly couldn't be given away. It wasn't that the wise virgins were unwilling to share but that the oil was interior. The foolish virgins needed to find oil for themselves. Similarly, the priest who offered my Mass focused on the oil. He asked, "What is our oil? What fills our lamps?" We each have unique oil inside that allows our light to shine.

I continue to ponder the meaning of the oil in that parable. What is the oil that fills my lamp? What is the oil that fills your lamp? Wisdom and understanding can be ours if we take the time to look and listen. For this, we need quiet time and a prayerful space—such as at daily Mass?

Prayer: Holy Spirit, infuse the oil of Your wisdom into my heart. Amen.

Respond to His Call: Light a small candle and watch the flame consume the wax. Meditate on how quickly the wax is consumed in comparison to the time it takes to produce a candle.

Lucy H. Johnson

That's What Friends Are For

Oil and perfume make the heart glad, but the soul is torn by trouble. Proverbs 27:9

Let's face it. Sometimes a friend's kindness is expressed by a swift but gentle kick in the pants. And on the day of my mother's burial, I needed one badly.

My mother died on the Feast of St. Joseph, March 19, 2020, and thanks to the pandemic, we were limited to a small wake of ten people or fewer. No Mass, just a private Christian burial at the cemetery. I took some comfort knowing that she would be buried on my dad's birthday, March 25, the Feast of the Annunciation. Then her burial was moved to March 28.

It was difficult saying goodbye to my sweet Rosie Posie, but not being able to give her the proper Catholic send-off made it worse. The sense of loss and disappointment I felt led to an ongoing pity party—until two of my dearest friends, Kelly Wahlquist and Gail Coniglio, reminded me that they were there with me, and so was another friend, my feisty patron saint.

St. Teresa of Avila had an intense devotion to St. Joseph. Coincidence? Hardly, but I was not thinking about any of those spiritual connections as I watched the coffin being lowered into the ground. For a moment, I stopped feeling sorry for myself and checked my phone, which had been beeping almost nonstop. No wonder! Kelly and Gail had been trying to reach me all morning to let me know that it was St. Teresa of Avila's birthday. This time, the tears that flowed were tears of gratitude, and I thanked God for giving me friends on earth and in heaven who know what I need and when I need it, including a spiritual kick in the pants.

Prayer: Lord, thank You for friends. Please help me to appreciate how You speak to us through them, whether they are with us on earth or around Your throne in heaven. Amen.

Respond to His Call: Name the friends who support you in your spiritual life. Call or text them your gratitude for their prayers and support in the faith.

Teresa Tomeo

God Likes Your Company

Give thanks in all circumstances; for this is the will of God in Christ Jesus for you. 1 Thessalonians 5:18

"Sometimes, God's not funny," a friend once told me. Sometimes, I agree with that statement. God's particularly not funny when something isn't working out as I planned. That's when I feel God is trying to "grow me up," and frankly, I don't like it. At those times, I can choose to stay connected to God or disconnect and spiral into my misery. Staying connected doesn't necessarily mean the suffering goes away, or that I'm now experiencing joy, but at least I'm not alone.

Last year, I had a wonderful experience attending a Joy School workshop and learning about the neurology, psychology, and theology of joy. Our brains are hardwired for joy, and it is the most potent force of our minds.

How do we define joy? When we experience that someone is glad to be with us, it in effect turns on the brain. Joy is relational and contagious. We thrive through interacting with God and other people in loving relationships. God is always glad to be with us even when our pain, misbehavior, sadness, anger, shame, or fear interferes with our relationship with Him. He created us as relational beings, in the image of His Trinity.

Gratitude helps us stay connected to God. Gratitude returns our minds to a relationship with God, even when we are suffering. When we practice gratitude toward God, our brains remember what our connection with Him is like, making it easier to find our way back to Him. Living and practicing gratitude in good times helps us practice gratitude in times of suffering. Gratitude deepens us through constant giving thanks back to God. Let us recognize that everything, even our next breath, is a gift from God.

Prayer: Lord Jesus, thank You for all the prayers, works, joys, and sufferings of my life. May my daily gratitude be a song of praise to You. Amen.

Respond to His Call: What are you grateful for today? Tell God and listen to His response.

Katsey Long

Jesus, the Wounded Healer

He himself bore our sins in his body on the tree, that we might die to sin and live to righteousness. By his wounds you have been healed. 1 Peter 2:24

When my daughter was five years old, she was involved in a household accident that left a deep gash in her upper thigh. Horrified, I scooped her up and took her to the emergency room, where they cleaned and sutured it. It healed remarkably fast, and the leg is fully functional, but twenty-one years later, a scar remains as a reminder of the accident.

There's an expression, "walking wounded," that describes people who are by all appearances functional but who carry in their bodies or psyches the traces of injury. Cuts and abrasions leave scars on the skin; abusive treatment, tragic events, and acute losses leave scars on the soul. None of us are immune; we're all "walking wounded," projecting images of well-being while hiding the evidence of those wounds.

According to the Gospel of John, Thomas remained unbelieving until he felt the nail marks in Jesus' hands and the wound in His side—blemishes that remained even in Jesus' resurrected body (20:27–28). One would expect that all traces of His torture on the way to Calvary would have faded away, but they endured, to be seen and touched.

Why would Jesus the Healer, victorious over suffering and death, choose to reveal Himself as a wounded person? Perhaps He wanted to remind us that healing is not a restoration to a state of pristine perfection. Our wounds, like His, have the power to heal. Our sufferings, transformed by the love of a resurrected Savior, become a source of empathy for others. By putting aside misplaced shame and guilt and ministering to one another in our woundedness, we become healers as well, according to the image of Christ, by whose wounds we are healed.

Prayer: Lord Jesus, help me to bear my scars in a way that deepens my compassion for others who are suffering. Amen.

Respond to His Call: Think of a wound in your soul that you have brought to the Lord for healing. Without shame, honestly share that experience with someone else who needs the healing touch of Christ.

Sharon K. Perkins

Luke and the Lost Coin

Or what woman, having ten silver coins, if she loses one coin, does not light a lamp and sweep the house and seek diligently until she finds it? And when she has found it, she calls together her friends and neighbors, saying, "Rejoice with me, for I have found the coin which I had lost." Luke 15:8–9

Get out the fireworks; it's St. Luke's feast day! Now I love the whole Gospel, and I am particularly fond of the Nativity stories and the parable of the prodigal son, but I will never forget one line from Luke that meant everything to my coming home to the Church.

Nestled between the parable of the lost sheep and the story of the prodigal son is the parable of the lost coin. In it, Luke describes a woman with ten coins who diligently searches her house when one of them is lost. She rejoices with her friends and neighbors when she recovers the coin. Jesus ends the parable by saying, "Just so, I tell you, there is joy before the angels of God over one sinner who repents" (v. 10).

It was the spring of 1999, and I was making my first adult Confession to Bishop Paul Dudley. After Confession, he referred to the parable above and said, "Alyssa, imagine the rejoicing in heaven today for one sinner coming home." In one sentence, he welcomed me back to the fold. Later, as I was leaving, he emphatically stated, "Alyssa, God has forgiven you. Now, go home and do the hard work of forgiving yourself."

So today, in honor of St. Luke, get to the confessional if you need it. After God forgives you, do the work of forgiving yourself, and stand back and get ready . . . angels will be rejoicing! Imagine their joy in celebrating the return of your very soul to God!

Prayer: St. Luke, pray for me to rejoice in the gift of forgiveness, especially as offered to me through the Sacrament of Reconciliation. Amen.

Respond to His Call: Regardless of anxiety or fear, resolve to *go to Confession!* Make an appointment or go incognito at another parish—just do what you have to do to receive the grace and the assurance of your sins being forgiven by Jesus Christ Himself.

Alyssa Bormes

Case No. 05-12046-RGM

My sheep hear my voice, and I know them, and they follow me.
John 10:27

It was the most humbling day of my life. In the course of a twenty-plus-year marriage, more than $200,000 in credit card debt had been incurred in my name or jointly, and it was all on me to deal with it through chapter 13 bankruptcy repayment. I sat in a little room with a dozen or so other people, watching videos and hearing speakers talk about making your own coffee, selling vehicles you can't afford, and playing board games instead of going on vacation. These were all practices my parents had instilled in me. But none of that mattered; I was just Case No. 05-12046-RGM. Finally, after meeting with the bankruptcy trustee, I started home, feeling as if everyone on the street knew what a loser I was. I hadn't been a churchgoer for decades and thought maybe I'd give that a try since nothing else was working.

A couple of Sundays later, the bulletin had a notice about a returning Catholics program. The first session was pretty nonthreatening. But there was a catch: we had to tell our "faith journeys," and the date I drew was September 28—the same day my bankruptcy repayment plan was to be reviewed by a judge. If the plan was accepted, I would be handing over all of my monthly take-home pay for the next three years except what was needed to cover my rent. That night, I reluctantly talked about why I quit going to church as a teenager and how my personal and financial life was such a mess. And no one threw a single stone.

The blessings I received that night powered me through navigating my reentry into the Church. I learned a new language of monstrances and surplices—and redemption and transformation—as Jesus revealed His name for me was not Case No. 05-12046-RGM but Beloved Sister.

Prayer: Jesus, close my eyes to what the world calls me, and open my soul to You. Amen.

Respond to His Call: Journal about your favorite encounter between Jesus and one of the gospels' unnamed women. Imagine what she called herself after that encounter.

Melanie Rigney

October 20

A Redemptive Experience

The Spirit of the Lord God is upon me, because the Lord has anointed me to bring good tidings to the afflicted; he has sent me to bind up the brokenhearted . . . to comfort all who mourn.
Isaiah 61:1–2

Divorce is horrible. It violates the whole family, the poison of it reaches into every part of our community, and, yes, God hates it (Mal 2:16). But there's another part of this challenging reality: from the tragedy of divorce can come great blessings, renewal, restoration, and even redemption. That is precisely the *good news* of our faith. Our whole Christian religion is about a God who takes our mess and brings something good out of it, even greater than we had.

Those I've ministered to over the last few decades often speak of a redemptive experience in the aftermath of divorce. Many are the times I've heard exclaimed, "I found God! I'd been running from Him for years." Or, "I started going to Confession again after thirty years," and "I started reading the Bible, and it's changed me." Often they delight: "I'm a much better Mom/Dad than I ever was." Some help others through their sufferings with the help of the Lord: "I started a divorce ministry in my parish where God is healing so many." And some learned more about themselves: "I was grossly selfish, and through this painful time, I've learned how to love rightly."

Whether a person chose to leave the marriage, or had to leave, or was abandoned, every heart must stay open to God's healing and the abundant mercies that can flow from the wound and bless others nearby. Don't despair—beauty will rise from ashes. Trust that God will make good on His promises to you or someone you know who is suffering.

Prayer: Dear Jesus, help me be less afraid, critical, or judgmental of those I know who are suffering from divorce. As You are for me, let me be a light of love and truth for them. Amen.

Respond to His Call: Call your parish and ask if there is a ministry to the separated and divorced. If not, offer your best resource: prayer.

Rose Sweet

Diamonds and God's Love

Behold, you are beautiful, my love, behold, you are beautiful! Your eyes are doves behind your veil. Song of Solomon 4:1

When we cleaned out the neglected house of my parents after the death of my only brother, our son helped us. Going through all the piled papers and debris in each room, our son found a small box on a nightstand by my mother's bed. He brought it to me, asking, "Do you recognize this?" Inside the dark, velvety jewelry box, on a bed of creamy satin, a slim gold necklace with five tiny diamonds gleamed. It instantly took me back to an evening when I saw my mother put it on while my father smiled proudly at her.

I remembered the way they used to look at each other. In all my family's craziness, I could always say my mother and father loved one another. Against all opposition of both their families, their love was steadfast. When they finally had money to celebrate that love publicly, Dad bought Mom that necklace. During her decline in health, beauty, wealth, and even security, she saved it, as she saved their love.

Seeing it out in the open on a nightstand, daring those who broke into this ravaged house multiple times to steal it away, reminded me that God loves *love*. He *is* love, loving the love we give one another. The symbol of Mom and Dad's love told me God wanted me to remember to love regardless of opposition, despite illness and aging, defiant of separation by death, on into eternity.

Thank You, God, for my parents, who saw each other as beautiful. Thank You, God, for their fidelity to their marriage vows. Thank You for their choice to live out love in front of me, so I learned Your love.

Prayer: O God, thank You for having created me within the love of my parents for each other. May my mother and father praise You in heaven forever. Amen.

Respond to His Call: Attend a Mass, offering your prayers and Holy Communion for both your parents, giving thanks for their love. If possible, send a card to them telling them how much you love them and thank God for them.

Dr. Carol Younger

Jesus Approaches on the Road

But they constrained him, saying, "Stay with us, for it is toward evening and the day is now far spent." Luke 24:29

Out for a morning walk, I consider all that is going on in my life. I worry for my children, feel uncertain about finances, and am confused about the world's direction. My pace quickens as my mind races through my cares and concerns. As I continue walking, I feel Jesus' presence. He is fully aware of what is rummaging through my mind, but I sense His invitation to tell Him about it anyway. As I pour out my heart, I remember another time He approached walkers on a road. He asked the two disciples on the way to Emmaus why they were so distraught, even though He already knew. The Emmaus story exemplifies Jesus' desire to have a relationship with us and to share in all things that concern us. That desire takes the form of pursuing each of us in various elements of our Catholic faith: prayer, Confession, scripture, and the Eucharist.

Prayer: Jesus wants me to come to Him with everything. He longs to be an intimate part of my life through prayer. By regularly talking with the Lord, I increase His involvement and constant presence in my life.

Confession: In the Sacrament of Confession, Jesus meets me where I am emotionally, mentally, and spiritually. Even in my foolishness, He patiently and attentively listens to all that lays heavy on my heart. He responds with forgiveness, mercy, and love.

Scripture: In scripture, I learn the history of God's plan and receive a personal invitation to be part of it. When I stay close to His Word, I remain in a place of trust in Him.

Eucharist: At every Mass, my eyes are open to the miracle before me. I recognize Jesus' Body, Blood, Soul, and Divinity in the Holy Eucharist. Oh, how my heart burns within me!

Prayer: Thank you, Jesus, for inviting me into a close relationship with You. May my heart burn with love for You, as Your Sacred Heart always burns with love for me. Amen.

Respond to His Call: Take your own Emmaus walk. What will you talk to Jesus about when He joins you?

Sarah Damm

Turning Obstacles into Opportunities

Pray at all times in the Spirit, with all prayer and supplication. To that end keep alert with all perseverance, making supplication for all the saints. Ephesians 6:18

I hate traffic! Wedged in like a sardine on Interstate 94, I noticed the license plate in front of me included my brother-in-law's initials, CPW. So, I thought, "I should say a little prayer for him," and I did. Then suddenly I was checking everyone's license plate to see who I could pray for next. I prayed for my cousin Jenny, JMS, and I think I even prayed for a lawyer . . . the license plate was ISUE4U. (He probably needed the prayers most!) What I thought was a miserable situation—a forty-five-minute commute to drive twelve miles—instantly became a win-win-win situation. I was distracted from the angst of the daily traffic rut, I was praying for others, and I was communing with my Creator.

St. Paul says, "Pray at all times in the Spirit, with all prayer and supplication." These words come on the heels of him encouraging the Ephesians to remain strong in battle and to put on the armor of God. He is telling his readers that we are in a spiritual battle, a battle that will require some serious armor.

We have many ways to draw power from the Lord to stand firm in our faith on the battlefield. As Christians, we have truth, righteousness, peace, and hope. As Catholics, we have the Mass, the Blessed Mother, the Communion of Saints, the sacraments, and especially the Eucharist. This spiritual armor not only protects and defends us but also takes us on the offense; we have the sword of the Spirit—the Word of God—and the power of prayer. We can turn any obstacle into an opportunity to pray. That's a pretty good superpower to have!

Prayer: Lord, give me the strength to persevere and overcome obstacles in my life. Give me the grace to see how I can make goodness shine through any situation. Amen.

Respond to His Call: Today, look for ways to "pray at all times in the Spirit," even if it means praying for the person who cuts you off in traffic.

Kelly M. Wahlquist

Our Lives Are Not Accidental

We know that in everything God works for good with those who love him, who are called according to his purpose. Romans 8:28

Have you ever felt you were in the wrong place at the wrong time? While taking a walk in my neighborhood one summer evening, I waited at the edge of a street for a break in the traffic so that I could cross. Since I was standing on a spot designated for crossing but that wasn't an official cross-walk, I wasn't expecting anyone to stop for me. One driver did, though. Unfortunately, a young man in the car behind him didn't see this Good Samaritan's brake lights and crashed into the stopped vehicle, causing significant damage to both cars. Thankfully no one was seriously injured. In the weeks that followed, I wrestled with the fact that the accident wouldn't have happened if I hadn't decided to go for a walk that night.

St. Paul reminds us that regardless of the decisions we make, God can bring good from them. Even though life events can seem painful or senseless, we can find comfort in knowing that God is transforming us through them. As St. Paul writes to the Thessalonians: "To this end we always pray for you, that our God may make you worthy of his call, and may fulfil every good resolve and work of faith by his power" (2 Thes 1:11). God loved the world so much that He gave us His Son, at just the right place and time, according to His will. Jesus will bring good out of all we put before Him.

Prayer: O God, how grateful I am that You work all things for good for those who love You. Please wipe away any unnecessary guilt I feel for situations I have faced that were beyond my control. Amen.

Respond to His Call: Compose a thank-you note to God for all the good you are experiencing from a current relationship or responsibility.

Susan Klemond

Who Do You Think You Are?

Beloved, we are God's children now; it does not yet appear what we shall be, but we know that when he appears we shall be like him, for we shall see him as he is. 1 John 3:2

Who do you think you are? Perhaps you have been confronted with this question, as a reprimand or an insult. But it is actually an important question. Your response might reveal whether you are in line or out of line with what God knows about you and has in store for you. Sadly, too many of us have a wrong idea about ourselves, one that does not match reality. And we act out of those mistaken beliefs.

On the one hand, our talents or giftedness, accomplishments, or the treasures we possess here on earth may make us think too highly of ourselves. We then have an inflated sense of worth, especially in relation to others. We must rethink and resize our own image, lest we dangerously deceive ourselves. Otherwise, we will likely be in for a great surprise on the last day. On the other hand, our inadequacies, limits and failures, or handicaps of any sort may make us think too poorly of ourselves. This leads to a deflated sense of self and a deficient estimation of our worth, painfully so in relation to others. We must rethink and resize our own image, lest we unnecessarily deprive ourselves. Otherwise, we will likely be in for a great surprise on the last day as well.

Aim to know yourself as God knows you—the original and finished product, the person He dreamed you to be from the beginning. Thank the Lord for who you are, and are both becoming and unbecoming, through the ongoing process of Christian conversion and growth.

Prayer: Lord, You have searched me and You know me. You perceive my thoughts from afar. I praise You because I am fearfully and wonderfully made. Help me to see that I am who I am in Your sight—nothing more and nothing less. Amen.

Respond to His Call: Prayerfully identify any distorted views you have of your unique self, asking for the grace to look at yourself with a sober, serene, and kindly countenance and to act accordingly, in relation to God and others.

Martha Fernández-Sardina

October 26

Pray for Holy Priests

For it is witnessed of him, "You are a priest for ever, according to the order of Melchizedek." Hebrews 7:17

On the day of my brother's priestly ordination, I watched in awe as the sacred ceremony unfolded. He prostrated himself, received his vestment, and pledged his allegiance to the Church. At ordination, a spiritual and ontological change occurs. The priest is still human, of course; however, this change imprints an indelible spiritual mark on his soul and allows Christ to work directly through the priest.

As a human, the priest still suffers loneliness, sorrow, poor health, envy, and the general messiness of life. This was brought home to me strongly one day during lunch with a priest friend, who told me he had just celebrated the funeral of a parishioner. He served at a small parish, and this man was a dedicated volunteer, showing up and helping the priest when no one else could. As my priest friend told me how beautiful the funeral was and how the family had leaned heavily on him for solace, tears welled up in his eyes. He looked at me and said, "I lost a very good friend whom I dearly loved." No one had thought to comfort him, the celebrant of the funeral. Yet he, like all good priests, strives to pour his life out in loving service to the Father, as Jesus did. He aches for our souls, and he has been charged by Christ to guide us safely home.

Let us follow the example of Mary, the mother of all priests, and use the gift of the feminine heart to receive the needs of others. Resist the temptation to see your pastor as the CEO of a business. Forgive his homilies and lousy singing, support him even if it's just with your smile, allow him to be a spiritual father to you and your family, pray for him, and above all, work on your own holiness.

Prayer: Mary, mother of all priests, bring my prayers for Fr. [*name*] to your Son. Amen.

Respond to His Call: Mail a thank-you note to each priest in your parish, letting them know that you see and appreciate their efforts to tend the Body of Christ. Include one example of something they said in a homily or wrote in a parish bulletin that contributed to your spirituality.

Sherry Kennedy Brownrigg

The Dizzying Depths of Divine Mercy

Go and learn what this means, "I desire mercy, and not sacrifice."
For I came not to call the righteous, but sinners. Matthew 9:13

One desolate winter I took an eight-day retreat, alone in a tiny house with a chapel on a deserted city street. Each morning a nun drove me to Mass. Each afternoon, a priest visited for one hour of spiritual direction. On the third day, I recalled a sin that I had never confessed. Asking for Reconciliation, I explained that I hadn't thought of this for twenty years—using birth control. Father asked only one question, "Have you talked to God about this?" "No," I answered a bit sarcastically. "I don't have to talk to God about this. I know it was wrong. I know what God will say."

Father insisted, "You must ask God about this." Over the next two days, we had the same conversation. Father was patient but firm. Finally, gritting my teeth, I entered the dimly lit, chilly chapel to talk to God about my sin. The next day, Father smiled when I said I had finally talked to God. "Well," he said, "what did God say?"

Taking a deep breath, I began. "God asked me how long I had taken birth control pills. I told Him I had taken them for one year." I looked up for Father's reaction—there was none. I continued. "God asked me how many foster children I'd taken in over the years." There were twelve. "Then God said to my heart, 'See? I gave you one child for every month you chose birth control.'" In an instant, my whole world had turned upside down. The very thing I thought that I was doing for God, *He* had been doing *for me*! I could not qualify for regular fostering because I was a single mom in a tiny two-bedroom apartment. I only qualified for children who were required to sleep in the same room with the parent—newborns!

Prayer: Take, Lord, and receive all my liberty, my memory, my understanding, and my entire will. Give me only Your love and Your grace; that is enough for me. Amen. (from the Prayer of St. Ignatius)

Respond to His Call: Is there a particular issue or decision with which you are struggling? Let go of your own ideas, agendas, and expectations, and ask God about it.

Lynne Keating

October 28

Living Water Promises

Jesus said to her, "Every one who drinks of this water will thirst again, but whoever drinks of the water that I shall give him will never thirst; the water that I shall give him will become in him a spring of water welling up to eternal life." John 4:13–14

One evening, as I returned home from parent-teacher conferences, I remembered being out of coffee. I didn't need anything else from the grocery store, but how could tomorrow begin well without my morning java? Walking into the grocery store to grab a pound of my favorite espresso blend, I spied my favorite spring flower in the floral section. How could I resist? Each year, they're only available for a short time. So I picked up a few bunches of daffodils and headed to the checkout line.

When I arrived home, I put my coffee in the pantry and filled a vase with water. I arranged the daffodils as best I could, but I have to admit that they didn't look like much. They were still closed pretty tightly, looking almost lifeless. The beauty this flower promises was nowhere to be seen. Early the next morning, though, as I shuffled into the kitchen to brew coffee, a stunning scene greeted me. All because of a little water, my tiny yellow beauties had opened to their fullest potential. They exemplified new life and restored hope.

Sometimes we feel like those daffodils when I initially brought them home: hidden, closed off, nearly lifeless. But Jesus tells us about the replenishing power of life-giving water for our weary souls. He desires to lavish this water upon us with the promise of healing and redemption. Once our thirst for this water is quenched, our inner beauty, like the daffodil, unfolds in all its splendor and can finally be shared with a world that desperately needs reminders of God's love.

Prayer: Jesus, I find You waiting for me at the well. I bring You my weary, restless, imperfect, and scarred heart. Fill me with Your life-giving water, and redeem me with Your overflowing love. Amen.

Respond to His Call: What are you thirsting or longing for? What makes you feel unknown and maybe even unloved? How do you need Jesus to replenish you today?

Sarah Damm

Share the Love

Go therefore and make disciples of all nations, baptizing them in the name of the Father and of the Son and of the Holy Spirit.
Matthew 28:19

Share the love! Easier said than done, right? I used to think so. Until recently, I wouldn't have opened my mouth about my faith. Since I awakened in my faith, God has given me many graced opportunities to share His love, mainly through my journey with breast cancer.

The waiting room in our cancer center has a dozen chairs. I always sit directly in front of the doors so I can give a big smile to whoever enters. If that seat is taken, I intentionally take a position next to someone else so that we can talk.

One day in February, "my" seat was taken, but I felt the Holy Spirit direct me to sit near a specific woman. When the doctor entered, she looked at us and said, "Look, two mothers of the brides!" I turned to the other woman with joy. "You have a daughter getting married, too?"

We compared notes on wedding plans, and I could see that this woman was struggling with her treatment. Before I knew it, I was offering to help plan her daughter's wedding! She looked relieved at my offer, and I knew it was the right thing to do. Later in an email, I evangelized about my faith and said that it was God's plan for us to meet. I was going out on a limb, but that is our call, right? I was pleasantly surprised by her reply to my email. She agreed that God's providence connected us, and she was grateful that He put us together.

Making disciples, bringing others to the Lord, helping our neighbor—all mean the same thing: share the love you have received from Jesus, and the Holy Spirit will provide the rest.

Prayer: Holy Spirit, empower me with every spiritual blessing I need to share my love for Jesus with whomever You place in my life. Amen.

Respond to His Call: Resolve to be open today to opportunities to share your love of Jesus.

Rhonda Zweber

Help My Unbelief

Immediately the father of the child cried out and said, "I believe; help my unbelief!" Mark 9:24

Faith is a gift from God that we cannot merely open and place on a shelf like a knick-knack. This precious gift requires familiarity with the instructions and frequent use to reap the most benefit. Do you remember the Tamagotchi toy craze of the 1990s? A Tamagotchi was an electronic pet that the owner had to tend to all day long. If the owner failed to follow the instructions, her little friend would "die." I've learned that my faith will do the same if I fail to give it the proper attention. Imagine if we treated our faith like our Tamagotchi! Jesus not only teaches us but also models for us how to keep our faith alive. He has given us lessons by example of how He prays, retreats, breaks bread, spends time with the Blessed Mother, and fasts.

Grace feeds our faith. God provides grace to us in abundance, especially through the sacraments, prayer, and the scriptures. Participating fully in the sacraments strengthens the weak spots in our faith. Lord, I believe, but I am too preoccupied most days to bolster my belief by partaking of the sacraments. Unfortified by the sacraments' efficacious grace, when trouble comes, I wonder if God can deliver on all His promises or if He's even real.

Daily prayer keeps the line of conversation open, so even when we are unsure, like the father in Mark's gospel, we bring our troubles to Jesus. I believe enough to know that Jesus can help, but there is always a part of me that wrestles with the uncertainty of whether He will. How many times have I begged for Jesus' help, but the outcome rocked my faith (and trust). For this very reason, I know all too well the prayer, "Lord, I believe; help my unbelief."

Prayer: Lord, I believe; please help me in all those places You find my unbelief. Fortify my faith through Your sacramental love. Amen.

Respond to His Call: Today, research one area of the faith you struggle to understand or adopt.

Allison Gingras

Halloween and Hand-Me-Downs

I am the light of the world; he who follows me will not walk in darkness, but will have the light of life. John 8:12

"In two years, I get to be Pluto for Halloween," I pronounced. The girls in the ballet carpool were confused. "How do you know that?" they asked. *Didn't everyone know their costume for the following years?* I thought. I knew what I was going to be all the way through sixth grade!

Every year a few days before Halloween, my mother would retrieve the costume box. It was its own holiday! As you grew, you graduated to the next costume. We started as a teddy bear and finished as an old man or an old lady. I also knew what dress was coming to me and when. All my sister's dresses were about eight years ahead of me—except that I eventually was much taller than her. Sometimes hand-me-downs would go to another family and then back to me.

A woman once told me that she couldn't think of anything worse than hand-me-downs. She thought it was damaging to expect children to wear them. She was an only child. "Oh, you're wrong—it was the best!" I explained the nuances. It seemed to make sense to her when I mentioned going shopping. If we shopped for new clothes, I might end up with one item. But when I received a box of used clothes from a sibling, whatever was in it was mine until I grew—then it was someone else's turn.

Hand-me-downs and Halloween costumes have everything to do with life. When you say yes to life, you might need to rely on hand-me-downs, and Halloween is a big yes to life. How? The kids in their costumes, holding a jack-o'-lantern full of candy and a flashlight to make their way, illuminate the night, saying we are not afraid of the darkness. This is All Hallows' Eve; tomorrow is All Saints' Day, which is exactly where we are headed!

Prayer: Holy men and women of heaven, pray for us to say yes to the life awaiting us in heaven. Illuminate the way. Let no fears keep us from joining you in the Church Triumphant. Amen.

Respond to His Call: Prepare a box of used clothing to donate to a Catholic charity. Try to include a costume in that box!

Alyssa Bormes

Stay Connected

Therefore, since we are surrounded by so great a cloud of witnesses, let us also lay aside every weight, and sin which clings so closely, and let us run with perseverance the race that is set before us. Hebrews 12:1

The Catholic faith boasts of so many faithful men and women who have gone before us to serve the Lord. The examples of fidelity chronicled throughout Hebrews 11 give us an idea of the variety of ways God uses His beloved people for His glory. St. Paul compares our journey of faith to a race that requires perseverance. He thus encourages the faithful to remain steadfast despite the many obstacles life presents.

I once ran the Disney half-marathon. To ensure the runners complete the 13.1 miles before the parks open, the starting gun sounds at 3 a.m.! In January, even Florida can be uncomfortably cold at that hour. Each runner begins wearing many layers of clothes, which you must be willing to donate as you shed them along the route. These comforts become burdens, slowing a runner down, as the heat of the day intensifies. Much like extra layers when running, the difficulties, challenges, and burdens of our life hamper our ability to reach our spiritual finish line.

During the half-marathon, we encountered many people offering assistance—high fives, nourishment, instructions, even medical care. They were there to give us whatever we needed to ensure we successfully finished the race. Help to complete the spiritual race is the role of the saints in our lives. These holy men and women feed us through their words, encourage us by their example, and some even guide our journey through their intercessory prayers. How good to know that we're never alone in this journey. God given us not only beautiful sisters in Christ to travel alongside but also a great cloud of witnesses—holy men and women who help us lay aside every weight and persevere.

Prayer: O holy men and women of heaven, pray for me, my family, and our world. Amen.

Respond to His Call: Pray with the saints for your intentions today.

Allison Gingras

It's November. Get Busy!

And just as it is appointed for men to die once, and after that comes judgment. Hebrews 9:27

November is dedicated to the souls in purgatory. Our job as the Church Militant is to pray for the souls of the faithful departed every time we pass a cemetery or have a spare moment to offer a quick prayer.

First, let's be clear on what the Church teaches—there is a heaven, purgatory, and hell, and depending on the state of your soul at death, you will spend eternity in one of two and, possibly, some amount of time in the other. The Church's teaching on this is explicit and is beautifully addressed in *Lumen Gentium*, n. 48, "Since we know neither the day nor the hour, we should follow the advice of the Lord and watch constantly so that, when the single course of our earthly life is completed (cf. Heb 9:27), we may merit to enter with him into the marriage feast and be numbered among the blessed, and not, like the wicked and slothful servants, be ordered to depart into the eternal fire, into the outer darkness where 'men will weep and gnash their teeth' (Mt 22:13 and 25:30)."

To enter heaven, every single trace of sin must be purged from the soul. We are the Church on earth, engaged in warfare with the devil, the flesh, and worldly powers of temptation and unrighteousness. It is our duty, privilege, and honor as Catholics to pray for those who are being purged of their last attachment to sin. We pray for their deliverance so that one day, as the Church Triumphant, they may pray for us: "Eternal rest grant unto them, O Lord, and let perpetual light shine upon them. May the souls of the faithful departed, through the mercy of God, rest in peace. Amen."

Prayer: Eternal rest grant unto [*insert name*], O Lord; let perpetual light shine upon them. And may they rest in the light of Your peace. Amen.

Respond to His Call: Visit a cemetery today and pray for the souls at rest there. Pray especially for those who have long since passed and may not have anyone left to pray for them.

Elizabeth Westhoff

To the Men Who Open Doors

The Son of man came not to be served but to serve, and to give his life as a ransom for many. Matthew 20:28

Throughout my life, I have done everything imaginable to avoid needing help. I never wanted to be a bother. Childhood wounds told me that I needed to manage on my own. I never thought my self-sufficiency hurt anyone; I tried not to upset or irritate others. Once, though, a gentleman guest of my sister-in-law asked her if I had a problem with him because I wouldn't let him open a door for me. She explained to him that it was nothing he did; it's just how I am. Needless to say, I felt terrible. I wondered, *How many other times have I hurt people by refusing to accept their kindness?*

Avoiding the help of others is, in reality, an excellent way to push them away. Love is a verb—by definition, an action. If we don't allow others to serve us in the way they can and want, we reject their love. As a beloved child of God, you actually practice selflessness when you accept assistance. You snuff out the flame of pride in your heart by saying no to your unwarranted desire to prove yourself.

We learn how to accept the help of others slowly, with God's grace. Jesus, always the gentleman, has my heart; He is the flawless example of a person who came to serve and not be served. Yet He allowed Himself to be loved and served during His public ministry. So here's to the men who open doors. May we accept their humble gift of love in service for the sake of Jesus.

Prayer: O my Jesus, may I learn to accept the graces You send by the hands of others, and may I bring Your graces to others. Make my humility like that of Your mother Mary, who went to help Elizabeth. Teach me to praise You and the Blessed Mother in thanksgiving, as Elizabeth did. Amen.

Respond to His Call: Volunteer at a charity for an afternoon as an act of love and humility. Or donate the cost of a day's meals to a charity that serves poor women.

Angela Koenig

Reap What You Sow

Do not be deceived; God is not mocked, for whatever a man sows, that he will also reap. For he who sows to his own flesh will from the flesh reap corruption; but he who sows to the Spirit will from the Spirit reap eternal life. Galatians 6:7–8

As a young child, I watched my mother grow an array of fruits and vegetables. My own family has gardened for twenty-two years, and I find it rewarding to provide food for our table this way. But I have come to appreciate agriculture beyond the thrill of harvesting what I planted. I most value the abundant spiritual analogies I can draw from my experiences and the numerous biblical references to agriculture that come alive for me.

Scripture often speaks of sowing and reaping. As an avid gardener, I can easily relate to this concept, for when I take time to sow seeds properly, I reap a bountiful harvest. The amount of effort I exert through preparing, weeding, and planting determines the harvest.

This same concept applies to all aspects of our lives. We reap what we sow. Our results are based on our actions. If we want to experience unfailing eternal love, then we must lead a righteous life. If we live our lives united to Christ, our actions will reflect our life in His Spirit. The seeds we sow will be life-giving and not life draining. They will fill our souls with beauty instead of ugliness and our hearts with peace instead of unrest.

We all have sown good seeds, yet we all have sown bad seeds as well. God calls us to sift through the weeds and the wheat in our lives and move forward in faith. Do not be afraid to uproot and replant if necessary. God can heal the areas where we have sown bad seed. Have the courage to do an inventory of the fruit present in your life and to weed and rearrange the garden of your soul. The Master Gardener awaits.

Prayer: God, please heal the places in my life where bad seed has crowded out my love for You and others. Amen.

Respond to His Call: Ponder what seems to be "good seed" in your life.

Kathleen Billings

It Is Good That We Are Here

And Peter said to Jesus, "Lord, it is well that we are here; if you wish, I will make three booths here, one for you and one for Moses and one for Elijah." Matthew 17:4

Lord, it is good that we are here. My heart has echoed this sentiment many times—attending the last day of school, singing with my sister, encountering Jesus anew. Have you caught glimpses of these heaven moments, perhaps surrounded by loved ones? During a retreat with faith renewed? These times of gladness might be likened to the Transfiguration on Mount Tabor. Jesus invites us to climb the high mountain with Him. He astonishes us by piercing our everyday mundane with His glory.

At first, we delight in the scenery and abundance. Our comfort slowly transforms when we offer that same suggestion as Peter. "Jesus! Maybe we should just stay a while longer. We have everything we need on the mountain, right? No need to go back down there into the messiness of real life." Love and mercy were in the cloud, which covered the mountain; God still uses these holy shadows. When the coffee grows cold, and the guests leave, are we still grateful for what we have been given? For the disciples, the wondrous glories from heaven drifted from present reality to mere memory. With the gentlest touch, Jesus reminded them (and us) that His humanity matches His divinity. While the Transfiguration was a beautiful time for the disciples, our hope lies in the knowledge that Jesus descended from the mountain with them.

Are you wearied by the hills and valleys of this life? Are your mountaintop moments vague memories? Be not afraid. The same Jesus who met you there has led you down the mountain and walks with you. Spiritual altitude aside, we can rest in the knowledge that His continual presence is transfiguring us every day.

Prayer: Jesus, transfigure me. Be with me on the mountaintop, and as I walk through the valley, protect my faith from being wearied. Amen.

Respond to His Call: Take a long walk outside today. Pay attention to how your thoughts, attitude, and energy level change during the walk back home, and on your arrival. Any lessons to take to prayer?

Katie Anderson

God Delights in Mercy

Who is a God like you, pardoning iniquity and passing over transgression for the remnant of his inheritance? He does not retain his anger for ever because he delights in mercy. He will again have compassion upon us, he will tread our iniquities under foot. You will cast all our sins into the depths of the sea. Micah 7:18–19

There's a popular saying going around on social media: "Resentment is like drinking poison and waiting for the other person to die." It makes me laugh because it's so true! I tend to hold on to my hurts and cultivate my wounds as if they were something precious and irreplaceable. But do I remember the good? Do I focus on it, as I should? I try, but . . . Lord, it's hard. Unfortunately, holding onto unforgiveness disfigures our once-beautiful, unique, and unrepeatable souls. It's an ugly habit, and it gets us nowhere holy.

So what's a girl to do? I find it refreshing to contemplate the Lord's delight in showing mercy. In fact, even a cursory read of Micah 7:18–19 reveals an ebullient God, extravagant in the delight He takes in smashing our iniquities like grapes and hurling our sins into the depths of the sea. (It's quite a sin-squishing romp!) God not only wants to let go of our failings but also practically makes a recreational sport of forgiving and forgetting. God is awesome. All the time. And I love to imagine Him, as I step out of the confessional, delightedly sending all my decimated yuck to the bottom of the sea and then showering me with affection—because forgiveness looks so good on me!

Prayer: Thank You for Your forgiving heart, Lord. Give me the grace to give every resentment to You. Redeem my thoughts, Lord, and attract my heart to all that is beautiful, true, and good in others. Amen.

Respond to His Call: Sit in silence with the Lord and ask Him to show you which resentment to start with. Then pray for the grace to release it for smashing and hurling!

Lisa Mladinich

What Do You Want on Your Tombstone?

For he was a good man, full of the Holy Spirit and of faith. And a large company was added to the Lord. Acts 11:24

In the 1990s, a pizza company created commercials featuring villains and people in dire straits. At the final moment, the villain would ask, "What do you want on your tombstone?" The victim would pause, reflect, and answer, "Pepperoni and cheese." This question remains relevant today. How do we want to be remembered? What will be our legacy?

One of the benefits of attending daily Mass is hearing different biblical readings. Throughout the years, my husband and I have picked favorites that we wish to have read at our funerals. Being a competitive person, I have always loved the reading from Timothy: "I have fought the good fight, I have finished the race, I have kept the faith" (2 Tm 4:7).

Recently, the first reading at daily Mass, from the Acts of the Apostles, described Barnabas as a "good man, full of the Holy Spirit and of faith." The homilist suggested how wonderful it would be if we were remembered in such a way.

Growing up, I recall my mother always saying, "When I die, don't wish me back. I'm going to a greater glory." When she passed at age ninety-eight, I felt certain that Mom had achieved her desire as she was a good woman, filled with the Spirit and faith. In the same way, I want our children to realize that the goal of this life is to get to heaven. By talking about funeral readings, songs, and the rewards of heaven, I hope they realize that what happens today is so much less important than what happens in eternity.

Prayer: Dear God, please don't let us fear dying. Remind us that it is a gateway to heaven. Help us to realize that our goal on earth is to spend eternity with You. Amen.

Respond to His Call: Talk with your children or loved ones about your funeral arrangements—what readings, songs, and food you'd like.

Lucy H. Johnson

The Art of Doing Nothing

Be still, and know that I am God. I am exalted among the nations, I am exalted in the earth! Psalm 46:10

"Be still and do nothing." That is what we tell our WINE & Shrine pilgrims to do in Italy. It might seem like a strange thing to suggest when traveling to a country overflowing with stunning churches, museums, piazzas, and other places of interest, but it's not weird at all. In Italy, being still is a way of life.

Italians excel at the "sweet art of doing nothing" (*la dolce far niente*). They don't rush through meals. There is always time to take a break in the middle of the day, and doing nothing is actually doing something very important. It gives one time to relax and to reflect.

One of the premier places in Rome for "doing nothing" is the old section of Trastevere, which translated means "along the Tiber river." This area of the Eternal City is a favorite stop on our pilgrimages. Filled with quaint cobblestone streets, lovely courtyards, terra-cotta rooftops, and relaxing coffee shops and wine bars, Trastevere is the perfect place to be still and take in the surroundings.

Embracing the sweetness of doing nothing gives us time to thank God for all the blessings surrounding us. The Psalmist sings, "Be still, and know I am God." It is in this stillness that we can come to know the Lord. When we slow down and quiet our hearts, we recognize His immeasurable love for us. Spending quiet time with the Lord helps us know His heart and better imitate Him, and that's what we are all called to do, to imitate the Lord—to be perfect as our heavenly Father is perfect. And there's nothing sweeter than that!

Prayer: Lord, help me quiet my heart today. Teach me to be still and to know that You are God. Amen.

Respond to His Call: Take a moment to practice the sweet art of doing nothing, and thank God for the blessings that surround you.

Kelly M. Wahlquist and Teresa Tomeo

In Jesus You Have Peace

I have said this to you, that in me you may have peace. In the world you have tribulation; but be of good cheer, I have overcome the world. John 16:33

This passage is taken from what is known as Jesus' farewell discourse, which spans chapters 14–17 in the Gospel of John. The farewell discourse is a profound and prophetic testament of Jesus' great love and respect for the apostles. It is also a testament of Jesus' great love and respect for you.

In the discourse, Jesus is preparing His closest friends for His departure. This is not the usual sort of leave-taking between friends. Jesus and His apostles have just concluded the Last Supper, where He alluded to His upcoming betrayal and denial. Now, on this eve of His Passion and Crucifixion, Jesus promises not to leave the apostles as orphans but to send them the Holy Spirit to remain with them and strengthen them. It's hard for the apostles to grasp all that Jesus is telling them. Jesus further instructs them that there are turbulent times ahead for them because of their association with Him.

Already grieved because their Friend, Teacher, and Confidant is about to leave them, the apostles must struggle with the news of their own persecution and suffering to come. Knowing their hearts have been shaken, Jesus comforts and encourages them to be at peace and of good cheer even during tribulation. Why? Because He has overcome the world.

Perhaps you can picture this scene playing out in your own home as you gather with your loved ones and our Lord. Jesus spoke His farewell discourse not only to His apostles but also to you and the people you love. He's speaking these words to you now. No matter what tribulation you face, Jesus has already overcome it. Be at peace.

Prayer: Lord, I want to be there at the table with You, listening to Your words of peace and hope. Help me to remember at every moment of my day that You have overcome the world. Amen.

Respond to His Call: Take a moment to picture yourself in the Upper Room, gathered at the table with Jesus. Ask Him what He has to say to you in your present circumstances. Then, listen to Him!

Marge Steinhage Fenelon

A Warrior's Tale: Wounded and Wonderful

You are all fair, my love; there is no flaw in you. Song of Solomon 4:7

Broken is beautiful. I didn't believe it before our pilgrimage to France, but some cathedrals preach without speaking a word. Let's start with stained-glass windows: thousands of bits of glass pieced together become something beautiful.

My favorite "broken" cathedral was built in the early thirteenth century in Chartres, France. It survived all the tragedies and disasters France has seen for the past eight hundred years. During World War II, the stained-glass windows were removed and hidden for protection.

The exterior of Chartres is genuinely remarkable. Over each entrance, stunning chiseled arches reveal the Genesis creation story, the twelve apostles, and numerous other expressions of our faith. The exterior also shows its troubled past: a disciple's hand is missing here, a staff chipped away there. But it's even more beautiful for its brokenness. This cathedral has endured through the ages to welcome pilgrims from every corner of the world. The imposing edifice still teaches and inspires, even with its imperfect statues and art.

Through every age, Chartres has stood strong in its purpose and mission as the House of God. Still not convinced that broken is okay? Just remember the Last Supper: "And he took bread, and when he had given thanks he *broke* it and gave it to them" (Lk 22:19, emphasis mine). Jesus broke Himself for us that we might not despise our brokenness. May we regard our littleness with humility and trust the Lord to do marvelous things with our brokenness.

Prayer: Come, Holy Spirit, and heal my every wound. May Your glory be revealed in my littleness, my poverty, and my brokenness. Nothing is impossible for You. Amen.

Respond to His Call: Ask Jesus today to show you the places where He finds you beautiful. Sit quietly in His presence and let Him love you.

Katie Anderson

The Appointed Time

And when I go and prepare a place for you, I will come again and will take you to myself, that where I am you may be also. John 14:3

Today, we remember the end of World War I. At the eleventh hour of the eleventh day of the eleventh month in the Year of Our Lord 1918, the Armistice halting the "war to end all wars" was signed in Compiègne, France. It was the appointed time to end the misery of war in Europe that took seventeen million lives. Sadly, it became the First World War in what would become a century of wars.

War releases hell on earth, and earlier that year in February, the Spanish flu had begun its wrath. It would continue until April of 1920, infecting more than 500 million and claiming as many as 50 million lives. These were among the darkest of days, except that God has appointed times and seasons.

God is always near, and He is especially close in the hour of suffering. Job suffered to the point that He called out to God the ultimate question sequestered in each human heart: "If a man die, shall he live again?" (Jb 14:14). Then Job surrendered all to the God in whom he placed his hope: "All the days of my service would I wait, till my release should come" (14:14).

A life lived in harmony with God is a series of divine appointments, seasons, and changes. When we have tasted and seen that the Lord is good, the memory of His goodness sustains us during the times of waiting, testing, and struggle. There is an appointed time for each of us living on the earth. For anyone who might wonder about reincarnation, the writer of Hebrews tells us, "It is appointed for men to die once, and after that comes judgment" (9:27). We will then see Jesus, who offered Himself to bear our sins. Face-to-face. Heart to heart.

Prayer: Lord, make me know Your times and seasons in my life. Reveal to me how Your ways are higher than my ways . . . that I may ascend to where You dwell. Amen.

Respond to His Call: Ask the Holy Spirit to search your heart and reveal to you the answer to this question: *Have I surrendered all to God?*

Deborah Kendrick

Life Lost and Found

He who finds his life will lose it, and he who loses his life for my sake will find it. Matthew 10:39

"What are you so afraid of?" my pastor asked about a task related to the parish council.

"Everything." It felt good to say it aloud finally.

I'd been away from the Church for thirty-three years, back for only a month, and found myself on the council. I was afraid that this divorced, childless, financially struggling mess of a middle-aged woman wasn't good enough for God. Check that—I knew it was true, deep in my heart.

Ten years earlier, everything seemed perfect: a dream job, a treasured husband, and a beautiful house. I lost all this through mistakes we both made, and in retrospect, I know that the lack of a faith-based marriage was part of the problem. Afterward, I struggled to repay a six-figure bankruptcy debt. Who wouldn't be afraid?

The loss of external trappings left me with nothing—except the slim hope that God might still be interested in me. In my previous job, I'd met many writers who had tragic stories, but it was the Christian writers who interested me. It wasn't that they celebrated pain, but they had a way of bearing it with grace. Even before my life crashed, I vaguely desired that peace, which eventually led me to a Catholic church. I never looked back.

Since my return, I've sacrificed things harder to lose than my marriage and house: pride, envy, anger, and a bit of each of the other deadly sins. These sacrifices have drawn me closer to Jesus and His will for me. Life is simpler; there are fewer material goods, and I have more peace and joy, even in challenging times. I now know He loves me, and there is no longer a need to be afraid. I lost my old life but found a new life in Him.

Prayer: Lord, may I find the fullness of my life with You, knowing no sacrifice is too big for Your love to fill. Amen.

Respond to His Call: Name some things you've lost over the years, and ask yourself why you still remember them. Ask Jesus to sit next to you. Let Him tell you why you still remember these things.

Melanie Rigney

Fill in the Blank

For I am sure that neither death, nor life, nor angels, nor principalities, nor things present, nor things to come, nor powers, nor height, nor depth, nor anything else in all creation, will be able to separate us from the love of God in Christ Jesus our Lord. Romans 8:38–39

I've learned there is always a reason to be on my knees, interceding before God. My daily prayers of petition are often filled with strife. How about yours? I find I need an everyday pep talk from God. And that is why praying with scripture is part of my daily routine. That brings me to St. Paul's amazing eighth chapter in the epistle to the Romans. It has long inspired me.

One of my favorite confidence-building exercises is to fill in the blank in this passage with whatever is ailing me or name the things that might be making me fearful or fretful. Like this: "I am sure that neither death, nor life, nor _____ will be able to separate us from the love of God in Christ Jesus our Lord."

What's nagging you? Family worries? Work stress? Sickness? Heartache? Grief? Give it a name and add it to the blank space above. Then pray aloud with that new verse a few times. Jesus already sees what's in that space. Nothing that the world dishes out can separate us from His love. The problems come when we take our eyes off of Him.

Prayer: Lord, increase my faith. Help me place all my concerns safely within Your divine providence. Amen.

Respond to His Call: Try it. Fill in the blank with your fear or worry, and pray over it with Jesus: "I am sure that neither death, nor life, nor _____ will be able to separate us from the love of God in Christ Jesus our Lord."

Pat Gohn

Adopted and Prepared

Then Jesus came . . . to be baptized by him. John would have prevented him, saying, "I need to be baptized by you, and do you come to me?" But Jesus answered him, "Let it be so now; for thus it is fitting for us to fulfil all righteousness." Matthew 3:13–15

Please do not tell my sons that I barely remember their baptisms. It wouldn't really be an issue unless they were aware of how vividly I remember every detail of their little sister's special day. Hers was many years later, and I was in a very different place—emotionally, mentally, and spiritually. My lack of recall in their cases does not diminish the importance of the day, which marks their adoption into God's family. Enter Faith—both the virtue and the adorable little three-year-old we had the blessing of adopting from China. When she entered our family, my reclaimed Catholic faith became everything to me, and the sacraments had meaning beyond the party and precious white baptism gown.

Faith's baptism held extra significance because I realized that although I had not been there for her birth into the world, I would be present for her birth into the Church and God's family. When I read the scripture account of Jesus' baptism, especially when God proclaims Jesus as His Son, my heart nearly explodes with joy as I contemplate what it means for each of us. Jesus is teaching us that through baptism, we too are claimed by God! We become His adopted sons and daughters. Welcoming Faith into our home has taught me in a personal way the beauty and blessing of a family bonded through adoption.

As a member of our family, Faith has a particular role that only she can fulfill. As members of God's family, we too are each given a plan (Jer 29:11) that only we can fulfill. And just as Jesus' baptism equipped Him for ministry, we can be confident that the graces we received in baptism will equip us for our particular mission.

Prayer: Jesus, may the grace of my baptism guide me to fulfill whatever You call me to, for Your glory and honor. Amen.

Respond to His Call: Look up the date of your baptism, put it on your calendar, and celebrate it in a special way each year.

Allison Gingras

140ish Years

Confident of your obedience, I write to you, knowing that you will do even more than I say. At the same time, prepare a guest room for me, for I am hoping through your prayers to be granted to you. Philemon 1:21–22

My mother was never more beautiful than when she was in her work clothes, ready to make sausage! My family has been making pork sausage for 140ish years. My mother's maternal grandparents taught their eleven children; eventually, it was passed to us. Let me give you the recipe: pork, salt, pepper, coriander, and then smoke it for about twelve hours with applewood. That's it—nothing more. But the technique is essential. Oops . . . I forgot one thing. There is always some arguing. The matriarch has the last word—but since my mother died, my brother John and I just argue a bit with each other, and my stepdad adds a word or two as he sees necessary. It makes the sausage taste better.

We have a guest book that friends sign when they come over. The same book is used for the yearly recap, including the comments of family and friends who have joined us for the first brunch with the links right from the smokehouse. Each year it is wonderful to look back on those who joined us. So many have died, not to mention all of the grandparents who gave us the tradition.

In a couple of days, I will journey back to South Dakota to make the sausage again. It is fitting that we make it in November, the month when we commemorate the dead. I will return home to visit the graves of my parents, and then I will go to my brother's home. And somehow this year, John will look more like my father than ever, and I hope that I can be even half as radiant as my mother, and we will touch their souls in this 140ish-year-old recipe.

Prayer: Lord, increase in us an appreciation for the gift of our senses, which connect us to each other and allow us to retain memories of those gone before us. Amen.

Respond to His Call: Make a favorite family recipe and invite a relative to share the meal, or call one to reminisce.

Alyssa Bormes

Your Call to Fruitfulness

In that day: "A pleasant vineyard, sing of it! I, the LORD, am its keeper; every moment I water it. Lest any one harm it, I guard it night and day." Isaiah 27:2–3

We came around the corner of our house after some time away and gasped. Massive tire tracks scored the yard. Piles of rocks and flagstones, dug up from the terrace, lay everywhere. The backyard was a rough, churned sea of mud and debris. *My garden!* was all I could think. Everything from lilies to raspberries—gone! Who knew that building a house addition would create so much collateral damage?

Reading Isaiah 27 with that disaster of a yard in mind, I could empathize a little bit with the Israelites back in the days when Babylon swept down and conquered them, carrying many off into exile and laying the land waste in the process. Israel was seen as the Lord's own vineyard, which He had planted with choice vines in fertile soil (see Isaiah 5). Now, due to their sin, the land was ruined.

Our lives feel like that sometimes, whether because of our sins, others' sins, or simply because we live in a fallen world. Like Israel, we go through times of upheaval and darkness. Times when we feel dry and barren or worse. Through Isaiah, God promised the Israelites that He would heal their ravaged lives and make them fruitful. God is the same today. His plans don't end in dust and dirt, even if sometimes our path goes through destruction and chaos. He is the master of bringing life from death, and He has called you to fruitfulness (see John 15:16). Even when everything looks wrecked around you, hope in God!

Prayer: Thanks be to God, who is my keeper, who has His eye on the vineyard of my life, and who wants me to bear fruit. Jesus, help me keep my eyes on You and off of the mess around me. Amen.

Respond to His Call: Today, tackle a space you need to clean up. Put on some praise-and-worship music to accompany your work.

Sarah Christmyer

Cultivating Good Soil

A sower went out to sow. And as he sowed, some seeds fell along the path, and the birds came and devoured them. Other seeds fell on rocky ground, where they had not much soil, and immediately they sprang up, since they had no depth of soil, but when the sun rose they were scorched; and since they had no root they withered away. Other seeds fell upon thorns, and the thorns grew up and choked them. Other seeds fell on good soil and brought forth grain, some a hundredfold, some sixty, some thirty. Matthew 13:3–6

As I prepared to plant vegetables in a corner of my yard this spring, I heard a dull sound as my spade hit rocks. After removing the big rocks, I raked over the small ones too numerous to pick out, hoping the plants could grow around them. It probably seems crazy to plant in this spot, but it's the sunniest place in my yard, and I harvested a good crop of tomatoes and peppers last year.

In the parable of the sower, Jesus teaches that seed landing on rocky soil has a somewhat better chance of surviving than seed dropped on the path. The seed that falls in rocky places springs up quickly in the shallow soil but tends to wither.

My soul is like my garden—there are rocks and thorns, but also a patch of good soil. Some seed finds rich, fertile ground, which I till by reading scripture, praying, reflecting on a homily, or heeding godly advice. The rocks in my spiritual life are the obstacles to prayer and my failure to follow through on the nudges I receive to do acts of service. With a landscape like this in my soul, it's a wonder I produce any spiritual fruit! But I'm confident there is some good ground, even if a gust of pride blows away a little topsoil now and then. Just as I remove the rocks from my garden to give plants space to grow, God continues to help me remove the thorns and rocks from my soul—as long as I let Him be the gardener!

Prayer: Lord, cultivate rich soil in my soul, that I may produce abundant spiritual fruit. Amen.

Respond to His Call: Find a garden to visit. Take a prayer book with you, and spend at least thirty minutes alternating between walking and reading.

Susan Klemond

Other Duties as Assigned

Behold, I send an angel before you, to guard you on the way and to bring you to the place which I have prepared. Exodus 23:20

I work for a large suburban church. Each year we sign new work agreements. Oh, wait. They changed the name to "appointments" this year. Part of what we sign is our job description, to make sure that we have an accurate list of our duties. My favorite is "must be able to lift thirty pounds." When you're short on maintenance staff and want stuff done, you'd better be able to lift a lot more than that!

"Other duties as assigned" is another good one. So many gifts can arrive when God extends such an open-ended invitation.

One very special gift actually came in a box, on a routine Wednesday morning. If I had known this day would bring a visitation from a tiny saint, I would have prepared a place for her. I didn't even know her name.

This baby was born and died the same day. She was to be laid to rest in our cemetery, but no one had called ahead to see who would receive her. I hurried to meet her.

My tiny guest and I went to my office. I placed her on my desk and looked at her little coffin. It was pretty and had a green ribbon around it, which held some papers that were important, I was sure. I wished I had a beautiful cloth to put under her. I sat next to her, waited, and prayed.

A couple of my coworkers stopped by. We talked about her, though we did not know anything about her. We imagined the sorrow of her parents and wondered about siblings. There were tears of both sorrow and gratitude. We knew she would never be home with her family, but that through Christ and His Church she had already made her way to her eternal home.

Prayer: Heavenly Father, please have mercy on the holy souls in purgatory and grant them pardon. Amen.

Respond to His Call: Have a Mass celebrated for someone who has died.

Teresa McCarthy

Giving Thanks for the Gray Skies and Big Talkers

Does he not speak entirely for our sake? It was written for our sake, because the plowman should plow in hope and the thresher thresh in hope of a share in the crop. 1 Corinthians 9:10

Late autumn is a contemplative time of year. Blustery gray skies serve to sweep my mind clear. I love bare trees against a blazing orange sunset. The world outside is simplified, tidied, waiting for the first clean blanket of snow. Am I nuts? Maybe.

For me, this bleak landscape provides the perfect backdrop for the enrichment of the interior life. The brisk fall days culminate in my favorite holiday, Thanksgiving. I have a couple of big talkers in my family, so it is a day off from talking for me. Also, I usually schedule my annual silent retreat for the weekend immediately following Thanksgiving; the big family gathering serves as preparation. How blessed am I? A treat, and then a retreat. I love my family, but sometimes I think I love silence just a bit more.

We will gather around our colorful, festive table laden with little candles and all the warm food and wine that makes us sleepy and goofy. Our cozy house will be filled with familiar voices and laughter. There are so many other blessings as well—such as the smell of cold in the children's hair, leaves stuck to their sweaters as they burst in from the yard to plunk themselves down in front of huge pieces of pie.

My Thanksgiving prayer this year is to be with my family whom I love and to be steeped in gratitude in the present moment, content to just let it all roll on, however it will—much like those layered clouds rolling by in the dark November sky.

Prayer: Today, Lord, help me to count my blessings, giving thanks for every good and perfect gift You have placed in my life. God, grant me the grace to see your gifts clearly and dearly before me this Thanksgiving—and to love as You love. Amen.

Respond to His Call: Find time today to sit in silence and reflect on your blessings.

Jill Mraz

Crosses That Save Me

Those who trust in him will understand truth, and the faithful will abide with him in love, because grace and mercy are upon his elect, and he watches over his holy ones. Wisdom 3:9

I wasn't the best mother in the world. I went through a very dark, traumatic time in my life: the unexpected death of my father (he was forty-three), separation from my husband and boys, a fallout with family, divorce, homelessness, being a single parent, unemployment, depression. I was angry with God because I couldn't see or hear Him in my darkness. I felt very alone.

This was my life for twelve years. I buried the pain deep within my soul. However, each cross I endured and each death I experienced led me closer to God. The powerful witness of others reminded me of the faith instilled in me as a cradle Catholic. I watched my grandmother reading her Bible despite the crosses in her life (there were many). I watched my mother embrace her faith, despite mourning the death of her beloved. During this time, God placed many special people in my path, which led to a closer relationship with Him. In my desperation, I reached out to Him, just like the hemorrhaging woman in the Bible. It was her faith that saved her. It was my faith that saved me.

Through Jesus' light, love, and mercy, He raised me from the dead. He made all things new again. I am now married to a godly man and live in a beautiful home. I am the mother of five wonderful children and six adorable grandchildren. Our family is very close, and our relationship is stronger than ever. Most importantly, God uses my painful past to allow me to be a "mother" to others and bring hope where there is none. Good Friday was not the end; it is the beginning. Each cross, each death brings us to new life—a new life in Jesus Christ. Embrace the Cross and celebrate the Resurrection!

Prayer: Lord, I believe You indeed make all things new again—for I have seen You do it! Amen.

Respond to His Call: Tell a friend about a renewal of life God has brought you through a trial or difficulty.

Donna Luna Hernandez

Dwelling in His Shadow

They shall return and dwell beneath my shadow, they shall flourish as a garden; they shall blossom as the vine, their fragrance shall be like the wine of Lebanon. Hosea 14:7

I once watched a documentary on Kim Peek. Remember who he was? Odds are if you went to the movies in the 1980s, you know him well. Kim Peek was the real-life inspiration for Dustin Hoffman's character in the film *Rain Man*. Kim was a "megasavant"; he had an exceptional memory. He could read one page in one second with a 98 percent retention rate. (That's impressive. I have to read the instructions on a box of rice at least eight times!) Though Kim possessed this phenomenal memory, he had an IQ of 87. He had a difficult time with daily activities such as getting dressed, brushing his teeth, and combing his hair. His father did all those things for him each day. In the documentary, Kim was asked about his relationship with his father. He replied, "My father and I share the same shadow."

Wow! To be so close to your father that you share the same shadow. Actually, it's what we are all called to do. We are called to be so close to our Father that we dwell in His shadow. It is there that we find healing, mercy, love, protection, and peace.

Often when I feel anxious, unsettled, or unbalanced, I turn to Hosea 14:7. Here I am reminded to return to God's loving protection. He's such a good Father that He even tells me how to return to Him—through the flourishing garden (in Hebrew, grain) and the blossoming vine (the wine of Lebanon). That's the Eucharist! My loving Father instructs me to return to Him and dwell in His shadow by putting my trust in His greatest gift of mercy, my Lord and my salvation, Jesus Christ.

Prayer: Father, help me to know the comfort and protection of dwelling in Your shadow. Let Your peace reside in my heart today so that I act at all times with Your fragrant love. Amen.

Respond to His Call: Spend time today in the shadow of the monstrance, sitting with Jesus in adoration.

Kelly M. Wahlquist

The Benedictus

And you, child, will be called the prophet of the Most High; for you will go before the Lord to prepare his ways, to give knowledge of salvation to his people in the forgiveness of their sins. Luke 1:76–77

Many years ago, I became familiar with the prayer called the Benedictus, taken from the Gospel of Luke and prayed daily in the Divine Office. It is the recitation of Zechariah's words at the birth of his son, John the Baptist. In it, Zechariah praises God for His faithfulness to His promises and prophesies his son's mission on earth.

Over the years, this prayer has turned into a sort of dialogue between God and me. I speak the words of Zechariah to Him, and He speaks Zechariah's prophecy over me. Sometimes I stand like a petulant child, hands on hips, to remind Him of His promises. Sometimes, like a firm but loving parent, He gently reminds me that He has called me to "prepare his ways," to bring "knowledge of salvation."

Still, trust in God's promises has to be a daily decision for me, because I am so aware of my unworthiness. At times, it can be difficult to even come to the Lord with my problems because my failings convict me. It helps to recall Romans 8:28: "We know that in everything God works for good with those who love him." The condition for this promise is only that we love God—not that we are always good, we deserve such a promise, or we never sin or have no faults. Nevertheless, it takes a very intentional act of will for me to move forward, trusting God's Word.

How grateful I am that God is so patient with me. He waits for me to come to Him like a child to her father's knee. So, every day, I will continue this dialogue of the Benedictus, praising God for His mighty promises and trusting in His call upon my life.

Prayer: Lord Jesus Christ, help me to lean on You rather than on my own understanding. Amen.

Respond to His Call: Google "Hauser Zagreb" to access a live concert that begins with the classical hymn entitled "Benedictus." As you listen, allow the words of the above scripture to speak to your heart.

Lynne Keating

Crying Out for Wine

There is an outcry in the streets for lack of wine; all joy has reached its eventide; the gladness of the earth is banished. Isaiah 24:11

Have you ever "cried out for lack of wine"? Specifically, have you ever felt you weren't being served in your church parish, that you didn't have a place or a program that fit your needs? Many years ago, I was a young mom of an eight-month-old girl. I had just quit my job to stay at home, was new to my parish, and felt a little lost and friendless. Through the grace of God, I made a new friend. One day we were complaining that our church didn't offer young moms any programs. Why wasn't it serving our needs? We were crying out because of "a lack of wine."

Hearing our grumbling, my friend's mother offered words of wisdom: "If you want a group for young mothers, start one. You are the Church, and the Church needs you. You want the Church to serve you. But it's you girls who need to serve the Church." Seeing her point, we decided to start a group, even though we didn't know what we were doing. Within two weeks, we had signed up more than thirty women, all looking for the same thing we were. We started meeting in homes and parks, letting the kids play while we moms gave each other support and much-needed encouragement. Soon we were serving the parish by providing Mass activity bags for parents of toddlers, making meals for families with new babies, and visiting nursing homes with our children in tow.

In the past twenty years, this same group has continued to grow and serve. It has headed fundraisers, provided meals for priests, and done service projects with the youth. If you've been crying out for lack of wine—wondering when your parish will serve you—perhaps you should be asking how you can help the Church with your gifts.

Prayer: Jesus, fill the places where I lack with Your generous love. Inspire me to serve where I am needed and to continuously listen for Your voice so I may do whatever You tell me. Amen.

Respond to His Call: Take the time this week to read your parish bulletin from front to back. Where might you offer some time to serve others?

Stephanie Landsem

Stand Up and Go

Then one of them, when he saw that he was healed, turned back, praising God with a loud voice; and he fell on his face at Jesus' feet, giving him thanks. Now he was a Samaritan. Then said Jesus, "Were not ten cleansed? Where are the nine? Was no one found to return and give praise to God except this foreigner?" And he said to him, "Rise and go your way; your faith has made you well." Luke 17:15–19

The lepers in Luke 17 reveal something about me and what I aspire to be. Although Jesus heals ten lepers, only one returns to thank Him. I am moved to contrition when I think of all the times the Lord has blessed me with grace or answered prayers, and I move on without thanks. Perhaps I am not intentional in my ingratitude, but my actions show self-absorption all the same.

The last leper, the Samaritan, was perhaps the least likely to receive healing from the Messiah, and yet he was the first to proclaim the Lord's mercy. He not only received healing but also recognized and acknowledged the source of that healing as the Lord Jesus Christ. I am heartened by his example to praise the Lord in all things, and especially to live my faith with a grateful heart.

Often, my lack of gratitude stems from my tendency to compare my own life with the lives of others and thus overlook the wealth of my blessedness. God gives us all that we need for salvation, and we should not question what He chooses not to give or forget to thank Him for the many gifts He does bestow. When I forget that all I have is from Him and deserves praise, this passage in Luke 17 reminds me to look outward rather than inward, graciously accepting everything from the Lord, whether difficult or not. We are so loved, and all the world is a gift.

Prayer: Lord, for all those times I have forgotten to run back to give You thanks, I offer my prayer today in gratitude. Let me lift my eyes and hands to You, O Lord, praising Your generosity in my life. Amen.

Respond to His Call: Call someone who deserves your thanks. Express your gratitude and promise specific prayers for their needs.

Maria Morera Johnson

How May This Wisdom Come to Us?

Happy is the man who finds wisdom, and the man who gets understanding, for the gain from it is better than gain from silver and its profit better than gold. She is more precious than jewels, and nothing you desire can compare with her. Proverbs 3:13–15

How may the wisdom spoken of in the verses above come to us? By choosing to make it our chief desire.

First, read the wisdom literature in the Bible. Proverbs has thirty-one chapters; read one chapter a day for a month. Dig into Job, Psalms, Ecclesiastes, and Wisdom. Also, spend time with the parables of Jesus and the book of James. Slow reading is best—this is not a race to get finished. Allow yourself to be melted by the warmth of wisdom entering your heart.

Also pray for wisdom. The consistency of seeking wisdom increases the desire for it. If we hunger and thirst for that which only God can give, He responds as the loving Father He is.

Know that wisdom is protection. Wisdom will shine a light on the path before us, causing us to know the potential consequences of our actions. Wisdom will also nurture in our hearts the courage we need to make the best decisions at the moment.

Finally, cooperate with wisdom. Seeking, embracing, and receiving wisdom makes life easier. The fruits of wisdom produce a respite from struggles and strife. "When a man's ways please the LORD, he makes even his enemies to be at peace with him" (Prv 16:7).

Prayer: Jesus, You are our wisdom. Enlighten our minds, still our hearts, subdue us with Your peace, and conquer us with Your love. May we seek to know You more fully and love You more deeply. Amen.

Respond to His Call: Make a schedule for regular reading of the wisdom literature of the Bible.

Deborah Kendrick

Morning Glory

The steadfast love of the LORD never ceases, his mercies never come to an end; they are new every morning; great is your faithfulness. Lamentations 3:22–23

My favorite time of day is the moment when God kisses the world good morning—sunrise. I have never been an early bird. For decades I missed those stunning few seconds. Recently I started rising early to go to Mass, and the sweetness of that moment has captivated me. Silly maybe, but every morning, when the sun first peeks over the trees, I say with all my happy heart, "There it is!" I feel the invitation in the warm rays to send the light radiating over me out into the connections I make in this hymn of a day that inches the earth toward its fulfillment.

I smell the prayerful incense in the fragrance of damp leaves and grass turned toward the sun for blessing. I feel the divine benediction throbbing in my own pulse and throughout the atmosphere, awakening every dewdrop, frolicking fawn, and sleepy head to its eternal purpose, beckoning an awareness of its miracle, its gift. There is no promise of another day. Indeed, today will be the last for many, maybe someone we know. Maybe me. My face may soon break the surface of this murky dimension to gasp with new breath the shocking clarity of all I forfeited while I focused on the mundane. Yesterday cannot be unlived yet, if faced with truth, might be transformed. The horizon leans forward.

What are we missing because we're sleeping? What glorious gifts is God's great, open hand showering on me while I blearily, blindly rush through my to-do list? What little miracle awaits my simple attention to my neighbor this day? May I receive the grace of this good morning and present my day at evening to its Maker as a cup running over with participation in eternity. "His mercies . . . are new every morning."

Prayer: Lord, give me eyes to see and ears to hear You, as You breathe Your constant love in me, around me, over me, and through me. My heart is open. Let me be a little ray of light over someone today. Amen.

Respond to His Call: Resolve to smile like a sunrise at every person you come in contact with today.

Sonja Corbitt

Be Not Afraid

But he who did not know, and did what deserved a beating, shall receive a light beating. Every one to whom much is given, of him will much be required; and of him to whom men commit much they will demand the more. Luke 12:48

The above passage from Luke is a rough kind of exhortation. It's not one of the uplifting, inspirational scriptures we can display with a pretty picture. Here the Lord makes a direct statement on the cost of our commitment to Christ. If we are going to be in, then we need to be all in.

Sometimes we are afraid to make this full commitment because we feel inadequate or insecure about our ability to do a good job. But when the Lord calls us, He equips us for the job—"much is given" to us. Sometimes we are afraid because we have an inkling of what sort of sacrifice Christ is asking of us. These are real fears—we can take them to the Lord. But again, He knows us and our capabilities. Take heart. Be not afraid! He will not take us anywhere without going ahead of us, leading us. Despite the upsets of our emotions, He asks us to rest and trust in His peace, surrendering totally to His divine will.

It's a lot to understand and ponder—and yet it's a direct call to live. This demand shows us how to live our Christian lives the right way, to use our gifts for His glory, every moment of every day until He comes.

Prayer: Jesus, whatever the sacrifice, whatever the cross, I will not fear because I know You are with me. I will make my life an offering to Your glory. Amen.

Respond to His Call: Make a specific small sacrifice today, just because you love the Lord your God and want to glorify Him. Tell no one about it.

Maria Morera Johnson

Some Days Are Longer Than Others

This is the day which the LORD has made; let us rejoice and be glad in it. Psalm 118:24

What a cheery verse! Can't you just see yourself rising with the dawn, looking out at the beautiful world, and singing this verse to creation?

Now try waiting in line at Costco, singing the same verse. Actually, don't try that. Wait until you get home and have the fabulous pleasure of lugging your industrial-sized jug of laundry detergent from the car into the house, plus the supersized package of paper towels and all the other stuff—don't we all agree?

Perhaps you could sing that verse while waiting for a bus in the rain or writing the check to pay for your neighbor's mailbox—the one shaped like a giant trout that your kid just ran over with your car.

Some days are longer than others. But the day that ended with writing the check for that hideous mailbox is the same day that began with a glorious dawn. It's still the day the Lord made. Try to let it end with the same kind of rejoicing. And maybe a glass of wine.

Prayer: Lord, I might not always be happy, but with Your help I can be cheerful. Help me be cheerful today. Amen.

Respond to His Call: Catch a sunset sometime this week. Rejoice in it.

Susan Vigilante

Gazing upon His Gaze

As he passed by, he saw a man blind from his birth. John 9:1

I've been a lifelong lover of Jesus, yet at times, I lose sight of Him by focusing on the next thing. We live life juggling the responsibilities of work and family. Our life may be full, but if we're honest, we may not be fully living. We are losing sight of Jesus. The blind man in the Gospel could not see Jesus, nor could he see that Jesus saw him. He was unaware that the Eyes of Love were resting on him until he could finally see. Imagine the joy when his eyes beheld the blue sky, or the tears when they rested on his parents' faces. He also beheld the beauty of Jesus, and he worshipped.

We lose sight of Jesus if our gaze is fixed on the next thing; we can't see Him seeing us. He sees you and pauses before you. While your gaze is focused on the next thing, His gaze is focused on you. He knows you; you are His work of art; He longs to free you of your burdens. What would happen if we rested under His gaze and focused on Him? How would our lives be different if we never lost sight of Him?

Jesus wants us to see life more clearly by seeing Him. His face is worth beholding. As we look into His loving eyes, we discover that we are seen, known, and cherished amid the whirlwind of daily life. When we pause to gaze on the face of Jesus in prayer, we begin to see Him everywhere. Every face becomes His face. When we rest in His gaze, we become His gaze of love for others—His gaze through our gaze enables people to see Him. Instead of looking toward the next thing, let us be His eyes of love for others.

Prayer: Protect me from losing sight of You, Jesus. Keep my gaze from being fixed on the next thing. I want to gaze at You as You pause before me. Amen.

Respond to His Call: Get a copy of the book *Gaze upon Jesus: Experiencing Christ's Childhood through the Eyes of Women* (www.CatholicVineyard. com). It's the perfect book for an Advent book club with friends!

Kristin Molitor

Me and the Fig Tree

> On the following day, when they came from Bethany, he was hungry. And seeing in the distance a fig tree in leaf, he went to see if he could find anything on it. When he came to it, he found nothing but leaves, for it was not the season for figs. And he said to it, "May no one ever eat fruit from you again." Mark 11:12–14

In the above passage, Mark clearly states that figs were not in season. When I first read this gospel story, I wondered, "What did Jesus expect to find on a fig tree if it wasn't time for that tree to bear fruit?" I thought it strange, harsh actually, that Jesus would curse the fig tree when figs weren't in season. I talked to a knowledgeable friend, who explained that the fig tree represented Israel and that as Jesus was approaching His Passion, His people weren't producing fruit. It was great information but didn't answer my question. I prayed, reread the passage, and was struck with fear. Am I producing fruit consistently, or could Jesus stop by and find me barren at any moment?

There are times when I feel energized and engaged in exemplifying the Word. These are the seasons when my life bears fruit. Then there are times when I am struggling to pray, and I feel far from God. In those moments, I'm weak and barely hanging on, and I have no figs. What if Jesus is hungry when I'm not in season?

As my thoughts spun out, the good Lord quickly rescued me. In my heart, I felt I was beginning to understand what He wanted me to understand. Don't ever let your tree be empty; produce something. Even when you're weary and worn, and it's not your season, produce at least one fig. When God allows you to be pruned back, it's only in anticipation of a season of fullness. Maintain your efforts, keep the faith, and you'll soon find you're in full bloom!

Prayer: Lord, help me to persevere in my pursuit of You so that I can produce fruit for Your kingdom. Let me recognize Your presence in all of the seasons of my life. Amen.

Respond to His Call: Though you may feel empty, persevere in prayer, keep reading scripture, and continue receiving the sacraments.

Michelle Schroeder

Present in Advent

Come, let us walk in the light of the LORD. Isaiah 2:5

We arose this morning and welcomed a new season. All around us, we notice the changes this newness brings. In the middle of the kitchen table, a wreath of four unlit candles accompanies us as we sip our morning coffee. A fresh start greets us as we turn the calendar to a new month. All of this newness captures our attention, ignites our imagination, and beckons us to enter into Advent fully—free from distraction, without reservation, full of anticipation and hope.

Christ is coming and our salvation is near, but how do we remain present to the Advent moment when Christmas decorating, music, movies, and parties swirl all around us? Be attentive and purposeful; seek to include the spiritual traditions of Advent in your season. Jesus commands us to be prepared for His coming. So, actively consider what needs to happen between now and December 25 for you to be ready to celebrate His birth. Be intentional about what matters most to you regarding the traditional holiday preparations (cards, decorating, baking, and gift giving). What is truly necessary, and what is optional? Invite the Lord into your preparations, and to guard against anxiety, do not be afraid to shorten your usual list.

Today, let us rejoice in the new season of Advent and the new liturgical year—with its beautiful simplicity, heartening hymns, and readings that beckon us to walk in the light. Let us journey through the Advent season with quiet prayerfulness, humility, and intention. When the hustle and bustle of the holidays swirl around us, let us ask for God's grace to stay present to the Advent moment, "as we wait in joyful hope for the coming of our Savior, Jesus Christ."

Prayer: Holy Spirit, help me to stay present to the Advent moment, as in expectant hope we wait. I will begin this season of waiting with rejoicing and my full attention. Amen.

Respond to His Call: This Advent, put together a stack of twenty-four prayers or prayer books (we all collect them, don't we?) and choose a different prayer each day to offer up to God.

Sarah Damm

Rites and Rules

Jesus answered her, "If you knew the gift of God, and who it is that is saying to you, 'Give me a drink,' you would have asked him and he would have given you living water." John 4:10

Rites and rules accompany liturgical seasons. I do my best with the rules and rites: Advent wreaths in Advent, lighted trees and crèches at Christmas. Lent follows with ashes, Stations of the Cross, and Friday fish fry. The paschal candle and Vigil Mass climax Easter season. In the languid summer, "God Bless America" rings out on Independence Day Sunday. Rites remind us of interior spirituality, but they do not cause it.

Rites should bring us a right heart, nearer to Jesus. It's the living of the rites that matters. When the doing becomes disruptive of time with Jesus, we are tempted to give up. Oops, we missed the third candle on the Advent wreath. Darn, the calendared gift exchange conflicts with the Friday penance service; what to do? In the past, often I would just give up, losing the battle to do all the activities. I'd resign myself to my self-imposed purgatory and wait until the next liturgical season. This season, I'd say, I'll do it right all the way through!

Now, I see things rightly. Each season focuses on another part of the journey toward God, who loves me beyond all telling. Perhaps I haven't completed all the demands of Christmas décor and secular events, or attended every scheduled parish devotion. But this Advent I am setting aside time each day, even just a little bit, to reflect on the love He wants to show me this season, this year. I draw near to Him present in a different season of my own life. I reflect on all He has done this past year, with sincere gratitude even for the bad moments when I learned necessary lessons. I count each individual grace, saying thank You. I prepare to encounter Him in my final season. My inconstant heart thus watches and prays through all the liturgical seasons.

Prayer: O my Jesus, I long for the living water of Your love and Your mercy. Envelop me in Your Sacred Heart daily and always. Amen.

Respond to His Call: Make a visit each day for a week to a nearby church or chapel. Sit quietly and listen to Jesus for five minutes.

Dr. Carol Younger

Make Room for Jesus

A voice cries: "In the wilderness prepare the way of the Lord. Make straight in the desert a highway for our God." Isaiah 40:3–4

It's barely December, and I'm ready for Christmas to be over. Ever since Thanksgiving, I've been baking, shopping, decorating, mailing, stringing lights, wrapping. It is a long, exhausting season. I wonder if whoever puts the Mass readings together thought of people like me when they decided to set the second Sunday of Advent in the desert. I so need to get away from it all, and enter a desert somewhere! To go where there is nothing to catch the eye but rock and sand, where the wind vanishes without a sound. Where I can leave behind the mounds of Christmas cookies and festive drinks that fill my kitchen and be thirsty again. I need to feel my need for Jesus so that I can welcome Him.

"Prepare the way of the Lord, make his paths straight!" cries John the Baptist, quoting Isaiah (Mk 1:3). Then everyone will see the Lord coming. There's no straight way through the wilderness He's in; it's full of hills and valleys. I realize I've gotten it backward. I've been filling up my inner life instead of emptying it. Creating hills and valleys and placing rocks instead of flattening out a highway for the Lord to ride in on. No wonder I can't see Him coming in the distance! No wonder I don't have the stamina to wait!

The scriptures are drawing my attention inward. All those other preparations might be useful, even needed, but they don't prepare my heart. By "preaching a baptism of repentance for the forgiveness of sins" (Mk 1:4), John the Baptist calls us to clear out the debris in our souls. It's time to take advantage of the Sacrament of Reconciliation and make room in our hearts to receive the Christ child. Come, Lord Jesus!

Prayer: Come, Lord Jesus, come! Prepare a way in the wilderness of my heart, through prayer and Your Word. Amen.

Respond to His Call: Cultivate a regular daily time of inner peace and quiet so there is room in your interior life for Christ. Use the time for spiritual reading, meditation, and prayer.

Sarah Christmyer

The Gift of Jesus

I love you, O LORD, my strength. The LORD is my rock, and my fortress, and my deliverer, my God, my rock, in whom I take refuge, my shield, and the horn of my salvation, my stronghold. Psalm 18:1–2

Contained within God are love and beauty. God is stronger than anything or anyone. Those who think the struggle between good and evil is a fight where we should be on the edge of our seats awaiting the outcome are delusional. God was never defeated. His sacrifice becomes our greatest triumph! God is love, and love is stronger than death. In every way conceivable, the good of God is more potent than evil. We know the rest of the story as believers, as this battle is not a movie. This struggle is life. Only God can give life, and only God can sanctify, which He did in becoming man.

He takes our sin upon Himself and dies for us. We could not redeem ourselves. Jesus' humility is breathtaking. He does not deserve any of the things He endures in His Passion, but He takes them all on for you and me. We should be humbled. Every day of our life, we should realize we could never merit the sacrifice. Jesus is worthy enough for all of us. He is the reason to be grateful for our existence. We ought to be joyful that He made us worthy and able to be kind, loving, and forgiving to one another because He is.

The Incarnation leads to the Crucifixion. That death leads to the Resurrection. The first Christians died for Jesus, for they had seen the risen Lord and would never be the same. When Jesus is back among His friends, He forgives those who were unfaithful during his arrest. He explains why He suffered and died and how He will never leave them or anyone who comes after. I hope you want to share that story with everyone. The joy and sacrifice are too great to keep to ourselves.

Prayer: Thank you, Jesus. You said, "I am the resurrection and the life" (Jn 11:25); therefore, we have life everlasting. Amen.

Respond to His Call: Today let your reaction to unwelcome situations be one of kindness and love.

Lynda MacFarland

Meeting Resistance in the Waiting

Hear, you deaf; and look, you blind, that you may see! Who is blind but my servant, or deaf as my messenger whom I send? Who is blind as my dedicated one, or blind as the servant of the LORD? Isaiah 42:18–19

December 2017 proved to be quite a different Advent for me. I went in to the hospital for a supposedly minimally invasive surgery on my right knee. The timing was good. I would have a long recovery period, and ample time to condition with my husband for a backpacking trip to Alaska the following summer.

To put things into perspective, earlier that year our oldest son endured two brain surgeries and a double hamstring lengthening with no complications. I felt that in comparison I had nothing to worry about. Boy, did things turn out differently!

Two months after my surgery, I continued to struggle with climbing stairs, walking, and sitting for long periods without pain. Though my resistance to be still was strong, my body told me otherwise. For me, this is no simple task; I find it easiest to be still in my mind and spirit when I am out in nature and hiking. After wrestling for a long while trying to determine how I could find my peace when I couldn't be in nature, I resigned myself to prayer. I asked God what He was showing me. He shared with me what stillness is and made me aware of how often I fight it. He revealed that life isn't about what I have accomplished but to whom I belong. I belong to a loving God who asks me to cease striving so much and to allow myself to receive His love and mercy. "Remember not the former things, nor consider the things of old. Behold, I am doing a new thing" (Is 43:18–19).

Prayer: Lord, thank You for calling me to a much-needed, unanticipated pause. Please help me to remember that it is often in such pauses that You invite me to a fresh perspective and to transformative growth. Amen.

Respond to His Call: Today, step away from your normal routine for a few minutes and take a deep breath. Notice what comes up for you. Is it peaceful or challenging? Share this experience with the Lord.

Heather Makowicz

The Wilderness

I am the voice of one crying in the wilderness. John 1:23

John's gospel describes John the Baptist as a voice crying out in the wilderness. The wilderness has always intrigued and attracted me. Perhaps this comes from living in a large metropolitan city, having seven children, and balancing work and volunteer activities—I have little time for quiet reflection, much less wilderness. Yet through the years, the concept of spending time in the wilderness has remained in my mind. About twenty years ago, I met a retiring priest going to Spain to walk the Way of St. James, the Camino. I remember thinking, *Someday, I might do that.* Years passed, but finally, when my youngest child went to college, I made plans to walk the Camino.

In September 2019, I left home to spend forty days in the wilderness and another ten days visiting religious sites, for a biblical fifty-day pilgrimage. At one stopover on the Camino, a priest shared three possible reasons why people make the pilgrimage. First, some undertake the journey out of gratitude for favors received, to meet the challenge of walking five hundred miles, and to enjoy the beauty of God's creation.

A second reason to walk the Camino is in prayer for a particular intention, such as an upcoming decision or forgiveness for a particular wrong. For some, God seems to have placed this journey in their hearts, and they don't know why they are walking.

Finally, this priest noted, some pilgrims walk because they are called to be "stars" for others on the journey. The Camino de Santiago is sometimes called "the way of the stars." In life, we, too, are pilgrims on an extraordinary journey—the journey to heaven. As you travel, may you be grateful, live intentionally, and let your light shine like a star for others.

Prayer: O God, I am grateful to be a pilgrim on this extraordinary journey of faith. May I always be guided by your Son. Amen.

Respond to His Call: For each of the days remaining in Advent, cut out a paper star and write on it a prayer for guidance from the Christ child. Place the stars at random places in your Bible, marking passages to explore during the Christmas season. See what the Lord has to say!

Lucy H. Johnson

He Sings Joyfully

Sing aloud, O daughter of Zion; shout, O Israel! Rejoice and exult with all your heart, O daughter of Jerusalem! The LORD has taken away the judgments against you, he has cast out your enemies. The King of Israel, the LORD, is in your midst; you shall fear evil no more. Zephaniah 3:14–15

Zephaniah tells us to shout for joy, for our Savior is in our midst. After weeks of waiting and preparing for His arrival, exult I will. But I won't be the only one. Just a few verses later, we hear that the Lord rejoices over us! "The LORD, your God, is in your midst, a warrior who gives victory; he will rejoice over you with gladness, he will renew you in his love; he will exult over you with loud singing as on a day of festival" (v. 17).

The book of Zephaniah consists of only three chapters. The first two chapters warn the people of Judah and Jerusalem of their impending judgment, encouraging them to repent. The last chapter speaks of hope in God's promise of mercy. Judgment and mercy share a close relationship, as St. Thomas Aquinas indicates in his *Summa Theologica*: "Mercy does not destroy justice, but in a sense is the fullness thereof." The word "justice" comes from a Latin word meaning "righteousness," and it relates to the right ordering of things. Jesus Christ has fulfilled God's righteousness, which allows us to be renewed in His love and receive His gift of mercy.

Jesus said to St. Faustina, "I cannot punish even the greatest sinner if he makes an appeal to My compassion, but on the contrary, I justify him in My unfathomable and inscrutable mercy" (*Diary*, 1146). As we make our way through Advent, be at peace, knowing that Jesus justifies us and renews us with His love.

Prayer: Jesus, please reveal to me who I have been struggling to forgive. Help me to practice justice by having mercy on them, just as You have mercy on me. Amen.

Respond to His Call: Play a worship song today and sing out joyfully to the Lord.

Susanna Parent

I Can't Give Birth Yet

All this took place to fulfil what the Lord had spoken by the prophet: "Behold, a virgin shall conceive and bear a son, and his name shall be called Emmanuel" (which means, God with us). Matthew 1:22–23

During my seventh month of pregnancy, one day something felt off; however, assuming it was normal thirty-two-week pangs, I ignored the symptoms. By the end of the day, it was clear something was wrong. My first thought was not the baby but the holy day of obligation for the Feast of the Immaculate Conception. Although I grew up Catholic, the concept of a holy day of obligation was new to me, and I was looking forward to attending my first holy day Mass that year.

My husband and I arrived at the hospital, and after a failed attempt to halt labor, the nursing staff told me I would be having a baby that day. My first response should have been concern for my two-month-premature child; however, I hadn't even wrapped my head around that idea. Instead, the first thing that came out of my mouth was, "I can't have a baby right now. I haven't been to church yet." The nurse chuckled and responded that she felt pretty confident God would understand in these circumstances. I remember the disappointment I felt in missing this long-anticipated Mass. A new "revert" to the faith, I'd only just learned that the Immaculate Conception referred to Mary and not Jesus!

During my pregnancy, it had been Mary that I turned to in prayer for comfort with every fear and insecurity. I knew it was her intercession that brought peace to my heart. It seemed only fitting that this defining moment of motherhood, my baby's birth, would come on her special day. My son was born on December 8 at five pounds but, miraculously, was home before Christmas. Gratefully, I've not missed Mass on the Immaculate Conception since.

Prayer: Blessed Mother, thank you for treating me as your beloved daughter. Please continue to guide me to your Son. Amen.

Respond to His Call: During Mass today, listen carefully to the readings about Mary.

Allison Gingras

Bee Busy This Advent

In the morning sow your seed, and at evening withhold not your hand; for you do not know which will prosper, this or that, or whether both alike will be good. Ecclesiastes 11:6

Mary O'Connor wrote, "It's not so much how busy you are, but why you are busy. The bee is praised. The mosquito is swatted."

In this season of hustle and bustle, busyness abounds. There are presents to buy, parties to attend, trees and homes to decorate, cookies to bake, and Christmas cards to mail. Ironically, it is a season when we spend so much time preparing that we can lose sight of what it is we are preparing for—the coming of the Word Made Flesh. In the midst of the usual seasonal preparations this year, let's be sure to spend time preparing our hearts to be a dwelling place for the living God. This Advent I will busy myself to receive Jesus like never before, and I invite you to join me. Let's enter into our relationship with Him in the way in which we are created to relate to Him—with our feminine soul.

And let's not wait until Christmas to open our gifts, either. Each day of Advent, let's unwrap the gifts of the feminine genius that God has given us and make ready to receive Jesus anew. We can unwrap the gifts of receptivity, generosity, and sensitivity each day, and we can do it in very simple ways through prayer and spending time with the Lord.

May we all "bee" busy this Advent preparing a dwelling place for Jesus so that on Christmas, we receive the Christ child in our maternal hearts like never before.

Prayer: Lord, help me receive You into my heart in a new way today. Amen.

Respond to His Call: This Advent, spend an hour in adoration each week, embracing God's love so you can love like Him. Fix your gaze on Jesus and respond to His presence within your heart.

Kelly M. Wahlquist

To the Daughters of the King

You are the light of the world. A city set on a hill cannot be hidden. Nor do men light a lamp and put it under a bushel, but on a stand, and it gives light to all in the house. Matthew 5:14–15

The world can be a dark place, but the light of Christ Jesus, who lives among and within us, can illuminate the blackest of nights. Do not allow the darkness to consume you; instead, be the light by allowing the grace and joy of our Savior to radiate from you. Our world needs your light. You are the beautiful daughter of the King of heaven and earth. John reminds us, though, that the world does not know us, because it does not know Him (1 Jn 3:1). Now is the time to make our Father known in this world, because His children, our brothers and sisters, still wander aimlessly in the desert of their despair.

The enemy will try to convince you that you were made for worldly comfort and pleasures. This idea of worldliness is a lie. Do not shy away from honoring the Lord in all you do. Sacrifice your comfort for the sake of the kingdom. You were made for the perfection of heaven. How could any momentary pleasure hold a candle to eternal joy with the Lord in your true home?

Let us build each other up, choosing to see the good in each other. Let us resolve to help those around us become saints. Our prayers and our works can move mountains. We must join together on the spiritual battlefield against sin, even little sins. Though the enemy hates us daughters of the King, the Father gives us the grace to defeat the enemy. Our hearts united with our Savior, we can reach the summit and plant our victory flag. Then the darkness will be no more.

Prayer: O Jesus, be with me in troubled, dark times. Increase my faith in Your Father's loving providence. Give me Your grace to defeat the enemies of my soul and the souls around me, so we may all be ready for Your return in light. Amen.

Respond to His Call: Spend an hour in eucharistic adoration, reflecting on the scriptures or praying the mysteries of the Rosary.

Angela Koenig

Rededicating the Days

Abide in me, and I in you. As the branch cannot bear fruit by itself, unless it abides in the vine, neither can you, unless you abide in me. John 15:4

Like the cousin in *Mary Poppins Returns*, I often feel that my world has turned topsy-turvy. There is little downtime; if I have a few minutes of solitude, I struggle to keep awake. I survey social media in checkout lines, in a parking spot, or while on hold. I'm sure many of you can identify with me.

We have been fed the lie that we must be busy every moment. We must go places, earn money, spend money, and accomplish tasks. The deception continues: if we aren't busy, then we are lazy; if we aren't doing, we are wilting. Even Mary and Martha made it to social media after a Sunday gospel. Many women connected with Martha and felt the gentle rebuke of Christ as He admonished her for being anxious. The problem is that when we are always busy, we may stop hearing God. We risk losing our connection with Him, especially on our daily journey.

It's time to take action and change now—a change you will feel in the depths of your bones, the recesses of your soul. Carve some time on your calendar for peace, for relaxing, and for prayer. Perhaps add one daily Mass to your week, include twenty minutes in adoration, and attend Confession once a month, spending some extra time in prayer after the penance is completed. The change could be rising a little earlier—or staying awake just a little later—than the rest of the household, to focus on hearing God.

Make room in your calendar to banish the lie we have been fed—to rededicate your days to your relationship with Christ. He is worth it . . . and so are you.

Prayer: Lord, I will move You to the top of my to-do list, knowing there is no better gift than a relationship with You. Amen.

Respond to His Call: Add preparing your heart for Christmas to your holiday to-do list.

Ann Aliese Harry

Mama!

And a great sign appeared in heaven, a woman clothed with the sun, with the moon under her feet, and on her head a crown of twelve stars. Revelation 12:1

Children cry out for their mom when they are hurting, upset, afraid, or in need. So do God's children!

Our Lady of Guadalupe, the ever-virgin Holy Mary and mother of the one true God, appeared December 9–12, 1531, to St. Juan Diego and promised aid when we cry out for help. Do you see Christ's mother as your loving mama and powerful intercessor? Is there anything you need? Confidently bring everything to Jesus through Mary. Remember, at her bidding and before His hour had come (see John 2), Jesus performed His first miracle and changed water into wine. Mary and Jesus wanted to spare the newlyweds and their parents the embarrassment of running out of wine. This story reminds us that the best is yet to come—that we will receive the best wine at the eternal Wedding of the Lamb, where Christ Himself will be our groom and gift, food and friend, drink and dowry.

When in need, cry out, "Mama!" She will intercede with Jesus for whatever you and those near you need most. Like Juan Diego, be docile and witness God's glory on full display for all to see for eternity. Repeat Mary's soothing words to your own disquieted heart and to others in their trials: "Do not be troubled or weighed down with grief. Do not fear any illness or vexation, anxiety, or pain. Am I not here who am your mother? Are you not under my shadow and protection? Am I not the source of your joy, your fountain of life? Are you not in the hollow of my mantle, in the crossing of my arms? Is there anything else you need?" (Our Lady's words to her servant Juan Diego).

Prayer: Our Lady of Guadalupe, make our hearts temples for your Son. Give us all your love, compassion, help, and protection, for we believe that you are indeed our merciful mother and the mother of all. We love you, invoke you, and confide in you. Amen.

Respond to His Call: In this world gone mad with grief and disbelief, discern who needs you to speak of the marvels of Christ and His mama.

Martha Fernández-Sardina

You Are a Gift

Father, I desire that they also, whom you have given me, may be
with me where I am, to behold my glory which you have given me
in your love for me before the foundation of the world. John 17:24

Have you ever appreciated someone so much that you felt in your heart
that they must be a gift to you from God? Perhaps a spouse or a child? Or
a friend that comes over with a bottle of wine when you are seriously con-
sidering jumping off the roof? I have an Aunt Babe. Aunt Babe is hilarious. For the past thirty years, whenever our family has gotten together,
my brother, sisters, cousins, and I look for Aunt Babe. She never fails to
be fun, and we always laugh. She is truly a gift to our family.

Before Jesus suffered on the Cross, He raised His eyes to heaven and
prayed for us to our heavenly Father. The entire chapter 17 of John's gospel is Jesus' prayer to God the Father before His arrest. He prays for the
disciples given to Him by the Father, and also for "those who believe in
me through their word" (v. 20). That's you, and that's me. And then He
says something very special. He refers to us as those whom the Father
has given Him (v. 24). Put another way, Jesus calls us a gift to Him!

So often we think of Jesus as the gift of the Father—a Savior who gave
His life for us. But remember, Jesus told the Father that you and I are a
gift to Him. No matter how much you love another person, Jesus loves
you even more. Reflect on that. He wants to be with you. He wants you
to be with Him in heaven. He doesn't want you to suffer. He is with you
when you suffer.

When we laugh and giggle, Jesus is also filled with joy. Jesus is rooting
for us and praying that we will be the saints God the Father designed us
to be. When you wonder, *What does Jesus think of me?* the answer is that
He thinks you are a gift.

Prayer: Dear Lord Jesus, thank You for loving me. Please help me to feel
Your love in a special way today. Amen.

Respond to His Call: Tell someone today how grateful you are for the
gift of their friendship and love.

Amy Brooks

December 14

Mary and Martha

But the Lord answered her, "Martha, Martha, you are anxious and troubled about many things; one thing is needful. Mary has chosen the good portion, which shall not be taken away from her." Luke 10:41–42

The story about Jesus' visit to Mary and her sister Martha's home has a message for everyone. Although I have slowed down the pace of my life quite a bit in the past few years, there are still times when I find myself living like Martha, when I really should be living like Mary.

On the one hand, I see Martha as doing her best to serve Jesus, and that is what we have been called to do. But her attitude toward Mary blinded her to the true sense of service. She was jealous that Mary was simply sitting at the feet of Jesus, listening to Him. I remember the first time I read this passage. I could relate. I come from a large family, and there were always chores to do. Dusting was one of my least favorite chores, and no matter what anyone else had to do, I was jealous of my siblings because I felt their chores were easier than mine. That childhood feeling came rushing back to me when I read about how Martha felt that day. That feeling quickly dissipated, though, as I read Jesus' message to Martha.

As I reflected on this passage, it occurred to me that although Mary had chosen to sit at Jesus' feet and learn from Him, her job wasn't as easy as it may seem. Most likely, Jesus told Mary, and all who listened, what He wanted them to do to glorify God. It's quite possible that He was challenging Mary and the others to do things outside of their comfort zone. As we know, sharing our faith can be difficult at times, but if we listen and learn from Jesus, we will receive grace and courage to talk to others about our faith. And that is one thing that is indeed needful these days—sharing Jesus!

Prayer: Dear Jesus, help me to know when to be like Martha and when to be like Mary. Amen.

Respond to His Call: Try to be aware of when you are acting like Mary and when you are acting like Martha.

Rhonda Zweber

No Ordinary Christmas

> But you, O Bethlehem Ephrathah, who are little to be among the clans of Judah, from you shall come forth for me one who is to be ruler in Israel. Micah 5:2

How do you celebrate the first coming of Jesus? That's the focus of Advent, celebrating the first coming of the Savior and anticipating the Second Coming. Some years ago, my usual Advent preparations were anything but ordinary. I was pregnant during Advent and delivered on December 23. Complications kept me and the baby in the hospital. Despite record snows, my husband visited. Finally, mid-January, I came home on bed rest. Not an auspicious beginning for a first-time mother. Nonetheless, looking back, I can see God's wisdom.

Every Advent, I reflect on the Blessed Mother, Mary. She didn't wonder precisely where and when she would deliver her baby. She was sure of many other things. She knew the prophecies, and Micah 5:2 stood out. Gabriel had said her Son would be a king and rule His people (Lk 1:32–33). She also remembered the words of Jeremiah, that Judah shall be saved and Jerusalem shall dwell secure (33:14–16). The prophecies and the annunciation sustained her in times of uncertainty. What then would have been her prayerful petition?

Mary would pray: "Teach me your paths. Lead me in your truth and teach me, for you are the God of my salvation" (Ps 25:4–5). This is my continued prayer today, for my first-born Advent son and all my family, into eternity! Christmas is about looking forward. Eternal life is coming, and Jesus will return, redemption accomplished. The good news angels heralded still applies today: Glory to God in the highest, and on earth, peace to men of goodwill. Emmanuel, God with us, is on His way!

Prayer: Come, O long-awaited Jesus! In humble faith, we wait for You as Mary did. With confident hope, we carry You in our hearts, imitating Your mother. Amen.

Respond to His Call: This Advent season, write Christmas cards and deliver them to those confined to their homes or in nursing homes, enclosing the promise of some prayers for each.

Dr. Carol Younger

Open the Door to Your Heart

Behold, I stand at the door and knock; if any one hears my voice and opens the door, I will come in to him and eat with him, and he with me. Revelation 3:20

Jesus continually knocks at the door of our heart. He loves us and wants more than anything to be the center of our lives. He allows us free will to choose to open the door to Him or to keep Him out.

Have you surrendered your life to God and opened the door of your heart to Him? A man named Holman Hunt painted a picture of Jesus in a garden knocking on a big oak door. He called his friends and family together to be the first to see the painting when he unveiled it. As they began to comment on what they liked about the picture, one friend asked Hunt why there was no handle on the door. Hunt explained that when Jesus knocks on the door of our hearts, the handle is on the inside.

The painting was based on Jesus' words recorded in Revelation 3:20. The Lord tells us that He is standing outside the door, and if we hear His voice and open the door, He will come in. But our Lord is good and generous. He will do more than just come into our hearts; He'll nourish and strengthen us for the journey that culminates in our dwelling with Him in everlasting glory. He says, "I will come in to him and eat with him, and he with me." Our Lord feeds us with the Bread of Life and draws us ever closer to eternal communion with Him.

God's grace requires our cooperation. Jesus is knocking on the door of our hearts, eager to come in. All we need to do is open the door and invite Him in.

Prayer: Dear Lord, I open the door to my heart and invite You to come in. Amen.

Respond to His Call: Set a place at dinner tonight for Jesus. See how it changes the conversation at that meal.

Deb Hadley

Jesus! I Know Him!

But now thus says the LORD, he who created you, O Jacob, he who formed you, O Israel: "Fear not, for I have redeemed you; I have called you by name, you are mine." Isaiah 43:1

Many have seen the Christmas movie where Buddy the Elf travels to New York to see his father. Along the way, he hears that Santa is in town. Clapping and jumping, his face filled with joy and awe, he exclaims, "*Santa? Here? I know him! I know him!*" His childlike innocence and love for Santa are contagious. We have also seen videos of soldiers surprising their loved ones with their return home. These tear-jerking scenes often include a touching moment when their eyes meet and they run toward each other with arms outstretched and tears streaming down their smiling faces as they end twirling in an enormous embrace. What an amazing picture of two hearts longing for each other.

The ability to feel so overjoyed, your heart so overwhelmed that your eyes well with tears and a scream of excitement escapes your mouth, is a true gift of deep and tender love.

As Christmas quickly approaches, we know Jesus is coming. He is near. Pray that our response to Him will be one of awe and excitement, of sheer joy at His presence, one that will include a new and surprising encounter with the gift of His incredible love. Picture Him coming—let's run with open arms and tears of amazement to His warm embrace, saying, "Jesus, You're here! I know You! I love You and have been waiting for You! Thank You for coming so we can truly know You now and forever!" You will hear His tender response, "Of course I know you, my precious daughter. Fear not, for I have redeemed you; I have called you by name; you are mine."

Prayer: Jesus, we come to You today, longing to know You more deeply and to love You more fully. Thank You for calling us by name. In Your loving embrace, we are fully known—accepted in all our strengths and weaknesses. Fill us with overwhelming love and joy. Amen.

Respond to His Call: With childlike innocence, share your contagious joy with all those you meet.

Heidi Harvey

Final Countdown to Joy

But watch at all times, praying that you may have strength to escape all these things that will take place, and to stand before the Son of man. Luke 21:36

It's the final countdown! Are you ready? Or is there more to prepare? I'm not referring to Christmas shopping—there's always plenty to do; we may never feel finished. There's meal planning, gift wrapping, and home decorating to do. It's a frantic time. However, I'm not asking if you are ready for Christmas in the worldly sense. Rather, are you prepared to celebrate Christ's birthday?

On the third Sunday of Advent, the rose-colored candle represents joy in the coming of Christ. It reminds us of Mary's joy, the joy of the Wise Men, and Anna and Simeon's joy in the Temple. We seek the same joy found only in Christ, even amid pain and suffering, centuries after His Death, Resurrection, and Ascension.

Christ is coming again. Wait, are we truly ready for Christ? Advent is a time not only to reflect on the joy of Christ and how it manifests in our lives but also to ponder whether our hearts are ready for the coming Lord.

When was the last time we made a thorough examination of conscience? How recently have we met Christ in the confessional? These questions may make us a little uneasy. Yet, the season of Advent is a beautiful time to recognize that Christ is waiting for us. He's waiting for each of us with His loving and merciful arms outstretched in the confessional. There, we as a Christian people are joyously anticipating not just Christmas Day but ultimately Christ's Second Coming!

On this joyous third Sunday of Advent, are we excited? Are we ready? Or do we need to clean house spiritually? May the blessings of Advent turn into the most joyous Christmas season!

Prayer: Lord, I rejoice in You. I prepare my heart and my home for Your coming. Amen.

Respond to His Call: What is one thing you can do today to prepare your heart for Christmas?

Ann Aliese Harry

December 19

Prepare Your Heart

In my Father's house are many rooms; if it were not so, would I have told you that I go to prepare a place for you? And when I go and prepare a place for you, I will come again and will take you to myself, that where I am you may be also. John 14:2–3

In the Gospel of John, Jesus tells us that He is preparing a place for us in His kingdom in heaven. He doesn't tell us when He will return for us, but He assures us that it will happen, and when it does, our hearts need to be ready.

Imagine arriving at your friend's house for dinner, and you're standing outside the door, about to knock. How have you prepared for this moment? You've probably dressed up, maybe made an appetizer, perhaps purchased a good bottle of wine. You've put thought into this moment because it is important to you. How much more important is entering heaven?

How can you prepare your heart to be ready to enter the kingdom of God? Here are a few ways: Claim Jesus Christ as your Savior. Build a relationship with Him. Spend time in His presence, read His Word, repent of your sins, surround yourself with people who lift you up, and trust that He has a purpose and plan for your life.

Life is uncertain, so we should live each day as if it were our last. The Lord could bring us home today, tomorrow, next week, or decades from now. If you knew today was your last day on earth, how would you live it? Let us spend all of our days loving the people God has placed in our lives, embracing the many blessings He has bestowed on us, and shining His love and light on all that we meet. If today is your last day—make it great!

Prayer: Dear Lord, thank You for the promise of eternal life. If You choose to keep us here on earth another day, help us to see the beauty and blessings before us. If You choose to bring us home, please bring peace and serenity to our hearts as you lead us home. Amen.

Respond to His Call: What is something you can change today to live with eternity in mind?

Deb Hadley

December 20

New Life in Christ

Therefore, if any one is in Christ, he is a new creation; the old has passed away, behold, the new has come. 2 Corinthians 5:17

Six weeks after our son Joseph's birth, my husband and I watched with immense gratitude as the priest poured water on his forehead, saying, "I baptize you in the name of the Father, Son, and Holy Spirit." Dressed in a white gown, he sweetly cooed. I smiled, filled with the joy of the moment, recalling how my father and I had worn the same gown during our baptisms. I felt a profound sense of thanks for faith traditions and my family's participation in this big day.

Cherishing this long-awaited gift and celebration of this new life in Christ, I offered sincere gratitude to God for His wisdom and plan for my life, my husband, our adoptive son, and that of his birth family. Accompanied by God and the promise of our bright future, I felt confident in my ability to solve any issues that might come our way. Despite this confidence, I had no idea what self-sacrificial love entailed. So many aspects of the life of Christian discipleship awaited my discovery.

As a mother and disciple of Christ, I am called to love, serve, and surrender to God's will for my child. My son Joseph, as a son of God, is called to love, to go out and share the light of Christ's love with others. All the while, he is called to hope and search for God's healing touch for himself and his birth family. I pray that the light of Christ, bestowed on my son and each of us during the Sacrament of Baptism, will continue to grow, inflame, and attract all those we encounter, so they, in return, will desire to know its source, Jesus Christ our Lord, the King and Savior of the world.

Prayer: O God, adoption into Your family set my heart ablaze to be Your beloved daughter. May that light, enkindled at baptism, shine forth brightly for all to see in this season of Your Son's birth. Amen.

Respond to His Call: Find out your baptismal date, write "Celebrate!" on the calendar for next year, and plan a party at which you'll give out candles signifying the light of Christ.

Karen Schwaner Sheehy

Dilemma of a Restless Mind

Can a woman forget her suckling child, that she should have no compassion on the son of her womb? Even these may forget, yet I will not forget you. Isaiah 49:15

It's been years since I've had a newborn at home, but there is one thing I remember about infants: when they're wet, they cry. When they're hungry, they cry. When they're sleepy, they cry. They focus on their essential needs, and their parents' quick responses assure them that they are cared for. But as we get older and more self-sufficient, we often can become fixated not only on our essential needs but also on our more trivial concerns, even to the point of absurdity.

I was reminded of this a few years ago when I visited the site of Jesus' anguished prayer in the Garden of Gethsemane. Even as I knelt before the ancient stone where His sweat had fallen as drops of blood, my restless mind started wandering. *Did I pack my umbrella? What is the hotel dinner menu this evening?* The irony of this self-centered train of thought in such sacred surroundings was not lost on me. I was ready to berate myself for my inattentiveness. But then I wondered, *Would I rebuke my newborn's hungry cries? Would I take personal offense at my sleepy toddler's grumpiness? Or would I take into account her limitations and respond accordingly?* To be sure, the Lord knows my tendency to be easily distracted—and distraction during prayer has troubled many a saint greater than me!

While single-mindedness in prayer is certainly a worthy goal, the Lord cares more that I'm making the effort to pray. It's His place to judge my heart. So rather than worry, I'll gently poke fun at my distracted self and pick up that Hail Mary where I left off.

Prayer: Lord, you know my difficulties with distraction and self-centeredness. Please help me to bring to You in prayer my human weaknesses with honesty and humility. Amen.

Respond to His Call: The next time your prayer becomes distracted or unfocused, instead of reproaching yourself, gently bring your thoughts back to the Lord, who lovingly rejoices in your efforts to commune with Him.

Sharon K. Perkins

God's Promise for Your Generations

Know therefore that the LORD . . . keep his commandments, to a thousand generations. Deuteronomy 7:9

One of my favorite parts of the holidays is hearing my relatives tell stories about our ancestors. One story I think about often concerns my great-grandparents from Italy. They had a great love for the Lord and our Blessed Mother, which they shared with their ten children.

Every night after dinner, the family would gather around the fireplace and pray the Rosary. Afterward, they would have a snack together, and my great-grandfather, who was very funny, would tell jokes. This simple time of prayer and laughter bonded them to one another and to their Catholic faith—a bond that would last for generations.

In the book of Deuteronomy, Moses spells out the first commandment. He instructs the Israelites to teach these words diligently to their children because God will be faithful to His covenant for generations. How comforting for those who worry about the faith of their children or grandchildren! In the New Testament, we read of Lois, a faithful Jewish woman whose daughter married a Greek man. Their son, Timothy, was not circumcised according to Jewish law, which must have distressed Lois. But God had different plans!

Lois and her daughter Eunice became believers in Jesus Christ, and their faith spanned generations. Little Timothy grew up to be like a son to St. Paul. What an answer to prayer—Timothy loved and was loved by one of the greatest evangelists of all time!

Prayer: Lord, we lift up our families and our future generations to You. Hear our prayers even as You heard the prayers of Lois for her grandson Timothy. We ask that You open the hearts of our descendants that they may all be followers of Jesus Christ. Amen.

Respond to His Call: Don't despair for your children or grandchildren who may not have deep faith in Christ. Pray for them constantly, and trust God to be true to His promises. You may be surprised at the great ways God will use them!

Dianne Davis

All Good Gifts

What father among you, if his son asks for a fish, will instead of a fish give him a serpent; or if he asks for an egg, will give him a scorpion? Luke 11:11–12

When it came to presents, my mother never got us what we wanted. She meant to, I'm sure. Taking care of us children, being the primary emotional support for her mother, and being married to a guy who worked all sorts of hours, she had other priorities above getting our gifts just right.

The Christmas when a light blue cotton bathrobe was on my list, I got a pink chenille one. When I wanted a brunette Barbie with a ponytail, I got a blond one with a bubble cut. For one of her birthdays, my sister asked for a small camera with a flash attachment; the camera she received didn't have one.

Yet my mom's gifts would generally work just as well, maybe better, than the original requests. In our drafty old house, chenille kept me warmer than cotton would have, and pink probably suited my coloring better. My bubble-cut Barbie's hair stayed neat, while the ponytails on my friends' Barbies got ratty. My sister learned how to take excellent photographs in natural light.

Sometimes, we don't immediately appreciate God's gifts either. However, if we trust, we may discover that what appears to be a snake when we've asked for a fish, or a scorpion when we've asked for an egg, actually is precisely what we need to grow closer to Him. The loss of a loved one may enkindle in us the compassion we need to minister to others. A disappointment at work may lead to the trust and patience we need to wait for God's larger plan to unfold. May we appreciate God's gifts as we receive them each day, and pray for the faith to embrace them with a loving heart.

Prayer: Jesus, in Your infinite wisdom, You answer my prayers in the absolute best way according to Your plans for me. Wrap each response in grace, so I may see it as a gift. Amen.

Respond to His Call: Buy thank-you notes and stamps and plan to use them to thank all those who give you gifts this Christmas.

Melanie Rigney

O Come Let Us Adore Him

Now when Jesus was born in Bethlehem . . . Wise Men from the East came to Jerusalem, saying, "Where is he who has been born king of the Jews? For we have seen his star in the East, and have come to worship him." Matthew 2:1–2

When I was a little girl, the tiny baby Jesus lying in a manger captured my heart. Everything about the Nativity scene was mysterious—the times, the setting, and the visitors who had traveled so far. I loved the name of the town, Bethlehem. As the years go by, the longing and mystery surrounding Christ's birth reach even more deeply into my heart.

As Joseph and Mary made their way from Nazareth in Galilee to Bethlehem in Judea, three men from a faraway country were also on a journey that would be told and retold through the centuries. In all likelihood, the Magi were from Babylon, a place where fourteen generations ago the Jewish people were exiled because they failed to keep their covenant with God. Departing Jerusalem, the Wise Men traveled south until the star they followed rested over a dwelling place in Bethlehem. There they found Mary, Joseph, and the baby Jesus. When they saw the Child, they bowed prostrate in worship and presented their gifts of gold, frankincense, and myrrh.

Jesus invites us this Christmas season to return again to Bethlehem and remember His birth. It is in Bethlehem that Jesus is born in our hearts anew. Christianity was born in the womb of a young Jewish woman. God sent His Son through Mary, incarnate as an infant, to receive gentle care and love. How many hearts melt at the remembrance of the tenderness of Jesus' birth? For many, like me, the first touch of God's love came in childhood as we beheld the tiny Baby in a manger. The story of Bethlehem, no matter how many times it is retold, remains both mysterious and glorious, reaching to capture all hearts with tenderness.

Prayer: Jesus, with an open heart, I receive You into my arms. May my celebration of this season be my cherished gift back to You. Amen.

Respond to His Call: Today, contemplate how Jesus is reborn in your heart this Christmas.

Deborah Kendrick

The Gift of God

O sing to the LORD a new song; sing to the LORD, all the earth! Sing to the LORD, bless his name; tell of his salvation from day to day.
Psalm 96:1–2

As the saying goes, "A picture is worth a thousand words." How clever God is! As the world struggled in faith, God sent us His image to clear our confusion about who He is. He sent us His Son. More than two thousand years later, and well beyond a thousand words, this picture still unfolds before our eyes in new and astonishing ways in the person of Jesus. No matter how many times we encounter God's Word, we come face-to-face with its newness, cutting through the confusion of the world around us and entering directly into our hearts.

Eclipsed in the rush of good intentions and honest generosity that characterize this season is a truth lying just below the surface of traditions and inspired music. We who believe in Jesus Christ, the Son of God, are ourselves, "of God." I wonder what it would be like to introduce myself with both a name and the title "of God." What would others expect of me? More importantly, what would I expect of myself? What would change about the choices I make, the words I use, my attitude toward others? Would I live my life with more explicit intention?

As my eyes take in the infant Jesus' tiny face on Christmas morning, this beautiful scripture comes to mind: "The time for singing has come" (Sg 2:12). When you join in the carols, be sure to include songs of rejoicing. God has shown His face. He has sent the picture that is the Word. Gaze on Jesus this Christmas and behold the greatest gift God has ever given.

Prayer: Lord God, I sing Your praise. Make my voice loud and clear so that all around me hear Your name and know I am of God. Bless the Lord, O my soul, and count all His blessings aloud! Amen.

Respond to His Call: Make up or learn a song of praise, even if you think you can't sing. In a quiet corner of your home or in your car, sing out loud your love of the Lord and praise Him for His gift of life.

Lynne Keating

Reliving the Christmas Story

And while they were there, the time came for her to be delivered. And she gave birth to her first-born son and wrapped him in swaddling cloths, and laid him in a manger, because there was no room for them in the inn. Luke 2:6–7

Upon entering the cave, I see a donkey, sheep, and chickens. They're doing their normal animal thing, but somehow they seem tamer. It's as if they're on their best behavior. Then, I notice that the other shepherds are kneeling. Some are bowing. I look in the direction they are facing, and before me is the most beautiful thing I've ever seen: a family.

The mother makes eye contact with me and smiles. She invites me closer. "You're beautiful," I tell her. She laughs and thanks me. She tells me that her name is Mary, and her husband is Joseph. He is strong, quiet, and has the kindest eyes. I look down at her Baby, sleeping peacefully. Love radiates from Him and pulls me into His presence. "Would you like to hold Him?" Mary asks.

I nod and sit down in the hay. Mary carefully places Him in my arms. I am mesmerized, and I have a hard time looking away. "The angel said this is our Savior," I tell Mary. I also tell her about how the angels came and how glorious they were. She and Joseph tell me about the times when angels visited them. "He's so small and precious. How will He save us?" I wonder. "With God, all things are possible," Mary assures me.

The other shepherds start to leave, and I reluctantly return the Baby to Mary. "I'm so glad you came," Mary says. "Thank you, Mary. I love Jesus. I love you and your family." "Hold us close to your heart. You will always be in ours," she replies. I hug Mary and Joseph. I kiss Jesus' head.

As I leave the stable, I realize God's love for me in a new way—in the face of the Baby Jesus.

Prayer: Blessed Mother, thank you for all the ways you bring me closer to your Son, Jesus. Amen.

Respond to His Call: As Mary brings you closer to Jesus this Christmas, how can you encourage someone in your life today to draw closer to Him?

Sarah Damm

We've Only Just Begun

Because your merciful love is better than life, my lips will praise you. Psalm 63:3

Visiting family members may have gone home and leftovers lost their glamour, but Christmas is not over. The precious baby Jesus has been born. Now what? A child came to earth, grew in wisdom and knowledge, became a man, and died on a cross for you. How does that change things? How does that change you? The way you live, the words you speak, or the decisions you make each day? Think about it.

Are you living your life with this idea in mind? The idea that is so much more than an idea—it is Jesus incarnate. Thinking of Him should be a daily reminder of the incredible truth that *you* are important enough for God to become a man and sacrifice Himself for you. An omnipotent God, the one who created the universe and every microcosm within it, loves you enough that He would give His life for you. Dare I ask again—how does that change you?

As you ponder that question, ask Jesus what changes He would like to make in your life. Examine your choices and ask Him what He would have you doing differently. Are you afraid to ask? Worried what He might say? Jesus said, "I did not come to judge the world but to save the world" (Jn 12:47). He wants to help you. He wants you to be with Him for all eternity. *You* are the reason the Lord of the universe came as a babe in swaddling clothes.

Prayer: Jesus, You gave Your life for me. Help me to respond to You by giving You my life in return. Amen.

Respond to His Call: Make the changes in your life that will allow you to follow Jesus more closely. Ask Him for His guidance and help.

Michelle Gelineau

The Third Day of Christmas

"And this will be a sign for you: you will find a baby wrapped in swaddling cloths and lying in a manger." And suddenly there was with the angel a multitude of the heavenly host praising God and saying, "Glory to God in the highest, and on earth peace among men with whom he is pleased!" Luke 2:12–14

Being only three days old, the tiny infant Jesus is hungry, and like all newborns, He is fed night and day. Because of the shepherds' report, there is a constant stream of visitors. As everyone knows, shepherds are notorious for creating wild tales during the long, eventless nights on the hillsides with the sheep. They spin sagas of robbers and wolves and bears, always exalting themselves as the saviors of their sheep. But this time their story is different. The people dwelling in Bethlehem have seen a great light. Granted, it was the shepherds' most outrageous story yet. Angels appearing in the night. The glory of God shining around them. A baby lying in a feeding trough. Yet, the sound of truth could be heard in the voices of those night watchers.

The beautiful mother appears in no way discomforted by her conditions. On the contrary, she glows with a radiance reflected from the Baby Himself. The father, so strong and protective, is already thinking of the next event. For in five days, the Babe would be circumcised. Joseph would take care of the details.

In Judaism, circumcision is the sign of the covenant with God, just as baptism is for Christians. The Jewish rabbi who performs this procedure is known as a mohel. On the eighth day of Jesus' life, the mohel will come and lay out his cloths and instruments and don his prayer shawl. He shall offer prayers. The Baby's name will be proclaimed, and then, in a moment, this covenant of God with Abraham is established again. This time with a difference—Jesus is God.

Prayer: O Lord, You created us to know You and love You. Born in tenderness, You took on the greatest vulnerability to know us and love us. Forever in gratitude, we will worship You. Amen.

Respond to His Call: Meditate on Isaiah 7:14.

Deborah Kendrick

Come Away, My Love

My beloved speaks and says to me: "Arise, my love, my dove, my fair one, and come away." Song of Solomon 2:10

We've all been called many names. Some of these names manifest joy in our hearts and provide us with a sense of belonging, of having a place in someone's heart. Other names have the opposite impact; they remind us of our failures, our mistakes, the ways in which this broken world has inspired us to live out of our woundedness, and not out of our identity. Unfortunately, many of us don't even know who we really are, where our identity truly lies. You, ravishingly beautiful woman, are love—His love.

We so often hear that we are created in the image and likeness of God, but the world distorts this image. We lose heart when we are hurt by the very people the Father sends to love us, and we find ourselves entangled in worldly allurements and the false promise of security that success in this world advertises.

When the weight of the world seems to be on your shoulders, when you've tried to handle everything on your own, when you are knee-deep in self-sufficiency, hear that still, small voice whispering to you, "Arise, my love, my dove, my fair one, and come away." Every moment in your life is an opportunity to respond to His call: to arise and leave behind anything that is holding you back from His love and the truth that you are His.

Whether you are struggling to overcome little worldly attachments that prevent you from total surrender to our Beloved's will, or you have been running from Him for far too long, hold fast to the knowledge that God is love, and therefore you, by your very being as His exquisite creation, are love.

Prayer: My Beloved, give me the grace to say yes to Your call to come away with You, that it may transform my heart into Your love. Amen.

Respond to His Call: Place a reminder near you of your identity as love. Whether it be a note with an affirming scripture on your computer screen or a rosary carried in your pocket, keep God's love on the forefront of your mind today.

Angela Koenig

Latin, Life, and Lessons Well Learned

Lord, now let your servant depart in peace, according to your word; for my eyes have seen your salvation which you have prepared in the presence of all peoples, a light for revelation to the Gentiles, and for glory to your people Israel. Luke 2:29–32

I held his hand and prayed this Canticle of Simeon over my grandpa just hours before he drew his final breath. To be with the dying in their last moments is a privilege and gift.

Few people enjoy talking about death, much less thinking about it. But a beautiful tradition is making its way back into the devotional life of the Church. The Latin *memento mori* is a call for all the faithful to "remember you must die."

C. S. Lewis pointed out, "If we find ourselves with a desire that nothing in this world can satisfy, the most probable explanation is that we were made for another world." Memento mori helps us keep our priorities in check. All things pass away. A wonderful family, successful career, good health, and beautiful home are all blessings, but none of these things will keep us from the moment Jesus calls us home.

God never changes. He has prepared a place for us, and He wants us to spend eternity with Him. When we approach each day in the light of this truth, we live memento mori. We thank God for blessings, but we don't despair when they leave or even when trials come.

A beloved high school teacher always told me to "begin with the end in mind." Her wisdom is memento mori applied. Our decisions are braver, our hearts more peaceful, our joy more sincere when we live in the hope of heaven. Be at peace, good and faithful servant, and cling to the Truth. Death is not the end. Our partings are not forever. There is life beyond this one, and Christ is our way home.

Prayer: Lord, open my eyes to see the gift of eternal life You have prepared for us. Jesus, I trust in You! Amen.

Respond to His Call: When driving by a cemetery, say a prayer for the departed souls. Offer a Hail Mary or pray, "Eternal rest grant unto them, O Lord, and let perpetual light shine upon them."

Katie Anderson

December 31

Here's the Plan and It's Quite Good

Many are the plans in the mind of a man, but it is the purpose of the LORD that will be established. Proverbs 19:21

We all have days when nothing seems to go as planned. When everything we worked up to shatters, the prize we were about to grasp is suddenly out of reach, or we are the only person not invited to the party. On days like these, it's easy to give up and give in to despair.

Yet even in the darkness of the soul, there is hope. For in the soul, there is an inner realization that we are made for more. We are made for union with God, and God has a plan for our lives—a plan that will lead us to Him. In fact, "God, infinitely perfect and blessed in himself, in a plan of sheer goodness freely created man to make him share in his own blessed life" (*CCC* 1).

God's plan is for us to share in His own blessed life. Ponder that sentence for a minute or two. Seriously.

Sometimes, in the midst of shattered dreams, it is hard for us to recognize God's plan of sheer goodness. During times of pain, suffering, or loneliness, we must trust God and believe that He did not abandon us, leaving us to navigate the journey back to Him alone. He gave us His Spirit to guide us on the way.

In the apostolic exhortation *Evangelii Gaudium* (*The Joy of the Gospel*), Pope Francis tells us, "The Holy Spirit, sent by the Father and the Son, transforms our hearts and enables us to enter into the perfect communion of the blessed Trinity, where all things find their unity." That's the ultimate sharing in God's blessed life; that's why it is a plan of *sheer goodness*.

Prayer: Lord, increase in me the virtue of hope. Give me the courage each day to trust in the plan of sheer goodness that You have for me. Amen.

Respond to His Call: Today, simply say, "God, infinitely perfect and blessed in Himself, has a plan of sheer goodness for me." And believe it. Better yet, live it!

Kelly M. Wahlquist

Scripture Index

Contributors

Katie Anderson is a young Catholic with an old soul working for a parish in the St. Croix River Valley. Sparkling water, a stack of books, and all the St. Teresa's are a few of her great joys!

Sherry Antonetti is a published author and freelance writer for multiple Catholic publications, including the *Catholic Standard*, *National Catholic Register*, and *Aleteia*.

Danielle Bean is an author, speaker, podcaster, and brand manager of *CatholicMom.com*.

Kathleen Beckman is a speaker and the author of *Praying for Priests, God's Healing Mercy, When Women Pray*, and *A Family Guide to Spiritual Warfare*.

Jennifer Beutz is a freelance writer whose work has appeared in *The Catholic Spirit* and *Star Tribune*. She also served as the small-group coordinator at St. Hubert Catholic Community.

Kathleen Billings lives with her husband, Troy, and their five children on their five-acre homestead in Greenville, South Carolina. She is a national Catholic speaker and writer and blogs at seasonsoftheheartandhome.com.

Amy Brooks and her husband, Matt, live with their three children in Pennsylvania. You can follow her on her blog PrayerWineChocolate.com. She is also the founder of CatholicsOnline.net.

Sherry Kennedy Brownrigg, a convert to Catholicism, runs a classical music radio station in Omaha, Nebraska. She and her husband, Steve, dote on their many nieces and nephews and golden retriever Gilly.

Anne Carraux writes mostly in prayer and to make sense of her journey. She hopes her words help readers keep looking toward God, especially when it comes to living joyfully with faith.

Emily Cavins is an author and holds a master of arts degree in Near Eastern archaeology and biblical history. She is a tour leader of pilgrimages to Israel and other Bible-related destinations with her husband, Jeff Cavins.

Sarah Christmyer connects Catholics to Christ through scripture with her writing, teaching, and speaking. She is the author of *Becoming Women of the Word*, and can be found online at ComeIntotheWord.com.

Kitty Cleveland is a music missionary who feels called to encourage people—whether through music, storytelling, or teaching from the great Catholic spiritual writers and her life experience. Learn more at KittyCleveland.com.

Caralyn Collar is the writer and speaker behind BeautyBeyondBones.com. She uses her story of total restoration to positively impact others and offer Christ's hope for others with eating disorders and other adversities.

Sonja Corbitt is the Bible Study Evangelista. She makes Bible study spinach taste like cake! Find her books, CatholicTV show, podcast, LOVE the Word® Bible study method, and events at biblestudyevangelista.com.

Sarah Damm is a Catholic wife and mother of six children. She writes regularly about faith, scripture, and prayer at sarahdamm.com. Two of her favorite things are coffee and good books.

Dianne Davis is a speaker and teacher. She serves as the director of mission expansion for ChristLife and is the coauthor of *Share Christ*. She and her husband have two sons.

Marge Steinhage Fenelon is an award-winning author and journalist, speaker, retreat leader, podcaster, and Catholic radio and television personality. She's written several books on Marian devotion and Catholic spirituality.

Martha Fernández-Sardina is an international speaker, teacher, and writer. She is also the founder and host of Remember You Are Loved. Find, friend, and follow her online at MarthaFernandezSardina.com.

Reagan Franklin is a Catholic wife, mother, and elementary school teacher who knows, lives, and shares her faith! She organizes events with the mission of spreading the joy of the resurrected Christ.

Michelle Gelineau wanted everyone to know how much Jesus loves them! Knowing His love changed her life and she never lost the joy of living in His love, even as she faced terminal cancer.

Andrea Gibbs and her husband, Jeremy, are proud homeschool parents to five wonderful children. She serves as a director of faith formation at Divine Mercy Catholic Church in Faribault, Minnesota.

Debby Giusti, a *USA Today* bestselling author with more than a million books in print, shares the love of Christ one story at a time. Visit her at www.DebbyGiusti.com.

Pat Gohn is a wife, mother, and grandmother. She's also an author, catechist, retreat leader, and podcast host, and she works as an editor of devotional booklets. Visit her at PatGohn.net.

Deb Hadley is an inspirational speaker and author, the creator of the Morning God Boost, the founder of the KT Humble Hearts Foundation, a hospice spiritual care provider, and a Servant of the Lord. Learn more at debhadley.com

AnnAliese Harry is a proud Army wife and mother to several children and can be found online at beautifulcamouflage.com where she writes about her Catholic faith through the lenses of her many vocations.

Heidi Harvey is a Blue Star mom with a warrior's heart. She and her veteran husband, Dave, have a blended family of five—including two Marines and one in waiting.

Dr. Mary Healy is professor of scripture at Sacred Heart Major Seminary in Detroit, Michigan; a bestselling author; and a member of the Pontifical Biblical Commission.

Judy Hehr is a wife and mother of four. She is a speaker, coach, author, and host who knows it is never too late to become who God created us to be.

Barbara Elaine Heil is a convert who, along with her husband, Jeff, continues in ministry sharing the Gospel. They reside in Iowa and together have eight children and ten grandchildren.

Lisa M. Hendey is the founder of *Catholic-Mom.com*, a bestselling author, and an international speaker. She serves internationally giving workshops on faith, family, and communications. Visit her at LisaHendey.com.

Donna Luna-Hernandez lives in Midland, Texas, and is a wife, mother, grandmother, and sister. She is passionate about Catholic women's ministries and, in 2018, was named the West Texas WINE specialist.

Patti Jannuzzi is the director of new evangelization, stewardship, and adult faith formation at Church of the Immaculate Conception in Somerville, New Jersey, where she also teaches theology at Immaculata High School.

ValLimar Jansen is an inspirational speaker, composer, recording artist, storyteller, and author. She also has experience as a university professor, leader of worship and prayer, and international workshop presenter.

Lucy H. Johnson, wife to Jeff, mother of seven, grandmother of nine, has been a pharmacist since 1981. She previously served as president of the Archdiocesan Council of Catholic Women.

Maria Morera Johnson is an award-winning Catholic speaker, retreat leader, and bestselling author. Read more at mariamjohnson.com.

Annie Karto is Catholic singer-songwriter and inspirational speaker who hopes to imitate Our Lady by proclaiming the greatness of the Lord! Her focus is sharing the healing power of God's mercy.

Lynne Keating is a prolific writer who loves to teach scripture and Confirmation classes to children and adults.

Deborah Kendrick came into the Catholic Church through her interaction with Catholics in Europe, where she was a conference speaker and retreat leader. Her heart is to see people receive God's love.

Julie E. Kenney is a mother, educator, speaker, writer, and a pro-life and pro-marriage advocate who believes in miracles and the power of prayer. She enjoys family time, watching sports, and traveling.

Susan Klemond is a Minnesota writer who loves delving into faith, Church, vocations, and family and life issues. She enjoys interviewing inspiring people of all backgrounds for her stories.

Angela Koenig is head over heels in love with Jesus and the beauty of His creation. She blogs about her love story with Him at www.spiritu-allyspokenfor.com.

Stephanie Landsem is the author of The Living Water series of novels—*The Well*, *The Thief*, and *The Tomb*—which bring the unknown women of the Bible to life.

Joan F. Lewis retired from Vatican Information Service and formerly served as EWTN's Rome bureau chief. She is the creator of the *Joan's Rome* blog and videos and the author of *A Holy Year in Rome*.

Katsey Long is a licensed clinical social worker who actively integrates her Catholic faith into her profession. She executive produced *The Secret of Peace*, a documentary film about Fr. Ubald Rugirangoga.

Lynda MacFarland is a blogger and author of *Drowning in Lemonade*. She loves Jesus and wants everyone else to know Him, too!

Heather Makowicz is a certified spiritual director, retreat leader, founder and president of Peak Encounter Ministries, and outdoor adventure guide with a passion for bringing the love of Christ to others.

Margie Mandli is founder and owner of GEM Communications and Consulting, LLC, where she serves Fortune 100 companies in marketing and communications strategies. She is married and has three children.

Joelle Maryn is a Catholic speaker, evangelist, and actress. In 2012, she had a major reversion to the faith and now spreads a message of God's healing love, radiating hope and purpose to many around the world.

Teresa McCarthy and her husband live in Minnetonka, Minnesota. They have five children and one grandson. She works at a large suburban parish.

Kerry McGuire writes for the *Texas Catholic Herald* and formed two ministries: Catholic WE, which helps women deepen their relationship with Christ, and Loving Stones, which equips parishes in forming apostles.

Marie Miller is a singer-songwriter and mandolin player from the Blue Ridge Mountains in Virginia. Her full length project, *Little Dreams*, is available on all streaming platforms. Visit her at mariemillermusic.com.

Lisa Mladinich is a certified Gallup strengths coach helping Catholics live their best lives by developing their natural talents. A podcast host and bestselling author, she also teaches for HomeschoolConnections.com.

Kristin Molitor serves as the New Evangelization coordinator for the central Minnesota Catholic parishes of Holdingford, St. Anna, and St. Wendel.

Jill Mraz, Catholic mother, poet, and essayist, enjoys summer road trips marveling at the stunning beauty of God's natural world. Her writings reflect upon motherhood and her beloved Catholic faith.

Michelle Nash lives a life intentionally filled by and centered on Christ. Her dynamic, joyful, witty, and enthusiastic approach to sharing her Catholic faith offers an encounter with Christ that cannot be missed.

Susanna Parent is a wife, mother, and freelance writer who begins her mornings brewing French press coffee in the home she shares with her family in the Twin Cities.

Pamela Patnode, EdD, OblSB, is a Catholic wife, mother of five, author, speaker, educator, and Benedictine oblate. She homeschooled her children and now teaches at Chesterton Academy of the Twin Cities.

Sharon K. Perkins is a wife and mother with forty years' experience as a published writer, speaker, course instructor, retreat leader, and director of evangelization and catechesis in the Diocese of Austin, Texas.

Letitia M. Peyton, wife to Deacon Scott Peyton, homeschooling mom to six beautiful children and grandmother to one beautiful granddaughter, is a women's Bible and book study facilitator and WINE gatherer.

Marilyn A. (Dee) Ray, RN, CTN-A, PhD, FAAN, FNAP, is a professor emeritus at the Christine E. Lynn College of Nursing at Florida Atlantic University and retired from the United States Air Force as a colonel.

Dr. Carol Razza is a faculty member and formation advisor at St. Vincent de Paul Seminary. She has worked as a psychotherapist for more than twenty five years. She is an international speaker.

Melanie Rigney is a contributor to Living Faith and the author of several books about saints. Learn more about her at www.rejoice-beglad.com.

Paige Freeman Rosato is a lawyer and legal writer who resides with her husband, children, and granddaughter in Mandeville, Louisiana.

Roxane B. Salonen is a children's author, pro-life memoir coauthor, religion writer for her city's daily, columnist for her diocese, and Catholic radio host. View her work at roxanesalonen.com.

Hilary Scheppers is a religious poet and writer from Minnesota. She holds an masters in writing from Sarah Lawrence College and a bachelors in humanities and theology from Loyola Marymount University.

Lindsay Schlegel is a podcast host and the author of *Don't Forget to Say Thank You: And Other Parenting Lessons That Brought Me Closer to God*. Follow her work at LindsaySchlegel.com.

Michelle Schroeder is a married mom of two teenagers from Louisiana. She is the author of three volumes in the Handy Little Guide series: *Adoration, Confession*, and the *Holy Spirit*.

Karen Schwaner Sheehy is a devout Catholic, wife, mother, motivational speaker, author and certified spiritual director. She obtained her masters in theology from the University of Holy Cross in New Orleans.

Rose Sweet is a sparkling speaker, author, and certified life and relationship coach. Her books—written to help others heal and strengthen relationships—are charming and practical and offer beautiful spiritual depth.

Katie Lee Taylor is passionate about equipping leaders in the New Evangelization. She is a wife, mother, and Air Force veteran with a masters in marriage and family counseling. Find out more at rosesweet.com.

LeAnn Thieman is a Hall of Fame speaker and author of *Chicken Soup for the Soul, Living Catholic Faith* and the series Everyday Catholicism.

Teresa Tomeo is a Catholic talk show host, author, and journalist with thirty years of experience as a media consultant/activist. She is also the founder of Teresa Tomeo Communications. Learn more at www.TeresaTomeo.com.

Lori Ubowski is a Catholic musician, speaker, coauthor of *Side By Side: A Catholic Mother-Daughter Journal*, and a contributing writer in *Our Friend Faustina*.

Susan Vigilante lives in Minnesota. She is the author of *Breakfast with the Pope* and blogs at desperateirishhousewife.blogspot.com.

Katie Warner is a homeschooling mom and popular author. She holds a graduate degree in theology and is the manager of communication and evangelization at Catholics Come Home. Visit her at KatieWarner.com.

Elizabeth Westhoff is a communications pro dedicated to sharing the beauty and truth of Catholicism. She is a daughter of St. Francis de Sales and a dame of the Equestrian Order of the Holy Sepulchre of Jerusalem.

Sharon Agnes Wilson is a wife, mother, writer, speaker, and WINE specialist with a degree in education. She has worked as a respect life coordinator and in youth advocacy. Follow her at SharonAgnesWilson.com.

Dr. Carol Younger is an author and educator whose teaching career spans elementary through graduate school, parish ministry, and Catholic conferences. She is also a senior fellow for the St. Paul Center.

Rhonda Zweber's mission since being diagnosed with breast cancer has been to bring others to Christ. She enjoys sharing how her relationship with Jesus has sustained her throughout her journey.

Kelly Wahlquist is a Catholic author and speaker, and the founder of WINE: Women In the New Evangelization. She is the director for the Archbishop Flynn Catechetical Institute in the Archdiocese of St. Paul and Minneapolis.

Wahlquist is the author of *Created to Relate*, the editor of *Walk in Her Sandals* and *Gaze Upon Jesus*, and a contributing writer for WINE. Wahlquist leads women's pilgrimages through Italy and Ireland and travels around the country speaking on the New Evangelization. She lives in Minnesota with her husband, Andy, and their children.

catholicvineyard.com
Facebook: WomenIntheNewEvangelization

Alyssa Bormes is a theology teacher at Chesterton Academy, the author of *The Catechism of Hockey*, and writes for the WINE: Women In the New Evangelization blog. She also hosts *Catholic Kaleidoscope* on Radio Maria.

alyssabormes.com

Allison Gingras is a Catholic speaker, podcaster, and author. She created the Stay Connected Journals for Catholic Women. She facilitates the book club and online activities for WINE: Women In the New Evangelization.

ReconciledToYou.com

ALSO BY

wine®
Women IN *the* New Evangelization

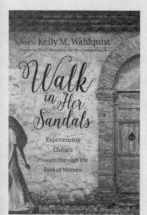

Walk in Her Sandals, edited by Kelly M. Wahlquist, takes you deeper into your relationship with Jesus by helping you relate to him in a profoundly intimate way. Looking at six universal gifts of women through the eyes of women in the gospels, the book guides you on a prayerful and creative journey through the days of Holy Week, Easter, and Pentecost.

"A devotional tapestry."
—Sonja Corbitt
Catholic speaker, radio host, and author of *Unleashed*

This six-week scripture study follows the infancy and early years of Christ as seen through the eyes of Mary and other familiar and imagined women in the gospels. You will dig deep into each of the scriptural vignettes and grow in your faith as you learn about virtues such as humility, patience, charity, reverence, prudence, and courage.

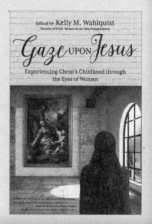

"You will be renewed and refreshed."
—From the foreword by
Teresa Tomeo
Syndicated radio host and author of *Intimate Graces*